ASIAN/OCEANIAN HISTORICAL DICTIONARIES
Edited by Jon Woronoff

Asia

1. *Vietnam*, by William J. Duiker. 1989. *Out of print. See No. 27.*
2. *Bangladesh*, 2nd ed., by Craig Baxter and Syedur Rahman. 1996. *Out of print. See No.48.*
3. *Pakistan*, by Shahid Javed Burki. 1991. *Out of print. See No. 33.*
4. *Jordan*, by Peter Gubser. 1991
5. *Afghanistan*, by Ludwig W. Adamec. 1991. *Out of print. See No. 29.*
6. *Laos*, by Martin Stuart-Fox and Mary Kooyman. 1992. *Out of print. See No. 35.*
7. *Singapore*, by K. Mulliner and Lian The-Mulliner. 1991
8. *Israel*, by Bernard Reich. 1992
9. *Indonesia*, by Robert Cribb. 1992
10. *Hong Kong and Macau*, by Elfed Vaughan Roberts, Sum Ngai Ling, and Peter Bradshaw. 1992
11. *Korea*, by Andrew C. Nahm. 1993
12. *Taiwan*, by John F. Copper. 1993. *Out of print. See No. 34.*
13. *Malaysia*, by Amarjit Kaur. 1993. *Out of print. See No. 36.*
14. *Saudi Arabia*, by J. E. Peterson. 1993. *Out of print. See No. 45.*
15. *Myanmar*, by Jan Becka. 1995
16. *Iran*, by John H. Lorentz. 1995
17. *Yemen*, by Robert D. Burrowes. 1995
18. *Thailand*, by May Kyi Win and Harold Smith. 1995
19. *Mongolia*, by Alan J. K. Sanders. 1996. *Out of print See No. 42.*
20. *India*, by Surjit Mansingh. 1996
21. *Gulf Arab States*, by Malcolm C. Peck. 1996
22. *Syria*, by David Commins. 1996
23. *Palestine*, by Nafez Y. Nazzal and Laila A. Nazzal. 1997
24. *Philippines*, by Artemio R. Guillermo and May Kyi Win. 1997

Oceania

1. *Australia*, by James C. Docherty. 1992. *Out of print. See No. 32.*
2. *Polynesia*, by Robert D. Craig. 1993. *Out of print. See No. 39.*
3. *Guam and Micronesia*, by William Wuerch and Dirk Ballendorf. 1994
4. *Papua New Guinea*, by Ann Turner. 1994. *Out of print. See No. 37.*
5. *New Zealand*, by Keith Jackson and Alan McRobie. 1996

Historical Dictionary
of Kyrgyzstan

Rafis Abazov

Asian/Oceanian
Historical Dictionaries, No. 49

The Scarecrow Press, Inc.
Lanham, Maryland, and Oxford
2004

SCARECROW PRESS, INC.

Published in the United States of America
by Scarecrow Press, Inc.
A wholly owned subsidiary of the Rowman & Littlefield Publishing Group, Inc
4501 Forbes Boulevard, Suite 200, Lanham, Maryland 20706
www.scarecrowpress.com

PO Box 317
Oxford
OX2 9RU, UK

British Library Cataloguing in Publication Information Available

Library of Congress Cataloging-in-Publication Data

Abazov, Rafis.
    Historical dictionary of Kyrgyzstan / Rafis Abazov.
        p. cm. — (Asian/Oceanian historical dictionaries ; no. 49)
    Includes bibliographical references.
    ISBN 0-8108-4868-6 (alk. paper)   ISBN 978-0-8108-4868-9
    1. Kyrgyzstan—History—Dictionaries. I. Title. II. Series.
DK918.12 .A23 2004
958.43'003—dc22   2003019174

Contents

Editor's Foreword

There is an increasing tendency to give countries, especially developing countries and most particularly newly independent ones, "report cards" showing how well they've been doing and even to indicate their respective positions. Under these conditions, Kyrgyzstan might receive something like "needs improvement" or come in—more or less—in the second-to-bottom quarter. Shortly after it became independent in 1991 with the collapse of the Soviet Union, Kyrgyzstan was regarded as one of the more promising new states. But when the lessons it was obliged to learn were poorly digested (or perhaps the lessons themselves were poorly thought out), it gradually slipped and lost favor. More recently, however, this small country with a mixed population and limited natural resources has been making headway for many reasons: its political system and democracy, civil society, human rights, economic development, equality, and cooperation with the international community.

It is much easier to understand Kyrgyzstan's indifferent performance as an independent state with some insight into the previous decades and even centuries. The country began as a collection of tribes, and was then poorly absorbed and assimilated into the Russian Empire. Even before becoming an independent state, Kyrgyzstan was more or less rejected by its Soviet masters, classified as a semi-independent "republic." Not many scholars have studied it, including its own, and not many have written about it; the country has for the most part been lumped together with the Russian and Soviet Empires, and even today normally appears just as part of the Central Asian Republics. So this *Historical Dictionary of Kyrgyzstan* is particularly welcome because it makes up for previous omissions and fills a gap by providing basic information in a readily usable format. The dictionary contains the standard entries on significant people, places, and events; organizations and institutions; ethnic and political groups; and salient aspects of the economy, society, and culture. Both the chronology and introduction are unusually helpful in providing an overview of the country's often halting progress, and the bibliography supplies references in English and other languages.

This volume is one of the last Asian/Oceanian Historical Dictionaries, not surprising given the deficit in scholarship on this area of the world. I was therefore quite pleased to find a more than suitable author for this addition to the series. Rafis Abazov graduated from Kyrgyz State University, later receiving his *kandidat nauk* (roughly equivalent to a Ph.D.) from a research institute in Moscow. He subsequently worked with the Centre for Social Research of the Kyrgyz National Academy of Science and has received fellowships to the University of Tokyo and the United Nations University in Tokyo, the University of Reading in the U.K., and La Trobe University in Australia. Abazov has written on economic and other topics on Central Asia and Kyrgyzstan for the *Encyclopaedia of Modern Asia*, and is currently a visiting scholar at the Harriman Institute of Columbia University.

Jon Woronoff
Series Editor

Reader's Notes

The Kyrgyz Republic (also known as Kyrgyzstan and by convention called "Kirgizia" until 1991) was established on 14 October 1924, as an autonomous republic within the Russian Federation. It comprised parts of former Semirechenskaya, Syrdar'inskaya, Ferganskaya, and Samarkandskaya regions (*oblasts*). On 5 December 1936 Kyrgyzstan was granted the status of the Kyrgyz Soviet Socialist Republic (Kyrgyz SSR), which gave it constitutional rights to maintain some autonomy in cultural, administrative, and social affairs. Kyrgyzstan declared its independence from the USSR on 31 August 1991. The Kyrgyz language obtained the status of state language after the introduction of the Law on Languages in 1989. The independence of 1991 encouraged the conversion of the state documentation and educational system into the Kyrgyz language and prompted changes in spelling of major geographic and personal names according to Kyrgyz pronunciation.

LANGUAGE

The modern literary Kyrgyz language was standardized at the beginning of the 20th century. However, there are several dialects that differ noticeably. Two major dialects are northern—spoken in the Chui, Ysyk-Kol valleys, and the capital—and southern—spoken by the Kyrgyzs in the Ferghana valley. The latter has been influenced by the presence of a big community of Uzbeks in the southern *oblasts* of the republic, especially in the usage of some common words. For example, in the south younger people use the word *ake* (*aka*), which shows respect, in polite reference to an older male person, while in the north the same meaning is conveyed by *baike*.

During the Soviet era the Kyrgyz language extensively borrowed from the Russian language, especially in the fields of science, technologies, and social sciences. However, since the late 1980s there has been a strong trend to replace the words of Russian origin with words of Kyrgyz or Turkic origin. For example, *uchak* replaced the Russian word *samolyot* (an airplane), *synalgy* replaced *televizor* (a TV set), *el tashychuu avto* replaced *avtobus* (a bus), *chong zhol* replaced *avtomagistral* (a highway), *til zym* replaced *telephone*, and so on.

The more recent trend is the appearance of English words in the Kyrgyz language, especially among youth and students and in independent media. Some English loans replaced both Russian and Kyrgyz equivalents in informal everyday interaction. For example, EVM (*elektronno-vychislitel'naya mashina*) became *komp'uter*, *sabak (okuu) barakchasi* became *study-kard* (student ID card), *okuu tartibi* became *taim-teibl* (time-table), *tyshkyy tamak* became *lanch* (lunch), and the like.

TRANSLITERATION AND PRONUNCIATION

During the 20th century the Kyrgyz language underwent two significant changes from the Arabic script to Latin in 1926, and then from the Latin script to the Cyrillic (Russian) alphabet in 1940. Despite government support in the early 1990s to convert the alphabet from Cyrillic to Latin script, as in Turkmenistan or neighboring Uzbekistan, there are no indications that it will happen in the near future. Currently there are 36 letters in the Kyrgyz alphabet, 33 Russian plus three additional Cyrillic-based characters used for characteristic Turkic sounds not found in Russian.

Transliteration of modern Kyrgyz into English was problematic and inconsistent. One of the main reasons is that in the past many words, especially geographic and personal Kyrgyz names, underwent double transliteration, first from Kyrgyz into Russian and then from Russian into English. A good example is transliteration of a sound that was traditionally represented by "dzh" in Russian ("John" would be transliterated into "Dzhon"). Until the 1990s the "Jalal Abad *oblast*" and "Jany Jol *raion*" were transliterated as "Dzhalal Abad *oblast*" and "Dzhangi Dzhol raion." Personal names were also double transliterated, for example, "Dzhumashev" or "Dzholdoshev." This type of transliteration could be found in the indexing of the Library of the Congress and in many publications on Central Asia. The present trend, however, is to avoid the double transliteration. The direct transliteration implies the usage of the letter "J," for example: "Jalal Abad," "Jumashev," or "Joldoshev." However, both variations could be equally found in the modern literature.

Many russified geographic names were written with a dash in the past—Dzhalal-Abad *oblast,* Kara-Balta, and so on. The current trend is to drop the dash in the Kyrgyz spelling of geographic names (Jalal Abad, Kara Balta, etc.). Because the process of the transition from the russified version to the Kyrgyz form has not been completed yet, there are some inconsistencies. Some maps and geographical publications still hyphenate the geographic names; others do not use the dash. There are even publications that sometimes use both variations. In this dictionary most of the names of the cities and towns are given in accordance with the current Kyrgyz language standards, with some exception, such as "Tian-Shan."

There is also no unanimity in transliteration of personal names. For example, the name "Akayev" could be found in two forms "Akayev" and "Akaev." The former spelling is used throughout the dictionary.

In the 1990s there was a broad trend for a direct transliteration of geographic or personal names from Kyrgyz into English. For example, "Kirgiz" became "Kyrgyz," "Issyk Kul" became "Ysyk Kol," "Dzhangi Dzhol" became "Jany Jol," and so on. In everyday life, especially in northern Kyrgyzstan, both forms are still used.

TRANSLITERATION TABLE OF SOME KYRGYZ CONSONANTS AND VOWELS

Kyrgyz letters	Transliteration	Russ. spelling	Kyrgyz spelling	Double transliteration	Direct transliteration
Ж	J	Джалал-Абад	Жалал Абад	Dzhalal Abad	Jalal Abad
Y	U	Тюрк	тYрк	Turk	Turk
Ө	O	Иссык-Куль	Ысык КӨл	Issyk Kul	Ysyk Kol
Ы	Y	Киргиз	Кыргыз	Kirgiz	Kyrgyz

This new type of transliteration (direct), as shown in the table above, is used throughout this dictionary. At the same time, the alternative form of spelling of the most common names can also be found with a *See* or *See also* reference to the latest transliteration.

KYRGYZ NAMES AND TITLES

All Kyrgyz names in this dictionary are given in a standard form—the family name first, followed by the first name in the entry title, and first name followed by the family name in the text.

The Kyrgyzs traditionally refer to each other by their first names, followed by the father's name. For example, Askar Akai-uulu (son of Akai), Roza Isak-Kyzy (daughter of Isak). However, during the Soviet era, there was a change to a russified version, where the father's name ended with russified "-vich" for male and "-ovna" for female. For example, Usen Asanovich, Roza Isakovna. The form of family names also experienced Russian influence, as "-ov" or "-ev" was added to the end of family names for male and "-ova" or "-eva" was added to the end of family names for female. For example, Alikbai Nazarbayev, Zamira Urstanbekova. In the post-Soviet era, people increasingly turned to the traditional writing of their family names. One way of doing it is by replacing the suffix "-ov," "-ev" or "-ova," "-eva" with "-uulu" or "-kyzy": Urstanbekova becomes Urstanbek-kyzy. The other way is to drop the suffix "-ov," "-ev," or "-ova" and use a shorter version of their names. For example, "Roustem Zholamanov" becomes "Roustem Zholaman," "Askar Shomanov" becomes "Askar Shoman."

Traditionally the Kyrgyzs, like most of the peoples in Central and East Asia, have been using various titles with their names (usually with their first names) and have been very sensitive to proper titles. For example, a younger person is encouraged to refer to an older person as *baike* or *ake*, while an older or senior person refers to younger person as *uke* or *uka*. In the pre-Soviet era, there were titles like *khan*, *bek*, *bai*, *myrza*, and others, which were widely used in addressing nobility, landlords, and officers of the state administration. The title *aiym* (i.e., madam) was used to address a female member of the upper class. It was traditionally added to the first name. For example, Ormon Khan or Kadyr-bek. During the Soviet era, the noble titles were abolished and all titles were replaced by the formal *joldosh* (*dzholdosh*) (i.e., comrade). In the post-Soviet era, *joldosh* is rarely used and the usage of pre-Soviet titles is slowly coming back, especially in the rural areas and among traditional groups of the society, though there is no strict regulation of their usage.

HOW TO USE THE DICTIONARY

All entries in the *Historical Dictionary of Kyrgyzstan* are arranged alphabetically. Entries with variant spellings direct the reader to the more commonly spelled entry through a *See* reference. Cross-references to relevant entries are indicated in **bold** within the entry or listed at the end of the entry under *See also*.

Acronymns and Abbreviations

ADB	Asian Development Bank
CAEU	Central Asian Economic Union
CAF	Central Asian Forum
CC	Central Committee
CEC	Central Election Committee
Centrasbat	Central Asian (Peacekeeping) Battalion
CIA	Central Intelligence Service
CIS	Commonwealth of Independent States
CP	Communist Party
CPK	Communist Party of Kyrgyzstan
CPSU	Communist Party of the Soviet Union
CU	Customs Union
DKV	*Dogovor o Kollektivnoi Bezopastnosti* (CIS Collective Security Treaty)
DMK	Democratic Movement of Kyrgyzstan
ECO	Economic Cooperation Organization
EEC	Eurasian Economic Community
EIU	Economic Intelligence Unit
FDI	Foreign Direct Investments
FTUK	Federation of Trade Unions of Kyrgyzstan
FTZ	Free Trade Zone
GDP	Gross Domestic Product
Goskomstat	*Gosudarstvennyi Komitet po Statistike* (National Statistical Committee)
HDI	Human Development Index
IMF	International Monetary Fund
IMU	Islamic Movement of Uzbekistan
KGB	*Komitet Gosudarstvennoi Bezopastnosti* (Committee on State Security)

KGS	Kyrgyzstani Som (national currency)
Kolkhoz	*Kollektivnoye Khozyaistvo* (collective farm)
KOMSOMOL	*Kommunisticheskii Soyuz Molodezhi* (Youth Communist League)
Kyrgyz ASSR	Kyrgyz Autonomous Soviet Socialist Republic
Kyrgyz SSR	Kyrgyz Soviet Socialist Republic
NATO PfP	North Atlantic Treaty Organization's Partnership for Peace (program)
Natstatcom	National Statistical Committee
NGO	Nongovernmental Organization
OIC	Organization of the Islamic Conference
OSCE	Organization for Security and Cooperation in Europe
RSFSR	Russian Soviet Federal Socialist Republic
SADUM	*Tsentralno-Aziatskoye Dukhovnoye Upravleniye* (Central Asian Spiritual Board)
SCO	Shanghai Cooperation Organization
Sovkhoz	*Sovetskoye khozyaistvo* (Soviet farm)
TASSR	Turkistan Autonomous Soviet Socialist Republic
TCP	Turkistan Communist Party
TSSR	Turkistan Soviet Socialist Republic
UNDP	United Nations Development Program
UNESCO	United Nations Educational, Scientific, and Cultural Organization
USSR	Union of Soviet Socialist Republics
WTO	World Trade Organization

Department of Public Information
Cartographic Section

Map No. 3770 Rev. 3   UNITED NATIONS
August 1998

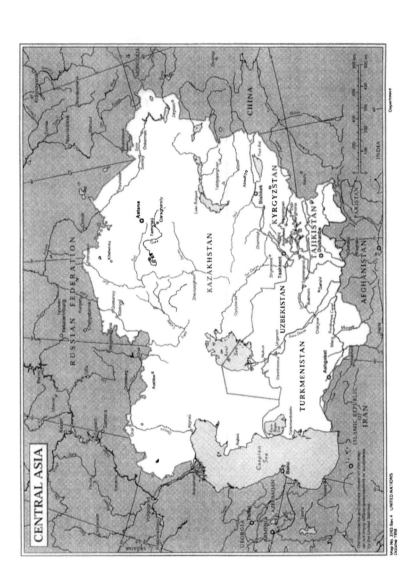

CENTRAL ASIA

Chronology

Early History up to Around 500 A.D.

2,000–1,000 B.C., Bronze Age Irrigation systems were developed in Central Asia. Bronze utensils and equipment were found, also some jewelry (Naryn region).

First Millennium B.C. The Sogd, Bactria, and Khorasm mentioned in ancient chronicles.

12th–7th centuries B.C. First settled communities, settlements around modern Osh.

6th–3rd centuries B.C. Tribal unions of Saks in Tian-Shan.

329 B.C. Alexander the Great conquered Central Asia.

4th–1st centuries B.C. Shurabashat culture in the Ferghana Valley.

3rd–2nd centuries B.C. Greco-Bactrian states in Central Asia.

2nd century B.C. The Great Silk Road starts to function.

1st century B.C. The Huns conquered ancient Kyrgyz tribes.

4th–5th centuries A.D. The Kushan Empire in Central Asia.

Khanates, Arrival of Islam: 552–1722 A.D.

552–744 Turk Khanate.

568–571 War between western Turks and Iran.

581 Factual division of Turk Khanate into western and eastern parts.

582–593   Civil strife between western and eastern Turks.

603   *De jure* establishment of Western and Eastern Turk Khanates.

7th century (1st half)   Establishment of ancient Turk alphabet.

622   Beginning of Muslim (Hijra) calendar.

654–683   First incursions of Arabs into Central Asia.

682–744   Second Khanate of Eastern Turks.

704–746   Turgesh Khanate.

711   Defeat of Turgesh Khanate by Eastern Turks Khanate.

716   Resurgence of Turgesh Khanate.

751   Battle between Chinese troops and joint troops of Arabs and Karluks on the Talas River.

766–940   Karluk Khanate.

8th century   Establishment of the legendary Kyrgyz Khanate on the Yenisey River.

9th century   The Kyrgyz tribes began to move from the Yenisey River basin to the Tenir-Too mountains (territory of present Kyrgyzstan).

940   Balasagun is conquered by the Karakhanids.

960   Islam is proclaimed an official religion of the Karakhanids.

992–996   Karakhanids' armed incursions into Bukhara.

999   Karakhanids conquered Maveranahr.

10th–11th centuries   Architectural and cultural complex Burana was built.

1015/1016   Yusuf Balasaguni was born.

1069/1070   Creation of Turk poem *Kutadgu Bilig* [Knowledge which brings happiness] by Yusuf Balasaguni.

1070   *De jure* formations of two Karakhanid states—Eastern and Western.

1072–1974   Creation of *Divan Lugat at-Turk* [Dictionary of Turk dialects] by Makhmud Kashagari.

11th–12th centuries   Uzgen architectural complex was built.

12th century   Shakh Fazil Mausoleum was built.

1219–1224   Genghis Khan (also spelled as Chingis Khan, first known as Temujin) turned his war campaign toward Central Asia.

1348   Establishment of Mogulistan.

1370–1380   Invasion by troops of Tamerlane (Timur) into Mogulistan.

15th–16th centuries   The Kyrgyzs established their first legendary state on the territory of contemporary Kyrgyzstan. First historical reference to the Ala-Too mountain areas as the "land of Kyrgyzs" (Kyrgyzstan).

14th–15th centuries   Manas Mausoleum was built in the Talas region.

16th century   Creation of *Majmu at-Tavarikh* [Historical essays] where some episodes of Manas are mentioned for the first time.

1500–1512   Sheibani Khan conquered Central Asia; Timurids were defeated.

1635   Establishment of Jungar Khanate.

1710   Kokand Khanate declared its independence from the Bukhara Khanate.

Russian Interest in Turkistan: 1722–1917

1731–1854   Russia acquired the Kazakh steppes (territory of present Kazakhstan).

1758–1759   Defeat of Jungar Khanate; Tsins conquered the Eastern Turkistan.

1758   Several representatives of the Kyrgyz tribes arrived in Beijing. Kyrgyz tribes recognized Chinese suzerainty.

1762–1831   The Kokand Khanate acquired territories populated by the Kyrgyz tribes.

1774–1782   Phillip Semenovich Efremov traveled through Kyrgyz land to India.

1785   Kyrgyz delegation led by Abdrakhman Kuchak(ov)-uulu arrived in Saint-Petersburg.

1786 Book by Filipp Efremov was published, which gave first information about southern Kyrgyzs.

1787 Reciprocal visit of Russian delegation led by Muslim Agafyorov to Kyrgyz land.

1814 Kyrgyz delegation from Ysyk Kol arrived in Russian Siberia with a letter requesting Russian protection from the Kokand Khanate.

1821 Kyrgyz riot in the Talas valley against the Kokand Khanate.

1822 Kyrgyz riot in Osh against the Kokand Khanate.

1824 Kyrgyz delegation arrived in Russian Siberia with another letter requesting Russian protection.

1825 Madali Khan attacked Kyrgyzs in the Chui valley. The Kokand Khanate built outposts Pishpek (Frunze and now Bishkek) and Tokmak in the Chui valley.

1827 Diplomatic mission led by A. L. Bubyonov arrived in Kyrgyz land.

1830s Riot of the Kyrgyzs of Naryn region led by Tailak against the Kokand Khanate.

1838–1842 First Anglo-Afghan war.

1839–1840 Russians undertook their first unsuccessful expedition to Khiva.

1842 Entire British garrison was slaughtered in the outskirts of Kabul. British retreated from Afghanistan. Two British officers, Colonel Charles Stuart and Captain Arthur Connolly, traveled through Turkistan but were captured and hanged in Bukhara. Riot of Kyrgyzs of Ysyk Kol region against the Kokand Khanate.

1844 Kyrgyzs of Ysyk Kol region requested Russian protection from the authorities in Western Siberia.

1845 Kyrgyz riot in the Alai valley and in Osh against the Kokand Khanate.

1847 Kyrgyz delegation from the Chui valley asked for Russian Empire protection.

1847–1848   Kyrgyz riot in Namangan against the Kokand Khanate.

1851   Kulja Agreement between the Russian and Tsin Empires.

1855   Kyrgyzs from the Ysyk Kol valley accepted the Russian protectorate.

1856–1857   Expedition to Central Asia of Petr Semyonov-Tianshanski and artist P. M. Kosharov.

1856–1858   Chokan Valikhanov, a Kazakh aristocrat in the Russian service, travels through the territory populated by the Kyrgyz tribes. Later he wrote scholarly accounts of his travel. He was the first to write down excerpts from Kyrgyz oral epic "Manas."

1860   Russian troops with Kyrgyz assistance stormed the Kokand military outposts Pishpek (now Bishkek) and Tokmak.

1861   Kokand reclaimed Pishpek and Tokmak.

1862   Russian troops together with Kyrgyzs took back Pishpek.

1863   Successful riot of Kyrgyzs against Kokand Khanate in Toguz Toroo. Kyrgyzs of Ak Sai and Chatyr Kol accepted the Russian protectorate.

1864   Kyrgyzs from Chatkal accepted the Russian protectorate. Establishment of Russian outpost Tokmak.

1864–1867   Nikolai Severtsov traveled through the Kyrgyz land.

1864–1933   Toktogul Satylganov—famous Kyrgyz *akyn* (poet) and composer.

1865   Russian troops captured Tashkent, an important trade center and a strategic outpost of the Kokand Khanate. Russian authorities established the Turkistan *oblast*, which included the territory of present-day northern Kyrgyzstan.

1867   Russian ethnographic exhibition was opened in Moscow; among the Kyrgyz handicraft works were paintings by P. M. Kosharov. Turkistan *oblast* was reorganized into Turkistan Governor-Generalship (later Turkistan province), which included territory of present-day northern Kyrgyzstan.

1868–1871 Expedition of Alexei Fedchenko to the Kokand Khanate and southern territories of Kyrgyz land.

1869 Agreement was reached on acceptance by Kokand Khanate of its vassal dependence on Russian Empire.

1869–1870 Artist Vasilii Verechshagin spent some time in Kyrgyz land and brought back to Russia a number of paintings reflecting the lifestyle of Kyrgyz people.

1875 Russian troops captured the city of Kokand.

1876 Kokand Khanate was abolished.

1878–1880 The Second Anglo-Afghan War. The British establish control over Afghanistan's foreign relations.

1878 Pishpek (now Bishkek) obtained city status and became the capital of the *uyezd*.

1895 Convention was concluded between Great Britain and Russia (division of spheres of influence in the Pamirs area).

1898 Popular uprising in Andijan against the Russians.

1916 Widespread uprising in the Chui valley against the Russians and the Tsar's decree to mobilize the Kyrgyzs and other Turkistanis for World War I.

Soviet Era: 1917–1991

1917 Russian Duma forced the abdication of Tsar Nicolas II, the last Tsar of the Russian Empire, and establishment of the Russian Republic. **7 April:** Establishment of Turkistan Committee of the Provisional Government in Tashkent. **Summer:** Bolshevik newspaper *Pravda* was delivered to Pishpek public library. **25 October:** The Bolshevik Revolution in Saint-Petersburg. **28 October–1 November:** The Bolsheviks came to power in Tashkent. **8 November:** Vladimir Lenin's *Decree on Land* was published in the newspaper *Nasha Gazeta* [Our newspaper]. **29 November:** Establishment of antirevolutionary Government of Kokand Autonomy. **12 December:** Old judicial system was abolished.

1918 January–February: The Soviet power was established in Pishpek. **19–22 February:** Antirevolutionary Kokand Autonomy was liquidated. **16 April:** Antirevolutionary riot of Semirechie Kazaks began. **20 April–1 May:** The Turkistan Autonomous Soviet Socialist Republic (TASSR) was formed within the Russian Soviet Federative Socialist Republic (RSFSR). **21 April:** Turkistan People's University was opened in Tashkent. **15 May:** Antirevolutionary riot of the Czech corps began. **22 July:** Semirechie front was opened. **13 September:** First Soviet regiment was formed in Pishpek. **5–15 October:** The Constitution of Turkistan ASSR was adopted during the VI Extraordinary Session of Turkistan Soviets. **6–28 December:** Anti-Soviet revolt in Pishpek *uyezd.*

1919 19–21 January: Antirevolutionary riot in Tashkent led by Osipov. **25 February:** Ferghana front was opened. **19–31 March:** Second Congress of the Turkistan Communist Party (TCP) and establishment of the Muslim Bureau of the TCP. **7 April:** Establishment of the Revolutionary Military Council (government) of the Turkistan ASSR **15–19 May:** First Congress of Communist Party in the Naryn *uyezd.* **14 August:** Turkistan front was opened. **September:** Orenburg front was liquidated. Turkistan and Russian republics were re-united. **December:** Establishment of Muslim Bureau of Bolsheviks in Osh.

1920 3 February: Government of the Turkistan ASSR issued a decree on providing assistance to those Kyrgyz refugees who escaped to China during the popular uprising of 1916. **March:** Anti-revolutionary armed forces in Semirechie were defeated. Semirechie front was liquidated. **September:** Turkistan State University was established. **5–22 November:** Anti-Soviet riots in the Naryn *uyezd.*

1921 February–May: Water and land reforms in the Talas valley and in Pishpek and Przhevalsk *uyezds.*

1922 4 August: Enver Pasha, a Turkish military officer and one of the leaders of the *Basmachi* movement in Central Asia, killed in a battle. **30 December:** Union of Soviet Socialist Republics (USSR) was established with the capital in Moscow.

1923 28 October: Government of Turkistan issued a decree on liquidation of illiteracy in Central Asia.

1924 21 January: Lenin died. **28 April:** Resolution was issued on necessity and timeliness of national state delimitation of Central Asia.

Provisional territorial committees were formed—Uzbek, Turkmen, Kyrgyz, Kazakh, and Tajik. **12 June:** Resolution was issued on the "nation-state delimitation in Central Asia." **14 October:** Kara-Kyrgyz (later Kyrgyz) Autonomous *Oblast* (province) was established with its center in Pishpek under the jurisdiction of the Russian Federation. **7 November:** First Kyrgyz newspaper *Erkin Too* [Free Mountains] was established, on 29 August 1927 it was renamed *Kyzyl Kyrgyzstan* [Red Kyrgyzstan]. **1924:** Osh Teaching College was opened.

1925 **March:** First women's club opened in Kyrgyzstan. Newspaper *Batratskaya Pravda* was established (renamed later *Sovetskaya Kirgizia*). **25 May:** Kara-Kyrgyz Autonomous *Oblast* became Kyrgyz Autonomous *Oblast*. **10 November:** Establishment of the Kyrgyz Institute of Education.

1926 Kyrgyzstan Mamlekketik Basmasy, the first publishing house, was established in Kyrgyzstan. First radio center was established in the capital. First census was conducted in Kyrgyzstan. **1 February:** Resolution was adopted on granting the Kyrgyz Autonomous *Oblast* the status of Kyrgyz Autonomous Soviet Socialist Republic (KASSR). **11 May:** Pishpek was renamed Frunze. **13 July:** First passenger steam boat on the Ysyk-Kol Lake. **14 October:** Committee was established on transformation of Kyrgyz alphabet from Arabic script to Latin.

1927 **March:** Central Museum of Kyrgyzstan was opened. **July:** Government issued a decree on water and land reforms in Jalal Abad and Osh *kantons*.

1929 **5 February:** Kyrgyz government issued decree on deportation of *manaps* and *biis* from the republic and confiscation of their land and property. **April:** Kyrgyz ASSR adopted its first Constitution. **29 November:** Decision was adopted to complete transfer of Kyrgyz alphabet from Arabic to Latin script by 1 January 1930. **10 December:** First five-year plan of economic development was adopted. Mass deportation of Kyrgyz *manaps*, *biis*, and former opposition leaders began.

1929–1931 First wave of Stalin purges.

1930 Mass collectivization and settlement programs began. **August:** Primary education became compulsory. **7 November:** First season of Kyrgyz State Theater began. **30 November:** Newspaper in Kyrgyz language *Sabattuu Bol* [Be literate] was established.

1931   First literary journal *Chabyyl* (later *Ala-Too*) in Kyrgyz language was published.

1932   5 November: Establishment of first tertiary education center in the republic—Kyrgyz State Pedagogical Institute.

1933   Kyrgyz Agricultural Institute was established.

1934   First art exhibition of Kyrgyz painters was organized in Kyrgyzstan. First Kyrgyz Congress of writers.

1935   Russian Drama Theater was established in Frunze. **October:** First Kyrgyz Congress of female youth.

1936   Kyrgyz State Philharmonic was established. **5 December:** The Kyrgyz Autonomous Soviet Socialist Republic became Kyrgyz Soviet Socialist Republic (Kyrgyz SSR).

1936–1938   Mass purges against the Kyrgyz intelligentsia and political leadership were launched in the republic. Thousands were sent to labor camps or executed, accused of opposing the political regime.

1937   23 March: New Kyrgyz Constitution was adopted, changing some arrangements in the previous Constitution including the addition of a section that Kyrgyzstan had the right to leave the USSR.

1939   Decade of Kyrgyz Literature and Art in Moscow. Census conducted in Kyrgyzstan.

1939–1940   Widespread construction of large irrigation systems

1940   Kyrgyzstan converts its alphabet from Latin to Cyrillic script. **10 May:** Beginning of construction of Big Chui Canal.

1940s   Uranium mining began in Kyrgyzstan. The uranium was later used to produce the first Soviet atomic bomb.

1941   Government announced that illiteracy was liquidated among the majority of the adult population.

1941–1945   Soviet Union fought against the Nazis in World War II.

1942   First cinema-producing center was established. **August:** Kyrgyz State Theater of Opera and Ballet was established.

1943   Kyrgyz branch of the Academy of Science of the USSR was opened.

1951 Kyrgyz State University was established in Frunze (now Bishkek).

1953 Josef Stalin died in Moscow. The Kremlin began political changes and the rehabilitation of the Kyrgyz intelligentsia.

1954 Kyrgyz Academy of Science was established.

1957 Kyrgyz SSR was awarded the order of Lenin for successes in agricultural development.

1958 Second Decade of Kyrgyz Literature and Art in Moscow.

1959 Census conducted in Kyrgyzstan.

1963 Kyrgyz SSR was awarded the order of Lenin.

1967 Kyrgyz State Institute of Arts was established.

1973 Kyrgyz SSR was awarded the order of Friendship of the Peoples.

1974 Kyrgyz SSR was awarded the order of the October Revolution.

1979 Toktogul hydroelectric power station was launched. Census conducted in Kyrgyzstan.

1985 Michael Gorbachev came to power. Beginning of the campaign against corruption in Kyrgyzstan.

1985 Turdakun Usubaliyev was dismissed from his position.

1986 Dinmuhamed Kunayev, long-standing Kazakh leader, was dismissed and replaced by Genadii Kolbin. Students in Alma-Ata organized unsanctioned meetings and demonstrations in protest of Kunayev's dismissal. Students in Frunze were warned to refrain from any political activities.

1989 **August:** Draft of Kyrgyzstan's Law on Languages was published in main newspapers, sparking heated debates. **23 September:** Jogorku Kenesh (Parliament) passes the Law on Languages, declaring Kyrgyz the official language of the Republic.

1990 **June:** Interethnic conflicts occurred in Osh region of southern Kyrgyzstan; Leaders of Central Asian Republics gathered in Bishkek (then Frunze) and agreed to establish a Central Asian Union. **October:** Democratic Movement of Kyrgyzstan (DMK) was established in Bishkek.

27 October: Jogorku Kenesh elected Dr. Askar Akayev as the first President of the Kyrgyz Soviet Socialist Republic. **15 December:** Jogorku Kenesh adopted the Declaration on Kyrgyzstan's Sovereignty.

Independence, Kyrgyz Republic

1991 18 February: President Akayev and President Nursultan Nazarbayev of Kazakhstan stated that the Gulf War should be stopped. **17 March:** All-Union referendum on the future of the Soviet Union. **6 April:** First Secretary Absamat Masaliyev resigned from his position. **19 August:** Anti-Gorbachev coup d'etat in Moscow. **25 August:** Communist Party of Kyrgyz SSR dissolved. **28 August:** President Boris Yeltsin declared that the Russian Federation established control over key Soviet Ministries. **29 August:** Supreme Soviet adopted a resolution dissolving the Communist Party. **31 August:** Jogorku Kenesh adopted the Declaration on political independence of Kyrgyzstan. **10 September:** Kyrgyz Komsomol dissolved. **2 October:** Political Consultative Council met to discuss the Union Treaty. **12 October:** Dr. Akayev was elected as Kyrgyzstan's president by popular vote. **18 October:** Kyrgyzstan signed the Treaty on Economic Community. **22 October:** President Akayev stated before the United Nations General Assembly that the Soviet Union ceased to exist. **14 November:** Kyrgyzstan declared that it was ready to sign the new Union Treaty. **8 December:** Belarus, the Russian Federation, and the Ukraine, founding members of the USSR, signed a treaty dissolving the Soviet Union. Kyrgyzstan joined the Commonwealth of Independent States (CIS). **17 December:** Yeltsin and Gorbachev agreed that the Soviet Union would cease to exist on 1 January 1992. **16 December:** Turkey recognized the independence of Kyrgyzstan. **21 December:** Kyrgyzstan signed the Alma-Ata Declaration and became a member of the CIS. **25 December:** Gorbachev resigned from the post of president.

1992 30 January: Kyrgyzstan was admitted into the Conference for Security and Cooperation in Europe. **1 February:** The United States opened its embassy in Bishkek. **17 February:** Kyrgyzstan joined the Economic Cooperation Organization (ECO). **27 February:** Felix Kulov was appointed vice-president. **2 March:** Kyrgyzstan became a member of the UN. **25 March:** Chairman of Supreme Soviet on Military Affairs declared that Kyrgyzstan would not establish its own army. **27 March:**

Kyrgyzstan was admitted to the International Monetary Fund (IMF) and World Bank. **22–23 April:** Kyrgyzstan signed an agreement with neighboring Central Asian states recognizing existing borders. **May:** Kyrgyzstan signed the CIS Security Treaty (Tashkent Declaration). **1 June:** Kyrgyzstan established its control over all military units on its territory. **16 July:** North Atlantic Treaty Organization (NATO) delegation visited Kyrgyzstan. **28 July:** Free Uiguristan Party held its congress in Bishkek. **1 September:** Kyrgyzstan freed food prices. **30 November:** Kyrgyzstan joined the CIS Peacekeeping force in Tajikistan. **3 December:** Kyrgyzstan signed an agreement on demilitarization of its borders with China.

1993   March: Turkic Orthographical Conference called for the change from Cyrillic to Latin script for all Central Asian Turkic languages. **10 March:** Commission set up to investigate allegation that Felix Kulov was involved in the sale of weapons to Tajikistan. **7 April:** Turkish President Turgut Ozal visited Kyrgyzstan. **April:** Kyrgyzstan received the status of a "developing nation." **5 May:** Jogorku Kenesh adopted new Kyrgyzstan's Constitution. **10 May:** Kyrgyzstan introduced its currency, the *Som.* **27 May:** President Akayev asked President Islam Karimov of Uzbekistan to lift trade and customs restrictions between the two countries imposed due to the introduction of the Kyrgyz currency. **7 July:** Kyrgyzstan and Russia signed a military agreement. **22 July:** Janybek Umetaliev, chairman of the Committee on Defense, resigned. **9 December:** Kyrgyz Parliament demanded resignation of Prime Minister Tursunbek Chyngyshev over gold scandal. **12 December:** U.S. Vice-President Al Gore arrived in Bishkek on an official visit. **13 December:** President Akayev appointed Apas Dzhumagulov as prime minister.

1994   16 January: Kyrgyzstan joined the Central Asian Economic Union (CAEU). **21–23 January:** People's Assembly of Kyrgyzstan was established. **31 January:** National referendum on constitutional changes held in Kyrgyzstan. **1 February:** Kyrgyzstan agreed to remove customs controls on its borders with Kazakhstan and Uzbekistan under the CAEU agreement. **4 March:** Kyrgyzstan and Russia signed an agreement regulating rights of Russian citizens in Kyrgyz military service. **1 June:** Kyrgyzstan joined NATO's Partnership for Peace program. **8 July:** CAEU leaders agreed to extend their cooperation into the defense area. **15 July:** Esengul Omuraliyev, chairman of State Property

Fund, dismissed on mismanagement allegations. **21 July:** Kyrgyz and Russian Defense Ministers signed a bilateral agreement on military cooperation. **22 October:** Referendum was held on constitutional changes and introducing a new bicameral parliament.

1995   5 February: Elections to the Jogorku Kenesh. **16 February:** A parliamentary candidate was assassinated in Bishkek. **24 April:** The CAEU prime ministers signed a five-year economic integration plan. **7 July:** Agreement signed with Cameco Corporation (Canada) on joint development of the Kumtor gold field. **4 September:** Celebration of the 1,000th anniversary of Kyrgyz oral epic *Manas*. **20 September:** Parliament rejected a proposal for a referendum prolonging President Akayev's term in office until 2000 without an election. **15 December:** The CAEU members declared their intention to establish the Central Asian Peacekeeping Battalion (Centrasbat). **24 December:** Akayev won the presidential elections.

1996   3 January: A new constitutional referendum announced aiming to increase presidential powers. **10 January:** Agreement on establishing a Custom Union with Russia is discussed. **10 February:** National referendum approved constitutional changes. **19 February:** Kyrgyzelbank was declared bankrupt. **26 February:** The government resigned. **11 March:** Russian language was granted the status of "official language." **29 March:** Kyrgyzstan joined the CIS Custom Union. **27 April:** President Akayev agreed to resolve border disputes with China within the Shanghai Forum (now Shanghai Cooperation Organization). **19 July:** Three bombs exploded damaging government buildings. **25 November:** President Akayev approved private ownership of land. **17 December:** Topchubek Turgunaliyev, a leading opposition figure, was arrested on corruption charges.

1997   10 January: Agreements signed between Kazakhstan, Uzbekistan, and Kyrgyz Republic on eternal friendship. **12 March:** NATO secretary-general visited Bishkek. **5 June:** Committee on Protection of Journalists protested against detention of independent journalists. **1 July:** Foreign Minister Roza Otunbayeva replaced. **9–15 July:** President Akayev visited Washington and held meetings with Al Gore. **21 July:** Official opening of Andijan-Osh-Kashgar highway. **15 September:** Kyrgyzstan joined the Centrasbat military exercises in Kazakhstan. **12 November:** Hillary Clinton visited Kyrgyzstan.

1998 **22 January:** Space flight of first Kyrgyz cosmonaut, Salizhan Sharipov, with an American space expedition. **April:** Establishment of a new government led by Kubanychbek Dzhumaliyev. **17 October:** Referendum on adoption of the law on amendments of the Kyrgyz Constitution. **December:** Prime Minister Dzhumaliyev was dismissed. Jumabek Ibraimov was appointed as a new prime minister.

1999 The year 1999 was proclaimed the Year of Health. **8 February:** Several ministers dismissed on corruption allegations. **9 February:** Kazakhstan imposed custom duties on all Kyrgyz goods in response to Kyrgyzstan's admission to the World Trade Organization (WTO). **24 March:** Census of the Kyrgyz Republic began. **4 April:** Prime Minister Ibraimov died of cancer. **2 May:** Arrest of a group suspected of plotting terrorist actions. **14 May:** Security Council approved a new Foreign-Policy Concept. **May:** *Jogorku Kenesh* adopted Law on Land, Law on Cooperation, and Law on Farming. **22–23 June:** Several Parliament members arrested on corruption charges. **9 July:** Ar-Namys political party established. **6 August:** Militant incursion in Batken *oblast*; four Japanese geologists were taken hostage. **30 August:** Uzbek air force planes bombed militants' position but hit civilians. **7 September:** Bolot Dzhanuzakov appointed as new head of the Security Council. **24 October:** Four Japanese hostages were released allegedly for US$4 million ransom. Batken *oblast* was formed. **November:** Kyrgyz troops with military assistance from Russia and Uzbekistan expelled militants from Kyrgyzstan.

2000 **February:** Parliamentary elections held in Kyrgyzstan. **12 March:** Kulov was arrested on charges of embezzlement and abuse of power allegedly committed, but released in August. **Summer:** Incursion of militants of the Islamic Movement of Uzbekistan into the territory of Kyrgyzstan. **4–5 October:** Osh celebrated its 3000th anniversary. **29 October:** Akayev won his third term as president. **21 December:** Kurmanbek Bakiyev was appointed prime minister. **26 December:** Law on Status of the Teacher was adopted by the Jogorku Kenesh.

2001 The year 2001 was declared the Year of Tourism in Kyrgyz Republic. **January:** A closed military trial convicted Kulov of abuse of power while serving as national security minister and sentenced him to seven years in prison. **29 May:** National Forum adopted the National Strategic Program of Complex Development for 2001–2010. **June:** The Shanghai Forum was renamed Shanghai Cooperation Organization

(SCO) and members emphasized the need for military cooperation against terrorism. **August:** Topchubek Turgunaliyev, a leading opposition figure, was released from prison. **November:** The U.S. military airbase was established at Manas Airport. **16 December:** First American contingent arrived in Kyrgyzstan.

2002   **5 January:** Azimbek Beknazarov, a member of the Jogorku Kenesh and opposition figure, arrested. Opposition groups began hunger strikes and meetings of protest in Bishkek and Jalal Abad *oblast.* **18 February:** General Richard Myers, chairman of the U.S. Joint Chiefs of Staff, met President Akayev and said the United States planned to expand military cooperation with Kyrgyzstan, including joint military exercises and training of Kyrgyz military personnel in the United States. **17 March:** Large meeting in support of Beknazarov organized in Kerben, in Aksy District. Police attempted to disperse people killing six and injuring dozens of civilians. **April:** James Wolfensohn, the president of the World Bank, visited Bishkek. The CIS Rapid Reaction Force exercises held in Kyrgyzstan and Tajikistan. **10 May:** The Kyrgyz Legislative Assembly ratified the Kyrgyz-China border agreement signed in 1999. **23 May:** Government resigned. New government declared a program "Kyrgyzstan is a Home for Human Rights." **June:** The United States extended the lease of Manas airport. Kyrgyzstan agreed to host the Russian military base and leased to Russia the facilities of the former Soviet airbase in the city of Kant. **August:** Constitutional Commission was established. Kyrgyz population passed the five-million mark. **19–24 September:** President Akayev visited the United States and presented a speech at the 57th session of the UN General Assembly. **October:** Kofi Anan, UN secretary-general, visited Kyrgyzstan. **23–28 December:** Joint Kyrgyz-Tajik intergovernmental commission on border delimitation held meeting in Bishkek to discuss procedures of the border delimitation process.

2003   **January:** Kyrgyz government declared 2003 as the Year of Kyrgyz Statehood. John O'Keefe, the U.S. ambassador to Kyrgyzstan, announced that the Kyrgyz Justice Ministry officially registered an international publishing house. Police confiscated property and the bank account of the independent newspaper *Moia stolitsa* [My Capital City]. The Japanese Embassy to Kyrgyzstan was officially opened in Bishkek. **27–28 January:** U.S. Assistant Secretary of State Elizabeth Jones met

with President Akayev to discuss the war on international terrorism.
2 February: National referendum approved constitutional changes
with a turnout of 86 percent and support for changes of 75 percent.
March: *Kurultai* (congress) of peoples of Kyrgyzstan was held in
Bishkek. **April:** Kyrgyzstan called for the resolution of Iraq problem
with active participation of the UN and offered its assistance in the postwar restoration of Iraq's economy. **June:** the Jogorku Kenesh granted
President Akayev a lifelong immunity from prosecution. **August:** Chinese defense delegation visited Kyrgyzstan. Kyrgyz troops took part in
the Kyrgyz-Kazakh-China joint military exercises.

Introduction

Kyrgyzstan (also known as the Kyrgyz Republic and by convention called "Kirgizia" until 1991) was established on 14 October 1924 as an autonomous republic within the Russian Federation. It comprised parts of the former eastern provinces of the Kokand Khanate. On 5 December 1936 Kyrgyzstan was granted the status of the Kyrgyz Soviet Socialist Republic (Kyrgyz SSR), which gave it constitutional rights to maintain some autonomy in cultural, administrative, and social affairs. Kyrgyzstan declared its independence from the Union of Soviet Socialist Republics (USSR) on 31 August 1991.

LAND AND PEOPLE

Kyrgyzstan is located in Central Asia, sharing 858 kilometers (km) of its borders with China in the east, 870 km with Tajikistan in the south, 1,099 km with Uzbekistan in the west, and 1,051 km with Kazakhstan in the north. Shaped as an arrowhead its territory lies along the southern borders of Kazakhstan and points toward the western borders of China. The country has a land area of 198,500 square kilometers (76,640 square miles) and is the second smallest in the Central Asian region after Tajikistan. The total area of Kyrgyzstan is approximately the size of England and Scotland combined or the state of Nebraska in the United States. It stretches between latitudes 39 and 43 degrees north of the equator and lies between longitudes 69 and 81 degrees east of Greenwich meridian.

There are three distinctive parts in the country, northern Kyrgyzstan (comprising the Chui and Talas valleys), southern Kyrgyzstan (covering parts of the Ferghana valley), and the highland Kyrgyzstan—the Tian-Shan mountains, which separate the three valleys. The mountains cover almost 87 percent of Kyrgyzstan's territory and nearly 60 percent of the country is elevated higher than 2,500 meters (approximately 8,200 feet). Northern Kyrgyzstan is divided into three administrative provinces (*oblasts*): Chui, Talas, and Ysyk Kol, and it stretches along the southern borders of Kazakhstan. This is the largest and most developed area of the republic. Bishkek, the capital city, is located in the Chui valley. This part of the country is characterized by relatively low mountain ranges. The valleys are watered by two major rivers—Chui and Talas—and by numerous small rivers and creeks that take their waters to Lake Ysyk Kol, the second largest mountain lake in the world. The area of the lake is 6,330 sq. km, and it is the largest salt-water lake in the region, which is free of ice in the winter. Hence the name of the lake means "hot lake."

Southern Kyrgyzstan is divided into three *oblasts*: Batken, Jalal-Abad, and Osh. It borders with Uzbekistan and Tajikistan. This is the most densely populated area of the country. Osh city, the second largest city in the republic, is situated in Osh *oblast*. This part of the country is characterized by the most fertile land along the Uzbekistan border, where the majority of the population lives. Batken *oblast*, which lies in the extreme south, is an exception in terms of population density. It shares parts of the Pamir mountain range (Trans-Alai range) with Tajikistan and is one of the least populated and smallest *oblasts* of the country.

The major highland mountain ranges stretch from the northwestern borders to the central parts of the country and then to the east and southeastern parts of the country. Most of these ranges are in the Naryn *oblast*, which is the largest province in the republic, covering nearly one-quarter of the country's territory. The Tian-Shan mountain range hosts *Pik Pobedy* (*Jenish Chokosu* in Kyrgyz or Victory Peak in English), the highest summit in Kyrgyzstan and in Tian-Shan, and the second highest peak in the Commonwealth of Independent States (CIS) (7,439 meters, or 24,406 feet). The peak is located close to the Kyrgyz-China border in northeastern Kyrgyzstan. This part of the country holds most of its water reserves, as Kyrgyzstan's and Central Asia's major glaciers may be found here. The country's largest water artery is the Naryn River; it flows westward through the middle of the country to the fertile Ferghana valley. The mountain passes in central Kyrgyzstan are covered with snow for at least four to five months a year and often impenetrable during winter. The Osh-Bishkek roadway is the only road through this region, which connects northern and southern Kyrgyzstan.

It goes through several mountain passes and is practically impassable during heavy snowfalls. The route is often closed for weeks during the fall and winter, thus making communication between the two parts of the country extremely vulnerable to the weather.

The climate in Kyrgyzstan is continental. The temperature and condensation vary widely depending on the region. In the valleys of northern Kyrgyzstan the climate is relatively mild and dry, the temperature ranging from -14°C (7°F) to +7°C (45°F) in January and the average daily temperature between +26°C (78°F) and +29°C (84°F) in July. In most parts of the Ferghana valley the climate is subtropical, ranging from +5°C (41°F) to +18°C (65°F) in January and from +26°C (78°F) to +33°C (92°F) in July (sometimes the temperature may exceed 40°C [100 F°]). The weather in the mountains, however, is characterized by extremes. In the mountain ranges with low altitudes the climate is dry continental with a temperature ranging from -18°C (2°F) to +5°C (41°F) in January and between +10°C (78°F) and +22°C (71°F) in July. The climate is more severe in the high elevated mountains (3,000 meters and higher), ranging from -28°C (-18°F) to -14° (7°F) in January and from +5°C (41°F) to +18°C (65°F) in July. Rainfall might vary between 180 millimeters (7 inches) in eastern Kyrgyzstan to 1,000 millimeters (40 inches) in southwestern parts of the country.

In the late 1990s the global warming and drying up of the Aral Sea in Uzbekistan began to have an effect upon the republic. For several years in a row, a harsh drought plagued the Ferghana valley, and vast areas of southern Kyrgyzstan experienced a water shortage. Moreover, the summers were drier in northern Kyrgyzstan (according to local reports the frequency of droughts with various degrees of intensity has doubled in the Chui valley), and winters were much colder in mountainous regions of the republic. Deforestation of the mountain slopes increased the chances of landslides in many parts of the republic. If this trend continues, it might negatively affect Kyrgyzstan's ecosystem, especially its water reserves and glaciers. According to the Ministry of Environmental Protection, 1,081 glaciers in the Pamir-Alai and 71 glaciers in the Zaili Alatau mountain range disappeared between 1957 and 1980, and water inflows in some parts of the Naryn River aqua-area decreased by up to 25 percent.

Kyrgyzstan is rich in various mineral resources, mainly nonoil mineral deposits. This includes deposits of coal, gold, uranium, mercury, antimony, nepheline, bismuth, lead, zinc, and some others. However, due to the remoteness of the country from world markets, rudimentary transportation infrastructure and high mountains, relatively few resources are exploited. Gold, coal, and antimony are more significant resources produced by the mining sector in Kyrgyzstan.

The proven gold deposits consist of between 500–700 tons. Gold was discovered in the early 1960s, but only in the mid-1970s were there attempts at industrial exploitation of gold reserves in the republic. Major investments, however, were made in the early 1990s, and since the middle of the 1990s, the country has been extracting between 19 and 22 tons of gold a year, mainly for export.

The republic has significant reserves of coal, which are estimated at around 31 billion tons (2001). Coal was first discovered in Kyrgyzstan in the early 1900s and by 1913 there were four major fields exploited commercially in southern Kyrgyzstan. Coal extraction gradually increased and peaked at around 4.2 million tons in 1980. It was, however, significantly reduced in the 1990s due to cuts in subsidies and economic restructuring. In 2000 Kyrgyzstan extracted 419,000 tons of coal.

Kyrgyzstan's oil reserves are estimated at around 700 million barrels in the southern provinces of the republic, and 1,500 million barrels of oil reserves in the northern and eastern provinces. Oil was first discovered in Kyrgyzstan in the early 1900s and by 1913 the first oil-field in Mailu-Suu district (southern Kyrgyzstan) was producing 3,000 tons of oil annually for industrial consumption. Oil extraction gradually increased and peaked in 1960, with a total of 464,000 tons. However, the country considerably reduced oil extraction in the 1970s and 1980s, switching to imported petroleum. In 2002 Kyrgyzstan only produced between 75,000 and 80,000 tons of oil.

The country's hydroelectric power resources are significant, as Kyrgyzstan is in third place in the CIS (after Russia and Tajikistan) for potential hydroelectric power resources.

Only 7 percent of the total land area is cultivated in the republic and only around 12 percent of the territory is used for pasture. Nonetheless, due to a favorable climate and intensive irrigation, the agricultural sector produces enough crops to cover the country's food requirements.

The population in Kyrgyzstan was estimated at 5 million at the end of 2002, up from 1 million in 1926. It doubled since the 1960s due to improved health, longer life expectancy, and immigration of people from other parts of the USSR in the 1960s and 1970s. In 2002 the birth rate stood at 26.11 births per 1,000, while the death rate stood at 9.1 deaths per 1,000 (CIA est.). The population growth rate in Kyrgyzstan is 1.45 percent (2002), and if the current trend in the fertility rate remains unchanged it is estimated that the population would double by 2044. In the 1980s and 1990s, however, the rapidly rising emigration of people, both permanent and temporary, offset the demographic growth. The major destinations for migrants from Kyrgyzstan are Russia, Ukraine, Germany, Turkey, and Kazakhstan. Temporary workers are mainly employed in the low-skill and low-wage construction and services sectors and in agricultural plantations in neighboring Kazakhstan and in Russia. According to the *CIA World Factbook,* the emigration rate stood at the 2.66 migrant(s) per 1,000 population in 2001, or approximately 13,000 a year, although it is significantly lower than the peak of about 110,000 people in 1994.

Kyrgyzstan's population is unevenly distributed, with almost three-quarters, or 3.5 million living in the most urbanized *oblasts* of Jalal-Abad, Osh, and Chui. The average population density is about 25 persons per square kilometer; however, it ranges from 40 in the Osh and Chui valley to 5.5 in the Naryn valley. Some parts of northeastern Kyrgyzstan are uninhabited due to the high mountain elevation and harsh climate.

Kyrgyzstan is a multiethnic country with a very diverse population. The Kyrgyz (singular Kyrgyz) make up 68 percent of the population (2002 est.). Ethnic Uzbeks, the second largest ethnic group, make up 14 percent of the population; Russians comprise 10 percent, and various other groups, including Dungans, Uigurs, Kazakhs, and Tajiks, together make up the remaining 8 percent of the population. The current ethnic structure was largely formed during the 20th century, when the tsarist and then the Soviet administrations encouraged migration from central Russia, Ukraine, and the Caucasus. Kyrgyzstan's population is young, with 34.4 percent (male 838,224; female 821,230) below the age of 14 and just about 6.2 percent of the population above 65 (CIA 2003 est.).

Urbanization did not penetrate Kyrgyzstani society very far. In 1999 just over 34.8 percent of the population lived in urban areas, up from 33.5 percent in 1959, but down from 38.3 percent in 1979. Kyrgyzstan along with Tajikistan are the only countries in the CIS that experienced a population decline in urban areas. This was mainly attributed to the emigration of the Slavic population from the major urban areas. The country's capital city, Bishkek (known as Frunze between 1926 and 1991), is home to 700,000 people (2002) or 14 percent of the population. However, independent experts estimated this figure as between 1 and 1.3 million people, including temporary and seasonal workers and migrants.

Religion plays an increasingly important role in the republic after 70 years of the Soviet policy of promoting secular identity. Nearly all Kyrgyzs and Uzbeks are Muslims, although religious fervor varies widely between people living in urban and rural areas and between northern and southern Kyrgyzstan. The population of the latter is traditionally more religious than the population in other parts of the country. In the 1990s several Christian missionary groups (Protestants and some others) were established in the republic, and reportedly between 1,000 and 4,000 Kyrgyzs were converted to Christianity. The majority of Russians, Ukrainians, and other Russian-speaking people are Christians (Eastern Orthodox Church), although in the 1990s some of them joined Protestant and other Christian groups.

ECONOMY

At present, agriculture, industries, and services are the three main pillars of post-Soviet Kyrgyzstan's economy, contributing 37.9, 27.3, and 34.8 percent, respectively, to the Gross Domestic Product (GDP) (2002, World Bank est.). Kyrgyzstan's exports are narrowly based on sales of raw materials in international markets. The country's main exports are nonferrous metals (accounting for almost 41 percent of total export earnings in 1998), garments and textiles, electricity, and agricultural products. The mining industry is largely concentrated around the single largest gold mining field, Kumtor. The country depends heavily on imports of machinery, fuel, industrial consumer goods, and food products. Due to the transitional recession and the disappearance of aid from the former USSR, Kyrgyzstan's economy increasingly relies on foreign aid and credits. Total external debt has reached almost US$1.4 billion (2002), a large figure for a nation of only 5 million people, although in 2002 a significant proportion of these debts was written off.

Kyrgyzstan is one of the poorest countries of the former Soviet Union, as according to various calculations between 48 and 63 percent of the population live below the poverty line. Since the 1990s a sizeable number of people have been leaving for other countries in search of jobs and better living standards. In 2002 the United Nations Development Program's Human Development Index (HDI) placed Kyrgyzstan in 102nd place out of 173, behind nearly all of the former Soviet countries, although ahead of Moldova and Tajikistan.

The structure of Kyrgyzstan's economy changed significantly over the 1990s. According to the World Bank, the contribution of agriculture to the country's GDP increased from 34.2 percent in 1990 to 37.9 in 2002, and this sector still provides employment for over 55 percent of the population. Along with some other Central Asian states, Kyrgyzstan experienced de-industrialization in the 1990s, as the share of manufacturing declined significantly from 27.7 percent of GDP in 1990 to 8.1 percent in 2002. The service sector is still underdeveloped in terms of quality and diversity. Tourism, for example, is in a rudimentary stage, although the government has prioritized it since the mid-1990s.

In the economic sphere, from the early 1990s the Kyrgyzstan government adopted an IMF-designed program of radical economic changes (the so-called shock therapy approach). This program is based on three main mechanisms: broad mass privatization, rapid price liberalization, and currency reform with the assistance of international organizations such as the World Bank and the International Monetary Fund (IMF). The government quickly abandoned the centrally planned economy and focused on mass privatization, promotion of private entrepreneurship, liberalization of its trade, and opening of the national economy to international investment. It was able to privatize most of the enterprises in the industrial and agricultural sectors, establish a freely convertible currency system (Kyrgyzstan's som was introduced in May 1993 and has remained relatively stable), and achieve macroeconomic stabilization. At the same time, the state downsized the social welfare system, and privatized medical services, educational institutions, and the pension system. Due to its rapid and extensive economic liberalization, Kyrgyzstan became the first among the Commonwealth of Independent States to be accepted into the World Trade Organization (WTO) in 1998.

However, the state's sudden change of economic policy and withdrawal of subsidies, combined with the disintegration of the Soviet market, led to a sharp de-industrialization and transitional recession affecting almost all sectors of the economy. According to the IMF, Kyrgyzstan's economy declined at an average annual rate of 4.1 percent between 1989 and 1999 (between 1992 and 1995 the industrial sector alone declined at an average annual rate of 20 percent). The country increasingly relies on the export of raw materials to the international market, and it is extremely vulnerable to fluctuations in world prices for its major exports—gold and agricultural products. Kyrgyzstan needs considerable foreign direct investments and international assistance to modernize existing technologies and to carry out major economic reforms. However, both local and foreign investors are reluctant to invest in the economy due to the low level of purchasing power of the population, the weakness of the legal system, corruption, and the inability of state institutions to implement property rights and contract law.

EARLY HISTORY

Contemporary Kyrgyzstan has a fascinating history, which reaches back to the first Turkic empires of the sixth–eighth centuries A.D. At the same time, it must be remembered that nomadic history is very difficult to trace. The nomads did not build big cities, towns, or castles. For them it was important not to disturb the natural landscape by erecting large monuments or buildings. The ancient Kyrgyzs very seldom used scripts to record events and changes in their life. A significant part of their history is oral, and their narratives are spoken by *akyns* (nomad bards) and accompanied by the *komuz* (musical instrument). The history of the nation was and still remains a highly politicized issue in Kyrgyz society. During the Soviet era it was dictated by the ideological nature of the Soviet state. After gaining independence, some parts of the history were rewritten for various political purposes, including legitimization of the borders of the state, which were arbitrarily established in 1924, and to promote legitimacy of various competing groups or clans in the political life of the republic.

Yet there is still some consensus among Kyrgyz historians about their history. Most of them agree that the pagan Kyrgyzs originally lived in Siberia, close to the basin of the Yenisei River (which many Kyrgyz narratives translate as "mother river"). There is no known date when the ancestors of contemporary Kyrgyzs moved from Siberia across the Altai to the Tian-Shan mountain range. Most probably the process was quite long and took several centuries. The Kyrgyz scholars consider that by the 10–11th centuries, this area was already fully inhabited by Kyrgyzs. To justify this claim, they often refer to the oral epic "Manas" that narrates the life of Manas, the great Kyrgyz hero. The Kyrgyzs grandiosely celebrated the epic's 1,000th anniversary in 1995. It is believed that many actions and events depicted in the epic had taken place in close proximity to the territory of contemporary Kyrgyzstan.

The Kyrgyz tribes played an important role in the ancient Great Silk Road, the old trade road between China and the West in medieval times, as they controlled vital passages and routes. Probably sometime between the 12th and 15th centuries the Kyrgyzs began to convert to Islam, the religion of numerous Persian, Arab, and Turkic traders and warriors who traveled along the road. Nonetheless, conversion of the Kyrgyzs to Islam was a long process and took several centuries, as even in the 19th century some travelers reported shamanistic traditions among the Kyrgyzs.

An extensive consolidation of Kyrgyz tribes took place between the 15th and 17th centuries, when the Kyrgyzs began to form a distinct language, identity, and culture. This process reached an advanced stage by the beginning of the 19th century. Yet, even early in the 19th century foreign travelers noticed that the Kyrgyzs had no single Sultan or Khan, a leader recognized by all tribes: each tribe was ruled by tribal leaders, *Manaps*. The Kyrgyzs were organized into an amorphous confederation of numerous tribes, who spoke the same Kypchak dialect of the Turkic language and shared a similar culture and a sense of common ancestors, glorified in their oral epics, such as "Manas" and "Semetey." In fact, one of the translations of the name "Kyrgyz" derives from the Turkic "qyrq" and "yz," which means 40 tribes (clans). The tribes were subdivided into two groups. The "Ong Kanat" (right wing) united those Kyrgyzs who lived in what is now northern Kyrgyzstan, to the north of the Ala-Too, in the Tian-Shan mountain range. The "Sol Kanat" (left wing) united those Kyrgyzs who lived to the south of the Ala-Too, what is now southern Kyrgyzstan. The Kyrgyzs fiercely resisted the Kokand invasion in the late 18th and early 19th centuries, but they were too divided and too weak to fight off the large Kokand forces. They gradually began to look for outside allies to beat off the Kokand.

Tsarist Colonization

Political Development

By the beginning of the 19th century the Kyrgyz tribes were clearly distinguished from neighboring Kazakhs, Uigurs, or settled Uzbeks but they lacked a strong national identity, political unity, universal literacy, and high culture. The "land of Kyrgyzs" was associated with Tian-Shan and Pamiro-Alai, the mountain ranges of inner Central Asia, which stretch from the east (at present the borders between Kyrgyzstan and China) to west and southwest, although there were no clear borders in the Ferghana and Jetisuu (Semirechiye) valleys. Not only did these high, often impenetrable mountain ranges form natural geographic boundaries and a valuable base for defense during numerous conflicts and wars, they also created the unique climate and a unique basis for the economy of the so-called vertical pastoral nomadism. At the same time these mountains had few passes, limiting communications between different Kyrgyz tribes, which were spread over five major valleys: Chui, Ferghana, Ysyk Kol (Issyk Kul), Naryn, and Talas.

This geographical division weakened the ability of the Kyrgyz tribes to resist the advancement of the Kokand Khanate from its base in the Ferghana valley, as the Khanate troops outnumbered the Kyrgyzs and were better armed. Despite heroic resistance of the Kyrgyz tribes, between 1762 and 1831 the Kokand Khans established control over most of the territory that is now Kyrgyzstan. They confiscated the land to build numerous fortresses and trading outposts, imposed stringent levies, and conscripted young Kyrgyzs to military service. The Kyrgyzs could not find allies in the east, as they were aware of the fate of the Oirats (Dzhungars) who were practically exterminated for their resistance by the Chinese troops in Eastern Turkistan in the late 18th century. The independent-minded Kyrgyz tribes, which regularly rioted against the Kokand rule, began seeking allies in the north. During the late 18th and first half of the 19th centuries, leaders of northern Kyrgyz tribes several times contacted the Russian tsardom looking for possible support. In 1814 and 1824 Kyrgyz delegations from Ysyk Kol even traveled to Russian Siberia with a letter requesting Russian protection. But the Russian Empire was slow to make moves in Turkistan, because it was invaded by Napoleonic troops in 1812 and it was later engaged in military campaigns in Europe.

By the middle of the 19th century, however, the Russians became increasingly interested in establishing their influence in Turkistan, especially after the British gained control over north India and began to move toward Afghanistan. This race for influence in Central Asia and bitter Anglo-Russian rivalry became known as the Great Game. British and Russian strategists argued that most medieval nomadic invasions against India and Russia were undertaken through the territory of Central Asia. For the British, influence over Central Asia was pivotal to the defense of their interests in India against Russian advancement, while for Russia it was crucial to defend its communication lines with Siberia and the Russian Far East (the "soft underbelly" of the Russian Empire in Winston Churchill's words). Besides, there were legends about the wealth of the cities on the Great Silk Road and many hoped to make a fortune by exploring and reviving trade.

After defeat in the Crimean War (1853–56) Tsar Alexander II (1818–81) and his advisers decided to hasten Russia's advance into Turkistan in several directions. One was the Kyrgyz territory. In 1855 the tsar established a Russian protectorate over the Kyrgyz tribes in the Ysyk Kol valley and in 1864 over the Kyrgyz tribes in Chatkal, thus contesting the interests of the Kokand Khanate. Imperial troops soon collided with the Kokand Khanate directly. Mass uprisings of the Kyrgyz tribes, cruelty of Kokand's ruler, Khudoyar Khan, and internal conflicts of the Khanate considerably weakened its military power. Consequently, Kokand was unable to offer significant resistance to the imperial troops led by Generals Cherniaev, Von Kaufman, and Skobelev. Russian troops conquered Tashkent in 1865, Samarkand in 1868, and finally, Kokand, Osh, and Andijan in 1875. But it took more than a year before they overcame the popular resistance, a "holy war," supported by some of the Ferghana valley's Kyrgyz tribes. Finally, the Russians negotiated with Kurmanjan Datkha (the "Kyrgyz queen" as she was often called by the Russians), who was the leader of Kyrgyz tribes in Alai that the large Kyrgyz tribes under her leadership would accept the Russian protectorate.

Around the same time the Russians forced the Chinese imperial government to recognize Russian interests over western Turkistan, thus establishing official borders between the Chinese and Russian Empires, although this action did not solve all territorial disputes between these two great powers. Gradually, the Russians and British also agreed on their respective spheres of influence in Central Asia.

Economic Changes during the Tsarist Era

Traditionally, the Kyrgyzs were engaged in a form of subsistence semi-pastoral nomadic animal husbandry, raising horses, sheep, goats, cattle, and yaks in the ecologically fragile mountain valleys of Tian-Shan and Pamiro-Alai. Their technique, developed through hundreds of years, utilized the unique climate and land resources in their mountainous homeland without damaging them. The economy of vertical pastoral nomadism was based on seasonal migration to the valleys in the lower reaches of mountains during the winter (what they called *kyshtoo*), when deep snow covered the tops of mountain ranges and the temperature often fell below 20°C. In the summer they migrated to the *jayloo* (summer camps), the valleys in the higher reaches of the mountains, as melting water from glaciers and rains in the mountains helped the grass grow in the rich pasture-land of the *jayloo*. The *jayloo* provided enough grass for animals and an escape for people and animals from the summer heat. This semi-pastoral nomadism in the Tian-Shan mountains provided a unique economic niche for the Kyrgyz tribes, as the Uzbek and Tajik settlers controlled oases in the west and the Kazakh tribes controlled vast grasslands in the north. The Kyrgyzs often bought wheat, barley, and oats from their settled neighbors, although they also cultivated some crops. Hunting in the mountain forests was another source of livelihood for people, especially when diseases, conflicts, or *barymta* (animal theft often as revenge) damaged their animal stock. Animal husbandry provided the Kyrgyz tribes both with a living and the products for trade or exchange with settled neighbors or with traders from other countries, who continued to travel on what once was the Great Silk Road.

Capitalism arrived in the Kyrgyz land in the late 19th century with the establishment of tsardom's control over Turkistan and beginning of colonial exploitation of the natural resources in the region. Within a few decades the regional economy experienced significant transformations and changed the landscape of the cities and towns, which rose alongside the old Kokand fortresses and in place of large *karavan-sarais*. Capitalism created a powerful market force and economic initiatives for consolidation of the Kyrgyz economy and Kyrgyz society into more cohesive entities.

One of the most important consequences of the economic development from the 1890s until 1917 was a significant increase in and diversification of trade between Kyrgyzstan and various parts of Turkistan and with Russia and China. In the early 1800s it could take weeks of dangerous travel with trade caravans to reach Turkistan's bazaars from Russia. The number of goods traded was limited, and the market was tiny due to continuous political instability and economic stagnation. In 1888 the Russians completed the Transcaspian railway and in 1905 the Orenburg-Tashkent line. Before World War I (1914–18) the railways provided access to important areas of Turkistan reaching as far as Andijan. The new mode of transportation made trade between Russia and Turkistan easier and faster. Steel, glassware, and other industrial goods, as well as grain, were brought to the Turkistan markets in exchange for agricultural products, such as leather, silk, cotton, and the like.

At the same time the development of capitalism brought new technologies to the Kyrgyz people as some products were processed locally. Hundreds of small workshops and plants were opened in major towns and cities all over the Kyrgyz land, producing or repairing agricultural equipment and processing agricultural products (like leather, wool, etc.) for exports to Russia or China. New technologies in land cultivation and a better quality of the agricultural equipment led to significant increases in productivity. New commercial crops were introduced to local farmers, as many people gradually began to cultivate tobacco and cotton in the Ferghana valley. By 1917 several small mines (lead, copper, coal, etc.) were opened in southern Kyrgyzstan and in some other areas.

Economic changes and growing trade contributed to changes in the social structures. More families were abandoning subsistence agriculture and switching to commercial crop cultivation or animal husbandry. However, at that time capitalism also dramatically increased the polarization of society. Local landlords, *manaps* and *bais*, increasingly concentrated wealth in their hands, while many other social categories lost traditional tribal and communal support. Some of the poorest members of society left agriculture altogether in search of new sources of income. They accepted wage labor in various workshops or plants, accumulating industrial and managerial skills. Others were trapped in misery, hunger, and hardship. The new economic realities also began to erode the tribal and regional isolation and affected the nucleus of traditional Kyrgyz society—the extended family, as people began to engage in various economic activities outside their families and tribes. Market relations also undermined traditional lifestyles and values among Kyrgyz people, who were previously mainly engaged in subsistence agriculture and animal husbandry, and in limited barter (exchange) trade with their neighbors.

Administrative and Demographic Changes

During most of the 19th century, there was no clear administrative delimitation in the territory populated by the Kyrgyz tribes, as the boundaries between different tribes and communities were regulated by traditional law (*adat*) and by customary courts. The *manaps, biis,* and *batyrs* (warriors) negotiated and settled conflicts over pastures or arable lands, or conflicts over migration routes during the seasonal movement of cattle. The Kokand Khanate did not establish clear administrative boundaries and largely left the administrative control to traditional intertribal or intercommunal arrangements. Most of the administrative duties were in the hands of the loyal Kyrgyz tribal leaders who were willing to accept the authority of the Khan. Usually people referred to the various administrative units as "the land of Sarybagysh," "the land of Bagysh," or "the land of Kypchaks." With the establishment of tsardom's control the Kyrgyz intertribal relations underwent significant changes, as Russia began reshaping administrative borders according to its own administrative needs and thus crossed many centuries-old tribal boundaries.

After abolishing the Kokand Khanate in 1876, most of the territory of what is now Kyrgyzstan was divided between different administrative units (*oblast, uyezd,* and *volost'*) under the Turkistan governor-general (Turkistan province from 1886 to 1917). The principal difference from British rule in the Indian subcontinent was that the Russian administration was, in Lord Curzon's words, "military, not civil in character."

Tsardom established several initiatives for local leaders to cooperate with the tsarist administration. It left local administration and jurisdiction in the hands of the native tribal leaders (*ak-suek*). It also required that the legitimacy of native administrators should derive from elections, not through inheritance or nobility. This was the most important political change, as the introduction of an electoral system on the *volost'* and *uyezd* level brought together different tribal and kinship groups replacing traditional inheritance of the leadership. Most of the land that is now Kyrgyzstan was divided between four *oblasts* (provinces): Ferghana (Andijan, Namangan, and Osh *uezds*), Semirechiye (Tokmak, Przhevalsk, and Pishpek *uezds*), Syrdar'ya, and Samarkand. Tsardom also tolerated Islamic beliefs and left most of the traditional legal system intact, as local criminal cases had to be handled by *biis* or *kazis,* and to be resolved under *Shariah* (Islamic law) or *adat* (traditional law).

Along with administrative reforms the tsarist government sponsored a large settlement program and brought thousands of newcomers, mainly ethnic Russians and other Slavic groups, into Turkistan. This move made Russian colonization of Central Asia different from the British pattern in India where there was no large migration of British people to their Indian colony. Those British who did migrate to India usually came temporarily, to work in various administrative, military or managerial positions. On the contrary, tsardom sponsored thousands of peasant families from Central Russia and from the Ukraine, who migrated to Turkistan, providing them with support and land, which was often seized from the Kyrgyzs and other local inhabitants of Turkistan. Moreover, in 1867 the tsar ordered creation of several Cossack settlements in Semirechiye *oblast*. In Imperial Russia in the 19th century, the Cossacks had special privileges in exchange for their military service.

The first Russian settlers appeared on the territory of Semirechiye *oblast* as early as 1868. However, the first large influx of settlers arrived in the late 1870s and 1880s and by the late 1880s there were several villages in Pishpek and Przhevalsk *uyezds*, including Buruldai, Kulanak, Nikolayevskoe, Tokmak, and some others with the total number of migrants reaching 15,100 or 4.8 percent of the total population in these *uezds*. In the 1890s the imperial administration established the first Russian settlements in Osh and Andijan *uezds*, reaching 2,000 people in 1897. At the same time approximately 500 Germans arrived from the Samara and Stavropol *oblast*s of Russia.

There are no reliable data on the ethnic composition in the region in the late 19th century. According to the census of 1897, there were approximately 233,700 Kyrgyzs in the Semirechiye *oblast* and 373,700 Kyrgyzs in the Ferghana, Syrdar'ya, and Samarkand *oblast*s. Meanwhile, the total number of Russians and Ukrainians in the same areas reached approximately 30,000 in that year.

The second large wave of migrants arrived in the Kyrgyz land mainly during and after the agrarian reforms of 1906–10. According to some estimates between 1897 and 1914 almost 73,000 new settlers arrived from Central Russia and Siberia and settled in the territory, which is now Kyrgyzstan. During this period previously small Kokand fortresses grew into significant towns and cities, with a mixed population. These urban centers increasingly served not only trade but also the industrial needs of the local people, repairing and producing agricultural and other equipment. Many newcomers established medium-size farms, specializing in commercial production of wheat and other grains, as well as potatoes and vegetables, and other crops. These centers also hosted the first medical and health facilities, which began the first ever vaccinations against major diseases. The improving agriculture and medical services gradually led to higher population growth in the Kyrgyz territory (from 0.5 percent in 1871–85 to 1.4 percent in 1900–1913).

Official calculations indicate that there were approximately 770,100 Kyrgyzs in Semirechiye, Ferghana, Syrdar'ya, and Samarkand *oblasts* according to the census of 1913. Meanwhile, the total number of Russians and Ukrainians in the same areas reached approximately 122,000 or around 15 percent of the total population in 1914.

Relations between the newcomers and the Kyrgyzs were not always smooth. Dissatisfaction grew gradually, especially among the poorest parts of society, who blamed the Russians for increasing social disparities, growing poverty, and loss of lands and pastures. There were a number of newcomers, especially among unauthorized settlers, who simply seized the land and pastures from local Kyrgyz families or tribes and mistreated and exploited the Kyrgyz workers. There was also mounting anger against rampant corruption among local administrators, and especially tax collectors. The first indication of emerging uneasiness was the Andijan popular uprising in 1898, widely supported by various Kyrgyz tribes. Even after its suppression small armed groups of Kyrgyzs continued to periodically ambush Russian settlements and administrative officers.

It was the popular uprising of 1916 in Turkistan that was driven by the strongest anticolonial sentiments. It was triggered by the June 1916 decree on mobilization of about 250,000 Turkistanis (who were traditionally exempted from military service) to carry out war-related duties in the unpopular war of Russia against Germany and its ally Turkey, the guardian of the Holy Places and culturally close to the Turkic people. But the uprising had much deeper roots as it was also a reaction to an economic depression, caused by World War I, and to additional war taxes and skyrocketing food prices. The local rioters attacked the Russian settlements, administrative centers, and gendarmerie headquarters, destroying property and killing settlers and representatives of the local administration. In retaliation the Imperial administration mobilized its armed forces and Cossack regiments who fought back against poorly armed local people, killing thousands, burning their houses and their crops, and driving tens of thousands of civilians out of their land and homes. In late 1916 many Kyrgyz families, even whole tribes, were forced to escape to Chinese Kashgar through high mountain passes, often covered with impassable snow at this time of the year. Many people died frozen or starved in the high mountains and later in Kashgar, as they lost their animals and belongings while escaping from the Cossack-led punitive expeditions. This remains the most tragic period in the memory of the Kyrgyzs, as they lost approximately 140,000 people, who were either killed, died of starvation, disappeared in war calamities, or migrated to Chinese Kashgar.

Social and Cultural Changes

The arrival of capitalism and Russian control over the Kyrgyz land wrought a social transformation in Kyrgyz society. During the early 20th century there was a significant rise in literacy, which fulfilled what Ernest Gellner considered "the minimal requirement for full citizenship, for effective moral membership in a modern community." At the same time, there were significant changes in cultural areas, including consolidation of numerous dialects into the Kyrgyz literary language, and the beginning of the Russification policy. There also was a technological revolution, which brought new agricultural and industrial skills and new modes of communication, including railways, telephone, and mass media.

During the first decade of the 20th century tribal and extended family ties were further weakened as Kyrgyz people began to travel frequently beyond their traditional *ails* (villages) in a search for jobs and trade opportunities. Some of them settled down in cities and towns, thus changing their traditional lifestyles and often their professions, and absorbing the new culture. The Kyrgyz elite, especially those who were employed in the local administration, completely changed their lifestyle, abandoning the traditional rural pattern of socialization and adopting a new urban lifestyle, working skills, and work habits. The pattern of settlements also changed, as many people began to build larger permanent houses in the *kyshtoo,* while taking only part of their families to the *jayloo* during the seasonal migration. New and better equipment allowed building of better roads. New modes of transportation increased and facilitated communication between different parts of the Kyrgyz land and significantly expanded the boundaries of what Benedict Anderson called the "imagined community."

Changes in the market and in the economy demanded new skills and new knowledge. Local communities needed more literate people who could help them to calculate taxes, read official documents, and write letters or other documents. Meanwhile, tsardom needed more educated native administrators who would be able to handle the increasingly complex issues of local governance. This led to an increasing number of schools, changes in the curriculum, and consequently, a significant rise in the literacy rate among the indigenous population.

By the middle of the 19th century a network of *medrese* (religious schools) had developed mainly in the areas with a traditionally sedentary population. This network generally did not cover areas with a traditionally pastoral-nomadic population, that is, most of the areas of what is now east and northeast Kyrgyzstan. In the late 19th century Tsardom attempted to establish a primary education network for the Russian population as well as for Kyrgyz children, where children could study in mixed classes (*Rusko-Tuzemnyie shkoly*). At the beginning of the 20th century there was an attempt to establish a network of secular schools—*maktabs*—to promote primary education in Russian among Kyrgyz children as well as among the adult population. These *maktabs* used a new curriculum and the primary education was in both languages, native and Russian. Such subjects as mathematics and literature, and some others were taught as well. At the same time, Muslim reformers from other parts of the Russian Empire attempted to introduce new educational curricula (*usul-i dzhadid*) with greater emphasis on the study of science in Turkistani's *medreses.*

According to official reports on Semirechiye *oblast*, by 1912–13 the literacy rate among Kyrgyz males increased to 8.2 percent, among Kyrgyz women to 0.2 percent, although only 2.20 percent of the Kyrgyz population could read and write in Russian. However, the efforts at increasing the literacy rate among the Kyrgyzs and development of education in Russian were quite inadequate as tsardom provided rather limited funding for education. Besides, these efforts were undermined by the inefficiency of the colonial administration. Increasingly, a number of people from Turkistan, including Kyrgyzs, traveled to foreign countries, especially to Turkey, in order to get a better education. The new class of literate, trained, and russified Kyrgyz intelligentsia was very small, but they began to think about themselves in profoundly new ways, rising above tribal identities and thinking in terms of a new national consciousness— *"Kyrgyzdar byz"* (we are the Kyrgyzs).

At the beginning of the 20th century, in addition to the development of the new educational system the first newspapers were published in the region, first in Tashkent and later in most of the major regional centers. Initially the local newspapers were in Russian and were intended for the Russian population only. However, gradually, especially after 1905–07, local publishers began producing several newspapers and other periodicals in native languages, covering mainly local news and cultural events and intended for the native intelligentsia. A number of books, which were published mainly in the cities of Kazan and Ufa, often in Chagatai dialects of the Turkic language but in Arabic script, as well as Turkish publications from Istanbul, began to arrive in public libraries and private collections. During this time the first attempts were made at recording the great oral Kyrgyz poem, "The Manas," which is a story about a legendary hero of the Kyrgyz people and an encyclopedia of Kyrgyz oral history and traditions.

After the Revolution of 1905, some of these publications absorbed the pan-Turkic ideas of Ismail Gasparali (1851–1914) and other Muslim reformers (*Dzhadids*), especially of Muslim members of the *Duma*, the Russian parliament. During the 1910s liberal-democratic and socialist ideas began spreading not only among the Russians of the Russian Empire, but also among Turkistanis, although on the territory of what is now Kyrgyzstan this was on a far lesser scale than in Kazan, Bukhara, or Tashkent. There was also a growing self-assertiveness among the Turkistani intelligentsia, which included some young Kyrgyz people. Inevitably, this intelligentsia was politically divided. Many of them became critical of the colonial administration and colonial policies in the region, rejecting Russian rule and calling for the restoration of Islamic values and what they called the golden age of the Khanate. Others were increasingly involved with revolutionary ideas and joined the Bolshevik movement. There were also people who advocated Westernization, but rejected Russian colonial rule and looked on Turkey as an example to follow. In the end, political, economic, and intellectual polarization in the Russian Empire exploded in the liberal-democratic revolution of February 1917, forcing the abdication of Tsar Nicolas II and bringing the establishment of the Russian Republic.

KYRGYZSTAN UNDER THE SOVIET SYSTEM

Creation of the Soviet Kyrgyz State

The 1917 Bolshevik Revolution and the abolition of the powerful Russian Empire caught people in Turkistan by surprise and many of them were not ready to accept the new regime. Throughout 1919 and 1920 many groups within Kyrgyz society vigorously resisted the establishment of the new political regime, supporting what was known as the *basmachi* movement. The basmachi (from Turkic *basma*—assault) fought either against the Bolsheviks or the representatives of the pro-tsarist White Army or both, resisting the imposition of any outside control in their land. During the civil war Turkish general Enver Pasha attempted to unite the basmachi movement in order to establish a pan-Turkistan Republic, but failed, creating deep mistrust toward pan-Turkic ideas among the Kremlin policymakers. The Soviet government led by Vladimir Lenin won the support of the Kyrgyz farmers and peasants in its single most important step as it confiscated the land of rich Russian settlers, the kulaks, and Cossacks, who backed the pro-monarchist anti-Bolshevik forces. According to Lenin's decree, large plots of arable land were returned to the Kyrgyz communities. This action extinguished the heat of the political resistance in the Kyrgyz land against the Bolsheviks.

The revolution also gave a great impulse to the rise of nationalism in Kyrgyz society similar to that of other parts of the former Russian Empire. During the turbulent years of 1918 and 1919 many ethnic groups in Turkistan expressed their desire to establish independent states (*Alash Orda*) or in some cases to reinstate old ones (for example, the Kokand Autonomy). In response to the rise of nationalism, the Soviet authorities promised to support the national drive and to break with Tsardom's practice of suppressing cultural and political developments on the outskirts of the empire. The new nationality policy, as the Bolsheviks called it, was built on a pledge to give people the land that had been the most valuable asset for Kyrgyz peasants and farmers. The Kremlin embraced the ideas of those Central Asian leaders who suggested dividing the region along vague ethnic lines, rejecting the suggestion of creating a Central Asian federation or pan-Turkic republic. As the Soviet government proceeded with the delimitation of the borders of the Kazakh Autonomous Republic in 1920 (until 1926 Kazakhs were often called "Kyrgyzs" or "Kaisak-Kyrgyzs" and Kyrgyzs were called "Kara-Kyrgyzs") and of the Uzbek Republic in 1924, the Kyrgyz leaders also pressed for delimitation of the "Kyrgyz land."

On 14 October 1924 the Soviet government issued a decree on establishment of the Kara-Kyrgyz Autonomous Oblast as part of the Russian Federation. This became a turning point in Turkistan's history as the region was divided not on the basis of cultural, religious, or political realities but exclusively on ethnic considerations. As Shirin Akiner put it "the formulaic Marxist-Leninist concept of national identity [was] thoroughly internalized, consequently, they [Kazakhs, Kyrgyzs] acquired an emotional validation that largely outweighed traditional ties and even objective historical realities."[1] The delimitation of the Kyrgyz land clearly contributed to national consolidation, despite the weakness in the national identity of the Kyrgyz people, who at that time considered themselves first as Muslims, Turks, Turkistanis, and members of their tribes, and only then identified themselves as the Kyrgyzs. In 1925 the Kyrgyz Autonomous Oblast became the Kyrgyz Autonomous Soviet Socialist Republic (KASSR) within the Russian Federation and adopted its first constitution. Until then the constitution of the Russian Federation was in force.

It took, however, almost two years from 1924 to 1926 before the territorial delimitation was completed in ethnically mixed areas. Thus the Ferghana valley was divided between Kyrgyzstan, Tajikistan, and Uzbekistan, and the Jetysuu (Semirechie) valley was divided between Kyrgyzstan and Kazakhstan. In 1926, for administrative purposes, Kyrgyzstan was divided into seven *kantons* (*oblasts*): Frunze, Chui, Talas, Karakol, Naryn, Osh, and Jalal Abad. This administrative division was preserved with some minor changes until Kyrgyzstan's independence in 1991. This division reflected both the geographical features of the republic, as the *kantons* were built around large cities or towns and, implicitly, the tribal subdivision of Kyrgyz society. In 1936 there was yet another change as the Kyrgyz Autonomous Soviet Socialist Republic became the Kyrgyz Soviet Socialist Republic (Kyrgyz SSR) and in 1937 it adopted its new constitution.

One of the most important political changes introduced by the Bolsheviks was the elimination of all political parties other than the Communist Party, the gradual abandonment of pluralism, and the suppression of even the slightest sign of dissent within the ruling party. These drastic measures were justified by the fact that most of the opposition parties fought against the Soviet regime during the civil war of 1918–22 or resisted radical changes in the 1920s. At the same time the Kremlin attempted to win the political loyalty of the Kyrgyzstani leaders by adopting two major measures: the policy of *tamyrlashtyruu* (indigenization) and the elimination of the influences of the pre-Soviet leaders. The policy of *tamyrlashtyruu* or *korenizatsia* in Russian implied involvement of the native Kyrgyzs in the ruling party apparatus, administration, and management at all levels through a complicated system of quotas and promotions. Since Abdulkadyr Urazbekov was elected in

1926 as the first head of the Kyrgyzstan government, this position was traditionally reserved for the Kyrgyz, although overall the representatives of Slavic nationalities occupied about half of the government and party apparatus posts. The policy of political isolation and elimination of the influential pre-Soviet intelligentsia and tribal leaders was initially through their exclusion and prohibition to hold state or party positions and later through deportation to other parts of the Union of Soviet Socialist Republics (USSR) (the first large deportation of *bais* and *manaps* took place in 1929). Josef Stalin's purges within the ruling party took place in 1933–34 and 1937–38, claiming the lives of at least 10,000 party members, who were executed or sent to prisons or to *Gulag* labor camps in Siberia.

The Soviet reorganization also introduced completely new political and bureaucratic systems with a single-party Parliament (Supreme Soviet), the Council of Ministers, the new administrative division of Kyrgyzstan, and a new centralized system of state planning and management. Control by the *nomenklatura,* the carefully crafted cadres from the Communist Party introduced by Stalin in the 1930s, was an essential part of the system throughout the whole Soviet era. Stalin's successor— Nikita Khrushchev—denounced Stalin's terror and mass purges. He introduced political and economic liberalization in the late 1950s and a system of political and economic incentives for fulfilling Moscow's plans and campaigns. Under the next leader—Leonid Brezhnev (who led the USSR from 1966 to 1982)—the Soviet government went even further, rewarding the Kyrgyzstan leader, then Turdakun Usubaliyev, with additional investments in exchange for full political loyalty to the central authorities. It was not surprising that with all political and government institutions in place and greater assertiveness, Kyrgyzstan's government, as well as the governments of other union republics, began to demand greater autonomy from the Kremlin.

By the end of the 1980s there was growing pressure from all union republics, including Kyrgyzstan, to revise the Soviet Union Treaty of 1922 and to give them greater sovereignty in their internal and external affairs. This culminated in 1989 and 1990 in a bitter political struggle between the central government and union republics, between conservatives and reformers, which diminished both the Kremlin's ability to control political developments and the Communist Party's exclusive grip on power, and led to numerous constitutional changes both at the union and republic levels. Mikhail Gorbachev (who led the USSR from 1985 to 1991) believed that greater pluralism and democratization would help to reduce political tensions in the USSR. His support of new liberal factions in the Supreme Soviet and his reform-minded elite throughout the USSR undermined the power of the conservative Communist Party leaders not only in Moscow but also in the union republics. In October 1990 Kyrgyzstan's Communist Party leader, Absamat Masaliyev, was forced to hold presidential elections on a competitive basis for the first time in the history of the republic and he lost the elections to the democratic candidate Dr. Askar Akayev, the president of the Academy of Science. This event ended the 70 years of Communist Party rule in Kyrgyzstan, but only in the following year after the collapse of the USSR was Kyrgyzstan able to declare its independence.

Soviet Modernization and Economic Changes

The modernization policy was an essential part of state building in Central Asia as the Kremlin leaders believed that only those nations that were united by common economic interest and engaged in the modern industrial and state-controlled agricultural sectors of the economy could overcome their economic "backwardness." Thus the Soviet government channeled sizable investments into building big industrial enterprises, agriculture based on large-scale centrally controlled farming, and services in Kyrgyzstan. At the same time the republic was tightly integrated into the Soviet division of labor and centralized economic planning.

Kyrgyzstan's economic development has been limited by its landlocked position, remoteness from major markets, mountainous landscape, and small population. The country had significant reserves of natural resources, including gold, uranium, and antimony; it also had huge potential for developing hydroelectric power stations. However, their development required enormous investments to modernize the virtually subsistence economy, which was largely ruined during the civil war of 1918–20. Ever since launching the first Soviet five-year plan in 1929, the republic lobbied Moscow for new investments so intensively and often successfully that its long-standing first secretary Turdakun Usubaliyev won the title of "resource hungry leader."

Industrialization began in Kyrgyzstan in the 1930s with large investments from the Central Soviet budget going into the production of heavy and agricultural machinery, electric motors and light manufacturing, and also mining. A number of industrial plants were built there during the first stage of industrialization (1929–39), mainly in and around the capital, Frunze (Pishpek until 1926), and Osh. During the 1930s, industrial production in the republic grew at an average annual rate of 14 percent and by 1937 the industrial sector had grown overall 20-fold since 1913. During and after World War II there was a second wave of industrialization: a number of industrial plants (mainly military) were relocated to Central Asia along with their workers, engineers, and technical staff from the European part of the USSR, where their functioning was threatened by military actions and postwar turbulence. These factories and plants remained in the republic after the war, and they became the backbone of Kyrgyzstan's heavy industry. A third wave of industrialization occurred in the 1960s and 1970s, when Moscow allocated large investments to the republic's hydroelectric power-producing sector, and to mining and metallurgy plants, although due to construction delays some of them could not start full scale operation until the late 1980s. By 1991 Kyrgyzstan produced 38 percent of its gross domestic product (GDP) in the industrial sector, specializing in processing raw materials (uranium, antimony, mercury, molybdenum, etc.) and agricultural production (cotton, silk, fruits, vegetables, etc.), and in the agricultural machinery and electric motor plants, mining, and light and military equipment manufacturing.

The agricultural sector, in which livestock breeding and crop cultivation have together been of great importance, underwent major restructuring as the Soviet government attempted to eliminate the subsistence economy by bringing together thousands of private households into large state-run collective farms (*kolkhozs*). In 1929 the Soviet authorities launched a campaign of collectivization and Sovietization of Kyrgyz *ails* (*ail* is a kind of tribal and extended family unit) and incorporated (often forcibly) most of the Kyrgyz peasants into *kolkhozs* within six or seven years. This campaign had two long-lasting consequences. Large-scale farming and the mechanization of the agricultural sector were introduced for the first time in the history of the republic. This dramatically increased the output of agricultural products, elevating most of the farmers out of poverty and social disparity. Kyrgyzstan provided meat, fruits, and vegetables for Russia's retail market (the so-called collective farms' *bazaars*), and cotton, silk, and some other crops for Russia's light industry in exchange for Russian-made industrial products like machinery and consumer goods. By 1991 Kyrgyzstan produced around 40 percent of its GDP in the agricultural sector, becoming an "agricultural basket" of the Russian Federation.

The Soviet modernization and extensive industrialization were implemented persistently, if not brutally. They accelerated industrial development and economic growth to unprecedented levels, virtually doubling Kyrgyzstan's GDP every 10 to 15 years between the 1930s and 1970s. However, by the 1970s the economic development increasingly relied on unsustainable exploitation of natural resources. By the 1980s a combination of factors, including the accumulated distortions in the economy, the sharp decline of the oil price in the international market, and unsustainable military spending, knocked the Soviet economy into a decade-long recession and stagnation. During the 1980s, together with the USSR, Kyrgyzstan entered a decade of stagnation, as the Soviet system was unable to catch up with the latest wave of the technological revolution and to adopt technological innovations and policy changes.

The Gorbachev-Ryzhkov administration's ineffective attempt to revive the economy largely failed and even aggravated the existing difficulties, and as a consequence the union republics, including Kyrgyzstan, began to question the wisdom of centralized control over the economy. In 1989 a group of Kyrgyzstan politicians, led by the influential economist Turar Koichuyev, argued that Kyrgyzstan's economy would be better off if the all-Union economic system were revised. Koichuyev and his supporters pointed out that Kyrgyzstan had been selling its mineral resources, water, electricity, and so on at prices that were disproportionly lower than world prices. In addition there was an argument about over-extensive exploitation of Kyrgyzstan's pasture and arable lands and falling prices for its agricultural products. They also argued that Kyrgyzstan's foreign trade with countries outside the USSR had been unfairly under direct centralized control from Moscow. Even if the goods from the republic reached markets in 60 countries, it did not benefit from this trade. Finally, because there was no competition, consumer products in the Soviet Union were of lower quality than goods in the international market. The Kyrgyz government suggested that only greater economic autonomy and the decentralization of the Soviet system would help the republic to prosper.

Soviet Nationality Policy and Demographic Changes

Just as the Soviet approach to nation-state building was very complex and in Anatoly Khazanov's words "quite contradictory," so was the Soviet nationality policy. This nationality policy was an attempt to reflect the Marxist-Leninist theoretical construction and vision of the nations and interethnic relations, as well as changing views within the Soviet ruling elite. By and large, it attempted to "force the social, cultural, and linguistic unification of all nationalities in the USSR on the basis of Russian, or more accurately, Soviet-Russian culture."[2]

In the 1920s and 1930s the Soviet modernization policy aimed to create a large intelligentsia and working class among the Kyrgyzs. But the reality was that most of them lacked the skills and education necessary for working in newly created factories and enterprises as only 15.1 percent of the Kyrgyzs were literate in 1927. In response, the government launched a *vydvizhenchestvo* program (promotion campaign) that aimed at intensive training of locals and promoting them to managerial positions and giving them priorities during recruitment to the newly created factories. Yet Kyrgyzstan still experienced shortage of skilled labor that was often filled by migration of people (voluntary and forcible) from the European part of the USSR. According to official statistics, the number of ethnic Russians in Kyrgyzstan increased from 116,000 in 1926 to 302,000 in 1939 and Ukrainians from 64,000 to 134,000 within the same period.

During the turbulent years of World War II and the postwar restoration of the Soviet economy, some plants, along with their entire workforce (mainly people of Slavic origin), were relocated to the republic. Between 1939 and 1959 the number of Russians in Kyrgyzstan increased from 302,900 to 623,500. Almost all of them settled in urban areas, such as the capital, Frunze, and its suburbs. In addition to this category of migrants, there was a huge inflow of people who were forcibly relocated from the areas of military actions. These included Germans (descendants of 18th-century migrants to Russia), Turks, Crimean Tatars, Greeks, Koreans, and so on.

Thus Kyrgyzstan became one of the most diverse republics among the former Soviet Union's members in terms of ethnic composition, although the structure of the population fluctuated all the time. The proportion of the ethnic Kyrgyz population declined from 66.7 percent in 1926 to 40.5 percent in 1959; however, their proportion increased to 52.3 percent in 1989, mainly due to the higher birth rate. From the 1920s until the 1970s the ethnic Russian population was growing in absolute and relative figures due to migration and natural increase from 11.7 percent in 1926 to 29.2 percent in 1970, although between 1979 and 1989 the proportion of ethnic Russians dropped to 21.5 percent. There was considerable growth in the Ukrainian population in Kyrgyzstan from 6.4 percent in 1926 to 9.4 per cent in 1939, but it fell to 2.5 percent in 1989. A rather similar process happened with the German community, which increased from 0.4 percent in 1926 (mostly descendants of German settlers and prisoners from World War I) up to 1.9 percent in 1959 (mostly due to the forced migration of the German descendants from Russia and the Ukraine). By 1970 their proportion rose to 3.0 percent, but it declined to 2.3 percent (101,000 people) by 1989. Throughout the Soviet era, the Uzbek community in Kyrgyzstan constituted between 10 and 12 percent of the population, making the Uzbeks the third largest ethnic group in Kyrgyzstan after the Kyrgyzs and Russians.

Overall, Kyrgyzstan's population doubled every 25 to 30 years due to high birth rates and improved health services combined with a high immigration rate. The population doubled from approximately 1 million in 1926 to 2 million by 1959, and again to 4.2 million by 1989, developing pressure on natural resources and a rising competition for social benefits.

In Kyrgyzstan, as in many developing countries, urbanization arrived in the 1950s and 1960s, creating distinct social, economic, and cultural differences and divides between the urban and rural populations. The republic's urban population steadily grew until the end of the 1970s but largely stabilized in the 1980s. According to Kyrgyzstan's statistics, in 1979, 38.7 percent (or 1.36 million) of the republic's population lived in urban areas, and 61.3 percent (or 2.16 million) lived in rural areas. In 1989, the urban population declined to 38.2 percent (or 1.64 million); meanwhile, the rural population reached 61.8 percent (or 2.65 million).

The native Kyrgyz population was primarily employed in the agricultural sector and lived in the rural areas. They faced increasing population pressure, rising unemployment, a shortage of arable land, and lower incomes. These problems became especially severe in the 1970s and 1980s, as young people, who tried to move from their villages to the Slavic-dominated cities, could not find enough jobs, accommodation, or training opportunities. Deteriorating economic and social conditions led to an increase in tensions between various communities, which were especially flammable in the rural areas. In the summer of 1990 these tensions exploded into a conflict between the Kyrgyz and Uzbek communities in the south (Osh) *oblast* of the republic. Intensive riots and clashes between these two communities continued for almost two weeks and took the lives of more than 300 people.

Social and Cultural Changes

The cultural and social changes introduced by the Sovietization policy had two major dimensions that were intended to further strengthen the "Soviet Kyrgyz nation" and, gradually, to make it an inseparable part of the "Soviet nation." First, during the seven decades of Soviet rule the Soviet authorities carefully crafted the educational system, the "new" Kyrgyz cultural setting (including the written "scientific" history of Kyrgyzs and Kyrgyzstan and new forms of modern art), and the "new" social organization of society. Second, the Sovietization policy aimed to decrease social differences between Kyrgyzs and Russians as these differences were perceived to be an obstacle on the way to consolidating the Soviet identity.

The development of literacy was part of the Soviet cultural revolution policy among the masses and a campaign to raise the literacy rate was launched in the 1920s. At the same time, the Soviet authorities attempted to limit the cultural influences of the past. Thus, among the first steps in the Soviet modernization was a change of the Kyrgyz alphabet from Arabic to Latin in 1929 and then from Latin to Cyrillic in 1940 and modern Kyrgyz literature and art was developed based upon the Cyrillic script. Between 1924 and 1933 the first tertiary education institutions were opened in major Kyrgyzstan cities, maintaining the Kyrgyz language as the primary language of instruction. The government also invested substantial resources in establishing a network of 1,700 schools and colleges, which by the late 1940s covered all cities and towns in the republic (comparatively, there were just 107 schools in 1913). In the 1960s and 1970s the Kremlin leaders took Sovietization policy even further by more vigorously implementing the Russification policy. By 1989, the newspaper *Sovetskaia Kirgizia* reported, for example, only three out of 69 schools in the capital taught subjects in Kyrgyz.[3] According to the 1989 census almost 35.2 percent of the Kyrgyzs (the second highest proportion among the Central Asian nations, after the Kazakhs) claimed that they had advanced knowledge of the Russian language.

The establishment of the cultural infrastructure was, in the Kremlin's eyes, one of the ways to strengthen the national Kyrgyz and Soviet identities. During the 1920s and 1930s the first groups of talented young

Kyrgyzs were sent to study modern art and sciences; with their return to Kyrgyzstan, the government opened public libraries, theaters, art exhibitions, the academy of sciences, and several museums. The newly established publishing houses produced hundreds of books, newspapers, and magazines, initially mainly in the Kyrgyz language, but after World War II, an increasing number of publications in the republic were produced in Russian. Between 1925 and 1971 20,000 books and brochures were published with a total print run of 128 million copies (in comparison, before the revolution there was only one publishing house in Kyrgyzstan, which produced a few dozen titles). In 1924 a few hundred copies of the first Kyrgyz newspaper, *Erkin Too,* were published but by the end of 1970 the total print run of 90 newspapers in the republic reached 184 million copies. In 1942 the first film-producing center was established, which became an essential part of the Soviet ideological machinery. In 1961 the center was transformed into *Kyrgyzfilm* studio.

But all these cultural changes were inseparable from the Soviet social experiment. During the 1920s and 1930s Stalin's regime eliminated the old Kyrgyz intelligentsia, as well as the religious, political, and tribal elite, first by sending them into exile in Siberia or other parts of the Soviet Union, and then by executing them in labor camps and prisons. The Islamic leaders were particularly targeted in this campaign, as from the 1930s the Soviet government persistently and brutally implemented the policy of atheism, closing mosques and *medreses (madrasahs)* and prohibiting religious practice. At the same time the Soviet leaders attempted to create a new Kyrgyz intelligentsia and a new Kyrgyz elite by promoting the most gifted and ambitious young people from the lower social strata of society. They were mostly promoted according to their talents and abilities rather than their social status or descent (as in traditional society). These young Russified intelligentsia contributed to the rise of what Alec Nove called the "Communist Model of Development," and they remained largely loyal to the Soviet system, implementing the Sovietization and modernization policies mostly without resistance.

Despite these considerable social changes, and the success in industrialization and social engineering in the republic, Kyrgyz society preserved some important characteristics of the traditional lifestyle that curiously mixed with certain elements of modernity. The traditionalism in Kyrgyzstan showed its ability to oppose the innovations and social transformations that were imposed by the Soviet system. Despite all social changes, the Kyrgyzs continued to preserve some of the features of the patriarchal society and strong tribal and kinship traditions. In this regard, some particularities of the Soviet modernization contributed to the preservation of these features. For example, whole Kyrgyz *ails* were brought into *kolkhozes* during the collectivization campaign and the *kolkhozes* kept the extended family ties alive throughout the Soviet era. Traditionally, the extended family social network provided support to all members of the *ails* and developed a kind of economic welfare net. The "patron-client" relationship outside the *ails* continued the traditional line of the Kyrgyz tribal regional confederations (the so-called clans).

Over time, however, the shortcomings of the Sovietization and nationality policy and, especially, the increasing pressure of Russification, sparked a growing uneasiness among the Kyrgyz population and even among the Kyrgyz russified intelligentsia. The situation was worsened by a growing gap between propaganda and reality, failure of the state to improve significantly standards of living, and rising unemployment, especially in the cities. The Kyrgyz intelligentsia began to talk about the *Mankourtisation* ("forgetting the roots"—the term introduced by Chingiz Aitmatov) of the society, as people increasingly were losing their cultural roots and facing the destruction of the traditional fabric of Kyrgyz society. The first sign of resistance to the Russification policy appeared in the 1970s. However, only with the liberalization of the Soviet political regime under Gorbachev in the 1980s could these popular feelings be expressed openly. The Kyrgyz community began to demand the opening of schools in Kyrgyz; switching teaching in major colleges and universities from Russian to Kyrgyz; increasing the amount of publications, television, and radio broadcasting in Kyrgyz; as well as demanding that the Kyrgyz language become the state language in the Kyrgyz Republic.

In 1989–90 frustrated people took the law in their own hands, seizing the land around the capital and other large cities and forming a first national opposition movement, *Ashar.* Emotions were boiling over as the conservative views of the old party *nomenklatura* increasingly came into conflict with the opposition's demand for radical political and economic reforms and the introduction of a more open and pluralistic society.

Disintegration of the Soviet Union

On 31 August 1991 the Jogorku Kenesh (Parliament) declared Kyrgyzstan's independence from the USSR, peacefully ending more than

70 years of the Soviet system in Kyrgyzstan. However, there was an ambiguity in articulating Kyrgyzstan's nationality and language policy, in consolidating national identity among the citizens of the newly independent republic, and in formulating political relations with Russia and neighboring countries. This reflected not only the political uncertainty in relations with the external world but also the controversies and differences of opinion among people in their evaluation of the Soviet past. This step also sparked wide debates about the legacy of the Soviet era, which was different for various groups of society.

Some emphasized the brutality of the Soviet system and political and cultural oppression. This group claimed that the Soviet border delimitation from 1924 to 1926 in Central Asia artificially divided Russian Turkistan into several republics endorsing Soviet identities and enforcing an imported political system on these republics. The state delimitation ignored the historical and cultural traditions of the Central Asians, instigated conflicts over the historical heritage that was shared between people who became members of different countries, and established a ground for territorial disagreements among Kyrgyzstan, Kazakhstan, Tajikistan, and Uzbekistan. The Soviet settlement program was the most criticized part of the Sovietization program as it sent thousands of Kyrgyzs into exile in Siberia and other places and brought hundreds of thousands of Russians, Ukrainians, Germans, and other nationalities into the region, enforcing the policy of russification. This migration often left ethnic Kyrgyzs outside the large cities, which became predominantly Russian centers, and in some degree marginalized the Kyrgyz people in their own republic. At the same time, the Russification policy created a large social stratum of Russified intelligentsia and Russified elite, who in Chingiz Aitmatov's words "forgot their national roots."

Others pointed to the huge social and economic changes and the increasing economic achievements of the republic. This group claimed that the economic changes during the 70 years of the Soviet system radically transformed the face of the republic, creating a diversified national economy, an advanced educational system, science, technology, public health, and a welfare system. The development of modern modes of transportation and communication broke down the isolation of different parts of the country, initiating the free movement of people, labor, and goods within the national borders. There was a noticeable improvement in the standards of living and consumption patterns throughout the republic. In the 1980s Kyrgyzstan was in a better position according to the human development indicators (HDI) than countries such as India, Pakistan, and China. According to the United Nations Development Program (UNDP), in 1991 the republic was in the 31st place in the HDI ranking (ahead of Bulgaria, Romania, and Turkey and just behind the Czech Republic, Malta, and Hungary).

During the Soviet era the entire system of political mobilization and administrative division among the Kyrgyzs was altered. The Kyrgyz state was established, with all the attributes of a modern society, including a national anthem, a flag, and strong state institutions. By 1991 an independent Kyrgyzstan had became a reality and Kyrgyz society largely accepted and strongly approved the existence of the Kyrgyz identity. Soviet social policy included the elimination of the old tribal elites and replaced them with a new intelligentsia, who thought about themselves in terms of Kyrgyz society. Although the Soviet system contributed to the elimination of illiteracy and the development of Kyrgyz culture, it perceived with suspicion the consolidation of *Kyrgyzchylyk,* or civic identity and awareness of belonging to one society, which was becoming stronger throughout the 1970s and 1980s. The Soviet social policy promoted large population movements enriching the Kyrgyz culture and language and bringing in new technologies, skills, and cultural elements, and promoting the achievements of the Kyrgyz culture internationally.

Most probably these debates will never end, as the Soviet legacy has indeed been controversial. The modernization, industrialization, urbanization, and technological revolution, all the changes that many countries in Asia and Europe underwent during the 20th century, were brought to Kyrgyzstan during the Soviet era. The economic changes were the most profound, as huge investments broke down the subsistence economy and helped to establish modern industrial and agricultural sectors. The economic changes, especially collectivization and sedentarization, also eliminated the thousand-year old traditional culture of pastoral nomads as people moved to cities and industrial centers embracing new lifestyles and new cultures. But, at the same time, the Soviet leaders were unable to abandon their political, economic, and ideological dogmas, which ultimately corrupted the Soviet system.

After 1991 the Soviet system left behind a much stronger base for independent development, including developed and diversified industries, administrative and technical skills, an established educational system, and strong state institutions, than the colonial powers left in Asia and Africa after their withdrawal. But it also left behind deep political and economic crises, ethnic conflicts, and growing instability. Kyrgyzstan's declaration of independence in 1991 brought new challenges and new problems, which tested the ability of Kyrgyz society to consolidate itself into a truly independent nation and a stable political entity.

INDEPENDENT KYRGYZSTAN

Experimenting with Democracy

Among its first steps as a newly independent nation the Kyrgyz Republic introduced a broad range of political reforms and set up political institutions. This inevitably included dismantling the Soviet-style one-party political system, building institutions of a sovereign state, preparing a new constitution, and enhancing the legitimacy of the *Jogorku Kenesh* and the presidential power and, in Gregory Gleason's words, "seeking to develop European-style democratic institutions."[4] In addition, there was a need to establish political equilibrium among various political parties and nationalist movements in order to avoid a civil war similar to that of Tajikistan and to build a national consensus over the direction of the future development of the republic.

Some fundamentals were laid down on the eve of independence. Already in 1990 the Kyrgyzstani leadership was exposed to what E. Huskey called a "serious rift in the republic" as "fault lines emerged within the elite itself."[5] The government removed an article in the constitution, which formulated the dominant position of the Communist Party of Kyrgyz SSR (CPK). Instead it adopted the Law on Public Organizations. In October 1990, following the constitutional changes, the Jogorku Kenesh introduced the post of president of the republic. The president was to be initially elected by the parliamentarians. The hopes of Absamat Masaliyev, the CPK candidate, to become the first elected president were not realized, as he could not obtain a decisive majority. After several rounds of elections Dr. Askar Akayev, the former head of Kyrgyzstan's Academy of Sciences, who emphasized the establishment of a democratic, pluralistic society and a liberal democratic multiparty political system, emerged as the first Kyrgyzstani president.

The first tough test of the president's credentials occurred in August 1991, when an attempted anti-Gorbachev military putsch in Moscow provoked a dramatic confrontation between the Kyrgyz president and democratic parties on the one hand and the CPK on the other. The Communist Party of Kyrgyz SSR, which supported the antidemocratic forces, was banned and its property was confiscated, and Kyrgyzstan declared its independence from the USSR. A number of political parties and independent mass media emerged on the eve and during the first years of independence as Kyrgyzstan established one of the most liberal political environments in the Central Asian region. This earned the title of "Island of Democracy" for the republic and millions of dollars of international assistance from Western donors and international organizations.

On 5 May 1993 Kyrgyzstan adopted its first post-Soviet constitution that provided a legislative framework for further political transition. New Kyrgyzstan's constitution embraced the constitutional ideas of the modern Western liberal democracies, as it strengthened the division of powers between the executive, legislature, and judiciary. Unlike some Baltic states, Kyrgyzstan guaranteed citizenship and full political rights to all people of the republic without discriminating on language, residency, or ethnic bases. The constitution gave substantial power to the president but provided the parliament with a mechanism to check and balance the presidential power. According to the constitution, the president is the head of state; he has the power to appoint the prime minister and the members of the Constitutional Court (with the approval of the parliament). He also has the right to initiate new laws and to veto the decisions of the Jogorku Kenesh. However, the Jogorku Kenesh has preserved its power, including the final say on the state budget, ratification of international treaties, and the ability to deter presidential decisions.

As the next step, the Soviet-style single-chamber 350-seat Jogorku Kenesh was dismissed by presidential decree in October 1994, sparking a constitutional crisis and sharp criticism from the political opposition. This dismissal was justified by the argument that it would help the government to implement the radical economic reforms and to reflect what Akayev called the "tradition and culture of people."[6] On 6 December 1994 the president suggested changes in the constitution, replacing the old single-chamber Jogorku Kenesh with a new, two-chamber Jogorku Kenesh. It was suggested that the new Parliament would consist of 35 seats in the Myizam Chygaruu Jyiyny (Legislative Assembly) and 70 seats in the El Okuldor Jyiyny (Assembly of the People's Representatives). Parliamentary elections were held on 9 February 1995, in a hotly contested environment as a total of 1,021 candidates representing approximately 40 parties and organizations were standing for 105 seats. The Social-Democratic Party won the largest number of seats, although the opposition Asaba, Unity of Kyrgyzstan, Erkin Kyrgyzstan, Ata-Meken, Communist Party of Kyrgyzstan, and the Republican Party also made their way into the parliament.

In the same year Akayev called for early presidential elections (the elections were initially planned for 1996). These were the first competitive popular presidential elections (in 1991 Akayev was the only candidate in the popular elections), and two opposition candidates were registered by the Central Electoral Commission (CEC), Absamat Masaliyev and Medetkan Sherimkulov. Akayev carefully built his platform, highlighting the importance of further liberalization of economy. He argued that only radical economic reforms, mass privatization, and structural adjustment recommended by the World Bank and International Monetary Fund could transform this small mountainous country into what he called the "Switzerland of Asia." He also appealed to the ethnic minorities by elevating the Russian language to the status of an official language despite the resistance of some nationalistic parties and some members of the Jogorku Kenesh (the Kyrgyz language had the status of state language). Meanwhile, the other two candidates for the presidency critically approached his policy from the left. Absamat Masaliyev represented the Communist Party platform, emphasizing the values and achievements of the Soviet era and suggesting the revision of privatization and a return to state control over the economy. The other candidate for the presidency, Medetkan Sherimkulov, put forward a political platform emphasizing the need to go further with economic reforms, preserve social guaranties, lower taxes, and develop a socially oriented policy. He based a considerable part of his election platform on criticism of the economic and social policies of President Akayev.

The presidential elections were held on 24 December 1995, achieving a voter turnout of 81.1 percent of the eligible electorate. President Akayev won the elections, receiving 71.6 percent of the votes. Masaliyev received 24.4 percent of the votes, and Sherimkulov only 1.7 percent of the votes.

The years following the 1995 elections were among the most difficult for independent Kyrgyzstan as the economic problems worsened, the political environment deteriorated and accusations of corruption and mismanagement pursued Akayev and his government. The 2000 parliamentary elections became an important benchmark testing public support for the president and government's policies. Pro-presidential political parties hoped to strengthen their presence in the Jogorku Kenesh, underlining the extensive political and economic changes and success of economic stabilization. Meanwhile, the opposition hoped to consolidate numerous small parties and to establish a political base for the autumn 2000 presidential elections, utilizing general dissatisfaction with the falling standards of living and deepening regional disparity.

Altogether 230 candidates contested for the 45-seat Legislative Assembly, and 186 candidates contested for the 45-member People's Assembly. Fifteen seats in the Legislative Assembly were allocated on the basis of proportional representation. The pressure on the opposition before and irregularities during the parliamentary elections seriously undermined the chances of the opposition. Observers stated that the Kyrgyz authorities "did not fulfill their commitment to organize fair parliamentary elections and the elections were neither democratic nor fully lawful."

The parliamentary elections were held on 20 February 2000, followed by a run-off on 12 March. On both occasions the turnout was exceptionally low, with 57.8 percent of the electorate casting votes in the first round and 61.86 percent in the second round. Direct elections were held for 45 seats in the Legislative Assembly and 45 in the People's Assembly.

Only three candidates received the required 50 percent plus one vote in the first round of the election, and a second round was needed. According to the CEC, after the second round 43 deputies were elected to the Legislative Assembly and 42 deputies were elected to the People's Assembly. Five seats remained undecided. Ultimately, however, seven opposition candidates made their way into the new Kyrgyz parliament wining in direct elections. Several prominent opposition politicians were simply disqualified on legal grounds. General Felix Kulov, leading opposition leader, had good results in the first round, but lost in the second. Those, who did make it into the parliament represented the El (People) Party, the Communist Party, the Ata-Meken (Fatherland) Party, and the Kairan El (Never-Do-Well People's) Party.

The parliamentary elections were soon followed by the presidential elections as in June 2000 the Myizam Chygaruu Jyiyny (Legislative Assembly) announced the date for presidential elections. According to the electoral procedures, it established the deadline for nominating and registering candidates, and passing a special Kyrgyz language examination.

In the presidential election campaign, the incumbent president and his team emphasized Akayev's ability to preserve political stability in the country and to deliver results. Meanwhile, the opposition focused on allegations of corruption during the privatization process and growing nepotism and social costs of the "shock therapy" approach to economic reform and of the IMF-designed structural adjustment program. In the end the CEC officially registered five candidates, including Akayev. These candidates were Omurbek Tekebayev, the chairman of the Ata-Meken (Fatherland) Party; Almazbek Atambayev, an industrialist; Melis Eshimkanov, a journalist and one of the leaders of the Asaba party; Tursunbay Bakir Uulu, one of the leaders of the Erkin (Free) Kyrgyzstan Party; and Tursunbek Akunov, a human rights activist. However, the two strongest candidates, Felix Kulov, the former vice-president, and Daniyar Usenov, a former parliamentarian and chairman of the opposition People's Party, were barred from the elections. Daniyar Usenov was barred on a legal ground (due to a past criminal conviction on charges that he always denied). General Felix Kulov decided not to take the Kyrgyz language exam (his spoken Kyrgyz was very weak), and he gave his support to Omurbek Tekebayev, the chairman of the moderate opposition Ata-Meken (Fatherland) Party.

According to the results published by the CEC, the turnout at the polls on 29 October 2000 was 77.3 percent. Kyrgyzstani president Askar Akayev won in the first round, securing 74.4 percent of votes. The alliance between Omurbek Tekebayev and Felix Kulov received a surprisingly low 13.9 percent of votes; Almazbek Atambayev received 6.0 percent, Melis Eshimkanov received 1.1 percent, Tursunbay Bakir Uulu received 1.0 percent, and Tursunbek Akunov received 0.4 percent.

Although the incumbent president won the election, the price was extremely high as the irregularities in both the parliamentary and presidential elections tarnished the image of the "island of democracy." According to Freedom House, in 2002 Kyrgyzstan was ranked in the 22nd place out of 27 transitional countries of the Commonwealth of Independent States and Eastern Europe, behind the Ukraine, Albania, and Armenia, although it was ahead of Bosnia, Kazakhstan, and Azerbaijan. In the short term, it seems that international sponsors, on whom the republic is heavily dependent, accepted the situation as it was, but in the longer term it could be more difficult to get extended political support and economic assistance as the democratic experiment has faltered.

Nationality Policy and Cultural Changes

The consolidation of ethnic groups on the territory of the country into the Kyrgyzstani nation has been the major objective of Kyrgyzstan's government since gaining independence. There was no unanimity, however, in the ethnic policy approach among the Kyrgyz elite. One view was that, like the Baltic republics of the former USSR, Kyrgyzstan's government should move toward an ethnocratic state. It should declare that the land belongs to the Kyrgyzs and should demand compulsory knowledge of the Kyrgyz language from all people who seek Kyrgyz citizenship, irrespective of their ethnic origin. The other view was that Kyrgyzstan's government should adopt a moderate stance. The ethnic policy should be based on development of a Kyrgyzstani state identity and loyalties of all citizens to the newly independent state, unification of all ethnic groups within the territory of the nation-state into one Kyrgyzstani nation, and maintenance of the multicultural nature of the society and moderate Islamic revivalism. The government should move toward a civil state, which guarantees equal opportunities to all citizens of the republic without ethnic or religious discrimination.

The decision on the policy choice was difficult for several reasons. First, the multiethnic composition of the country: in 1991 the Kyrgyzs, or the titular nation of the republic, constituted roughly 52 percent of the population, there were around 22 percent Russians, 13 percent Uzbeks, 2.4 percent Germans, and so on. Second, the interethnic relations in the republic were especially tense at the beginning of the 1990s because of the interethnic conflicts in the southern provinces of the republic in 1989 and 1990. Third, the Kyrgyzs themselves lacked national cohesiveness and they often defined themselves as members of different tribes or tribal groups with distinct dialects, cultural features, and political affiliations.

In 1989 the Law on Languages suggested that the Kyrgyz language should become the state language (Article 1), symbolizing Kyrgyzstan's sovereignty (Article 2), and replacing Russian. It also required compulsory usage of the Kyrgyz language by management and administrative personnel (Article 8) and gradual transfer of all documentation in the state and provincial administrative institutions into Kyrgyz. The law also required translation of signs in all public places, cities, and streets into Kyrgyz. During public debates on the law some members of the public suggested converting the Kyrgyz alphabet from Cyrillic to Latin, following the example of Turkey. The law (Article 22) sought to "create conditions for researching opportunities of changing Kyrgyz alphabet" to the Latin script. The Law on Land, adopted in 1991, declared that the land and natural resources should be the exclusive possession of the Kyrgyz people.

Akayev's government chose to moderate language and nationality policy, emphasizing a civil identity, guaranteeing citizenship to all people who live within the territory of the republic, and maintaining the multi-ethnic nature of the state. The government argued that in this multiethnic state, where the native Kyrgyz people constituted slightly more than half of the population in 1991, a strict ethnocentric policy would have provoked an escalation in interethnic tensions. Akayev vetoed both the Law on Land and the Law on Languages.

At the same time the government reintroduced symbols of Kyrgyz cultural traditions, changing the names of streets, squares, public places, cities, and towns. The names of many cities and towns were changed from Russian to Kyrgyz names, for example Przhevalsk and Rybach'ye became Karakol and Ysyk Kol, respectively. The new Kyrgyz flag and coat of arms, which symbolically refer to traditional Kyrgyz colors and symbols, were introduced along with the new national anthem, national currency, and passport. The Manas epic was elevated to the status of a national symbol and in 1995 Kyrgyzstan celebrated the 1,000th anniversary of its national hero. The idea of switching the Kyrgyz alphabet from Cyrillic to Latin was postponed due to scarce financial resources, although a number of Kyrgyz students began studying Turkish in various Turkish universities and in colleges in Turkey and in the republic. Meanwhile, the Turkish government supported the establishment of the Turkish Manas University and International Ataturk Alatoo University and several colleges in Bishkek and other cities. Kyrgyzstan's government also lifted restrictions on religious practice and a number of mosques and *medresse* were built or rebuilt. Islam come into prominence and most of the Kyrgyzs would highlight that the Hanafi Mazhab, to which they belong, has been the most liberal school in Islamic thought.

There were also dramatic demographic changes due to the economic recession, fears of conflicts, and collapse of the social welfare system. One of the consequences of these changes was the mass emigration of people from the republic. According to official statistics, more than 590,000 people (almost 15 percent of the population) left Kyrgyzstan between 1989 and 1995, mainly Russians, Ukrainians, Jews, Germans, and some other ethnic groups as well as some Kyrgyzs. According to the 1999 population census, the Russian population declined from 21 percent in 1989 to around 11 percent in 2002.[7] It is expected that it would further decline to 6 percent within the next 15 to 20 years (according to a recent survey 20.4 percent of the respondents expressed their desire to leave the republic "forever").

As some ethnic groups moved out, others moved in. There were reports that up to 10,000 Chinese citizens settled in Kyrgyzstan in the 1990s, although there were no reliable statistics. Thus most probably the ethnic composition of the republic would continue to change. Kyrgyzstan is slowly becoming ethnically more monolithic with the proportion of Kyrgyz approaching 68 percent in 2002 (52 percent in 1989). However, the reality is that the country will maintain its multiethnic composition for decades to come, especially with the growing proportion of Uzbeks and Chinese.

Economic Policy

Overcoming dependency on Moscow and building the national economy of the independent state were the two main tasks for the Kyrgyzstani government following independence in 1991. This was especially important since the Soviet system emphasized centralized control and distribution of resources and linked Kyrgyzstan's industrial and agricultural sectors to the all-union economy. Therefore, during the first stage of reforms Kyrgyzstan's government focused on decentralization, on building national banking and financial systems, and on introduction of the national currency.

When in 1991 Kyrgyzstan declared its independence after dissolution of the Soviet Union, many experts, including those from the IMF and World Bank, anticipated that Kyrgyzstan might rapidly undergo a transition similar to that of western European countries under the Marshall Plan. This plan channeled massive financial and technical assistance enabling war-torn Germany, France, and other countries to rebuild their economies in less then a decade. Independent Kyrgyzstan was among the IMF's favorites. In 1990 it was ranked 31st in the UNDP Human Development Index, ahead of many Asian countries, and it had a per capita GDP of US$1,160, rather similar to the rapidly growing Newly Industrialized Countries (NIC) of Southeast Asia in the late 1980s. Kyrgyzstan's economic structure was also similar to the economies of the rapidly transforming countries of Eastern Europe, as it had a well-established industrial manufacturing sector (32 percent of GDP), large agricultural sector (42 percent), and a sizeable energy sector. The literacy rate, which was close to 99 percent among both men and women, was among the highest in Asia. The well-educated population was backed by the well-established and free tertiary educational system.

From the early days of independence the Kyrgyzstani government accepted and steadily followed the "shock therapy" approach, in line with the recommendations of the IMF and the World Bank. In 1992 the government introduced the Program of Economic Reforms, which the IMF described as a program designed "to transform the economy from one dominated by central planning and administrative control of resource allocation to one in which economic decisions are determined primarily by market forces." The republic significantly liberalized economic activities on the domestic market and its foreign trade, expecting that foreign direct investments would flow into the country. Kyrgyzstan's rich reserves of mineral resources, such as gold, uranium, and some others, were considered valuable assets, which would attract foreign investors from Canada, Turkey, the United States, and Germany. International organizations also noted the advantage afforded by the country's small population, which stood at around 4.4 million in 1991, and the consequent fact that the country's economy would require lesser amounts of international assistance.

Kyrgyzstan together with the Baltic states was among few former Soviet countries that abolished most of its central planning institutions by the end of 1992. It also withdrew subsidies to major state-owned enterprises and simultaneously liberalized all consumer prices. Under pressure from the IMF, Kyrgyzstan's government tightened its belt in order to achieve macroeconomic and financial stabilization, cutting government and social welfare expenditures. In 1991 and 1992 the government adopted a program of mass privatization, which was conducted through a voucher scheme distributed among all Kyrgyz citizens.

Initially it aimed at the privatization of housing and small enterprises in the retail and service sectors. Later the government moved toward the privatization of medium and large enterprises and the banking and finance sector, retaining state control only over the so-called strategic enterprises (the energy and military sector). Between 1991 and 1998 the government privatized the major segments of its public assets. According to an official report, almost 80 percent of industrial enterprises, 97.2 percent of trade and food services, and 100 percent of household services were privatized by 1998. In November 2000 the Jogorku Kenesh approved the privatization of the largest enterprises such as KyrgyzTelekom, KyrgyzEnergo, KyrgyzGaz, and the National Airline.

Kyrgyzstan was first among the Central Asian Republics (CARs) to leave the rouble zone under the pressure of 1,300 percent inflation in the Russian rouble zone. In May 1993 it introduced its own currency, the som. Gradually, the government stabilized the macroeconomic situation cutting inflation from around 1,200 percent in 1993, to 278 percent in 1994, and to 45 percent in 1995 and kept it below 20 percent between 2000 and 2004. As part of the liberalization program, the government maintained free exchange of the som for hard currency. It also opened several free trade zones for foreign investments. After five years of steady decline, the exchange rate of Kyrgyzstan's som stabilized, fluctuating around 50 som per US$1 between 2000 and 2003.

Throughout the 1990s Kyrgyzstan's government opened its economy to globalization and free trade, focusing on attracting foreign investors, establishing trade relations with developed countries, and geographically diversifying its trade. After 1991 the republic lifted all the trade restrictions of the Soviet era and began to trade directly with China, Turkey, Germany, the United States, and other countries. The average annual trade turnover has stabilized above 1 billion dollars with the principal exports in nonferrous metallurgy (mainly gold from the Kumtor gold mine), electricity, agricultural, and light industry products and principal imports in machinery, oil, and gas. According to the *Economist Intelligence Unit (EIU) Country Report,* between 1999 and 2003 annual exports fluctuated from about US$480 to US$510 million, while imports fluctuated from US$440 to US$540 million. But foreign investments arrived in Kyrgyzstan at much slower rate than expected, forcing the government to rely heavily on international loans and credits.

Yet Kyrgyzstan's government attracted the attention of leading international organizations and individual states, which offered substantial assistance for its radical economic and political reforms. In 1993 the IMF and World Bank provided financial backing for the introduction of the som. Also in 1993 Turkey together with other major donors agreed to support an initial aid program of US$400 million designed to increase Kyrgyzstan's capacity to import investment goods and industrial and agricultural inputs. From 1994 until 1997 Kyrgyzstan received funding and international expertise crucial for its structural economic reforms. In 1999–2002 Kyrgyzstan received US$100 million under a three-year enhanced structural adjustment program from the IMF and 45 million from the Asian Development Bank (ADB). On the negative side, foreign debt increased from zero in 1991 to US$1.4 billion in 2002, although the Kyrgyzstani government managed to repay or renegotiate its debt obligations, avoiding default, and to remain a moderately indebted country.

The policy of radical reforms helped to restructure the national economy; however, it failed to generate the promised economic growth. For five consecutive years from 1991 until 1996 Kyrgyzstan's economy shrank by 45 percent. The republic began to experience a moderate economic recovery in 1996 and 1997 at an average annual rate of 5 percent, but was hurt by the Asian and Russian financial downturns in 1997 and 1998; and in 1999 Kyrgyzstan's real GDP was less then 70 percent of the 1991 level.

The economic restructuring imposed a heavy social cost on most of the population, creating sharp regional and social disparities. In Kyrgyzstan, as in many developing countries, business activities and investments were increasingly concentrated in the major urban centers such as Bishkek, while other regions, especially small towns and villages in the south and east of the country, experienced a steep economic decline. Throughout the 1990s the symbol of hasty privatization was the widespread stripping of assets and sale of expensive machinery and equipment as scrap metal to neighboring China. Many industrial enterprises were closed because they could not compete with cheap foreign imports, and they lacked managerial expertise and capital for upgrading technologies. The official statistics claimed that unemployment remained at around 3 percent or around 60,000 registered unemployed throughout the 1990s. Meanwhile, local experts produced unemployment figures between 20 and 25 percent of the labor force, insisting that in remote rural areas the rate may be between 30 and 35 percent. In 2003 average monthly salaries stood at around 1,500 som (US$32), placing them among the lowest in the CIS. However, these figures do not reflect social polarization in the country as some people had significantly profited from the "shadow economy." There are no reliable local studies on this phenomenon; however, in 2001 the *Economist Intelligence Unit* estimates that the "shadow economy" might account for up to 40 percent of GDP, which is among the highest in the CIS.

Only in 2000 and 2001 did Kyrgyzstan's economy show positive signs of stabilization and economic recovery. In those years the GDP, according to government's estimates, grew at an annual average of 6.0 percent. The output in the industrial sector grew around 10.3 percent, helped by an increase in gold, electricity, and cotton-fiber production (which are also the largest hard currency earners). Meanwhile, in 2000 agricultural production grew around 3.4 percent. This important sector of the Kyrgyzstani economy, which provides employment to 55 percent of the labor force, specializes in grain, cotton, tobacco, and vegetables production. Overall, in 2001 Kyrgyzstan's GDP remained below of the 1991 level and most probably only by 2010 would it fully recover from the so-called transitional recession of the 1990s. According to the World Bank's classification Kyrgyzstan belonged to a group of low-income economies with per capita income below US$755.

There is no satisfactory explanation as to why the shock therapy approach did not produce a quick economic recovery similar to Poland. According to international experts several problems undermine the attractiveness of Kyrgyzstan's economy for international investors, including the lack of respect for property rights, red tape, and corruption. In 2003 the Heritage Foundation ranked Kyrgyzstan in 104th place out of 161 countries in its Index of Economic Freedom, taking into consideration 10 major scoring factors (property rights, regulation, black market, etc.). Corruption and the bureaucracy's incompetence have also been a major problem. In 1999 Transparency International ranked Kyrgyzstan together with Pakistan in 87th place out of 99 countries in its Corruption Perceptions Index. Another problem that discourages investors is the diminishing purchasing power of the population. Kyrgyzstan slid from 31st place in 1991 to 102nd place in 2002 in the UNDP Human Development Index, behind Kazakhstan, Jordan, Albania, and Iran, although it was ahead of China, Turkmenistan, and Uzbekistan.

In July 1999 the World Bank together with the Kyrgyzstani government launched a joint project "Integrated Basis of Kyrgyzstan Development on 2000–2010." In 2001 President Akayev presented a national strategy titled "The Comprehensive Development Framework of the Kyrgyz Republic to 2010." This strategy was designed in order to address pressing economic, political, and social issues, including reducing mass poverty at least by half, dealing with social polarization, and decreasing political instability.

Vision 2010

President Akayev presented a national strategy "The Comprehensive Development Framework of the Kyrgyz Republic to 2010" as his view of the past and vision for future changes in the country and as a promise to maintain continuity in the new round of reforms.

Independence indeed brought many changes to the Kyrgyz Republic. After gaining its independence Kyrgyzstan managed to consolidate its society and introduce a civic identity and new nationality policy without calamities, which haunted many other young nations after gaining their independence. But from a historical perspective, a decade of independence is a very short period and it is still too early to arrive at any firm conclusions. The social, demographic, and migration indicators are constantly changing, as the process of forming the "Kyrgyzstani nation" is far from complete. Nevertheless, certain changes struck firm roots in society, as the nostalgia over the Soviet past is gone almost entirely and people accept the post-Soviet realities, acknowledging that the disintegration of the Soviet Union is an irreversible fact. The majority of the population understands that Kyrgyzstan is their only home country, regardless of their ethnic background, and the people perceive themselves as the citizens of this state; although, a considerable number of people in the republic are still uncertain about their future and have indicated their desire to migrate. It is important to note that there is a strong shift in people's identities and loyalties toward the republic and a growing belief that they are citizens of Kyrgyzstan.

The economic changes in Kyrgyzstan clearly showed that there was no easy and fast road to sustainable economic growth. It also demonstrated that the country will need to readjust its economic program, taking into consideration new realities and difficult lessons from the past decade of reforms and changes. Moreover, it needs to pay more attention to improving its competitiveness, rules of law, and property rights as well as regional trade liberalization and economic cooperation. However, despite many promises the Kyrgyz government failed to tackle red tape and corruption and raise living standards among the majority of the population. The war against corruption was arbitrarily used to bring to trial leading opposition figures, such as Felix Kulov or Daniar Usenov and many others, on dubious charges. In the meantime, many high-ranking government officials were accused by the independent media in multimillion som scandals and many state officials at provincial level ran local administrations as their own fiefdoms and behaved like feudal lords.

In the political field the results of the changes in the post-Soviet era were even more controversial. The government succeeded in dismantling its centralized political system, introducing democratic institutions and democratic procedures. Political opposition and independent mass media can express themselves relatively freely, although during the past few years the government has become less tolerant of criticism. Despite some quarrels over domestic affairs, during the 1990s the country remained politically stable and comparatively democratic. However, since the late 1990s the Akayev regime increasingly turned to authoritarian measures in dealing with the opposition and independent media. These authoritarian actions, combined with the government's inability to deal with rampant corruption, angered many political groups in the country and led to rising tensions.

On the eve of 2002 the public and especially the opposition were outraged by the revelations of the secret concession of part of the Kyrgyz territory to China and Uzbekistan during clandestine border delimitation negotiations. The behavior of the government, which initially denied the existence of territorial transfers related to the border deals and then declared that the deals were the best possible option for the national interests, raised suspicions in the Jogorku Kenesh. Members of parliament launched their own independent investigation over the secret deals, thus bringing thousands of people into the streets demonstrating against the deals.

Yet the government continued to ignore the opposition's demands. Indeed, it attempted to make a resolute move against the opposition by arresting parliament member Azimbek Beknazarov, one of the leading critics of the secret deals and a prominent opposition figure from southern Kyrgyzstan. As in the case of former vice-president Felix Kulov, Beknazarov was arrested on dubious charges of professional misconduct several years earlier.

The tensions gradually boiled over and consequently resulted in tragic events. On 17 March 2002 a group of Beknazarov supporters in his native Aksy district attempted to organize a public rally in his support in the district center, the town of Kerben. As the angry unarmed demonstrators gathered in front of the local police station, the police and security forces opened fire, killing six unarmed citizens and injuring more than 60 people. It was the first violent civil confrontation since the republic's independence in 1991.

The death of the civilians and the government's mishandling of the event and its aftermath outraged and radicalized even the moderate opposition. The full range of opposition groups and the public joined in demands to investigate and bring to justice those responsible for the tragic events. They also called for the resignation of the president and the government, as he and his ruling cohort in their view had lost all political credibility. In May 2002 several opposition groups organized a Kurultai (People's Congress), and then established a popular movement "People for the resignation of President Akayev."

In response to the criticism, in May 2002 the Kyrgyz government did resign, and a new one was established bringing in a significant number of new young ministers led by a new technocratic prime minister Nikolai Tanayev. However, President Akayev refused to follow suit, offering instead constitutional changes and introduction of a national program under the slogan "Kyrgyzstan is a Home for Human Rights." To defuse the tensions the government released Beknazarov and announced public debates on constitutional changes. A Constitutional Council established in September began looking into possible constitutional changes, including the establishment of a parliamentary system in which the position of the president could cease to exist or could be purely symbolic.

The constitutional referendum was held on 2 February 2003 and it wrought significant changes in the Kyrgyz constitution, including the return to a one-chamber parliament and giving additional powers to President Akayev. This created a new basis for possible tensions and political instability during the run up to parliamentary and presidential elections scheduled in 2005.

NOTES

1. Shirin Akiner, *The Formation of Kazakh Identity from Tribe to Nation State* (London: Royal Institute of International Affairs, 1994), 34.

2. A. Khazanov, *After the USSR: Ethnicity, Nationalism, and Politics in the Commonwealth of Independent States* (Madison: University of Wisconsin Press, 1995), 12.

3. *Sovetskaia Kirgizia,* 13 September 1989.

4. G. Gleason, *The Central Asian States: Discovering Independence* (Boulder, Colo.: Westview Press, 1997), 94.

5. Eugene Huskey, "The Rise of Contested Politics in Central Asia: Elections in Kyrgyzstan, 1989–1990." *Europe-Asia Studies,* vol. 47, no. 5 (1995): 821.

6. *Slovo Kyrgyzstana,* 7 December 1994.

7. *Sotsialno-ekonomicheskoye razvitie Kyrgyzskoi Respubliki, 1997–2001* [Social and Economic Development in the Kyrgyz Republic] (Bishkek: 2002), 91.

The Dictionary

– A –

ABDIMOMUNOV, KARIMSHER (1953–). Kyrgyz politician. Born in Aravan village in **Osh** *oblast* (southern Kyrgyzstan). Karimsher Abdimomunov graduated from Odessa Technological Institute (Ukraine) in 1975. He started his career as an engineer at the Kara Suu wine-processing plant in 1975. From 1975 to 1991 he held various managerial positions in Osh *oblast*. In 1991 Abdimomunov was appointed as chairman of the Kyzyl Kiya city council and in 1992 as *akim* (head) of the Kyzyl Kiya city administration. In 1994 he became the *akim* of the Kadamzhai district administration.

Abdimomunov launched his political career in **Bishkek** in 1996, when he was appointed minister of **Agriculture** and Water Resources of Kyrgyzstan. In 1997 he was appointed vice premier for agricultural policy. Throughout the 1990s Abdimomunov was among the leading and most influential figures of the Osh (southern) **clan**, negotiating a number of behind-the-scene political deals.

ABDRAZAKOV, ISHANBAI (1937–). Kyrgyz politician and diplomat. Ishimbai Abdrazakov played an important role in foreign and domestic policy formulation in President **Askar Akayev**'s administration. He was born in Cholpon Ata town in **Ysyk Kol** *oblast* (eastern province of the republic) in 1937. He graduated from the Moscow State Economic Institute in 1959 and worked as an engineer at the Kyrgyz *Gosplan* (state planning agency) from 1959 to 1962. From 1962 to 1964 he attended the *aspirantura* at the Institute of Economics at the Academy of Sciences of the USSR (Moscow). In 1965 he joined the Central Committee of the **Communist Party of the Kyrgyz SSR** and worked in the Department of Education and Sciences. From 1967 to 1970 Abdrazakov studied at the Diplomatic School under the Soviet Ministry of Foreign Affairs. Between 1971 and 1986 he worked as a secretary, consul, and advisor at the Soviet consulate in Sapporo and at the Soviet embassy in Tokyo. From 1986 to 1991 he held various positions in the Soviet Ministry of Foreign Affairs. From 1991 to 1993 he was the general consul in the Soviet and then in the Russian consulate in Sapporo (Japan).

Abdrazakov returned to Kyrgyzstan in 1994 and was appointed as a consultant-expert in President Akayev's administration. Since 1996 he has been the state secretary of the **Kyrgyz Republic**. As one of the most influential politicians in the presidential administration he supported the pro-Western policy of the Kyrgyz government, and he played a significant role in numerous negotiations with Western governments and international institutions, such as the International Monetary Fund and World Bank. He holds the rank of extraordinary and plenipotentiary ambassador.

ABDRISAYEV, BAKTYBEK (1958–). Kyrgyz politician and diplomat. Born in Frunze (now **Bishkek**), he graduated from the Frunze Polytechnic Institute in 1980 where he also completed his *aspirantura* in 1984. From 1987 to 1992 he worked as a researcher at the Frunze Polytechnic Institute and the Institute of Physics of the **National Academy of Sciences**. In 1992 Abdrisayev joined the international department in President **Askar Akayev**'s administration as an expert. From 1993 to 1996 he worked as head of the international department at the presidential administration. In 1995 he was elected as member of the **Jogorku Kenesh** (Parliament). In October 1996 he was appointed extraordinary and plenipotentiary ambassador of the **Kyrgyz Republic** to the United States and Canada and served until 2003, becoming the longest serving representative of the republic in this position.

Abdrisayev played an important role in the formulation of the republic's foreign policies after Kyrgyzstan's independence, and he participated in various negotiations with the United States and Western governments as well as international institutions such as the International Monetary Fund and World Bank. He holds the rank of extraordinary and plenipotentiary ambassador.

ABDURAKHMANOV, YUSUP (1901–1938). Kyrgyz politician and first chairman of the Council of People's Commissars. Born in 1901

Yusup Abdurakhmanov received little formal **education**. He became a political activist during the civil war in Kyrgyzstan (1918–20). In March 1927 he was elected as chairman of the Council of People's Commissars, becoming the first prime minister of the **Kyrgyz Autonomous Soviet Socialist Republic**. He served in this position from 1927 to 1933. In the middle of the 1930s he was accused of anti-Soviet activities. Abdurakhmanov was executed in 1938, but he was rehabilitated posthumously after the death of Stalin.

ABDUREKHMENOVA, ASYLGUL (1953–). Kyrgyz politician. Born in Bosteri village in **Ysyk Kol** *oblast* (eastern Kyrgyzstan), Asylgul Abdurekhmenova climbed the political ladder from village school teacher to minister in the Kyrgyz government. She graduated from the **Przhevalsk** Pedagogical Institute in 1974. From 1974 to 1978 she worked as a teacher at a secondary school in Chon Urukty village. Her political career started in 1978 when she got a job at the **Komsomol** organization. From 1979 to 1987 she held various **Communist Party of Kyrgyz SSR** apparatus positions in the Ysyk Kol district, and then in the Kara Suu and Dzhangi Dzhol districts of **Osh** *oblast*. From 1987 to 1996 she worked in various administrative positions in the Osh and then Karakol municipal administrations. From 1996 to 1998 Abdurekhmenova was the minister of labor and social protection.

ABDYKALYKOV, OROZMAT (1950–). Kyrgyz politician. Born in remote Tambashat village in **Osh** *oblast* (southern Kyrgyzstan), Orozmat Abdykalykov spent his entire career in the **Komsomol**, **Communist Party of Kyrgyz SSR** apparatus and **government**. He graduated from the Frunze Polytechnic Institute in 1971. He started his career as an engineer at the Maili-Sai (now Mailuu Suu) plant in 1971. From 1973 to 1978 he held various positions in the Osh *oblast* Committee of the Komsomol organization. From 1978 to 1982 he worked in the Central Committee of the Komsomol in Moscow. From 1982 to 1987 he served as first secretary of the Osh *oblast* Committee of Komsomol and then the first secretary of the republic's Komsomol organization. From 1987 to 1992 he held various party and administrative positions in **Karakol**.

Abdykalykov played an important role in the republic's domestic politics after Kyrgyzstan's independence. From 1992 to 1994 he was the chairman of the permanent commission of the **Jogorku Kenesh** (parliament). In 1994 he was appointed as head of President **Askar Akayev**'s administration, but he resigned after being accused of leaking state secrets to the mass media. From 1995 to 2002 he held the positions of minister of foreign trade and **industry**, deputy chairman of the social fund, and then head of the prime minister's administration. Abdykalykov played a significant role in reforming the social security and pension system in post-Soviet Kyrgyzstan.

ABILDAYEV, BOLOT (1963–). Kyrgyz politician. Born in Kirovskoye village in **Talas** *oblast*, Abildayev graduated from the economics department of the **Kyrgyz State (National) University** in 1985 and from the *aspirantura* of the Leningrad (now Saint Petersburg) Financial-Economic Institute in 1987. From 1985 to 1986 he worked as an economist in the **National Statistical Committee** of Kyrgyzstan. From 1990 to 1991 he was the commercial director of commercial enterprise in the Academy of Sciences (Moscow). From 1991 to 1993 Abildayev was vice-president of the Kyrgyz Stock Exchange. From 1993 to 1994 he worked as director of the Dasmia private enterprise and from 1994 to 1996 he was director of a Kyrgyz-Kazakh joint venture.

In 1996 Abildayev moved to a public position, becoming the senior inspector of the State Taxation Inspection. From 1997 to 1999 he was head of department and a treasurer of Sverdlovsk district in **Bishkek**. From 1999 to 2000 he was head of the Railways Customs Service under the Ministry of Finance. From 2000 to 2002 he was director of the Central Treasury of the Ministry of Finance. In 2002 Abildayev was appointed minister of finance.

At the time of appointment, Abildayev was one of the youngest ministers in the Kyrgyz **government** and among the few people in the 2002 government with extensive experience in the private sector.

ACADEMICIAN (also *akademik*). The highest academic rank in the **Kyrgyz Republic** given to a scholar or a distinguished researcher in a field. Academicians are selected from eminent scholars nominated by universities or research institutions to become corresponding members or full members of the **National Academy of Sciences** of Kyrgyzstan. According to the tradition inherited from the Soviet era, a candidate to the rank should possess a Doctor of Sciences degree and have made a recognized scientific discovery or contribution in the field.

ACADEMY OF SCIENCES. *See* NATIONAL ACADEMY OF SCIENCES OF KYRGYZSTAN.

ACHYLOVA, RAKHAT (1941–). Kyrgyz politician. Born in the remote village of Orto Boz in **Batken** *oblast*, Rakhat Achylova graduated from the **Jalal Abad** Pedagogical Institute in 1958, the history department of the **Kyrgyz State (National) University** in 1963, and the *aspirantura* of the Leningrad (now Saint Petersburg) State University in 1966. From 1966 to 1987 she worked as a lecturer and then as head of the philosophy department of the Kyrgyz State (National) University. From 1987 to 1992 she was rector (chancellor) of the Kyrgyz Women's Pedagogical Institute (**Bishkek**). From 1992 to 1993 Achylova was a professor in the philosophy department of the Kyrgyz State (National) University. From 1993 to 1995 she served as head of department at the Kyrgyz Agricultural Institute.

Achylova played a significant role in the post-Soviet era **women**'s movement, as she was elected a member of the **Jogorku Kenesh** (parliament) and became chairperson of the Parliamentary Committee on Education, Women, Family and Youth Affairs throughout the 1990s. She has authored numerous articles and brochures on philosophical and cultural issues. She was one of the experts who assisted in introducing and implementing a micro-credit program in Kyrgyzstan in the late 1990s.

ADAT. Customary law in traditional Central Asian society, guided by authoritative members of communities. It was practiced among the **Kyrgyzs** and other peoples of Central Asia until 1924–26, when the Soviet authorities banned the use of the Adat and replaced it with the civil law. However, in some parts of the republic the Adat was practiced well into the 1930s, regulating minor communal disputes and disagreements. In the 1990s people in some areas of Kyrgyzstan began to practice the Adat again as the republic experienced a decay in its legal and law enforcement institutions. *See also* SHARIAH.

ADMINISTRATIVE STRUCTURE. Kyrgyzstan is a unitary republic and its territorial administration is divided into *oblast* (province), *rayon* (district), *shahar* (city), and *ail* (village) levels. There were several changes in administrative division during the Soviet and post-Soviet eras. As of 2003 Kyrgyzstan is divided into seven *oblasts*

(**Batken, Chui, Ysyk Kol, Jalal Abad, Naryn, Osh, Talas**). Each *oblast* in turn is divided into *raions*. There are 40 *raions* and 21 cities. The activities of local administrations and legislatures have been regulated by the Law on Local Governance and Local State Administration in Kyrgyzstan (1991). According to the law, the president appoints the *oblasts' akims* (heads of an *oblast*) and of **Bishkek** city administration, upon the recommendation of the prime minister and by consent of the corresponding local *keneshes* (legislatures). In December 2001 the Kyrgyz **government** made a step toward the decentralization of local administration and conducted local elections of the heads (*akims*) of village and town administrations for the first time since independence. Previously, the prime minister had appointed them with the consent of the relevant local legislatures (*keneshes*).

ADYLET PARTY. *See* JUSTICE PARTY.

AFGHANISTAN. A country located southwest of Kyrgyzstan. Afghanistan and Kyrgyzstan have no common borders and are separated from each other by a 150-kilometer-wide land corridor of **Tajikistan**'s territory. Afghanistan has an area of 647,500 square kilometers and its population was estimated at about 26.6 million in July 2001. The Pushtuns account for 38 percent of the population, Tajiks about 25 percent, Hazara about 19 percent, Uzbeks about 6 percent, and others about 12 percent. About 20,000 **Kyrgyzs** live in Afghanistan, mainly in the northeast provinces of the country; some of them chose to move back to Kyrgyzstan after 1991.

Afghanistan had uneasy political and economic relations with Kyrgyzstan in the 20th century. After the Bolshevik revolution several thousand Kyrgyzs, who did not accept the Soviet system, escaped to Afghanistan. After World War II Kyrgyzstan sold its industrial production to Afghanistan through the Soviet Ministry of Foreign Trade. In the 1980s about 6,000 Kyrgyzstan citizens were sent to Afghanistan among the Soviet troops and political advisers. In the 1990s up to 18,000 refugees from Afghanistan moved to Kyrgyzstan, especially after the escalation of the civil war during the Taliban regime. In late 2001 the United States established a **U.S. military airbase** in **Kyrgyzstan** for military actions and rescue operations in Afghanistan. The base was used intensively in the winter and spring

2002 campaign in Afghanistan, as it is located within 50–60 minutes flying time from Kabul.

AGRARIAN PARTY OF KYRGYZSTAN (APK) *(Agrardyk Partiasy* **in Kyrgyz).** The organization was established in **Bishkek** and it was first registered on 26 November 1993. In its political program the party declared that it would defend the rights of farmers and rural settlers, as they experienced the greatest decline in income and social protection, and many of them lost their jobs and lived below the poverty line. The APK attempted to represent the interests of farmers and lobby their interests in the Kyrgyz **government.** The party claims that it managed to recruit up to 8,000 supporters in various parts of the republic, but its main stronghold is in northern Kyrgyzstan. The party was unable to become a real political force due to the general political apathy among the rural population of Kyrgyzstan. Esenkul Alyev, the chairman of the APK, was regarded as a moderate pro-government politician. Despite the promising start, the APK failed to win any seats in the **Jogorku Kenesh** (parliament) in the 2000 parliamentary elections.

AGRARIAN-LABOR PARTY OF KYRGYZSTAN (ALPK) (Kyrgyzstandyn Agrardyk-Emgek Partiasy in Kyrgyz). The organization was first registered on 14 October 1994. In its political program the party declared that it would defend the rights of farmers and rural settlers, and that the country's resources, including its land, forests, and pastures, should belong to its people and could not be sold to foreigners. The ALPK demanded that the Kyrgyz **government** slow down the process of economic reforms and take into greater consideration the needs of small farmers. The party claims that it managed to recruit up to 12,000 supporters in various *oblasts* of the republic, but it enjoyed greater support in **Jalal Abad** and **Osh** *oblasts*. The party joined the opposition in its criticism of the **Askar Akayev** administration. Usen Sydykov, the chairman of the ALPK, was considered to be an influential politician in the southern **clan**. The ALPK conducted an active political campaign and won a seat in the **Jogorku Kenesh** (parliament) in the 2000 parliamentary elections. In October 2002 Usen Sydykov's attempt to run for the Jogorku Kenesh sparked political controversy and mass public rallies, as he was banned from the second round of the election on the grounds of not registering all his property and incomes (he denied the charges), although he received 47 percent of votes after the first round of elections.

AGRICULTURE. Agriculture is an important contributor to the Kyrgyz economy, accounting for 39.4 percent of GDP (2000), and is a source of employment for about 55 percent of the **population**. Animal herding is an important subsector of Kyrgyzstan's agriculture and includes stock-breeding of **sheep, horses,** cattle, **yaks,** and goats. Kyrgyzstan has favorable conditions for producing cotton, silk, corn, wheat, tobacco, vegetables, and fruits, including grapes, apples, pears, and cherries. Most of the agricultural products were successfully exported to Russia during the Soviet era.

Most farmers in Kyrgyzstan are engaged in animal husbandry and intensive agriculture. The agriculture provides a source of income, everyday food, and mode of **transportation** for a significant part of the population in this mostly mountainous republic. Sheep wool and meat along with cotton and tobacco account for a significant share of Kyrgyzstan's exports. The rural **Kyrgyzs** usually move toward *jayloo,* higher and cooler mountain slopes, during the hot summer season, taking their horses, sheep, goats, and cattle to graze in the rich mountainous pastures. They move back to *kyshtoo,* their winter houses in the low-altitude valleys, during the winter to escape the harsh cold weather of the high mountains. In the 1930s the Soviet government imposed the policy of **collectivization** and most of the farmers were organized into large state-controlled *kolkhozes* and *sovkhozes*. By the 1970s and 1980s many *kolkhozes* and *sovkhozes* began to experience difficulties due to the extensive nature of the agricultural sector in the republic and overexploitation of the fragile mountainous land. In the 1980s the number of sheep in Kyrgyzstan, for example, was one of the largest in the world in proportion to the country's population.

In the early 1990s Kyrgyzstan's agricultural sector underwent major reforms as the state relaxed its control over this vital sector progressively liberalizing **government** regulation. In 1992 and 1993 the privatization of state-controlled *kolkhoz*es was introduced and most of the *kolkhozes* were dismantled. Kyrgyzstan has also made substantial efforts to achieve self-sufficiency in foodstuffs (cereals, potatoes, vegetables) after gaining its independence.

However, mismanagement, corruption, and unfavorable regional market conditions led to a depression in the agricultural sector and consequently in agricultural product-processing industries. After the privatization of large state-controlled farms and the creation of a system of small private farming, crop production fell sharply in the mid-1990s. Since 1992 many farmers have struggled to adapt themselves to new economic realities and turned to a subsistence economy. Moreover, since Kyrgyzstan's independence in 1991 Kyrgyz farmers have been forced to compete with neighboring **Uzbekistan** and **Tajikistan** as well as with major world producers as the ex-Soviet markets were opened to international competition. In 2002 the United Nations Development Program (UNDP) estimated that more than 55 percent of the rural population in Kyrgyzstan lived below the poverty line and the unemployment rate could run as high as 20–30 percent.

Kyrgyz agriculture recovered substantially between 1999 and 2004. The rise in agricultural production was attributed to a combination of private initiatives, restructuring of the sector, and increased funding from international organizations, including the World Bank and International Monetary Fund (IMF). According to the **National Statistical Committee**, in 2000 Kyrgyzstan produced 1.57 million tons of grain (up from 1.37 million tons in 1991), 1.05 million tons of potatoes (up from 0.326 million tons in 1991), and 746.8 thousands tons of vegetables (up from 170 thousand tons in 1991). Yet, in the 1990s, there was a significant decrease in livestock numbers due to the falling market demand and structural changes in the agricultural sector. The number of sheep and goats, for example, declined from 9.1 million in 1991 to approximately 3.2 million in 2001.

Other sectors of Kyrgyzstan's economy include forestry, fishery, and fur production, which are relatively small and do not have a significant impact on the economic development.

AIL. 1. Village, rural settlement, especially in the mountains. 2. A kind of tribal and extended family unit, as people who live in *ails* often (but not necessarily) represent members of the same tribal unit or community.

AIRLINES. Airlines represent an important mode of **transportation** in this landlocked and mountainous republic. The Soviet government built about 50 airports in the republic. They provide passenger and cargo transportation as well as medical access to the remote mountain villages. The national airline, established and heavily subsidized during the Soviet era as a branch of Aeroflot, experienced a severe decline in the 1990s. This was due to the dramatic fall in people's income, cuts of subsidies, shortage of fuel, and safety concerns. About 600,000 people were transported by the airways in 1996, down from about 1 million in 1991. In the middle of the 1990s there were several attempts to establish a private airline, which failed due to bureaucratic barriers and economic difficulties. According to official reports in 2001 about 197,000 people were transported by airlines, down from 465,000 in 1997. Several **Commonwealth of Independent States (CIS)** and international airlines opened services to Kyrgyzstan in the 1990s. *See also* KYRGYZSTAN ABA JOLDORU.

AITMATOV, ASKAR (1959–). Kyrgyz politician and diplomat. Born in Frunze (now **Bishkek**), Askar Aitmatov graduated from the Institute of Asia and Africa of the Moscow State University in 1981. He joined the Soviet Ministry of Foreign Affairs in 1982. From 1983 to 1987 he worked at the Soviet embassy in Turkey and from 1987 to 1990 in the Department of Information of the Soviet Ministry of Foreign Affairs.

In 1990 Aitmatov returned to Kyrgyzstan and was appointed head of the Department of Information of the Kyrgyz Ministry of Foreign Affairs. From 1992 to 1994 he served as deputy minister of foreign affairs. From 1994 to 1996 he was permanent representative of the **Kyrgyz Republic** at the United Nations (New York). From 1996 to 2002 he was a consultant and head of the International Department of President **Askar Akayev**'s administration. In May 2002 Aitmatov was appointed minister of foreign affairs.

Aitmatov played an important role in the republic's foreign policies, especially in the late 1990s and early 2000s, and participated in various negotiations with the United States and other Western governments, and international institutions, such as the International Monetary Fund and World Bank. He has the rank of extraordinary and plenipotentiary ambassador.

AITMATOV, CHINGIZ (1928–). Kyrgyz writer, publicist, and politician. He was born in December 1928 in Sheker village in **Talas** *oblast* (western province of the republic). Chingiz Aitmatov is a son of one of the leading Kyrgyz communists, who was repressed during the Stalin purges of 1937. In 1942, at the age of 14, he started work-ing in his village. During his studies at the Kyrgyz Agrarian Institute he began to write short stories. From 1956 to 1958 he attended the Gorky Literary Institute (Moscow). In 1959 he joined the **Communist Party of Kyrgyz SSR** and from 1959 to1965 he worked as a cor-respondent for the prestigious newspaper *Pravda*. From 1964 to 1969 he was the secretary and from 1969 to 1986 the chairman of the **Union of Cinematographers of Kyrgyzstan** and from 1986 to 1994 he was the chairman of the **Union of Writers of Kyrgyzstan**. From 1966 to 1989 Aitmatov became people's deputy of the **Supreme Soviet** (Soviet Parliament); he was also a member of the Central Com-mittee of the Communist Party of the USSR. Since November 1990 he has been Soviet and then Kyrgyz ambassador to Luxembourg.

However, it was Aitmatov's literary works that won him the reputa-tion of "one of the most distinguished non-Russian authors writing in Russian." His early writings combined the delicate psychological por-traits of ordinary people with the magical culture, landscape, and pas-toral lifestyle of traditional Kyrgyz society in such works as *Povesti Gor i Stepey* (1962); *Tales of Mountains and Steppes* (1969); *Proshchay, Gulsary!* (1966); *Farewell, Gulsary!* (1970); *Belyi Parakhod* (1970); and *The White Steamship* (1972). The stories *Dzhamilya* (1958) and *Pervyi Uchitel'* (1962) were screened and became classics of Kyrgyz cinema. Aitmatov was the first Kyrgyz author to raise the appreciation of traditional Kyrgyz folklore to the level of philosophical analysis. In his later writings, Aitmatov remained faithful to his early themes adding fresh nuances. His writing gravitated toward mystical imagery and philosophical parable. Aitmatov combined the traditional images of Kyrgyz folklore with motives of classical world literature within the context of precipitous social and political cataclysms in *I Dol'she Veka Dlitsya Den'* (1980); *The Day Lasts More Than a Hundred Years* (1983); *Plakha* (1986); and *Tavro Kasandry* (1997). Most of his novels, which were screened by the **Kyrgyzfilm** studio, have had a powerful impact on the formation of the Kyrgyz worldview.

Throughout the 1990s Aitmatov remained one of the most popular writers and politicians in post-Soviet Kyrgyzstan, though in the early 2000s he largely retired from politics. He was the person who pro-posed the candidacy of **Askar Akayev** for the presidency of Kyrgyz-stan in October 1990. Aitmatov supported the moderate nationalism of

Akayev against the extreme nationalists during debates on the Law on Languages and other issues in the 1990s. Aitmatov was elected to the **Jogorku Kenesh** (parliament) in 1995. He has been active in organizing various regional and international events in Kyrgyzstan, including the **Isyk Kol Forum,** and he has remained a prolific publicist.

In the former Soviet Union and in the present-day **Commonwealth of Independent States** (CIS) Aitmatov is one of the most celebrated non-Russian writers. His short stories and novels have been published in 130 languages with a total circulation of 40 million copies.

AITYSH. The art of improvised epic often accompanied by the *komuz.* These epics were traditionally devoted to the heroes or great events of the past and often carried philosophical reflections of the historical development. *Aitysh* has traditionally been popular among **Kyrgyzs** and other peoples of Central Asia and has been performed during mass gatherings for public celebrations or during the long evenings, when young herdsmen needed to be awake to protect their herds. *See also* AKIYEV, KALYK.

AKA (also *ake*). *See* BAIKE.

AKADEMIK. *See* ACADEMICIAN.

AKAEV, ASKAR. *See* AKAYEV, ASKAR.

AKAYEV, ASKAR (1944–). Kyrgyz politician and scientist; the first president of the **Kyrgyz Republic**. He was born in November 1944 in Kyzyl Bairak in Kemin District in **Chui** *oblast*. Askar Akayev, after completing his schooling in his native village, worked at the *Frunzemash* plant in Frunze (now **Bishkek**) for a year. He completed his university degree in 1968 and the *kandidat nauk* degree in 1972 at the Institute of Precision Engineering and Optics in Leningrad (now Saint Petersburg, **Russia**). From 1972 until 1986, he lectured in Leningrad and in Frunze. In 1987 he was elected as vice-president and in 1989 as president of the Kyrgyz Academy of Sciences (now **National Academy of Sciences).** During his academic career, he has authored more than 80 publications.

Akayev started his political career by joining the ruling Communist Party in 1981. From 1986 to 1987 he served as the head of the

Department of Sciences and Education of the Central Committee of the **Communist Party of Kyrgyz SSR**. In 1989 Dr. Akayev was elected as people's deputy in the **Supreme Soviet** (Soviet Parliament), where he was a member of the Council of Nationalities. In October 1990 he was elected the first president of Kyrgyzstan by the **Jogorku Kenesh** (parliament). The election was confirmed by a popular vote in 1991. In 1990 and 1991 Akayev was frequently voted by the Soviet newspapers among the 20 most popular politicians in the Union of Soviet Socialist Republics (USSR).

Akayev's views on the political process and national question were formed by his personal experience as a scientist and by his experience as a member of the Soviet parliament. The interethnic conflict in the southern part of the country in the summer of 1990 also left distinct marks on his political attitudes. In the early years after the disintegration of the USSR, he worked to reform the political system in the republic into one of the most democratic states in Central Asia and to ease tensions between the **Kyrgyzs** and other ethnic groups. He vetoed a provision of the Law on Land, which declared that the country's land resources are the wealth (*dostoyanie*) of the ethnic Kyrgyzs. He also advocated the liberalization of the Law on Languages and introduced the Russian language as the official language of the republic (**Kyrgyz language** is the state language). The new **Constitution of Kyrgyzstan**, adopted in May 1993, guarantees equal rights to all people of the state and maintains the secular nature of the republic.

In the economic field, the Akayev-led administration implemented the International Monetary Fund–designed Shock Therapy Approach, which included quick trade liberalization, mass privatization, and opening of the Kyrgyz market to international trade and investments. Yet despite political and economic liberalization Kyrgyzstan suffered one of the deepest economic recessions among the former Soviet republics at the rate of about 10–14 percent between 1991 and 1996. The opposition repeatedly claimed that Akayev's inability to focus on economic issues and his bold experiments with radical economic changes worsened the recession and led to impoverishment of the population.

After his election for a second term in December 1995, President Akayev, facing a growing economic meltdown, took a tougher stand toward the opposition and independent **mass media**. He also strengthened his wide-ranging powers through the referendum of 1996. Although the political opposition often claimed that there were some authoritarian tendencies in Akayev's political attitudes, Kyrgyzstan remained one of the most liberal states in the Central Asian region throughout the 1990s. Akayev was elected for a third term in October 2000 in highly controversial presidential elections, which were accompanied by various irregularities and harsh actions toward the political opposition and against **Felix Kulov** and **Daniar Usenov**, the most popular political rivals. Akayev's third term was tarnished by accusations of corruption and mismanagement, culminating in the **Aksy conflict**, in which police killed and wounded several civilians. In February 2003 he further strengthened his grip on power through a controversial constitutional referendum.

Nonetheless, Akayev retained strong support from the major Western powers for his pro-Western policies, opening the Kyrgyz market to international competition and cooperating with the major international institutions, especially with the International Monetary Fund and World Bank. In late 2001 Akayev joined the international war against terrorism and approved the lease of Manas airport to the **U.S. military airbase**. This step helped to further strengthen Kyrgyzstan's relations with Washington, despite the fact that Akayev declined to unconditionally support the U.S.-led war in Iraq in the spring of 2003.

AKBAGYSHEVA, ZAMIRA (1959–). Kyrgyz politician, publicist, and one of the leaders of the **women**'s movement in the **Kyrgyz Republic**. Born in San Tash village in **Chui** *oblast*, Zamira Akbagysheva graduated from the **Kyrgyz State (National) University** in 1981. She started her political career as an instructor of the department of women's policy at the **Komsomol** organization and worked in various Komsomol positions from 1981 to 1991. In 1991 Akbagysheva became vice-chairperson of Kyrgyzstan's Women Committee, a semi-independent public organization of women. From 1993 to 1994 she worked as the editor of the *Kazyna* newspaper. In 1994 Akbagysheva became the president of the Women's Congress of Kyrgyzstan, the largest and most influential **nongovernmental organization** of women in the republic.

Akbagysheva played a significant role in the post-Soviet era women's movement in Kyrgyzstan and contributed to the formulation of the **government**'s social policies toward women throughout the 1990s. She has authored numerous articles and brochures on the social and political activities of women in Kyrgyzstan.

AK CHII. *See* TALAS CITY.

AKENEYEV, ZHUMAKADYR (1954–). Kyrgyz politician and scholar. Born in remote Ulakhol village in **Ysyk Kol** *oblast* (eastern Kyrgyzstan), Zhumakadyr Akeneyev obtained a double degree as an engineer and an economist from the Frunze Polytechnic Institute in 1976. He started his career as a lecturer at the same institute. From 1978 to 1990 he held various administrative positions in the Frunze (now **Bishkek**) city administration, Ministry of **Agriculture,** and at a research institute of the Kyrgyz Agricultural-Industrial Complex. From 1990 to 1992 he worked as an expert of the State Commission on Economic Reforms under the **government** of Kyrgyzstan. In 1992 Akeneyev was a Preliminary Representative of the Kyrgyz Republic at the **Commonwealth of Independent States (CIS)** Economic Commission (Minsk, Belarus). From 1993 to 1997 he was the chairman of the **National Statistical Committee** of Kyrgyzstan and in 1995 he became (on rotation basis) chairman of Heads of the Statistical Committees of the CIS members. In 1997 he was appointed as minister of agriculture and water resources of Kyrgyzstan. However, his career came to an abrupt halt in December 1998, as he was arrested under corruption charges. He was later released.

In the 1990s Akeneyev played a visible role in the formation of the economic policies as a member of the State Commission on Sustainable Development, and a member of the Editorial Committee of the **Kyrgyz Encyclopedia.** He has authored around 40 articles and brochures.

AKIM **(sometime** *hokim* **in southern Kyrgyzstan; "the leader").** 1. Refers to any leader of the community. 2. In public life in the republic the term is used to refer to the appointed head of the local, district, or *oblast* administration (e.g., *oblastyn akimi*—the head of the *oblast* administration).

AKIYEV, KALYK (1883–1953). Prominent Kyrgyz poet, *akyn,* one of the founders of modern Kyrgyz poetry. Born in the remote village of Kul Zhygach in **Naryn** *oblast* (northern Kyrgyzstan), Kalyk Akiyev had no formal education; however, by the age of 14 he acquired a comprehensive knowledge of the Kyrgyz national oral epics and began to compose his own songs. He became a famous master of *aitysh*, the art of improvised epic accompanied by the *komuz*.

Akiyev, along with **Toktogul Satylganov,** had a positive attitude toward the Bolshevik Revolution of 1917 and created several songs expressing his support for social changes, which the Bolsheviks promised to introduce. He became one of the most influential authorities on Kyrgyz traditional epics in the 20th century. His version of several oral epics such as "Kurmanbek," "Zhanyzh-Baish," and "Kedeikan" were officially recorded in the 1930s and published in the 1930s and 1950s. Many of his songs and epics were translated into other languages of Central Asia and the USSR. In the 1990s there were literary debates concerning his heritage and controversies about his support of the Soviet policies in the 1920s and 1930s.

AKMATALIYEV, ALMAZBEK (1959–). Kyrgyz politician. Born in the remote village of Kara-Suu in **Naryn** *oblast* (eastern Kyrgyzstan), Akmataliyev graduated from the Kazakh State University in 1984. In 1988 he started his political career as an instructor at the sciences department of the Central Committee of the **Komsomol** organization. From 1989 to 1990 he worked in various positions in the Ministry of Education. From 1990 to 1992 he worked as the head of a department of the presidential administration. From 1992 to 1996 Akmataliyev worked as deputy head of the state administration in Naryn district and from 1996 to 1997 he worked as the head of Naryn district administration. In 1997 he was elected as chairman of the Naryn *oblast* council of people's deputies. He has authored around 20 articles and brochures.

AKMATALIYEV, TEMIRBEK (1958–). Kyrgyz politician. Born in **Naryn city** in **Naryn** *oblast* (eastern Kyrgyzstan), Temirbek Akmataliyev graduated from the Kyrgyz Agricultural Institute in 1981. From 1983 to 1995 he worked as an economist at the Kyrgyz Ministry for Fruit-Vegetable Farms. From 1985 to 1994 Akmataliyev held various managerial positions in Kemin district of **Chui** *oblast.* From 1994 to 1996 Akmataliyev worked as an expert and then deputy head of the agricultural department of the presidential administration. In 1996 he was appointed head of the Ala Buka administration in **Jalal Abad** *oblast.* In 2000 he was appointed finance minister and in January 2002 he became the minister of internal affairs. Akmataliyev was perceived as a rising political star with presidential ambitions.

Akmataliyev's political rise came to a sudden halt in 2002 due to civil casualties in the **Aksy conflict** in March 2002 as he was dismissed from his position.

AKMATOV, KAZAT (1941–). Kyrgyz writer and politician. Born in the remote village of Tambashat in **Osh** *oblast* (southern Kyrgyzstan), Kazat Akmatov graduated from the faculty of journalism of the **Kyrgyz State (National) University** in 1967. He started his political career in the **Komsomol** district committee in 1967, working in various positions. From 1971 to 1974 he was the editor and head of a department of the "Kyrgyzstan" publishing house. From 1974 to 1983 he held various administrative positions in the apparatus of the **Communist Party of Kyrgyz SSR**. Akmatov became the chairman of the **Union of Writers of Kyrgyzstan** in 1986. He was among the founding members of the **Democratic Movement of Kyrgyzstan** in 1990 and he played a significant role in ousting **Absamat Masaliyev** and electing **Askar Akayev** as president in 1990.

From 1990 to 1994 Akmatov was a member of the **Jogorku Kenesh** (parliament) and a member of the Commission on State Symbols that played a significant role in selecting all post-Soviet symbols of the **Kyrgyz Republic**, including its **flag**, anthem, **coat of arms**, and so on. From 1994 to 1995 he was chairman of the Public Committee on **Mass Media** under the president of Kyrgyzstan. Later he was appointed deputy chairman of the State Commission on Language, becoming one of the leading advocates of strengthening the role of the **Kyrgyz language** in **education** and public life.

Akmatov played an important role in the republic's domestic politics in the 1980s and 1990s, actively contributing to debates on the state language, Kyrgyz cultural development, and various other issues. He has authored eight books and numerous novels and articles (mainly fiction stories), becoming one of the prominent Kyrgyz writers in the republic and has regularly published his essays in the Kyrgyz media.

AKNAZAROVA, ROZA (1955–). Kyrgyz politician. She was born in the village of Iangi Bazar in **Jalal Abad** *oblast*. Roza Aknazarova graduated from the economics department of the **Kyrgyz State (National)**

University in 1978. From 1978 to 1981 she worked as a lecturer in the **Frunze Polytechnic Institute**. She completed the *aspirantura* from the Research Institute for Agriculture (Moscow). From 1985 to 1992 she worked as the senior research fellow and head of department at the Kyrgyz Research Institute for Economics and **Agriculture**.

From 1992 to 1996 Aknazarova was head of department and senior accountant of the National Bank of the **Kyrgyz Republic**. From 1996 to 1999 she was the director of the specialized Agency on Restructuring the Banking System and Debts of the National Bank of the Kyrgyz Republic. From 1999 to 2000 she was the chairperson and then the minister for the Social Fund of the Kyrgyz Republic. In 2000 Aknazarova was elected as a member of the **Jogorku Kenesh** (parliament). In 2000 she was appointed minister of labor and social protection. She managed to keep her position in May 2002 despite a radical **government** reorganization.

Aknazarova is considered to be one of the young technocratic ministers in the Kyrgyz government with high credentials for professionalism.

AKSAKAL (aqsaqal, oqsoqol; literally "white bearded" in Turkic). 1. Elder in a rural or town community or oldest member of an extended family. 2. Head of a craftsman shop or a craftsman order in Central Asia. 3. Administrator in a *mahallya* (a local neighborhood community) or in a town or village; elderly representative of a community. In northern Kyrgyzstan people sometime use the term "*chal*" as a synonym with *aksakal*.

AKSY CONFLICT (also known as Aksy events). In March 2002, a peaceful demonstration of about 1,000 people entered the town of Kerben (formerly Karavan) in **Jalal Abad** *oblast*, demanding the release of an opposition figure. A standoff between demonstrators and local police forces ended in clashes. According to official reports, the police opened fire with pistols and Kalashnikov handguns in response to the demonstrators' attempt to storm several public buildings, including the local militia headquarters. Six unarmed demonstrators were killed and several dozens of them were wounded (two of them died later in the local hospital). The violence spread to the streets of the town and nearby villages and demonstrations and meetings continued for nearly a week.

The immediate cause of the Aksy conflict was the arrest and trial of **Azimbek Beknazarov,** a parliamentary deputy from Jalal Abad *oblast.* He was arrested on 5 January 2002 and his trial began on 11 March 2002 on dubious charges of misconduct during his work in the mid-1990s. However, the real cause was a deep-seated discord between representatives of northern and southern Kyrgyzstan and sharp rivalry between elites of these two regions, which instigated the disastrous turmoil. It was widely perceived that the population of the previously prosperous southern Kyrgyzstan was the biggest looser from the post-Soviet transition, as most of them lost their jobs and lived below the poverty line throughout the 1990s. In the meantime it was felt that mostly representatives of northern Kyrgyzstan benefited from privatization and foreign investments and controlled most governmental positions. The arrest and trial of Beknazarov, who led the opposition against border agreements with **China, Kazakhstan,** and **Uzbekistan**, was regarded as a direct insult to southern Kyrgyzstan's political establishment.

The conflict became one of the bloodiest events in the post-Soviet history of the republic. It had a shocking effect, as it destabilized the political situation of the whole country, leading to numerous demonstrations and meetings. The opposition began to demand the resignation of President **Askar Akayev** as well as prosecution of the law enforcement officials. Both the Kyrgyz **government** and opposition established their own commissions to investigate the events, and they produced conflicting reports. The Aksy conflict resulted in the resignation of the government in May 2002 and led to constitutional referendum in February 2003. *See also* CLAN.

AKUNOV, TURSUNBEK (1959–). Kyrgyz politician. Born in the remote village of Eski Naryn in **Naryn** *oblast* (eastern Kyrgyzstan), Akunov graduated from the Kyrgyz Agricultural Institute in 1981. From 1981 to 1983 he worked as a veterinary doctor in his home village. He started his political career as a secretary of the **Komsomol** committee at a *kolkhoz* in his native district. From 1984 to 1987 he was the secretary of the Komsomol committee of the Kyrgyz Agricultural Institute. From 1987 to 1988 Akunov worked as a research fellow at Institute of Biochemistry of the Kyrgyz **National Academy of Sciences.**

Akunov relaunched his political career in 1991, becoming the executive secretary of the **Democratic Movement of Kyrgyzstan.** In 1993 he was elected as coordinator of the Human Rights Congress of the Central Asian republics, becoming one of the most vocal advocates for human rights in the republic. For his activities he was briefly detained in 1998 and in 2002. Akunov played an important role as a mediator in negotiations with the **Islamic Movement of Uzbekistan** for release of Japanese hostages taken during **militant incursions** in the southern **Batken** *oblast* in 1999, though his tactics and dealings with the militants were criticized by many politicians in the republic. In 2000 he was registered as a candidate for the presidential elections. His political platform called for greater democratization and respect for human rights. He lost the elections, obtaining only 0.4 percent of the votes. Akunov was among the leading figures who organized the protest campaign against President **Askar Akayev** in 2002, calling for his resignation and investigation of corruption in the government.

AKYN (also *aqyn*). 1. A popular bard, who sings and improvises traditional folk songs or epics; this makes him different from the *zhyrshy* (entertainment singer). 2. A respected member of the community to whom people traditionally turn for political advice, foretelling, or entertainment. In traditional Kyrgyz society *akyns* exercised significant influence over the people and tribal leaders. *See also* AKIYEV, KALYK.

ALA KIIZ. Traditional Kyrgyz woolen carpet with traditional national Kyrgyz patterns or pictures. Traditionally *Ala Kiiz* is made in two colors.

ALA-TOO (literary journal). A leading literary journal published in the **Kyrgyz language** in **Bishkek**. The *Ala-Too* was established in 1931 and became a leading literary journal in which a number of Kyrgyz classic writers published their first novels, poetry, or short stories. Under the leadership of **Tologon Kasymbekov** (1960–67) the journal became a tribune for the emerging Kyrgyz national intelligentsia. In the 1980s and in 1990s it initiated several debates about the development of Kyrgyz culture and Kyrgyz language. *See also* MASS MEDIA.

ALA-TOO MOUNTAINS (also Ala Too mountains—translated "Snowy Mountains"). A mountain system located in the central part of Kyrgyzstan, part of the **Tian-Shan mountains**. It stretches from east to west. It is up to 600 kilometers long and about 200 kilometers wide. The altitudes vary between 600 and 5,000 meters and it is one of the favorite destinations for mountain trekking for professional and nonprofessional climbers. Kyrgyzstan's population considers Ala-Too to be the heartland of the Kyrgyz nation. The Ala Archa Gorge, located on the northern part of Ala-Too and about 40 kilometers from **Bishkek,** is one of the most popular recreational destinations for local and international tourists.

ALAY MOUNTAIN RANGE. A mountain range located in southern Kyrgyzstan and part of the **Pamir-Alay mountain** system. It stretches from east to north up to 400 kilometers in length. Its width is up to 70 kilometers. The highest point of the range is 5,539 meters. There are more than 100 glaciers with a total area of about 568 square kilometers.

The Chong Alay mountain range, which stretches to the south from the Alay mountain range, forms a natural and difficult to penetrate border between Kyrgyzstan and **Tajikistan.** Several rivers, which flow from the Alay range, provide water to numerous *jayloo* and to **Batken** and **Osh** *oblasts*. The strategically important Osh-Khorog (Tajikistan) highway, the highest auto-road in Central Asia, crosses the range from north to south. The population of the Alay valley demonstrated significant resistance to the **Russian Empire**'s advance in the 19th century and to the Soviet government in the 1920s.

ALMA-ATA DECLARATION (also Almaty Declaration). A declaration signed by **Kyrgyzstan** along with other former Soviet republics in Almaty, **Kazakhstan**, in December 1991. The Alma-Ata Declaration formally ended the existence of the Union of Soviet Socialist Republics (USSR) and signified the beginning of independence for all members of the Soviet Union including five Central Asian republics (CARs). The declaration established the following major principles in dealing with the post-Soviet problems: "assurance of the territorial integrity and inviolability of national boundaries, creation of a system of political security, creation of a military system of security, and stabilization of interethnic relations within the former USSR." One of the most important outcomes of the Alma-Ata Declaration was that it endorsed the inviolability of existing political borders between the republics in principle and that the regulation of the rights of ethnic minorities was an internal affair of each state.

ALMAKUCHUKOV, OKMOTBEK (1960–). Kyrgyz politician. He was born in Semenovka village in **Ysyk Kol** *oblast*. Okmotbek Almakuchukov graduated from the **Frunze Polytechnic Institute** (FPI) in 1982. From 1982 to 1984 he lectured at the FPI and from 1984 to 1986 he worked as deputy-secretary of the **Komsomol** at the same institute. From 1986 to 1988 he was chairman of the **Trade Union** Committee at the FPI. From 1988 to 1990 he was deputy-commander of the students' *stroiotryady* (construction brigades) movement under the Central Committee of the Komsomol. From 1990 to 1991 he was chairman of the Komsomol's Bureau of International Tourism "Sputnik," after its privatization, and from 1991 to 1995 he was president of the joint-stock company "Sputnik-Kyrgyzstan." From 1995 to 2001 Almakuchukov was general-director of the Kyrgyz-Russian joint tourist company "Glavtur **Bishkek**."

In 2001 Almakuchukov moved to a public position, becoming the chairman of the State Committee on Tourism, Sport and Youth. Despite radical government reshuffling in 2002 he managed to keep his position.

ALMATY DECLARATION. *See* ALMA-ATA DECLARATION.

AMANBAYEV, ZHUMGALBEK (also Amanbayev, Jumgalbek) (1945–). Kyrgyz politician and Communist Party leader. Born in Chayek village in **Naryn** *oblast* (an eastern province of the republic), Zhumgalbek Amanbayev graduated from the Kyrgyz Agricultural Institute in 1966 and defended the *kandidat nauk* degree in 1971. From 1973 to 1985 he worked for the **Communist Party of Kyrgyz SSR,** holding various party positions at district and *oblast* levels. From 1985 to 1989 he was a secretary of the Central Committee of the Communist Party. In 1989 he was appointed as the first secretary of the **Ysyk Kol** *oblast* Communist Party Committee.

In April 1991 Amanbayev was elected as first secretary, replacing **Absamat Masaliyev**. However, he lost his position in August 1991, as the Communist Party of Kyrgyz SSR was banned for alleged support of the military putsch in Moscow and an alleged attempt to depose incumbent President **Askar Akayev**. In 1992 Amanbayev was elected as chairman of the reemerged **Party of Communists of Kyrgyzstan**. In 1993 he left the chairmanship. Between 1993 and 1996 he was a member of the **government**, as deputy prime minister. During 1996 presidential elections Amanbayev tried to challenge the incumbent president Akayev, but he was banned from registration due to legal irregularities. Since 1996 Amanbayev focused on his private business and became the director of the Kyrgyz-Chinese joint company "Kitlap," although he has continued to play a relatively active role in the political life of the republic.

Amanbayev is best known as the last leader of the Soviet era Communist Party of Kyrgyz SSR and for his attempt to return the party to political life on a moderate social-democratic platform.

ANDIJAN UPRISING. *See* POPULAR UPRISING OF 1898.

ANTI-TERRORIST CENTER IN BISHKEK. A center established jointly by the members of the **Shanghai Cooperation Organization** in **Bishkek** in 1999 to coordinate the organization members' efforts to fight international terrorism, religious extremism, separatism, and various forms of cross-border criminal activities. It was initially discussed during the summit in Bishkek in August 1999, as the members of the radical **Islamic Movement of Uzbekistan** entered Kyrgyz territory and captured several villages and significant numbers of hostages. Partly in response to the threat of the **militant incursions** the Shanghai Cooperation Organization members issued the Bishkek Statement, expressing their desire to tackle "international terrorism, illegal dealing in **drugs** and narcotics trafficking, arm smuggling, illegal immigration and other forms of trans-border crimes." They also set up the Anti-Terrorist Center in order to coordinate military and intelligence cooperation. Due to funding and coordination problems it became operational only in 2002; however, its size and presence was much smaller compared to the **U.S. military airbase** in Kyrgyzstan. *See also* RUSSIAN MILITARY BASE.

AQSAQAL. See AKSAKAL.

AQYN. *See AKYN.*

ARCHITECTURE. The architectural landscape of Kyrgyzstan was mainly formed in the 20th century, although there was a number of ancient cities on the territory of present-day Kyrgyzstan. However, few ancient and medieval monuments or buildings survived the numerous wars and feudal raids of the medieval era. Yet several mosques in **Osh, Uzgen,** and some other cities, **Burana, Manas Gumbezi** (mausoleum), as well as many smaller remains of towns, cities, and inns on the **Great Silk Road** represent a rich cultural legacy of the past.

Most of the cities in Kyrgyzstan were established in the 19th and early 20th centuries on the sites of ancient towns and fortresses. They largely expanded between the 1930s and in the 1950s and 1970s, and their architecture reflected a combination of Stalinist classicism and Soviet functionalism. In the 1930s many **government** and cultural building were built in the semi-classic monumental style in every *oblast*'s capital. In the 1960s many industrial centers were significantly enlarged and numerous four- or five-story apartment buildings were built of red bricks or concrete in the faceless style (locals often call them *Khrushchevka*—in the name of the Soviet leader who promoted building mass and cheap accommodation). In the 1980s there was an attempt to redevelop city centers in all major urban areas and significant numbers of modern office buildings, department stores, and cinemas were built in a composition of marble, glass, and concrete. During the post-Soviet era, the infrastructure in all major urban areas experienced visible decay, although the capital and major *oblast* centers still remained very green and unpolluted. In the 1990s only **Bishkek** grew considerably through private housing construction in its central and suburban areas.

ARCHIVES. The Department of Archives under the Ministry of Education, Science and Culture (the State Archive Agency between 1992 and 1998) regulates the activities and oversees the collections of all major archives in the **Kyrgyz Republic**. There were three central, seven *oblast*, 54 district and city archives, and seven archival departments under *oblast* administration in the republic in 2002. They managed more than 12,400 archival funds, which included 2.237 million archival entities. The Kyrgyz Republic became a member of the International Council of Archives in 1995. Most of the archives are open to the public, with the limited exception of specialized archives, such as the archive of the Ministry of Internal Affairs, **National Security Committee**, and some others. The Archive of the **Communist Party of Kyrgyz SSR**, one of the largest archives in the republic, was renamed the Central Archive of Political Documentation in 1992 and was also opened to the public.

The Kyrgyz archival system was established in 1924, and the Archival Bureau (Central Archive since 1927) was established in 1926 in Frunze (now **Bishkek**). In 1935, 35 archives were established, covering every district and city in the republic. Between 1929 and 1939 archives were established in all major *oblast* centers. In 1939 all archives came under control of the Narkomat (Ministry) of Internal Affairs (Russian abbreviation NKVD), but in 1960 they were transferred under the control of the Council of Ministries of the **Kyrgyz Soviet Socialist Republic**. During the Soviet era the archives were accessible to very limited numbers of scholars and many collections were not opened to the public at all. Instead, the **government** funded the publication of selected archival materials. Between 1960 and 2000 more than 40 collections of the selected archival materials were published. *See also* LIBRARIES.

ARKHAR. A rare mountain **sheep**, it lives in high alpine mountains on the territory of **Kyrgyzstan** and **Tajikistan**. The animals are large (90–110 kilograms), with long wool and large curved horns, which are highly valued as hunting trophies. By the middle of the 20th century the *arkhars* became an endangered species. During the Soviet era the animal was under state protection and the number grew to about 50,000–60,000. Since 1991 the Kyrgyz government has allowed limited *arkhar* hunting under a state licensing system in order to attract wealthy foreign hunters.

ARMY. All Kyrgyzstan's citizens (males) of the conscript age of 18 were drafted into military service in the Soviet army since the 1930s. They served both on the territory of the republic and outside, including Soviet military bases overseas. Independence brought up the issue of establishing national armed forces in Kyrgyzstan. It was especially important due to the geographic proximity of the republic to war-torn **Afghanistan**, to **Tajikistan**, and to **China**, the Cold War–era adversary of the Union of Soviet Socialist Republics (USSR).

In May 1992 Kyrgyzstan established its control over all military facilities and equipment of the Soviet army on the territory of the republic. Kyrgyzstan inherited from the Soviet army the equipment of the Eighth Motorized Infantry Division, an air force (attack helicopter) training center, some training air planes, air defense surface-to-air missiles, an early warning radar center, and some other military facilities. In 1992 President **Askar Akayev** issued a decree establishing the Ministry of Defense and appointed General Myrzakanov as the minister of defense. According to the **Constitution of Kyrgyzstan** the army consists of the infantry, defense airforce, border guards, and military training schools. In 1994 the **National Security Council** was established. It is the highest defense policy-making authority and it consists of key members of the government (president, prime minister, first deputy prime minister, ministers of defense, security and internal affairs, etc.).

In October 1992 the first draft for military service in the national army was held. Initially, the officer corps in the republic consisted mainly of officers of Slavic nationalities (Russians, Ukrainians, etc.). However, by the mid-1990s locally and internationally trained (mainly in **Russia**, Turkey, and some other countries) Kyrgyz officers replaced more than half of them. The morale in the army suffered from chronic underfunding and bullying. Currently, the Kyrgyzstan **government** maintains an army of 12,000 on an annual budget of US$13 million (1995).

Kyrgyzstan was among the **Commonwealth of Independent States (CIS)** countries that joined the North Atlantic Treaty Organization's Partnership for Peace (PfP) Program and actively participated in the PfP peacekeeping exercises. The republic also became a member of the **Organization for Security and Cooperation in Europe (OSCE)**.

In 1993 the republic sent its peace-keeping battalion of about 300 soldiers to Tajikistan, joining other CIS forces stationed there. Since 1997 representatives of the Kyrgyz armed forces have been taking part in **Centrasbat** joint training operations along with the United States, Turkey, and other CIS troops in **Kazakhstan**.

AR-NAMYS PARTY (Dignity Party). An organization established in **Bishkek** and first registered on 19 August 1999 under the slogan "Dignity, Order, Prosperity." It immediately became one of the most influential opposition organizations in the republic. It was founded by **Felix Kulov** in order to unite the opposition forces for the parliamentary and presidential elections of 2000. In its political program the party declared that it would fight corruption and poverty and restore order and prosperity. It promised to support a more balanced economic policy that would introduce protectionist measures to defend national industries and create job opportunities for every social group. It promised to reduce unemployment while defending the rights of the middle class. The party claims up to 11,000 supporters in various parts of the republic, although its strongholds are Bishkek and the **Chui valley**. Most members of the party come from the urban intelligentsia.

The party has been very active since its creation, but it was unable to win any seats in the **Jogorku Kenesh** (parliament) in the 2000 parliamentary elections. The party's activists claimed that this failure was due to active intervention by **government** officials and manipulation of the actual elections. The *Ar-Namys* Party suffered a severe blow in 2001 when chairman Felix Kulov was arrested on corruption charges and was sentenced to seven years of imprisonment. However, the party organized an active domestic and international campaign for Kulov's release claiming that the government had fabricated the charges.

In 2002 Ar-Namys was one of the major driving forces of the nationwide campaign against the government and President **Askar Akayev,** accusing them of mismanaging the **Aksy conflict** and of a cover up attempt to protect those responsible for civilian deaths. Although the government resigned in May 2002, President Akayev survived, promising constitutional reforms and significant concessions to the opposition.

ASABA. A leading opposition newspaper published in the **Kyrgyz language** in **Bishkek**. *Asaba* was established in 1990 and became a leading opposition tribune for radical nationalistic groups and for critics of the Soviet era modernization. The newspaper initiated vigorous debates on the Law on Languages, on the Law on Land, and on various constitutional changes in the post-Soviet era, which seriously affected political debates in the 1990s. Under the leadership of **Melis Eshimkanov**

(1990–2001) it became one of the most influential and largest Kyrgyz language **mass media** outlets. By 2000 the newspaper and its editor had become the most outspoken critics of President **Askar Akayev**'s regime. In December 2000 Melis Eshimkanov launched *Asaba-Bishkek*, a weekly supplement to *Asaba* newspaper in Russian.

In 2001 the newspaper was forced to file for bankruptcy, allegedly for being unable to repay a large financial loan, although its supporters claimed that the closure was politically motivated. In 2002 the journalists from *Asaba* attempted to launch a new newspaper under a different name.

ASABA PARTY (Asaba Partiasy in Kyrgyz). One of the oldest opposition political organizations in Kyrgyzstan. It was established in **Bishkek** and was first registered on 31 December 1991. It was one of the most active parties in the political arena throughout the 1990s. Initially it was part of a large opposition movement, the **Democratic Movement of Kyrgyzstan,** which disintegrated in 1992–93 due to internal disagreements. The Asaba Party was founded by Chapyrashty Bazarbayev, who remained its chairman. The political program of the party declared that it would defend the rights of ordinary **Kyrgyzs** and would pressure the **government** to defend the **Kyrgyz language** and culture. The Asaba was one of the most radical groups, which demanded tough measures for a quick transition of the republic's administration and education to the Kyrgyz language, then it vigorously resisted the introduction of the Russian language as the second official language of the state. The party claims up to 3,000 members and numerous supporters in various *oblasts* of the republic, and it was particularly influential among youth and rural voters. Due to its radical stands the Asaba could not recruit mass support in the country.

The party launched an active political campaign in 2000 in order to win a presence in the national parliament, but it failed. **Melis Eshimkanov,** one of the founders of the party, registered as a candidate for the presidential elections in October 2000, but received only 1.1 percent of the votes. The party leaders claimed that the failure was due to manipulation of the actual elections. The Asaba became particularly active during the 2001 and 2002 political campaigns against the government and President **Askar Akayev.**

ASANKULOV, ZHUMABEK (1927–). Kyrgyz politician and security services official. Born in Karl Marx *kolkhoz* in **Chui** *oblast*, Zhumabek Asankulov spent his entire career in the *Komitet Gosudarstvennoi Bezopastnosti* **(KGB).** He graduated from the Tashkent Regional School of the KGB in 1948. He joined the KGB ranks in Kyrgyzstan in 1948. After several years in service he completed his military-juridical studies in Moscow in 1955. From 1955 to 1961 he worked as a deputy head of the counter-intelligence department of the KGB of the **Kyrgyz Soviet Socialist Republic** (Kyrgyz SSR). From 1961 to 1966 he was head of the KGB in **Osh** *oblast.* From 1966 to 1967 he was head of the administrative affairs department of the Central Committee of the **Communist Party of Kyrgyz SSR.** From 1967 to 1978 he served as head of the KGB of the Kyrgyz SSR, becoming the longest serving head of the KGB in the republic's history. From 1978 to 1989 he served in various positions in KGB headquarters in Moscow. From 1989 to 1991 General-Lieutenant Asankulov was the chairman of the KGB in the Kyrgyz SSR. He played a controversial role during the military putsch in Moscow in August 1991 and was dismissed by President **Askar Akayev** in the same year.

Asankulov returned to service after Kyrgyzstan's independence, although he did not play an active role in the political process in the republic in the 1990s. He was appointed a deputy head of the General Staff of the Kyrgyz Ministry of Defense. He was one of the key experts who advised the Kyrgyz **government** on building the security and defense forces in post-Soviet Kyrgyzstan.

ASH (pronounced as a-sh ["a" as in "ask"]). 1. A refreshment or food, usually the term refers to whatever food is on the table. 2. The main dish at a dinner or lunch (i.e., *pilav,* a popular dish made of rice). *See also* ASH-KHANA.

ASHAR. 1. The term used in Kyrgyzstan to refer to a traditional mutual assistance at the community level to people in need. It may be in the form of fund-raising for poor members of society, families that have lost their breadwinner, or people affected by natural disasters, or building houses for the elderly,. 2. Free of charge mutual community assistance to those community members who decided to build a new house or extend an old one.

ASH-KHANA (also *osh-khona*). A traditional café, restaurant, or tea house, which serves national dishes such as *pilav*, *besh-barmak*, and others.

ASSEMBLY OF PEOPLES OF KYRGYZSTAN (APK) (also Asambleya narodov Kyrgyzstana). An organization initiated by the **government** of Kyrgyzstan in order to contain the interethnic tensions in the republic in the 1990s. It was formed as a nonpolitical and **nongovernmental organization**. Various cultural centers and groups and influential representatives of the cultural elite, who represented most of the ethnic minorities of Kyrgyzstan, contributed to the formation of the Assembly. The APK allowed various ethnic groups to voice their concerns such as the implementation of the Law on Languages and the needs of the various cultural centers. The government promoted the status of the Assembly in the mid-1990s making it the highest non-legislative consultation body. The APK played a significant role in moderating several clauses of the Law on Languages and in elevating the status of the Russian language to the second official language in the republic. In 1996 the APK established the "Informative and Research Center of the Kyrgyzstan People's Assembly," which began to monitor the development of interethnic relations in the republic.

The Assembly also contributed to stabilizing interethnic and political tensions throughout the 1990s and to promoting the national programs "Kyrgyzstan is our common home" and "Kyrgyzstan is a country of human rights." In 2002 President **Askar Akayev** signed the presidential decree "On enhancing of the role and status of the Assembly of Peoples of Kyrgyzstan" granting the APK the status of the "consultative and advisory organ under the President of the Kyrgyz Republic." President Akayev and his supporters actively used the APK to defuse interethnic anxieties and contain political tensions in the republic, especially the wave incurred by the opposition campaign for early resignation of the president in 2002.

ATA MEKEN PARTY (Ata Meken partiasy in Kyrgyz). One of the oldest and most influential opposition political organizations in Kyrgyzstan. It was established in **Bishkek** in 1992 but was required to re-register on 4 April 1998 and again on 28 December 1999. The party declared itself to be a socialist party that unites people regardless of their nationality, income, or social origin. It took a centrist position declaring that the policy of the state should be carefully balanced in order to defend the interests of ordinary people, to introduce the rule of law, and to provide check and balance mechanisms for the **government** and president. The Ata Meken was one of the most successful opposition groups, which regularly won parliamentary seats in the **Jogorku Kenesh** (parliament). Its representatives actively participated in drafting new legislation and various laws. The party claims up to 2,000 members and numerous supporters in all *oblasts* of the republic, although it is much stronger in southern Kyrgyzstan where its founders come from. Its chairman, **Omurbek Tekebayev,** was regarded as one of the most influential leaders among the opposition and he had serious presidential ambitions. He was one of the most vigorous advocates of increasing the role of political parties in the parliament and allocating parliamentary seats according to the party list. In 2000 Tekebayev registered as a presidential candidate and brokered an alliance with **Felix Kulov** to challenge President **Askar Akayev**. The Tekebayev-Kulov team came in second in the presidential race winning 13.9 percent of the votes. They claimed that the poor results were due to active government intervention.

The Ata Meken was particularly active during the 2001 and 2002 political campaign against the government and the president, criticizing the incumbent president for mismanaging the **Aksy conflict**. The party remains one of the most influential forces in the opposition, which may play a key role in the post-Akayev political process.

AZHIBEKOVA, KLARA (1946–). Kyrgyz politician. Born in **Naryn city** (eastern province of the republic), Klara Azhybekova graduated from the Kyrgyz Medical College in 1964, Kyrgyz Medical Institute in 1970, and defended the *kandidat nauk* degree in 1973. From 1983 to 1991 she held various party positions in the republic's House for Political Education and the Institute of Political and Social Management under the Central Committee of the **Communist Party of Kyrgyz SSR**. In 1990 she defended her doctoral dissertation at the Academy of Social Sciences under the Central Committee of the Communist Party of the USSR (Moscow).

From 1991 to 1999 Azhybekova taught in the Bishkek University of Humanities, the **Kyrgyz-Russian Slavonic University,** and some others. However, it was her active work in reviving the Communist Party after independence that won her a prominent place in Kyrgyzstan's political process. She was elected as first secretary of the **Communist Party of Kyrgyzstan** (officially registered in 1999), which challenged the political credibility of the **Party of Communists of Kyrgyzstan** led by **Absamat Masaliyev**.

Azhybekova is best known as an unreformed communist who supports the idea of the revival of the Union of Soviet Socialist Republics (USSR), restoration of the socialist political system, all social guarantees and state control over the economy and foreign trade, and calls for the return of "power to the people." She has authored more than 20 publications.

– B –

BABUR, ZAHERIDDIN MUHAMMAD (1483–1530). One of the greatest descendents of Tamerlane (Timur) and founder of the Mogul dynasty in the Indian subcontinent. In the early 16th century he was a *bek* of a small principality in the **Ferghana valley**. He ordered the building of several mosques and palaces, remains of which can be found in **Osh city** and in some other places. However, he lost his position in the bitter struggle with the neighboring feudal lords and fled the country, never to return. He moved to **Afghanistan** and then in 1526–27 to the Indian subcontinent where he gradually established a powerful state known as the Mogul Empire. His autobiography— *Babur-name*— is widely acclaimed in Central Asia for its depiction of life in the region in the medieval era.

BADAKHSHAN (also Gorno-Bodokhson or Gorno-Badakhshan Autonomous *oblast*). The autonomous *oblast* in **Tajikistan**, which borders **Batken *oblast***. It was formed in 1925 after the Soviet authorities finally managed to clear this region from **Basmachi** troops. Its total area is 63,700 square kilometers and most of its territory is elevated more than 3,000 meters above sea level and unusable for **agriculture**. Its total population stood at about 146,000, mainly Tajiks, **Kyrgyzs**, and Russians. Small groups of ethnic Kyrgyzs have been living in this area since the 18th century. Traditionally the populations of

Badakhshan and southern Kyrgyzstan maintained strong economic and social links. The **Osh**-Khorog (Khorugh) highway is the only route that allows transport of goods into Badakhshan on a large scale. It is a strategically and economically important route for trade and communication between the two countries. Since 1991 Badakhshan has lost its large subsidies and experienced a major economic recession. Its population turned to subsistence agriculture and illicit **drug** trafficking. In the 1990s the region became a major transit destination of the illicit drugs brought from **Afghanistan** through the Osh-Khorog highway to Kyrgyzstan and further to **Russia** and Europe.

BAI. 1. Rich person; sometimes used together with a person's name to show respect (e.g., *Alik-bai*). 2. The term refers to rich and influential political leaders among Kyrgyz **tribes** in the pre-Soviet society. 3. In the Tsarist colonial administration it referred to native heads of local administration or to landlords.

BAIKE (also *aka, ake*). 1. A polite form of reference used by a younger person to an older male person to show respect. It is also used together with a person's name (e.g., *Askar-baike*). 2. A polite reference to a male stranger.

BAKIR-UULU, TURSUNBAI (1958–) (also Bakirov). Kyrgyz politician. Born in the town of Kara Suu in **Osh** *oblast*, Bakir-Uulu graduated from the history department of **Kyrgyz State (National) University** in 1984 and completed the *aspirantura* at the Kiev State University in 1990. From 1984 to 1987 he taught at the Osh Pedagogical Institute. From 1991 to 1992 he was the deputy dean of the Osh Pedagogical Institute. In 1992 he became one of the leaders of the **Erkin Kyrgyzstan Progressive-Democratic Party**. In 1995 he was elected to the **Jogorku Kenesh** (parliament). From 1998 to 2000 he was the chairman of the Presidential Commission on Human Rights. He contested incumbent president **Askar Akayev** in the 2000 presidential elections but received only 1 percent of the vote in the elections that he claimed were highly rigged and full of irregularities. In late 2002 he became the first ombudsman in the republic.

Bakir-Uulu is best known for his controversial role in negotiating the release of the Japanese and other hostages during the summer

1999 **militant incursions** in **Batken** *oblast* of Kyrgyzstan. He personally met representatives of the guerrillas and allegedly negotiated the release of the Japanese hostages in exchange for US$4 million. He remained among the few politicians in Kyrgyzstan who continuously underlined the importance of the Islamic heritage and opposed the presence of the **U.S. military airbase** in the republic. He also played a significant role in stabilizing the political tensions in the 2002 political crisis ensuing from the **Aksy conflict**. In 2003 he was named one of the 20 most influential politicians in the republic.

BAKIYEV, KURMANBEK (1949–). Kyrgyz politician. Born in Masadan village in **Osh** *oblast* (southern Kyrgyzstan), Kurmanbek Bakiyev graduated from the Kuibyshev Polytechnic Institute **(Russia)** in 1972. He started his career as an engineer at the Kuibyshev plant in 1972. From 1972 to 1979 he worked as an electronics engineer at an electronics plant in Kuibyshev (Russia). He held various managerial positions at a factory in **Jalal Abad** *oblast* from 1979 to 1985 and from 1985 to 1991 he was a director of a factory in Kok Jangak town (Osh *oblast*). From 1991 to 1994 he held various party and administrative positions at district and *oblast* levels in Jalal Abad *oblast*. From 1994 to 1995 he served as deputy chairman of the State Property Fund in **Bishkek** and was the *akim* (head) of the Jalal Abad *oblast* administration 1995–97. From 1997 to 1999 he was the head of the **Chui** *oblast* administration. In 1999 Bakiyev was appointed prime minister.

Bakiyev played an important role in the republic's domestic politics in the late 1990s and early 2000s. He was considered to be a potential challenger to incumbent President **Askar Akayev**. In 2001–02 the opposition accused him of signing a secret memorandum with **Uzbekistan** to transfer Kyrgyz territory in southern Kyrgyzstan to Uzbekistan's jurisdiction in order to solve territorial disputes. Bakiyev resigned from the post of prime minister in 2002 under accusations of mishandling the **Aksy conflict**. He was elected to the **Jogorku Kenesh** (parliament) in autumn 2002. In 2003 he was named one of the 20 most influential politicians in the republic.

BALASAGUN (also Kuz-Ordu). One of the largest and most important centers of the Karahanid Khanate (9th–12th centuries) and a principal entrepot on the **Great Silk Road** during the medieval era. Its economy and wealth were built on the skills of craftsmen and merchants who traded from **China** to India and Europe. The rich architecture and culture of this city, which included Buddhist and Islamic monuments, were described by Arab traveler Al-Mukandisi (10th century A.D.) and by Turkic geographer Makhmud Kashgari (12th century A.D.). The power and might of the Karahanid state declined gradually. In the 13th century the Mongols led by Genghis Khan captured and destroyed Balasagun. The city never recovered and gradually ceased to exist probably in the 15th–16th centuries. It left behind vast ruins of buildings and palaces and a huge 11th-century minaret called the **Burana**.

At its zenith Balasagun was the home probably for more than 300,000 inhabitants. It was the birthplace of one of the most prominent early Turkic poets—**Jusuf Balasaguni.** His writing significantly influenced medieval Turkic literature and poetry.

BALASAGUNI, JUSUF (1021–not known). Prominent medieval Turkic writer and scholar in Central Asia. He was born in **Balasagun** city (some sources indicate that he was born in 1016) and received a basic education in his native city. From a young age he showed his talents and was sent to receive further education in the best schools of that era—in Farab, Kashgar, and **Bukhara**. In addition to the Turkic language he mastered Arabic and Persian. After graduation he proved himself in philosophy, poetry, politics, and sciences. However, it was his work *Kudagdu Bilim* (Knowledge which Gives Happiness), which he completed at the age of 54, that won him wide recognition. This was a philosophical and political encyclopedic work written in the Turkic language that presented the ideals of justice, knowledge, and human life. The most important innovation of the book was that it was written in Turkic not in Arabic or in Persian, which were the lingua franca of that era. According to the tradition of the time, he dedicated his work to a local ruler and immediately received a ministerial position in the **khan**'s palace. This book was regarded as one of the best works of the time and it represented the greatest achievement of Central Asian medieval philosophy.

Balasaguni's writing significantly influenced medieval Turkic literature and poetry. Western scholars first discovered the *Kudagdu Bilim* in 1796 when Austrian orientalist von-Khamer-Purshal acquired it in Istanbul and presented it to the Vienna Royal library. It was fully analyzed and published by Russian orientalist Vasilei Radlov between 1891 and 1900. In 1983 the Russian Academy of Sciences published the first full version in Russian. The Kyrgyz translation of the *Kudagdu Bilim* was published in Kyrgyzstan in the post-Soviet era and prompted wide public interest and debates.

BALYKCHI (literally "fishing place" in Kyrgyz; Rybachiye between 1954 and 1989 and Ysyk Kol City between 1989 and 1992). A city on the crossroads from the **Chui valley** to the **Ysyk Kol valley** located in northeast Kyrgyzstan, on the western shore of the **Ysyk Kol Lake**, about 180 kilometers southwest of **Bishkek**. Rybachiye was granted the status of city in 1954. Its population stood at about 41,700 (1999 census), up from about 33,400 (1979 census), consisting mainly of **Kyrgyzs** (80 percent), but also including Russians, Kazakhs, Uigurs, and some others. This is the seventh largest city in the republic. Balykchi is an entrepot in northeast Kyrgyzstan. It is the home of agricultural-processing plants, the Balykchi Industrial Institute (founded in 1979), a port, 10 secondary schools, libraries, two hospitals, a post office, railway station, and the like.

Balykchi was established in the late 19th century as a post-service center on the site of a small village. During the Soviet era it grew, becoming the most important industrial center and **transportation** hub of **Ysyk Kol** *oblast*. Its importance was enhanced by its strategic location on the only **railway** and **motor road** from Bishkek and Chui valley to major resorts on Ysyk Kol Lake and to **Naryn** *oblast*. The Soviet authorities invested in development of the agricultural products processing industries, dock, publishing house, and other facilities throughout the 1950s and 1980s, making Balykchi the *oblast* center of newly established Ysyk Kol *oblast* in 1939. Its importance was further increased as the Soviet torpedo testing complex relied on Balykchi port. Since 1991 Balykchi has been an important destination for tourists traveling on the **Great Silk Road** and from **Kazakhstan** and Kyrgyzstan to major lake and mountain resorts in Ysyk Kol valley. However, most of its industrial enterprises experienced a steep recession.

BANKS. Kyrgyzstan began liberalizing its banking sector in 1992, when the law on commercial banks was introduced. The law allowed the operation of independent commercial banks and by the end of 1992 the first commercial banks were set up. Later several state banks were privatized and commercialized. Most of the banks opened corresponding accounts with foreign banks and by the end of the 1990s they operated with most of the Western currencies, traveler's checks, and internationally recognized credit cards, such as Visa and Master Card.

The banking sector, however, proved to be weak as the republic experienced a steep economic recession and decline of living standards. Additionally there was a "dollarization" of the economy as Kyrgyzstan experienced hyperinflation from 1992 to 1994. People's confidence in the national banking system dried up after the collapse of the largest state-owned bank—*Sberbank*—in 1994. Between 1999 and 2001 about one-quarter of all commercial banks went bankrupt or were suspended, including the Kurulush-Bank—one of the country's largest, Maksat-Bank, KRAMS-Bank, and others. As a result the **government** reinforced regulation of the banking sector. By the end of 2002 there were 18 commercial banks. The largest bank, the Kyrgyz Investment Credit Bank (KICB), was established in 2001 (total capitalization around US$10 million) by the Aga Khan Development Fund, the European Bank of Reconstruction and Development (EBRD), and others. The Kairat Bank was the second largest bank, with a total capitalization of $2.7 million. In 2001 there were three foreign banks registered in Kyrgyzstan: Demir Bank, Bank of Asia, and Bank of Pakistan.

BARYMTA. The theft of domestic animals often as revenge against competing tribes or extended families. Traditionally, it was a one-night raid against herds that belonged to other tribes conducted by a group of young *jigits* for political or economic purposes or in search of personal glory. However, there was severe punishment arranged according to customary law—*adat*—if the people engaged in *Barymta* were caught.

BASHKARMA. 1. Head of a lower administration in Kyrgyzstan. 2. A traditional title for the head of a *kolkhoz* or *sovkhoz*.

BASMACHI MOVEMENT (singular Basmach—bandit, robber). The Basmachi movement was a popular movement of Central Asians against the establishment of Soviet rule. It appeared first in late 1917 to early 1918 in response to the Bolshevik Revolution, although some groups had acted against the **Russian Empire** administration since 1915–1916. The movement ended between 1929 and 1932. The *Basmachi* were particularly active in the **Ferghana valley** between 1918 and 1919. Their ideological support came largely from such native political movements as the Shura-i-Islam and Shura-i-Ulema. They also received substantial backing from the anti-Bolshevik Russian forces (Russian White Guards) and allegedly from the British military intelligence led by Lieutenant-Colonel Frederick Beiley. At its peak the Basmachi movement on Kyrgyzstan territory represented a powerful military force of between 10,000 and 30,000 people.

The first Basmachi groups led by Irgash-bai appeared around **Osh city** and gradually established control over most of the districts in the area. The other group led by **Madaminbek** appeared in the middle of 1918 and established control over the eastern parts of the Ferghana valley. In August 1919 the Basmachi groups united with the Russian White Guards and seized **Jalal Abad**, Osh, and some other cities and towns. However, in early 1920 the Red Army forces led by **Mikhail Frunze** defeated the Basmachi troops and established control over the major cities and towns of the Ferghana valley. The movement never recovered from this defeat, although occasionally it attempted to launch major offensive attacks in other parts of Central Asia like the Turkish General Enver Pasha–led assault from **Afghanistan** to **Bukhara** (territory of present-day **Tajikistan** and **Uzbekistan**) in summer 1922. In this campaign the Basmachi were defeated again and retreated to Afghanistan and **China**.

After this major setback the movement lost most of its spiritual leadership and gradually degenerated into small unconnected groups of fighters. They continued regular assaults against the Soviet administration and major communication lines, killing supporters of the Soviet regime and destroying crops. Between 1924 and 1926 the Soviet authorities sealed the borders with Afghanistan. At the same time redistribution of land and improvement of living standards combined with repression against Basmachi sympathizers undermined the movement's support base in the region. During the **collectivization** campaign (1929–32) and during World War II (1939–45) the Basmachi attempted to revive their attacks in Soviet Central Asia, but they were defeated again.

In the post-Soviet era there were attempts to revise the history of the Civil War in Kyrgyzstan and the role of the Basmachi movement there. However, this issue proved to be politically sensitive and the idea of revision has not fully materialized.

BATKEN. Batken was granted the status of city in 2000. A city on the crossroads from Isfara to **Osh** located in southwest Kyrgyzstan, about 480 kilometers southwest of **Bishkek.** Its population stood at about 12,000 (1999 census), up from about 9,000 (1979 census), consisting mainly of **Kyrgyz** (95 percent), but also including Uzbeks, Tajiks, Russians, and some others. It is an important military outpost in southwest Kyrgyzstan. There are agricultural-processing plants, Batken State University (founded in 2000), technical colleges, secondary schools, a library, a post office, headquarters of security and border guard units, and so on.

A small village has existed on the site of Batken since the early 20th century. During the Soviet era it grew, becoming an administrative center of the Batken district. Its importance was enhanced due to its strategic location close to Kyrgyzstan's border with **Tajikistan** and **Uzbekistan.** After **militant incursions** from Tajikistan to Kyrgyzstan territory in 1999 and 2000, the Kyrgyzstan government decided to establish **Batken** *oblast* with its center in Batken. It invested US$3.3 million in 2000, or almost a half of its military budget, in building border checkpoints and garrisons for border guards and security forces. Some 1,300 border guards were stationed in Batken and in Batken *oblast* in 2000, with the largest concentration of troops in southern Kyrgyzstan. Batken received large inflows of **government** subsidies and international assistance between 1999 and 2002 for rebuilding its infrastructure, especially its **transportation**, communications, and Kyrgyz **army** installations, and for developing job opportunities and social services in order to avert the growth of influence from militant Islamic groups.

BATKEN OBLAST. The youngest and the fifth most populous *oblast* in Kyrgyzstan, located in the southwestern part of the republic, bordered by **Osh** *oblast* in the east, **Tajikistan** in the south, and **Uzbekistan** in the north. Batken *oblast* was formed in 1999 and consists of Batken, Kadamjay, and Leylek *raions* (districts) and the cities of **Batken**, Kyzyl Kia, and Sulyukta. The *oblast* has a total area of about 17,000 square kilometers, or just over 8 percent of Kyrgyzstan's territory, and it is the second smallest *oblast* in the republic. Its population stood at about 382,500 (1999 census), up from about 237,500 (1979 census), or 8 percent of the country's population. Batken is a relatively homogeneous *oblast* in terms of ethnic composition, as the **Kyrgyzs** comprise nearly 74.3 percent of the population; others include Uzbeks (14.4 percent), Tajiks (6.9 percent), Russians (2.2 percent), Tatars (1.0 percent), and Turks (0.3 percent). The majority of the people (55 percent) live in rural areas. During the 1990s a significant number of people left the *oblast* permanently or temporarily in search of jobs. In 2001 the birth rate stood at about 34 births per 1,000, one of the highest birth rates in the republic. A sizable part of the *oblast* is located at 3,000 meters above sea level and is extremely inhospitable for human living.

Agriculture and mining are the two main sectors of Batken's economy. During the Soviet era the *oblast* specialized in coal mining in Kyzyl Kia (the oldest coal fields in the republic), with antimony in Kadamzhai (one of the largest fields in Central Asia) and mercury in Aidarken. The agricultural sector is well diversified and includes animal husbandry, tobacco, grain, and fruit production, although there was a notable decline in this sector in the 1990s.

The *oblast* was under siege in 1999 and 2000, as militants from the **Islamic Movement of Uzbekistan** (IMU) captured the small village of Zardaly in an attempt to move further toward Uzbekistan. In 1999 they took hostages, including Japanese geologists, local civilians, police officers, and even the commander of the Kyrgyz Interior Ministry Forces. The Kyrgyz defense and **National Security Committee** forces unsuccessfully battled the guerrillas for weeks. The Japanese geologists were allegedly released for a US$4 million ransom. Due to security concerns and Batken's vulnerability to political instability in Tajikistan, Kyrgyzstan's government decided to establish the Batken *oblast* in October 1999, investing considerably with the assistance of the United States and **Russia** in the building of viable border guards and defense forces in this *oblast*.

BATYR. 1. Strong man, hero. 2. The term refers to a professional warrior or commander in traditional Kyrgyz society, equivalent to the knights in Europe. To become *batyr* a person should possess exceptional military skills and capabilities or be born into a family of *batyr,* though in the latter case the status of *batyr* was not given automatically. 3. Professional warriors in the service of tribal leaders or *manaps*.

BEGALIYEV, SOPUBEK (1931–). Kyrgyz politician. Born in Chon Tash village in **Chui** *oblast* (northern Kyrgyzstan), Begaliyev graduated from the Moscow State Economic Institute (**Russia**) in 1954. From 1954 to 1961 he worked in various positions in the Gosplan (state planning agency) in Frunze (now **Bishkek**) and he worked as deputy head of a department of the Central Committee of the **Communist Party of Kyrgyz SSR** 1961–62. From 1962 to 1963 Begaliyev was minister of local industries, from 1963 to 1964 he was minister of communal services, and from 1964 to 1968 he was first deputy chairman of the Gosplan. From 1968 to 1991 he was deputy chairman of the Council of Ministers of Kyrgyzstan and he served as the economic adviser to President **Askar Akayev** 1991–94. In 1994 he was appointed chairman of the **Assembly of Peoples of Kyrgyzstan**.

Begaliyev contributed significantly to economic development and economic planning in the 1970s and 1980s. He remained one of the most influential moderate politicians throughout the 1990s and was called the "Kyrgyz High Commissioner for Ethnic Affairs," contributing to the establishment of a moderate nationality policy in the republic.

BEI-BECHARA PARTY (El [Bei Becharalar] Partiasy in Kyrgyz). This is one of the largest opposition political organizations in Kyrgyzstan. It was registered on 27 December 1995. The political program of the party declared that it would defend small entrepreneurs and revise the economic and social policy of the **government** to provide real social and economic protection and employment opportunities. It also declared that it would take decisive measures to fight criminal activities, the black market, and corruption. The party claims that it has up to 32,000 members and up to 200,000 active supporters in all parts of the republic. Its chairman, **Daniyar Usenov,** has been considered one of the leading opposition figures and one of the most experienced opposition parliamentarians. His political skills combined with his business success made him the most serious candidate to challenge incumbent president **Askar Akayev** in the 2000 presidential elections. However, in 1999 and 2000 the government refused to register Usenov for the parliamentary elections due to registration irregularities. This was a real blow to the party, and in the end the Bei-Bechara won only two seats in the **Jogorku Kenesh** (parliament) in the 2000 elections.

The Bei-Bechara was active in the political arena throughout the 1990s. In 2002 it also played an important part in organizing public rallies against the government and the president, demanding prosecution of those responsible for the **Aksy conflict**. The party remains one of the most influential forces in the opposition, which has the potential to become a key player in the post-Akayev political process.

BEISHENALIYEVA, BIBISARA (1926–). One of the most prominent Kyrgyz ballet dancers. Born in remote Tash Tube village, Bibisara Beishenaliyeva graduated from the Leningrad Choreography Institute in 1941. From 1941 to 1949 she was the leading solo ballet dancer at the **Kyrgyz State Theatre of Opera and Ballet**. In 1949, in addition to her ballet career she began to teach at the Music and Choreography Institute in Frunze (now **Bishkek**). She conducted at most prestigious theaters in Moscow, Leningrad (now Saint Petersburg), and other cities. In 1958 she was awarded the title of People's Artist of the USSR.

Beishenaliyeva was considered to be the first and one of the most prominent Kyrgyz ballet dancers who put the Kyrgyz school of ballet in the All-Union and international spotlight. Her performances became classics of Kyrgyz ballet and the Soviet authorities often presented her as the symbol of breaking the backward feudal past of Kyrgyzstan. She has authored several articles and works on ballet techniques.

BEK (also Beg). 1. The title used to refer to the tribal leader in Turkic society. 2. The title used in the medieval era to refer to the tribal and local administration leader in the **khan**'s (king) service. 3. In Kyrgyzstan the title is sometimes used with the name of a male person to highlight his honorary position in society (*Kadyr-bek*), equivalent to master or sir.

BEKNAZAROV, AZIMBEK (1956–). Kyrgyz politician. Born in **Jalal Abad** *oblast* Azimbek Beknazarov graduated from the Law College in Tashkent (**Uzbekistan**) and Faculty of Law of the **Kyrgyz State (National) University**. From 1984 to 1991 he worked at district court in Jany Jol *raion* (now Aksy *raion*). From 1991 to 1996 he was an investigator and senior investigator in the Jalal Abad prosecutor's office and from 1997 to 1999 he was a judge of the Oktiabrskii district court in Bishkek. In 2000 he was elected to the **Jo-**

gorku Kenesh (parliament), becoming one of the most vocal critics of the government, especially on the issue of legality of the border delimitation with China and Uzbekistan. His arrest on dubious charges in January 2002 provoked mass rallies in his support and led to a series of confrontations between government and opposition. In March 2002 a confrontation between demonstrators and *militsia* led to the Aksy conflict, when several demonstrators were killed. This situation seriously destabilized the political situation in Kyrgyzstan and led to the resignation of the cabinet and constitutional changes.

Beknazarov is best known for his active role in the opposition and for his vocal criticism of the government. He is considered one of the leading opposition figures in Kyrgyzstan. In 2003 he was named one of the 20 most influential politicians in the republic.

BISHKEK (Pishpek until 1926, Frunze between 1926 and 1991). This is the largest city in the republic and its most important industrial center. The city is located in the Chui valley in northern Kyrgyzstan, 30 kilometers south of the border with Kazakhstan. Its size is about 184 square kilometers, most of it located 750–900 meters above sea level. Its population stood at about 762,300 (1999 census), up from about 535,500 (1979 census), although city officials estimated that the figure is above 1 million people if all temporary workers and migrants from other parts of the republic are included. In 2001 the population consisted mainly of Kyrgyzs (52 percent) and Russians (31 percent), but it also included significant communities of Ukrainians (11 percent), Tatars (2.2 percent), Uygurs (1.7 percent), Kazakhs (1.6 percent), and some others. It is an important industrial and transportation center in northern Kyrgyzstan with light industries, machinery factories, consumer goods, and military production. It also hosts 28 tertiary educational institutions, including the Kyrgyz State (National) University (founded in 1932), Kyrgyz Technical University (founded in 1954), and Kyrgyz Agrarian University (founded in 1933). There are 22 libraries, 11 museums, and seven theaters. The republic's largest airport and railway terminal are also located here.

Bishkek is one of the youngest cities in Central Asia. It began as a small village and fortress on the Chui River. The Kokand Khanate established its fortress there in 1825, after conquering the Chui valley. The Russian Empire collided with the Kokand Khanate in the middle of the 19th century in the process of Russian colonization of Central Asia. In 1862 they took over the fortress and destroyed it. In 1864, however, they established their own garrison and a settlement, which became an important entrepot on the strategically important Semipalatinsk (now Semei in Kazakhstan)–Tashkent road. During the Tsarist era Pishpek became part of Semirechye *oblast* and grew rapidly, hosting new industries and businesses. After the Bolshevik Revolution of 1917 the city became the Bolsheviks' stronghold in this part of Central Asia. After the national delimitation of 1924 Pishpek became the capital of the newly established **Kara-Kyrgyz Autonomous *Oblast*** (part of the **Russian Federation**), which in 1926 was upgraded to the **Kyrgyz Autonomous Soviet Socialist Republic** and to the **Kyrgyz Soviet Socialist Republic** in 1939. In 1926 Pishpek was renamed Frunze after General **Michail Frunze**. The Soviet authorities invested significantly in the development of heavy and light industries during the 1930s. They relocated a large portion of Russian workers together with several large industrial plants during World War II, making Frunze a leading powerhouse of the republic. With independence the city was renamed Bishkek. In 2000 Bishkek produced 26 percent of the republic's machinery, 29 percent of its foodstuff, and 23.5 percent of its light industrial products and consumer goods.

During the Soviet era the city was predominantly Russian populated (up to 66 percent). Behind the façade of economic and political success there were growing tensions between major ethnic groups — Kyrgyzs and Russians — in the city in the late 1980s and early 1990s. These tensions culminated in 1990 and 1991, although Kyrgyzstan managed to resolve political and interethnic tensions without militant confrontation. In the post-Soviet era a significant proportion of the Slavic population, Germans and Jews (between 300,000 and 400,000) left the city, as social and interethnic tensions continued to affect everyday life, and the economy experienced a severe recession and industries downsized their activities.

The city was greatly expanded during the 1930s and between the 1950s and 1970s. Its **architecture** reflected a combination of Stalinist classicism and Soviet functionalism. In the 1930s many government and cultural buildings were built in the semi-classic monumental style. In the 1960s the city was significantly enlarged and several districts of four and five-story apartment buildings were built of red bricks or concrete in the faceless Khrushchev style. Yet it retained and expanded its park areas, becoming one of the greenest cities in Central Asia in terms of the number of trees per inhabitant. In the 1980s the city center was rebuilt in a bright composition of marble, glass, and concrete. During the post-Soviet era the city infrastructure experienced visible decay, although the city still remained green and in relatively better shape than many other cities in the republic. In the 1990s Bishkek grew considerably through private housing construction in its suburban areas. In order to revive its economy and attract Foreign Direct Investments, the Kyrgyzstan government established a **Free Economic Zone** Bishkek in 1995.

BOBULOV, KAMBARALY (1936–). Kyrgyz publicist and politician. Born in Osor village in **Osh** *oblast* (southern Kyrgyzstan), Kambaraly Bobulov graduated from the philology department of the **Kyrgyz State (National) University** in 1958. From 1958 to 1962 he worked at the *Ala-Too* literary journal in Frunze (now **Bishkek**). From 1963 to 1965 he was a correspondent of the Moscow-based *Pravda* newspaper. From 1965 to 1966 Bobulov conducted his postgraduate studies in the Academy of Social Sciences under the Central Committee of the Communist Party of the USSR in Moscow and in 1966 he defended his *kandidat nauk* degree. From 1966 to 1976 he was the editor of the *Kyrgyzstan Pionery* youth newspaper and he was head of department at the Institute of Kyrgyz Language and Literature of the Kyrgyz **National Academy of Sciences** from 1982 to 1992. In 1992 he became chairman of the Kyrgyz Til Society. In 1990 he was elected to the **Jogorku Kenesh** (parliament). In post-Soviet Kyrgyzstan Bobulov fiercely promoted the greater use of the **Kyrgyz language** in public and cultural life and in **education** and led a public campaign against the introduction of Russian as the second state language in the late 1990s.

Bobulov has published numerous articles, nonfiction stories, and novels and published his opinion articles, and his essays have appeared regularly in various newspapers (mainly in the Kyrgyz language).

BOKONBAYEV, KULUBEK (1940–). Kyrgyz politician. Born in Frunze city (now **Bishkek**), Kulubek Bokonbayev is the son of Joomart Bokonbayev, one of the leading Kyrgyz poets. He graduated from the Moscow Geological Institute (**Russia**) in 1963 and completed his postgraduate studies in 1968. From 1968 to 1992 he held various research and managerial positions at the Kyrgyz **National Academy of Sciences**. From 1995 to 1996 he was an executive chairman of the Kyrgyz State Agency for the Protection of the Environment. From 1996 to 1998 was minister of the environment.

Bokonbayev was in the center of the nationwide scandal relating to the contamination of the Barskoon River and **Ysyk Kol Lake**. The contamination was caused by the crash of a truck belonging to the Kyrgyz-Canadian gold joint venture Kumtor Operating Co., which spilled about 1,800 kilograms of highly poisonous sodium cyanide into the river. Bokonbayev was accused of taking a soft approach to the company that polluted a highly fragile natural environment, charges he denied. In 1999 he published his version of the events in a book, *Barskoon: Myths and Reality*.

BOLDZHUROVA, ISHENKUL (1955–). Kyrgyz politician. She was born in Tasma village in **Ysyk Kol** *oblast*. Ishemkul Boldzhurova graduated from the history department of the **Kyrgyz State (National) University** in 1973 and from the *aspirantura* of the Moscow State University in 1976. From 1977 to 1978 she taught at the Kyrgyz State (National) University. From 1978 to 1982 she worked at the **National Academy of Sciences** and was a senior research fellow at the Institute of History of the Communist Party under the Central Committee of the **Communist Party of Kyrgyz SSR** 1982–91. From 1991 to 1992 she taught at the Kyrgyz State Women Pedagogical Institute (Bishkek) and from 1992 to 1994 she was deputy-rector (vice-chancellor) of the same institute. From 1994 to 2002 she was rector of the Kyrgyz State Women's Pedagogical Institute. In June 2002 she was appointed minister of education. Boldzhurova has authored several articles and brochures on Kyrgyz history and **education**.

BORDER DELIMITATION IN 1924–1926. A program of the Soviet government to divide the ethnically diverse **Turkistan Soviet Socialist Republic** (TSSR) into several national entities. These nation-state entities were created along a relatively vague ethnic line, as the Soviet leaders both in Moscow and in the region rejected the idea of creating a Central Asian federation or pan-Turkic republic. As the result of the state delimitation the **Kyrgyz Autonomous** *Oblast* (KAO) was established in 1924. A special commission consisting of high-ranking officials of the Central Soviet government, representatives of the TSSR, and local officials from Semirechiye, Syrdaria, **Ferghana,** and Samarkand *oblasts* set up the borders between the KAO, **Kazakhstan,** and **Uzbekistan**. It took, however, almost two years, from 1924 to 1926, before the territorial delimitation was completed in ethnically mixed areas. This included the **Ferghana valley**, which was divided between Kyrgyzstan, **Tajikistan,** and **Uzbekistan**, and the **Jetysuu** (Semirechie) valley, which was divided between Kyrgyzstan and **Kazakhstan**. There were no clear criteria for setting the borders between the republics and the commission used various measures, primarily focusing on ethnic and language identities. Some borders were set arbitrarily as they did not play political, passport, or custom control roles and had no international significance. This created a basis for future border disputes after 1991. *See also* BORDER DELIMITATION IN THE 1990s.

BORDER DELIMITATION IN THE 1990s. A decade-long process of clarifying borders with neighboring countries in order to settle all border disputes. The Kyrgyz Republic inherited from the Soviet past highly disputed borders with practically all its neighbors, which became a major bone of contention in political relations with them. The most important negotiations included the **China-Kyrgyzstan border delimitation** within the multilateral framework of the **Shanghai Cooperation Organization**, and the bilateral negotiations framework of the **Kazakhstan**-Kyrgyzstan border delimitation, **Tajikistan**-Kyrgyzstan border delimitation, and **Uzbekistan**-Kyrgyzstan border delimitation. By the middle of 2002 **Bishkek** had completed negotiations and signed agreements with practically all its neighbors. However, the Kyrgyz-Tajik clashes on the border between Kyrgyzstan and Tajikistan in late 2002 indicated that the problem was far from over. *See also* BORDER DELIMITATION IN 1924–1926.

BORDER GUARDS (also *pogranvoiska*). Kyrgyzstan established its Border Guards force in 1992, although due to financial constraints and the absence of border guarding experience it relied largely on Russian assistance. In October 1992 Kyrgyzstan and **Russia** signed an agreement that settled the issue of responsibility for guarding Kyrgyzstan's borders with **China**. According to the agreement, Russia took control and agreed to finance (up to 80 percent) 2,000 border troops on the borders with China and to provide training to the Kyrgyz personnel and officers until a further agreement would be signed.

Between 1992 and 1999 the Kyrgyz border guards jointly with the Russian border guards patrolled the border with China and carried out border controls at all check points, including the airports. The borders with **Kazakhstan, Tajikistan,** and **Uzbekistan** were lightly guarded exclusively by Kyrgyz Border Guards. Kyrgyzstan heavily relied on Russians in training its border guards. In the 1990s Russian training centers provided training for more than 60 Kyrgyz officers and 150 solders. In 2000 and 2001 the United States and some NATO countries also provided equipment and limited training for the Kyrgyz Border Guards.

In 1999, however, the Kyrgyz **government** decided to take full control of the country's borders. After several negotiations with Russia, the issue was settled and it was agreed that by December 1999 Kyrgyzstan alone would establish control over its borders. In March 1999 the president of Kyrgyzstan signed a Decree on the State Borders of the **Kyrgyz Republic.** In May 1999 the president of Kyrgyzstan issued a Decree on Border Service of the Kyrgyz Republic, which established Kyrgyzstan's Border Guards of 3,000. In October 2002 Kyrgyzstan established the Department of Border Service (Upravlenie Pogranichnoi Sluzhby), which was designed to coordinate and prepare military planning for all Border Guard forces.

BUKHARA EMIRATE (also Bukhara Khanate). A Central Asian feudal state with its center in Bukhara (present-day Uzbekistan). The emirate was established in 1557 by a **khan** from the Sheybani family, after the defeat and disintegration of the Timurid state. At its zenith the state controlled vast territories of contemporary Central Asia, Iran, and **Afghanistan,** including the **Ferghana valley.** In 1753 a khan from the Uzbek tribal dynasty Mangyt captured Bukhara, but his successors exhausted the Khanate's army in a series of wars with Afghanistan, Iran, and the neighboring Central Asian states.

The Tsarist Empire defeated Muzzafar Khan, then the ruler of the Bukhara Emirate, in a series of battles in the 1860s. In 1868 the emirate became a **Russian Empire** protectorate, maintaining autonomy in internal affairs but surrendering its foreign policy. In 1920 Sayyid Alim Khan, the last ruler of the emirate, was overthrown and escaped to Afghanistan, where he headed the **Basmachi movement.** Most of the territory of the Bukhara Emirate was divided between **Uzbekistan** and **Tajikistan** during the **border delimitation in 1924–1926.**

BURANA (from Turkic *monara*—minaret). One of the most important historical sites in the **Chui valley,** about 60 kilometers east of **Bishkek.** The Burana monument is a minaret left from probably a larger architectural complex on the territory of the ancient city of **Balasagun,** which disappeared in the medieval era. The history of building the complex still remains a mystery. It was built around the 11th century and the minaret originally was about 45 meters high (one of the highest in medieval Central Asia). The city was captured by Genghis Khan in the 13th century and was heavily damaged. It never recovered again and gradually disappeared in the 15th–16th centuries, though travelers observed ruins of its mud buildings and palaces until the 19th–20th centuries.

During the Soviet era several archeological expeditions excavated areas around Burana and their findings can be viewed in the collection of the Historical Museum in Bishkek. After 1991 the site became one of the most frequently visited places in Kyrgyzstan on the route of the **Great Silk Road** tours.

– C –

CENTER OF THE STATE LANGUAGE AND ENCYCLOPEDIA. *See* KYRGYZ ENCYCLOPEDIA.

CENTRAL ASIAN FORUM (CAF) (also known as Central Asian Union [1990–1994] and Central Asian Economic Union [1994–2000]). Representatives of **Kazakhstan,** Kyrgyzstan, **Tajikistan,** Turkmenistan, and **Uzbekistan** established the Central Asian Union (CAU) during an informal meeting in Alma-Ata on 23 June 1990. The CAU was initially aimed at the promotion of cultural, political, and economic cooperation within the region and at coordinating a common stand in negotiating their relations with the Soviet Central government during the revision of the Soviet Union Treaty. The informal negotiations finally led to the signing of the **Alma-Ata**

Declaration in December 1991, which indorsed mutual acceptance of existing borders, the renunciation of any territorial claims on each other, and guaranties of ethnic minorities' rights.

Between 1992 and 1994 the CAU was largely inactive, as Tajikistan and Turkmenistan left the organization due to changes in their domestic and foreign policy environments. It was further undermined by the unilateral introduction of the Kyrgyz currency, the **som,** in May 1993, which led to a customs war on the borders between the republics and also negatively affected regional economic cooperation. In April 1994 Kazakhstan and Uzbekistan relaunched the Union as the Central Asian Economic Union (CAEU). Kyrgyzstan joined the organization in the same year. The CAEU members created several intergovernmental institutions, such as the Central Asian Bank, Council of Prime Ministers, Council of Defense Ministers, and various others. In early 1998 Tajikistan formally applied for membership in the CAEU and was accepted as a full member. These steps allowed an increase in intraregional trade of about 15–20 percent. However, the CAEU collapsed in late 1998, as Kyrgyzstan independently negotiated its entry into the **World Trade Organization (WTO).** Consequently the region faced a new cycle of conflicts over customs duties, import tariffs, cross-border trade, complications over border delimitation, and especially border mining and entry visa regimes. In 1999 security arrangements within the CAEU were further undermined as Uzbekistan decided to leave the **Commonwealth of Independent States Collective Security Treaty** and to join the GUAM (an organization that unites Georgia, Ukraine, Azerbaijan, and Moldova). Meanwhile, Kazakhstan, Kyrgyzstan, and Tajikistan decided to extend the CIS Collective Security Treaty for a further five years.

In January 2001 the CAEU was reconstituted as the Central Asian Forum (CAF). The new institution was intended to promote greater coordination and informal talks between government institutions, businesses and various regional **nongovernmental organizations** (NGOs). According to the CAEU-CAF, between 1991 and 2001 its members signed more than 250 treaties and agreements aimed at simplifying regional trade and the movement of goods and services. The organization played a positive role in the **border delimitation in the 1990s.** However, significant differences in the members' approaches to economic and political reforms and in their foreign policy orientations undermined regional cooperation within the CAF. In 2001 negotiations over the removal of customs and border controls within the region were halted and CAF members introduced entry visas for citizens of Kyrgyzstan and Tajikistan, thus ending CAF's visa-free travel regime. In 2001–02 the leaders of the member countries agreed to continue regular meetings to discuss regional problems and to resolve differences on such issues as the environment, population movements, defense policy, and cultural exchange. *See also* COMMONWEALTH OF INDEPENDENT STATES; RUSSIAN MILITARY BASE.

CENTRAL ASIAN PEACEKEEPING BATTALION (also known as CENTRASBAT). A peacekeeping unit jointly established in 1996 by **Kazakhstan**, Kyrgyzstan, and **Uzbekistan** and joined by **Tajikistan** in 1998. The idea of developing military cooperation between the Central Asian states was initiated in 1992 with the outbreak of the civil war in Tajikistan and the establishment of the **Commonwealth of Independent States Collective Security Treaty**. However, it took some time and a number of steps to realize the project.

In 1992–93 Kazakhstan, Kyrgyzstan, and Uzbekistan sent their defense units to Tajikistan in order to stabilize the situation there, but they disagreed over their objectives and also over the nature of the military cooperation preferred, such as whether a joint military unit should be created. Not until December 1995 did the Central Asian leaders agree on the forms of their cooperation and establish a Joint Council of Defense Ministers within the framework of the Central Asian Economic Union (*see* **Central Asian Forum**). In December 1996 the council worked out an agreement on the establishment of the Centrasbat. The unit's main objective was to promote cooperation and coordination between member countries' defense forces in cases of emergency, **militant incursions,** or other needs. It was intended that the participating countries would jointly finance Centrasbat's logistical support and military exercises.

In 1997 the United States Atlantic Command decided to sponsor the first joint military exercise to include Centrasbat and American troops. In August–September 1997 Centrasbat personnel underwent training at Fort Bragg, North Carolina (USA), and on 15 September 1997, 40 Central Asian and 500 U.S. troops were parachuted into Uzbekistan. For the United States it was the largest airborne operation on the territory of the former Soviet Union, and for the Central Asian republics it was the first operation on their soil with U.S. participation. To further develop the potential of such joint exercises, it was decided to continue them on an annual basis with the North Atlantic Treaty Organization (NATO) troops participating, sponsored primarily by the United States. The exercise's main objectives were to maximize the interoperability of the participating troops in actions against militant or terrorist groups and to improve their ability to conduct peacekeeping and humanitarian operations. It was also decided that further joint exercises should be conducted within the framework of NATO's Partnership for Peace (PfP) program. In 1998 Russian and Turkish forces teamed up with Centrasbat and U.S. troops in joint military exercises in Kazakhstan and Kyrgyzstan. In May 1999 the Centrasbat annual multinational exercises were conducted for the first time in a training seminar format at the U.S. Central Command Center at Tampa. In September 2000 the Centrasbat exercises took place in Kazakhstan, focusing on peacekeeping and humanitarian assistance in the field, but Kyrgyzstan and Uzbekistan were unable to participate because of militant incursions from Tajikistan into their territories.

In 2001–02 the U.S.-led war on international terrorism and against the Taliban regime in **Afghanistan** contributed to some changes in the format and operational tasks of Centrasbat. In 2001 the Centrasbat exercises were conducted at Ramstein, Germany, as a Command Post Headquarters Exercise. In February 2003 joint Kyrgyz-American military exercises, Balance Night, were held in the mountain area Chon Kurchak near **Bishkek**.

It is expected that the Centrasbat might play an increasing role in developing the Central Asian regional security architecture, although deep-seated mistrust between the Central Asian republics and differences in foreign policies still undermine the viability of the Battalion.

CENTRASBAT. *See* CENTRAL ASIAN PEACEKEEPING BATTALION.

CHAGATAI (also Jagatai). 1. Name of a large tribe in Central Asia, which traces its origin to the Mongols. 2. Extinct language, which was considered the lingua franca among Central Asian Turkic people in the 19th century. 3. Descendents of Chagatai—second son of

Genghis Khan—who formed a house of Chagatai and established the Chagatai Khanate. The Chagatai dynasty ruled Central Asia for several centuries after the death of its founder but was destroyed by Tamerlane (Timur) in the 16th century. The Turkic tribes assimilated the Chagatais by the 18th century.

CHAPAN. Traditional Kyrgyz cotton-quilted dressing-gown or buttonless overcoat. The *chapan* usually reaches the ankles and is worn by both men and women, though the style and color of men's *chapan* differ from women's. *Chapans* are often handmade and, therefore, they vary in colors and design. It was customary among the **Kyrgyzs** to present a brightly colored *chapan* to an honorable guest, *akyn*, or relative, as well as to give it to members of the family who were planning a long trip. This tradition still exits in some parts of Kyrgyzstan.

CHINA (official name People's Republic of China). This country is located east of the **Kyrgyz Republic**, and the two states share a border of 858 kilometers. China is Kyrgyzstan's largest neighbor with a territory of 9,596,960 square kilometers and with a population estimated at about 1,273 million in 2002. Han Chinese account for 91.9 percent of the population. Between 100,000 and 160,000 **Kyrgyzs** live in Xinjang autonomous province in western China.

During the 18th and 19th centuries the Kyrgyz tribes had uneasy relations with the Chinese Empire, as they vigorously resisted Chinese attempts to colonize the Kyrgyz land, though representatives of some Kyrgyz **tribes** expressed readiness to accept a Chinese protectorate. However, those attempts failed, and the powerful **Russian Empire** acquired the Kyrgyz land by the middle of the 19th century. After the Revolution of 1917 the Bolsheviks imposed the Iron Curtain on the Soviet border, including the Kyrgyz-Chinese border. In the 1940s and the 1950s Kyrgyzstan developed active trade and cultural exchanges with China, as the Soviet Union had positive relations with the Chinese leadership during this era. However, the Chinese-Soviet dispute in the 1960s and 1970s negatively affected the relations between Kyrgyzstan and China. This was complicated by the territorial disputes over the Kyrgyz-China borders. The relations significantly improved in the middle of the 1980s. After the dissolution of the Soviet Union in 1991 Kyrgyzstan and China established direct diplomatic relations, and China was among the first countries that opened an embassy in **Bishkek**.

Chinese immigration to Kyrgyzstan, **border delimitation in the 1990s,** and activities of Uigur separatist groups on Kyrgyzstan's territory were the three key issues in the relations between these two neighbors in the 1990s.

In the early 1990s Kyrgyzstan's public expressed concern about a large-scale immigration of Chinese to Kyrgyzstan; the fears were never proved. Experts reported about a large number of Kyrgyz and Chinese unregistered retail traders—*chelnoki*—who commuted back and forth between the two countries in order to buy and resell various consumer goods. According to **Kabar** news agency in 2002 up to 20,000 Chinese citizens visited Kyrgyzstan. Some Chinese traders did settle in Kyrgyzstan, but in small numbers.

In 1996 and 1997 Beijing and Bishkek negotiated and resolved their territorial disputes within the framework of the **Shanghai Cooperation Organization**. Kyrgyzstan agreed to cede around 100,000 hectares of its land; this act led to large-scale public protests throughout Kyrgyzstan in 2001 and 2002. In 2000 and again in 2002–03 Kyrgyz-Chinese diplomatic relations became tense due to assassinations of Chinese diplomats in Bishkek, allegedly by members of Uigur separatist groups, and the killing of more than 20 citizens of China in March 2003.

In 1999 and 2000 China provided substantial logistic and political support to Kyrgyzstan when the latter experienced the **militant incursions** from **Tajikistan** into **Batken** *oblast*. In exchange, Kyrgyzstan's government blocked activities of some Uigur groups on its territory. In 2001–02 Chinese policymakers expressed their disappointment with Kyrgyzstan's decision to host the **U.S. military airbase** at Manas airport, about 300 kilometers from the Chinese border. However, in 2003 security relations improved and the two countries agreed to conduct joint military and antiterrorist exercises.

China, along with Kyrgyzstan, is a member of the Shanghai Cooperation Organization and World Trade Organization.

CHINA-KYRGYZSTAN BORDER DELIMITATION. The **Kyrgyz Republic** shares 858 kilometers of its borders with **China**. These borders were disputed since the Soviet era, although there were no attempts from the Chinese side to forcibly enforce its territorial claims. After dissolution of the Soviet Union in 1991 **Kyrgyzstan** and China established direct diplomatic relations and began border delimitation negotiations. During several meetings with **Commonwealth of Independent States** members, Kyrgyzstan agreed to negotiate this issue jointly with **Kazakhstan**, **Russia**, and **Tajikistan**. Several major negotiations were conducted in Shanghai and the five countries decided to set up a joint organization—the **Shanghai Cooperation Organization**.

Kyrgyzstan completed major negotiations by 2001 and signed an agreement with China on settling all territorial disputes. According to the agreement, **Bishkek** agreed to cede to China around 100,000 hectares of its land, or around three-quarters of the disputed territories. This included some land close to **Khan-Tengri mountain**, which is sacred to the **Kyrgyz**. However, the Kyrgyz **government** completed these negotiations in secrecy, without constitutionally required consultations with the **Jogorku Kenesh** (parliament). In response, the Kyrgyz public and opposition organizations organized a series of mass protests throughout Kyrgyzstan in 2001 and 2002, which led to the resignation of the Kyrgyz government in May 2002. After intensive debates the Kyrgyz parliament agreed to approve the agreement in 2002.

CHUI *OBLAST*. Third most populous *oblast* in Kyrgyzstan, located in the northern part of the republic, bordered by **Naryn** *oblast* in the southeast, **Osh** *oblast* in the southwest, **Talas** *oblast* in the west, **Kazakhstan** in the north, and the **Ysyk Kol** *oblast* in the east. Chui *oblast* was formed in 1992 and consisted of Alamedin, Jayyl, Kemin, Moskovskii, Panfilov, Sokuluk, and Issyk Ata *raions* (districts) and the town of **Tokmak**. Kyrgyzstan's capital, **Bishkek** (formerly Frunze), is located in the north of the *oblast* and is the capital of the *oblast* as well. The total area of Chui *oblast* is about 20,200 square kilometers and it is the third smallest *oblast* of the republic, or just over 10 percent of its territory. Its population stood at about 772,200 (1999 census—excluding Bishkek), or 15 percent of the country's population, down from about 855,200 (1979 census). Local experts, however, estimated the population of the *oblast* at about 1 million people, including temporary workers, refugees, and displaced people. Chui *oblast* is the country's most heterogeneous *oblast* in terms of ethnic composition as it has the largest proportion of non-**Kyrgyzs** in the republic, including Russians, Ukrainians, Germans, Koreans, Turks, Uzbeks, Dungans, Kazakhs, and others.

Chui *oblast*, excluding Bishkek, is the home of almost 30 percent of the industrial enterprises of the republic. **Agriculture, industry, tourism**, and mining are the main sectors of its economy. During the Soviet era Chui *oblast* specialized in manufacturing consumer goods, producing and processing agricultural products for Bishkek and for export, mining (uranium fields were situated in the eastern part of the *oblast*), tourism, and services. There was a large helicopter-training airbase close to Kant city during the Soviet era (closed in 1992). Several military plants supplied the Soviet military with various equipment and other supplies, including enriched uranium, which was produced in **Kara Balta** city.

In the early 1990s the *oblast* experienced a severe economic recession due to structural changes, abolishment of state subsidies, and loss of the former Soviet market for its goods and services. But the *oblast* was quick to reinvent itself, restructure and revive its industries largely due to its proximity to the capital city. It attracted the largest share of foreign direct investments (FDIs), coming third only after Bishkek and Ysyk Kol *oblast*. In 2001 the U.S. military established the first **U.S. military airbase** on the site of the Manas civil airport; the airport was actively used for U.S. military and humanitarian operations in **Afghanistan** in late 2001 and throughout 2002. In response to these U.S. activities, the Russian military leased a former airfield and military facilities near the Kant airport for a **Russian military base** in June 2002.

CHUI RIVER. This river is 1,030 kilometers long with a basin area of around 67,500 square kilometers. The river, which forms a natural part of the Kyrgyzstan-**Kazakhstan** border, flows from the mountains of northeast Kyrgyzstan through the narrow Bo'omskoye canyon into the **Chui valley**. It continues further to Kazakhstan and then disappears in the Moun-Kum desert. The river's highest flow is from March to July, as snow melts in the high **Tian-Shan** glaciers, and it is at its lowest flow in November and December.

The Chui River is one of the most important sources of drinking and irrigation water for northern Kyrgyzstan. During the Soviet era several reservoirs were built on Kyrgyzstan's part of the river along with hydroelectric power stations and its water was excessively used for irrigation. It became the most polluted river in the republic in the 1970s and 1980s, as heavy and light industries were developed in the major cities along its course.

CHUI VALLEY. Located in northern Kyrgyzstan, it has an area of about 32,000 square kilometers, divided between Kyrgyzstan and **Kazakhstan**. The valley is bordered by the Kyrgyz **Ala-Too Mountains** in the south and the Chui Illyi mountain range in the northeast. The mountains protect the valley from the extremes of cold continental climate. Winter temperatures range between $-14°C$ and $+7°C$ in January, and the average daily temperature is between $20°C$ and $26°C$ in July. The warm summer and availability of drinking and irrigation water makes this area one of the most fertile and most densely populated *oblasts* in Kyrgyzstan.

Kyrgyzstan's archeologists claim that they dated the ancient settlements in the valley as early as the first or second millennium B.C. The valley was located on one of the routes of the **Great Silk Road**, which contributed to the *oblast*'s economic growth and strategic importance. However, it also made the area vulnerable to frequent incursions by the nomads of the steppe. The ancient cities of **Balasagun**, Shish Debe, and some others prospered in this valley, but disappeared in the Middle Ages. Between the sixth and 12th centuries the valley was controlled by various Turkic states and in the 13th century it was conquered by the Mongols under Genghis Khan. In the 19th century the **Kokand Khanate** extended its control over the area despite fierce resistance by the local Kyrgyz tribes. By 1876 the Khanate was brushed away by the Tsarist troops and was included in the **Turkistan Governor-Generalship**.

In 1924 the Chui valley was divided between newly created Kazakhstan and Kyrgyzstan. During the Soviet era the valley became one of the most important agricultural and industrial centers in Kyrgyz-stan. During the 20th century the population nearly tripled, making the valley the second most densely populated area in the republic with a total population (including **Bishkek**) of about 1.6 million. In the 1990s environmental issues, such as industrial pollution, became a serious problem for the valley.

CLAN. 1. In public life the term is often used in **Kyrgyzstan** to refer to a group or network of groups that act together to achieve political or economic advantages. The clans are often based on the regional patronage network and on close association by work in the same *oblast* (i.e., **Osh** or **Naryn** *oblast*) but not necessarily on descent from a common ancestor. 2. It sometimes refers to a kinship group based on actual or perceived descent from a common ancestor and is often used to identify members of the extended family or group of families. In post-Soviet Kyrgyzstan clan membership increasingly implies mutual support and defense of businesses or other social, political, and economic activities. The clan factor also plays an important role in arranging marriages. 3. It also refers to the two largest political groupings in Kyrgyzstan—southerners (representatives of **Batken, Jalal Abad,** and Osh *oblasts*) and northerners (representatives of **Chui, Ysyk Kol**, Naryn, and **Talas** *oblasts*). These two groups traditionally compete for power and influence in the political arena and in the **government** of Kyrgyzstan. Membership in the clans is formed by perceptions of common regional identities, and not by ideological inclinations. *See also* AKSY CONFLICT.

COAT OF ARMS. The **Jogorku Kenesh** (parliament) officially adopted the national coat of arms of the **Kyrgyz Republic** on 14 January 1994 to replace the Soviet era symbols. The centerpiece of the coat of arms is a white eagle against the backdrop of a blue lake, snowcapped mountains, and rising golden sun. The lake, mountains, and sun behind the eagle symbolize the beauty of nature and source of life and energy. The top part of the coat of arms is encircled by a golden wheat sheaf with the word "Kyrgyz" between them. The bottom part is encircled by cotton branches with opened boxes with the word "Respublikasy" between them.

COLLECTIVIZATION. Soviet policy in the late 1920s and 1930s, which aimed to create large agricultural enterprises (*kolkhozes* and *sovkhozes*) capable of producing agricultural goods on a large scale. In Kyrgyzstan, the collectivization also aimed at bringing together small, mainly subsistence farmers and sheepherders, eliminating wealthy feudal lords and landlords (*manaps* and *bais*) and sedentarization of **pastoral nomads** as well as establishing the Soviet local administration and Soviet political system in the rural areas of the republic.

A mass collectivization campaign in Kyrgyzstan began in 1928–29, and by 1937 nearly 90 percent of the population had joined *kolkhozes* and *sovkhozes*. Initially the policy of forceful collectivization and deportation of *manaps, bais,* and wealthy individuals to Siberia met considerable resistance, but it was subdued. It is believed that between 200,000 and 300,000 individuals perished during the campaign. On the positive side, the Soviet government invested heavily in developing the rural infrastructure and in producing modern machinery and farming techniques and significantly lifted living standards among the rural population. During the Soviet era Kyrgyz collective farms were specialized in the production of meat, sheepskins, wool, cotton, silk, vegetables, and fruits.

In the early 1990s Kyrgyzstan, with assistance from the International Monetary Fund (IMF) and World Bank, conducted a program of rapid de-collectivization, breaking up most of the *kolkhozes* and distributing land to the farmers.

COMMONWEALTH OF INDEPENDENT STATES (CIS) (also known as Sodruzhestvo Nezavisimykh Gosudarstv [SNG] in Russian). The organization was established on 21 December 1991 from the remnants of the Union of Soviet Socialist Republics (USSR), as the latter was dissolved following the collapse of negotiations on the new Union Treaty. It consists of 12 members: Armenia, Azerbaijan, Belarus, Georgia, Moldova, **Kazakhstan, Kyrgyz Republic, Russia, Tajikistan,** Turkmenistan, Ukraine, and **Uzbekistan.** The heads of state and government are required to meet at least every six months to discuss economic, political, security, and other issues. However, the decisions of the Council of Heads of State and the Council of Heads of Government are not binding on the members. Kyrgyzstan was among the founding members of the organization and signatory of several binding documents, including the **Commonwealth of Independent States Collective Security Treaty,** visa-free travel regime (amended in 2001), and some others.

Kyrgyzstan's trade with CIS members ranged between 50 and 80 percent of its total foreign trade in the 1990s. In 2002 the value of Kyrgyzstan's trade with CIS partners was estimated at about US$600 million, or approximately 60 percent of its trade. Since the mid-1990s the CIS was increasingly fragmented into subregional organizations, such as the **Central Asian Forum,** the GUUAM grouping, **Customs**

Union, and **Eurasian Economic Community**. *See also* RUSSIAN MILITARY BASE.

COMMONWEALTH OF INDEPENDENT STATES COLLECTIVE SECURITY TREATY (also known as the Dogovor o kollektivnoi bezopastnosti [DKV] in Russian). The Commonwealth of Independent States Collective Security Treaty was signed on 15 May 1992 in Tashkent in order to coordinate military reforms and security responses in the post-Soviet era. In 2003 it consisted of six members: Armenia, **Kazakhstan, Kyrgyz Republic, Russia, Tajikistan,** and Belarus (**Uzbekistan** left the organization in 1999). The Collective Security Treaty was enacted on 20 April 1994 and registered at the United Nations Secretariat on 1 November 1995. In order to counterbalance Russia's influence in the post-Soviet territory, Georgia, Ukraine, Uzbekistan, Azerbaijan, and Moldova established their own grouping, known as the GUUAM (abbreviation of names of member states), in 1997.

The treaty obliges the signatory states to refrain from using force between its members and from joining military alliances. In April 1999 all members extended the treaty for another five-year period. There are two major consultative bodies: the Council of Defense Ministers and the Council of Foreign Ministers. The Committee of **National Security Council** Secretaries was established in May 2000 in order to coordinate specific operations spearheaded against international terrorism. The post of the council's chairman was introduced in May 2001 (as of 2003, Vladimir Rushailo, secretary of Russia's National Security Council, was the chairman). National presidents chair the Collective Security Council during the sessions.

The treaty members established the Collective Rapid Deployment Forces, which were designed to counter terrorism in Central Asia. Under this treaty Kyrgyzstan received substantial military, logistic, and financial assistance in 1999 and 2000, during the **militant incursions** in Kyrgyzstan's territory. *See also* CENTRAL ASIAN FORUM; COMMONWEALTH OF INDEPENDENT STATES; RUSSIAN MILITARY BASE.

COMMUNIST PARTY OF THE KYRGYZ SSR (Kyrgyz SSR Kommunistik Partiasy—in Kyrgyz). A political organization established in 1924 after the creation of the **Kara-Kyrgyz Autonomous Oblast (Kyrgyz Autonomous Soviet Socialist Republic** [Kyrgyz ASSR] from 1926), as the *Oblast* Party Bureau. The first congress of the party took place on 23–26 March 1925. The party functioned as the *oblast* branch of the ruling Communist (Bolshevik) Party of the USSR. When the Kyrgyz ASSR was granted the status of **Kyrgyz Soviet Socialist Republic** (Kyrgyz SSR) in 1936, the organization was transformed into the Communist Party (Bolshevik) of the Kyrgyz SSR and its first congress was held on 4–16 June 1937.

The party congress, which was called regularly, was the highest decision-making organ of the Communist Party. It endorsed the appointments to the Central Committee and most important political, social, and economic decisions. The Central Committee of the Communist Party managed the day-to-day activities of the party between congresses and the first secretary of the Central Committee acted as the head of the republic. During the Stalin era the first secretary was traditionally appointed by the Kremlin and was approved by the Congress of the Communist Party of Kyrgyz SSR; this practice, however, changed during the regimes of Nikita Khrushchev (1953–64) and Leonid Brezhnev (1964–83), as the Congress began to elect the first secretary from the local *nomenklatura*. The Communist Party of Kyrgyz SSR established branches in every district, town, or city and maintained its party cells in every public organization, ministry, public enterprise, and *kolkhoz*.

Party membership rose as high as 154,000 members (1990), relatively evenly representing all ethnic and social groups and all regions of the republic. Despite the fact that it was a one-party political system and political competition was strongly discouraged, there was immense rivalry between various personalities and groups in the Communist Party. The power of these groups was based on extensive patronage networks (often called **clans**), which had strong roots in the traditional regional and even tribal rivalries.

During the regime of Mikhail Gorbachev (1985–91) there was an attempt to reform the one-party political system by transferring political power to the parliament and establishing a presidential post in every union republic. In 1990 the Kyrgyz Parliament introduced the post of president and presidential elections (the first presidents was elected by parliament) were conducted in October 1990. **Absamat**

Masalyev, the highly unpopular first secretary of the Communist Party, lost the elections to Dr. **Askar Akayev,** the president of the **National Academy of Sciences.** The political rivalry between the powerful Central Committee of the Communist Party of Kyrgyz SSR and the Office of the President ended in August 1990 when the Communist Party of the Kyrgyz SSR was banned and its property was confiscated. In September 1992 communist activists revived the party and registered it as the **Party of Communists of Kyrgyzstan,** which significantly modified its political platform and declared itself as the political successor of the Communist Party of Kyrgyz SSR. *See also* COMMUNIST PARTY OF KYRGYZSTAN.

COMMUNIST PARTY OF KYRGYZSTAN (CPK) (Kyrgyzstandyn Kommunistyk partiasy—in Kyrgyz). A party established as the result of the split among supporters of the communist ideology. It was registered on 13 September 1999. In its political program the party calls for a return to centralized state control over the national economy, direct regulation of prices, especially of food and other consumer goods, radical changes in the taxation system, liquidation of "capitalist exploitation," and restoration of the Soviet Union. The party claims that it has up to 10,000 members and many more active supporters in all *oblasts* of the republic, although its public actions and voting pattern indicate that the CPK receives support mainly from pensioners, war veterans, and some parts of the intelligentsia. Its chairman, **Klara Azhibekova,** who was a lecturer and head of the communist propaganda center, lacks significant political experience or organizational skills.

The CPK became particularly active in the political arena in 2001 and 2002 on the wave of the opposition campaign against large-scale corruption in the **government** and secret border negotiations with **China** and **Uzbekistan.** They also accused the government of mismanaging the **Aksy conflict.** The party's potential influence is seriously undermined by hostile relations with the **Party of Communists of Kyrgyzstan.** *See also* COMMUNIST PARTY OF KYRGYZ SSR.

CONGRESSES OF THE COMMUNIST PARTY OF KYRGYZ SSR. The party congress, which was convened regularly, was the highest decision-making organ of the Communist Party. It endorsed the appointments to the Central Committee and most important political, social, and economic decisions.

1st Congress of the Communist Party (Bolshevik) of Kyrgyz SSR—4–16 June 1937.

2nd Congress of the Communist Party (Bolshevik) of Kyrgyz SSR—3–16 July 1938.

3rd Congress of the Communist Party (Bolshevik) of Kyrgyz SSR—22–25 February 1939.

4th Congress of the Communist Party (Bolshevik) of Kyrgyz SSR—13–16 March 1940.

5th Congress of the Communist Party (Bolshevik) of Kyrgyz SSR—10–14 February 1949.

6th Congress of the Communist Party of Kyrgyz SSR—20–23 September 1952.

7th Congress of the Communist Party of Kyrgyz SSR—10–12 February 1954.

8th Congress of the Communist Party of Kyrgyz SSR—24–26 January 1956.

9th Congress of the Communist Party of Kyrgyz SSR—21–23 March 1958.

10th Congress of the Communist Party of Kyrgyz SSR—12–13 January 1959.

11th Congress of the Communist Party of Kyrgyz SSR—25–27 February 1960.

12th Congress of the Communist Party of Kyrgyz SSR—27–28 September 1961.

13th Congress of the Communist Party of Kyrgyz SSR—27–28 December 1963.

14th Congress of the Communist Party of Kyrgyz SSR—3–4 March 1966.

15th Congress of the Communist Party of Kyrgyz SSR—3–5 March 1971.

16th Congress of the Communist Party of Kyrgyz SSR—16–18 January 1976.

17th Congress of the Communist Party of Kyrgyz SSR—20–22 January 1981.

18th Congress of the Communist Party of Kyrgyz SSR—23–24 January 1986.

19th Congress of the Communist Party of Kyrgyz SSR—14–15 June 1990.

20th Congress of the Party Communist of Kyrgyzstan—13 March 1993.

21st Congress of the Party Communist of Kyrgyzstan—26 November 1994.

CONSTITUTIONAL COUNCIL. The Constitutional Council was set up by a decree of President **Askar Akayev** in September 2002 as part of the negotiation process between the **government** and opposition after the **Aksy conflict**. Events and confrontations that followed the Aksy conflict developed into a deep political crisis, which threatened to get out of control. In order to find a compromise both the opposition and the government decided to jointly develop proposals on constitutional changes. The Constitutional Council included prominent politicians, human rights activists, and representatives of various public organizations and **nongovernmental organizations** (NGOs), including opposition parties. Its work was conducted throughout autumn 2002 under the slogan of "Kyrgyzstan is a Home for Human Rights." The main objective of the council was to prepare proposals for a constitutional referendum. The constitutional referendum was held on 2 February 2003 and provoked considerable controversy and criticism from the opposition. *See also* CONSTITUTION OF KYRGYZSTAN.

CONSTITUTION OF KYRGYZSTAN. The first post-Soviet constitution of **Kyrgyzstan** was introduced in May 1993. The constitution declared that Kyrgyzstan was a "sovereign, unitary, democratic Republic, constructed on the basis of a legal secular state." The constitution stipulated major principles, such as the supremacy of the rule of law, guarantees of human rights and freedoms, distribution of power, and others. The constitution also declared the president as the head of the state, whose powers were balanced and checked by the legislature and judiciary.

The constitution stipulated that all citizens over 18 years of age were eligible to vote and all citizens over 25 years of age, who had resided in the republic for no fewer than five years before the elections, were eligible to be elected to the **Jogorku Kenesh** (parliament). There were no restrictions based on ethnic or racial grounds, though the Kyrgyz constitution bans all "religious political parties" and "organizations, that propagate war or violence against the state or any ethnic group" from participation in the political process.

There were several significant amendments to the constitution of Kyrgyzstan since 1991, conducted through national referendums. Some changes were introduced in 1994, 1996, and 1998. The **Constitutional Council** was set up in 2002, comprising representatives of various public organizations with the purpose of introducing some changes into the constitution. As the outcome of this work, a constitutional referendum was held on 2 February 2003. According to official reports about 95 percent of the voters approved changes to the constitution.

CUSTOMS UNION (also known as the Tamozhenyi Soyuz [TS] in Russian). The organization was established on 26 May 1996 in order to simplify trade and currency conversion and to coordinate the tariff regime and economic cooperation between the signatory members. It consists of five members: Belarus, **Kazakhstan, Kyrgyz Republic, Russia**, and **Tajikistan** (joined in February 1999). However, the idea of transforming the economic cooperation into economic integration similar to free trade agreements in Europe or North America failed due to economic and political disagreements. In October 2000 the members decided to transform the organization into the **Eurasian Economic Community**. *See also* CENTRAL ASIAN FORUM; COMMONWEALTH OF INDEPENDENT STATES.

– D –

DASTARKHAN. 1. Refreshments, dinner, or lunch. 2. Tablecloth or special piece of fabric on the floor, ground, or low height table. Traditionally Kyrgyz families had their meals on the floor or at a low-height table.

DAVLAT (also davlyat). 1. The term refers to the state or government administration. 2. Political power of the state.

DEKHKAN. 1. Peasant. 2. A farmer working on land and cultivating agricultural products, unlike a pastoral nomad, who moved with his herds in the mountains throughout the year.

DEMOCRATIC MOVEMENT OF KYRGYZSTAN PARTY (DMKP) (Kyrgyzstan Demokratialyk Kyimyly partiasy in Kyrgyz). One of the oldest opposition political organizations in **Kyrgyzstan**. The Democratic Movement of Kyrgyzstan (DMK) was established as a popular movement at the founding congress on 26–27 May 1990, which brought together 34 political groups, clubs, and **nongovernmental organizations** (NGOs). Most of these groups were established in Frunze (now **Bishkek**) in 1989–90 on the wave of the Gorbachev-led political liberalization in the Soviet Union. In the middle of 1990 the DMK claimed up to 300,000 active members and supporters. In September 1990 several prominent members of Kyrgyzstan's **Supreme Soviet** (parliament) defected from the **Communist Party of Kyrgyz SSR** and declared their support for the DMK. In October 1990 the movement organized a series of mass rallies in Bishkek demanding the resignation of the republic's political leaders. The DMK played a key role in uniting the opposition forces and in defeating **Absamat Masaliyev**, the Communist leader, in the first presidential elections in the Supreme Soviet in October 1990.

The DMK emerged as the largest and most influential organization after Kyrgyzstan's independence in 1991. However, very soon the movement split due to internal disagreements and rivalries. In 1993 it was officially transformed into a political party and on 26 November 1993 it was reregistered as the Democratic Movement of Kyrgyzstan Party (DMKP) under the leadership of **Zhypar Jeksheyev**. In its political program the party declared that it would adopt a liberal political platform and would demand greater democratization of the country, establishment of a civil society and rule of law, and improvement of the social conditions of the population. By the mid-1990s the DMKP had become one of the most outspoken opposition parties in Kyrgyzstan. In 2001 the DMKP claimed that it had up to 500 members and up to 15,000 active supporters. The party's moderate stand played an important role in ensuring the stability of Kyrgyzstan's political process in the 1990s, but its influence was declining. It performed poorly in the **Jogorku Kenesh** (parliament) elections in 2000.

The DMKP attempted to relaunch itself in 2001 on the wave of the mass campaign against the corruption of the **Askar Akayev**–led regime. In August 2002 the party became part of the "Movement for

Askar Akayev's Resignation and Reforms for the People," which united 22 opposition political parties and NGOs and demanded the immediate resignation of the incumbent president. *See also* ERKIN KYRGYZSTAN PROGRESSIVE-DEMOCRATIC PARTY.

DEMOCRATIC PARTY OF WOMEN OF KYRGZSTAN (DPWK) (**Kyrgyzstan Ayaldardyn Demokratialyk partiasy in Kyrgyz**). One of the largest **women**'s political organizations in Kyrgyzstan. It was registered on 14 October 1994. The party declared its support for market-oriented reforms, a privatization program, opening of the country to foreign investments, and restructuring of the national economy. It demanded that the **government** pay greater attention to the needs of women, families, and children; give greater social guarantees and equal rights in the workplace, in **education,** and in political life; and liquidate any form of exploitation of women. The DPWK claimed that it has up to 15,000 members and numerous supporters in all *oblasts* of the republic. Its chairperson, Tokon Shailiyeva, was regarded as one of the most influential political figures in the women's movement in the republic and she was an experienced parliamentarian.

The party was successful during the 2000 parliamentary elections, as it secured two seats in the **Jogorku Kenesh** (parliament). The DPWK traditionally supported the government in the parliament, although it occasionally criticized it for failing to improve living standards among women in Kyrgyzstan and for not increasing state social welfare payments to pensioners and families in need.

DMITRIEVSKOYE. *See* TALAS CITY.

DOKTOR NAUK (**DOCTOR OF SCIENCES**). The highest academic degree in the republic. The degree is awarded by the Specialized (Science) Council upon the successful completion of *doktorantura* (doctorate studies), which involves the writing and public defense of a doctoral dissertation. The Specialized State Commission must register and approve it. *See also KANDIDAT NAUK.*

DRUGS. In the early 20th century Kyrgyz farmers produced illicit drugs (mainly opium and its products) for local consumption and for smuggling into **China** and other neighboring countries. By the late

1930s the combination of harsh measures conducted by the Soviet authorities and agricultural reforms practically eliminated the production of illicit drugs for illegal trade, although there were reports of limited production of opium and marijuana for private consumption. In the 1960s several state farms were established in the **Ysyk Kol** *oblast* to produce a limited amount of opium for the Soviet pharmaceutical **industry**, but they were closed in the 1970s. In the 1980s northern Kyrgyzstan became a source of marijuana for Central Asia and **Russia** as the **Jetisuu** area had always been a region of natural growth of marijuana (cannabis) herbaceous plant (*Cannabis sativa*, family *Cannabaceae*). In the 1990s Kyrgyzstan also became a major transit destination of illicit drugs originating in **Afghanistan.** A combination of widespread unemployment and corruption and a low level of law enforcement contributed to an increasing involvement of Kyrgyz citizens in drug trafficking.

In 2000 and 2001 there were reports of opium growth in remote areas of Kyrgyzstan, although the republic was not named as a significant source of illicit drugs. There are no precise figures available for 2002–03, but various estimates indicate that the income from drug trafficking generates up to 40 percent of the shadow economy's revenue in some *oblast*s of the republic. In 2002 Kyrgyzstan's *militsia* confiscated 2,900 tons of various drugs. In April 2003 Kyrgyz **mass media** reported that the republic registered the highest proportion of drug addicts in Central Asia (1,644 addicts per 100,000 people).

DZHAI LOO. See JAYLOO.

DZHALAL ABAD. *See* JALAL ABAD.

DZHALAL ABAD *OBLAST.* *See* JALAL ABAD *OBLAST.*

DZHANGARACHEVA, MIRA (1952–) (also *Jangaracheva*). Kyrgyz politician. Born in Frunze (now **Bishkek**), Mira Dzhangaracheva graduated from the Faculty of History of the **Kyrgyz State (National) University** in 1974. From 1974 to 1978 she worked in the **Frunze Polytechnic Institute** and from 1978 to 1981 she studied at the *aspirantura* of the Moscow State University. She held the position of senior lecturer in the Frunze Polytechnic Institute 1981–88 and from 1989 to 1992 she worked on her doctoral dissertation at Moscow State

University. Dzhangaracheva started her political career as the director of the Center for Social and Political Problems in 1992. Soon she became the deputy head of the Bishkek city administration on social issues. In 1995 she was elected a member of the **Jogorku Kenesh** (parliament). In 1996 she was appointed deputy prime minister on social policies. In the late 1990s she emerged as one of the most influential female politicians. Dzhangaracheva has authored 40 articles and papers on social issues and interethnic relations in Kyrgyzstan.

DZHANUZAKOV, BOLOT (1948–) (also Januzakov). Kyrgyz politician. Born in Chym Korgon village in **Chui** *oblast* (northern Kyrgyzstan), Bolot Dzhanuzakov graduated from the **Frunze Polytechnic Institute** in 1970. From 1970 to 1972 he worked as an engineer at an industrial plant in the town of Sulykta (**Osh** *oblast*). From 1972 to 1977 he held various positions in the **Komsomol** in Osh *oblast*. From 1977 to 1982 Dzhanuzakov worked in the Central Committee of the Komsomol and from 1982 to 1987 he held various senior positions in the Frunze (now **Bishkek**) city administration. From 1988 to 1995 he was head of department at the Ministry of Internal Affairs in Bishkek and was the head of the defense department of the presidential administration 1995–96. In 1999 he was appointed secretary of the Security Council. In 2001 he was appointed head of the **National Security Service**, which was formed on the basis of the former **Komitet Gosudarstvennoi Bezopastnosti (KGB).**

In 2003 Dzhanuzakov was named one of the 20 most influential politicians in the republic. He was also regarded as the architect of the security service's reforms in response to both the **militant incursions** into southern Kyrgyzstan in 1999 and 2000 and increasing activities of the opposition parties in 2001 and 2002.

DZHETI-SUU. *See* JETISUU.

DZHIENBEKOV, SADRIDDIN (1964–) (also Jienbekov). Kyrgyz politician. He was born in Kyzyl-Kia town in **Osh** *oblast*. Sadriddin Dzhienbekov graduated from the economics department of the **Alma-Ata State Institute of National Economy** in 1986. In 1988 he worked as an engineer-economist in the Osh *oblast* Statistical Bureau. From 1988 to 1991 he was a research fellow of the Kazakh Research Laboratory of Economics (Alma-Ata, **Kazakhstan**). From 1991 to

1992 Dzhienbekov was senior expert of the Fund for State Property of the **Kyrgyz Republic** and from 1992 to 1996 he worked as head of department at the Ministry of Trade, Industries and Entrepreneurship. From 1996 to 1999 he was deputy-head of the Department of Economic, Market and Investments and from 1999 to 2000 he worked as an expert and head of the Department for Economic Policies, both in the presidential apparatus.

In 2000 Dzhienbekov was appointed chairman and minister for the Fund for State Property. In 2001 he became chairman of the State Committee for Management of State Property and Direct Investments. In 2002 he was appointed minister of foreign trade and industry. Dzhienbekov was the youngest minister in the Kyrgyz **government** and was appointed for his managerial skills rather than for political connections.

DZIGIT. *See* JIGIT.

DZHUMAGULOV, APAS (1934–) (also Jumagulov). Kyrgyz politician. Born in Arashan village in **Chui** *oblast* (northern Kyrgyzstan), Apas Dzhumagulov spent almost his entire career in the **Communist Party of Kyrgyz SSR** and state apparatus. He graduated from the Moscow Petrochemical Institute (**Russia**) in 1958. From 1958 to 1973 he held various managing positions in the Kyrgyzneft (Kyrgyzoil) enterprise. From 1973 to 1979 he was head of the Industrial and **Transportation** Department of the Central Committee of the Communist Party of Kyrgyz SSR. From 1979 to 1985 he held the position of secretary of the Central Committee and from 1985 to 1986 he worked as first secretary of the **Ysyk Kol** Committee of the Communist Party. From 1986 to 1991 Dzhumagulov was chairman of the Council of Ministers. In 1990 he was nominated as one of the candidates for the presidential elections but lost the elections to **Askar Akayev**. From 1991 to 1993 he headed the Chui *oblast* administration. In 1993 Dzhumagulov was appointed prime minister. He resigned from the post in 1998. From 1999 to 2003 he was an ambassador to Germany.

Dzhumagulov played an important role in the republic's **government** during the most difficult years for Kyrgyzstan's economy from 1986 to 1991 and from 1993 to 1998. He was considered a key actor in implementing market-oriented reforms.

DZHUMALIYEV, KUBANYCHBEK (1956–) (also Jumaliyev). Kyrgyz politician. Born in Kechuu village in **Jalal Abad** *oblast* (southern Kyrgyzstan), Kubanychbek Dzhumaliyev graduated from the Ryazan' Radiotechnic Institute (**Russia**) in 1978 and from the *aspirantura* of the **Frunze Polytechnic Institute** in 1982. From 1983 to 1986 he was an engineer and secretary of the **Komsomol** committee at the same institute. From 1986 to 1992 he held various research and administrative positions in the Frunze Polytechnic Institute and the **National Academy of Sciences** and from 1992 to 1997 he held various administrative positions at the Ministry of Education and in the presidential administration. In 1997 he was appointed head of the State Committee on Science and New Technologies, and then head of presidential administration. In 1998 Dzhumaliyev was appointed as prime minister, one of the youngest in the history of the republic. He was accused of mismanagement and inertia during the Russian financial crisis in summer–fall 1998 and he lost his position. In 1999 he was appointed minister of **transportation** and communications.

Dzhumaliyev proposed a number of initiatives as prime minister and was considered one of the more promising leaders of the Kyrgyz **government**. However, his ideas were poorly implemented and the weak management contributed to his downfall. Dzhumaliyev has authored more than 120 articles and research papers, mainly in electronics and optics.

– E –

ECONOMIC COOPERATION ORGANIZATION (ECO). An organization established in 1985 and including **Afghanistan**, Iran, Pakistan, and Turkey, although its original roots can be traced to a regional grouping established in 1964. The ECO was officially established to promote regional economic cooperation. In 1992 the Economic Cooperation Organization invited the newly independent Azerbaijan, **Kazakhstan,** Kyrgyzstan, **Tajikistan,** Turkmenistan, and **Uzbekistan** to join the ECO. The total population of the ECO members is about 300 million and their territories cover over 6 million square kilometers (twice the size of India). Almost immediately after its membership grew to 10, the ECO declared that it was "directed against no country or group of countries."

Kyrgyzstan sought to open an ECO market for its industrial production and to obtain another source of additional investments, credits, and assistance. The Kyrgyz **government** also hoped that through the territories of the ECO partners the republic would find alternative routes to the international market for its goods and commodities and the shortest access to commercial sea routes. In 1993 the ECO adopted the Quetta Plan of Action, which called for greater economic integration among the 10 members of the organization and the development of various regional infrastructure projects. In 2000 Kyrgyzstan completed a highway project from **Osh** to Karakorum (Pakistan), which was supported by the ECO. *See also* TRANSPORTATION.

ECONOMY. *See* AGRICULTURE; BANKING; INDUSTRY; INTERNATIONAL TRADE; MINING; SERVICES; TOURISM; TRANSPORTATION.

EDUCATION. The educational system in the **Kyrgyz Republic** has a strong Russian/Soviet influence and it is provided free to the general population.

During the precolonial era the **Kyrgyzs** were educated mainly in small *mektebs* and *medresse* (mainly in Arabic), primarily in the large cities in and outside the Kyrgyz land. In addition, some technical skills and professional expertise were passed on by *aksakal* and *ustoz* at craftsman orders. During the tsarist era, the colonial administration introduced a few dozens new *mektebs* for the native population and accepted the most talented Kyrgyz children into Russian schools. Yet, in 1913 about 95.4 percent of the population was illiterate, and there were only 195 primary schools and there were only about 220 qualified teachers. According to official reports on the Semirechye *oblast*, for example, in 1913 the literacy rate among Kyrgyz males stood at 8.2 percent and among Kyrgyz **women** at 0.2 percent; overall only 2.20 percent of the Kyrgyz population could read and write Russian.

During the Soviet era (1918–91) a comprehensive educational infrastructure and modern educational system provided free education emphasizing sciences, mathematics, and practical skills. By the 1930s the **government** had eradicated mass illiteracy. According to official statistics, in 1982 more than 909,600 students (out of total population of about 4.1 million people) or approximately 25 percent of the population attended 1,734 schools. More than 52,000 teachers taught at schools in the republic. About 60,000 students attended 122 specialized secondary schools and technical colleges. In addition, 55,000 students attended 10 institutes of higher (tertiary) education. The knowledge of Russian, which was the medium of instruction at most tertiary institutions, was comparatively strong, as 35.2 percent of Kyrgyzs stated in 1989 that they were fluent in Russian, the second highest percentage in the region after **Kazakhstan**.

After independence in 1991 the educational system in Kyrgyzstan underwent two major changes. First, there was a greater emphasis on the use of the **Kyrgyz language** as the medium of instruction, after the Kyrgyz language became the official language of the state. Second, there was a considerable reduction of state funding of the educational system.

The **Constitution of Kyrgyzstan** (1993) stipulates that general education is compulsory and free and that the state guarantees equal access to free general, vocational, specialized, and higher education in state-controlled educational establishments. Kyrgyz and Russian are the major languages of instruction, but many schools, colleges, and universities increasingly teach in English. The constitution also guarantees that all ethnic communities may use their mother tongue at primary educational institutions in the areas where those groups live as compact communities. In February 2003 the **Jogorku Kenesh** (parliament) adopted a Law on Education, which endorsed major changes in post-Soviet education in the republic.

At the age of seven, children begin an 11-year compulsory education program, composed of four-year primary schooling and seven-year secondary schooling. According to official statistics, in 2003 about 1.2 million students (out of total population of about 5 million people) or approximately 22 percent of the population attended 2,015 primary and secondary schools. This included 104 specialized secondary schools and 57 lyceums for gifted children. According to official statistics, approximately 96 percent of all those between the ages of seven and 16 were enrolled in some kind of educational institution, although the dropout rate is high.

After completing secondary school, students may enter a tertiary educational institution (university or institute), which usually offers a five-year program. According to official statistics, in 2001 185,200 students attended 40 higher education institutions. They may also continue their education at 115 technical colleges. Students may complete postgraduate studies at three- or four-year *aspirantura* programs, which combine coursework and dissertation writing. Upon completion of the *aspirantura* students receive a degree of **kandidat nauk** (equivalent to a Ph.D.). Students may also continue their study further at four-year *doctorantura* level and receive a degree of **doktor nauk** (Doctor of Sciences).

Throughout the 1990s the quality and accessibility of the educational system in Kyrgyzstan declined due to the severe economic recession and chronic shortage of funding. Many teachers and professors left the republic for **Russia** and other countries, or moved to the private sector where salaries are higher than in the schools. According to official reports schools experienced serious problems, including a shortage of about 2,800 teachers, the lack of and price of textbooks, high dropout rate of children from school, inadequate funding of educational facilities, among others.

The government of Kyrgyzstan is trying to reform its educational system by attracting private investment and international assistance to the educational sector. In 2001 there were 27 private schools, 14 higher educational institutions, and seven campuses of foreign (mainly **Commonwealth of Independent States**) universities. *See also* LIQUIDATION OF ILLITERACY.

ERKIN KYRGYZSTAN PROGRESSIVE-DEMOCRATIC PARTY (Erkin Kyrgyzstan progressivduu-demokratialyk partiasy in Kyrgyz). One of the opposition political organizations, which split from the **Democratic Movement of Kyrgyzstan** in 1991. It was first registered on 2 December 1991, but it was required to reregister on 21 February 1997. The party adopted a liberal nonviolence political platform; urged respect for human rights, genuine democratization of the country, and establishment of a market economy; and called for the cultural, spiritual, and religious resurgence of Kyrgyzstan. It was one of the few mainstream political organizations that advocated a greater role for **Islam** and Islamic traditions in public life. The party claimed that it had up to 12,000 members and numerous active supporters in all *oblasts* of the republic, although its real electorate came mainly from **Bishkek**. Its chairman, **Tursunbai Bakir-uulu,** was elected to the **Jogorku Kenesh** (parliament) in 1995 and was considered to be one of the most active opposition parliamentarians.

The Erkin Kyrgyzstan failed to relaunch itself in 2000 and was unsuccessful in its campaign during parliamentary and presidential elections. The party managed to get only 4.2 percent of the votes in the elections, according to the party list, and won only one seat in the parliament. Tursunbai Bakir Uulu, who was registered for the presidential elections, received only 1.0 percent of the vote. In August 2002 the party joined the "Movement for **Askar Akayev**'s Resignation and Reforms for the People," which united 22 opposition political parties and **nongovernmental organizations** and demanded the immediate resignation of the incumbent president.

ESHIMKANOV, MELIS (1965–). Kyrgyz politician and journalist. Born in **Naryn** city (in the remote eastern province of the republic), Melis Eshimkanov graduated from the Faculty of Journalism of **Kyrgyz State (National) University** in 1988. From 1988 to 1991 he worked as correspondent at the *Leninchil Jash* newspaper and the *Komsomolets Kyrgyzstana* newspaper. In 1991 he founded the *Asaba* newspaper (published in **Kyrgyz language**) and became its editor in chief.

Eshimkanov is best known as one of the most vocal voices of the radical nationalist groups. The *Asaba* newspaper gradually became the largest and most popular Kyrgyz-language newspaper in the republic, representing the views of the younger generation of the Kyrgyz electorate. He was among the active supporters of the Law on Languages, which established the Kyrgyz language as the sole state language and adopted a strict schedule for phasing out the Russian language from public institutions and **education**. He rigorously opposed the introduction of the Russian language as the second state language in the republic. In the late 1990s his sharp and critical articles caused a number of political scandals and consequently political reprisals. In 2000 Eshimkanov was registered as a candidate for the presidential elections, but he received an insignificant number of votes. In 2001 the *Asaba* newspaper was declared bankrupt and was closed, but Eshimkanov claimed that the charges were politically motivated. In 2002 he attempted to launch a new opposition newspaper but experienced financial difficulties.

EURASIAN ECONOMIC COMMUNITY (also known as the Evraziiskoye ekonomicheskoye soobshchestvo [EES] in Russian). The Eurasian Economic Community (EEC) was established in October 2000 and replaced the **Customs Union** of the **Commonwealth of Independent States (CIS)**. It consists of five members: Belarus, **Kazakhstan,** Kyrgyzstan, **Russia,** and **Tajikistan.** Initially the idea of establishing the

EEC was proposed by President Nursultan Nazarbayev of Kazakhstan in 1994. Following the European Union model, the EEC differentiates the participating states' voting power according to the size of their economies: Russia has four votes, Belarus and Kazakhstan two votes each, and Kyrgyzstan and Tajikistan one vote each. The EEC is aimed at simplifying customs border control between the member states, unifying taxation, and enacting legislation to increase economic cooperation. However, the move toward greater economic integration did not stop the EEC members from imposing additional tariffs or restrictions on imports from other EEC countries. For example, in 2000 Kazakhstan introduced restrictions on imports from Kyrgyzstan and Russia.

In 2002 Moldova and the Ukraine joined the EEC as observers, and in 2003 Armenia declared that it would consider joining the EEC. At the February 2003 meeting of the EEC International Council, its members declared that they would focus on joint development of the energy sector, cooperation in transportation, agriculture, and capital markets, and collaboration over immigration policies. *See also* CENTRAL ASIAN FORUM; RUSSIAN MILITARY BASE.

–F–

FERGHANA MOUNTAIN RANGE. Mountain range located in the **Tian-Shan mountains**, in the southwest of Kyrgyzstan. It stretches from north to southeast and is up to 225 kilometers in length. Its width is about 40 kilometers. The highest point of the range is 4,692 meters. There are more than 150 glaciers with a total area of about 125 square kilometers, although in the 1980s and 1990s some glaciers shrank or disappeared.

The southwest parts of the Ferghana mountain range were forested in the past (walnut trees and some other rare species), and its timber resources were intensively exploited. Thus, by the beginning of the 21st century deforestation had become a serious problem, although Kyrgyzstan's **government** established several national parks (Arslan Bob National Park and others). Several rivers, which begin in the range, provide water to **Jalal Abad** and **Osh** *oblasts*.

FERGHANA *OBLAST* (*Farghona veloyat* in Uzbek). 1. The Ferghana *oblast* was established in 1877 with its center in Ferghana city

(Yongi Margelan until 1910, Skobelev between 1910 and 1920), located in the **Ferghana valley**. In 1918 it became a part of the **Turkistan Autonomous Soviet Socialist Republic.** The territory of contemporary **Jalal Abad** and **Osh** *oblasts* were part of the Ferghana *oblast.* The eastern part of Ferghana *oblast* became part of southern Kyrgyzstan in 1924, when the *oblast* was divided between Kyrgyzstan and **Uzbekistan.**

2. Ferghana *oblast* is an *oblast* in Uzbekistan, with its center in Ferghana (Farghona) city. Its area is 7,100 square kilometers and its population was estimated at 2.584 million people in 2001, the second largest *oblast* in Uzbekistan in terms of population. It was established in the southeastern part of the Ferghana valley in 1938. The *oblast* is bordered by Kyrgyzstan in the south, **Tajikistan** in the west, Namangan *oblast* in the north, and Andijon *oblast* in the northeast. In the 1990s Kyrgyzstan and Uzbekistan had some territorial disputes over borders between Ferghana and Osh *oblasts*.

FERGHANA VALLEY (also Farghona valley in Uzbek). This triangular valley has an area of about 22,000 square kilometers, divided between Kyrgyzstan, **Uzbekistan,** and **Tajikistan.** The valley is bordered by the **Tian-Shan mountains** in the north and the Gissaro-Alay mountain range in the south. Due to the warm and dry climate and availability of drinking and irrigation water it is one of the most fertile and most densely populated regions in Central Asia. Central Asian archeologists claimed that they found settlements in the valley that were among the oldest human settlements in the world. The valley and its cities were mentioned in ancient Chinese sources and in the chronicles of Alexander the Great's conquest of Central Asia. Natural silk cultivation and trade along the **Great Silk Road** contributed to the growth of the region's legendary economic wealth and strategic importance. The Ferghana valley was acquired by the Arabs in the eighth century A.D., who introduced **Islam** to the local population. The Persians arrived in the region in the ninth century A.D., but later they were replaced by the Turks and then Mongols under Genghis Khan. The valley was part of Tamerlane's (Timur) Empire. In the 16th century the **Kokand Khanate** gained autonomy and made the region its stronghold. In 1876 the **Russian Empire's** troops conquered the Kokand Khanate and annexed it to the **Turkistan Governor-Generalship.**

The Ferghana valley was divided between the newly created Central Asian republics during the **border delimitation in 1924–1926**. Under the Soviet government the valley became one of the most important producers of cotton and natural silk. The government also invested intensively in the development of large industrial zones in the valley. The main centers of industrial development became the cities of **Osh** and **Jalal Abad** in Kyrgyzstan; Fergana, Kokand (Qoqond), Andijan (Andijon), and Namangan in Uzbekistan; and Khudjand in Tajikistan. During the 20th century the population in the Ferghana valley nearly tripled, and due to declining social conditions and competition for resources, including water and land, the valley witnessed bloody confrontations and clashes in the 1980s and 1990s.

Batken, Jalal Abad, and **Osh** *oblasts* of Kyrgyzstan are located in the Ferghana valley. These are the republic's most densely populated areas with a total population above 2 million people. Southern Kyrgyzstan is politically the most volatile area in the republic due to its proximity to war-torn Tajikistan and **Afghanistan**, increasing radicalization of some political groups, and growing **drug** trafficking.

FIVE-YEAR PLAN FOR THE DEVELOPMENT OF THE NATIONAL ECONOMY (also *Piatiletka*). Five-year plans of economic and social development were introduced in Kyrgyzstan as part of Soviet economic development planning. These plans were prepared by experts at the Kyrgyz GosPlan (State Planning Committee), with contributions of economists from the **National Academy of Sciences**, various ministries and the Central Committee of the **Communist Party of Kyrgyz SSR**, subject to approval of the GosPlan of the Union of Soviet Socialist Republics (USSR). After that the five-year plans were subject to approval by the **Congresses of the Communist Party of Kyrgyz SSR** and of the Congress of the People's Deputies of the Kyrgyz SSR. Kyrgyzstan introduced the five-year plans in 1928 and abandoned centralized planning in 1991. There were 12 *piatiletkas* in Kyrgyzstan:

The First, from 1928 to 1932
The Second, from 1933 to 1937
The Third, from 1938 to 1942
The Fourth, from 1946 to 1950
The Fifth, from 1950 to 1955

The Sixth, from 1956 to 1960
The Seventh, from 1959 to 1965 (actually seven-year plan)
The Eighth, from 1966 to 1970
The Ninth, from 1971 to 1976
The Tenth, from 1976 to 1980
The Eleventh, from 1981 to 1985
The Twelfth, from 1986 to 1991

FLAG. The **Jogorku Kenesh** (parliament) officially adopted the national flag of the **Kyrgyz Republic** on 3 March 1992 to replace the Soviet-era banner of red with a hammer and sickle. The Kyrgyz flag is red, which symbolizes bravery. In the center of the flag is a golden sun, which represents peace and wealth. The sun has 40 rays representing 40 Kyrgyz **tribes.** The center of the sun is diagonally crossed with two sets of three nearly parallel lines representing a stylized *tyundyuk* (*tyundyuk* is located in the upper part of the *yurt*). The *tyundyuk* signifies fatherland and universe in general. There is a one-to-two ratio between the total width and the length of the flag. *See also* COAT OF ARMS.

FOREIGN POLICY. After the unexpected dissolution of the Union of Soviet Socialist Republics (USSR) in 1991, the Kyrgyzstani government subordinated its foreign policy to achieving economic and political survival in a very complex Central Asian environment. Throughout the 1990s Kyrgyzstani diplomacy focused on three priorities. First, maintaining cooperation, coordination, and sustainable multilateral relations with the former Soviet republics, especially with neighboring countries **Kazakhstan, Uzbekistan,** and **Tajikistan.** Second, building security architecture. Third, establishing international political and economic relations with the Western countries, including the United States and Western Europe.

After the dissolution of the USSR Kyrgyzstan joined the **Commonwealth of Independent States** (CIS) in December 1991. Throughout the 1990s the CIS has been more of a temporary compromise among the former Soviet republics and a ceremonial institution, unable to promote closer economic integration among its members. By 2000 the CIS had sunk from being a strong supraregional organization into a club of several members who discussed political and economic development on the territory of the former USSR but had no desire to be bound by any agreements. In May 1992 Kyrgyzstan joined the **CIS Collective Security Treaty**, which became a key institution in dealing with the security issues and provided an institutional framework for relations with neighbors. Kyrgyzstan renewed the treaty in 1999 and received substantial assistance from it when radical militants from Tajikistan entered Kyrgyzstani territory in 1999 and again in 2000.

Kyrgyzstan was among the founding members of the Central Asian Union (CAU), which was created in 1990 as a consultative body for the Central Asian leaders. Although the creation of the CAU was largely driven by the idea of reintroducing political and economic integration among its members, by 1994 the CAU was on the brink of collapse. Kazakhstan, Uzbekistan, and later Kyrgyzstan formalized new common principles of integration, and in April 1994 they relaunched it as the Central Asian Economic Union (CAEU) (Tajikistan joined in 1998). The CAEU proved unable to help resolve trade, transportation, and border disputes or stop a devastating trade war in 1999 and 2000. In 2001 the CAEU was reformed again into the **Central Asian Forum**.

Kyrgyzstani leaders were attracted by what has been called "Turkey's secular model of development," and in 1992 Kyrgyzstan joined a summit of Turkic nations in Istanbul in order to extend economic and cultural relations. This opened the door for growing trade, investments, and travel, and for cooperation in **education** and cultural issues between the two countries. In 1997 Kyrgyzstan and Turkey signed an "eternal friendship agreement," but the expected large-scale investments from Turkey did not materialize.

In the security area Kyrgyzstan relied largely on Russian support, as it joined the CIS Collective Security Treaty in 1992. In order to resolve border disputes, in 1996 Kyrgyzstan joined the "Shanghai Five" organization, which includes **China**, Kazakhstan, Kyrgyzstan, Russia, Tajikistan, and, since 2001, Uzbekistan. In August 1999 President **Askar Akayev** hosted a "Shanghai Five" summit, which discussed regional security and expanding trade and economic cooperation. During this summit China, Kazakhstan, and Kyrgyzstan signed an agreement delimiting the borders between the three countries. The heads of states also signed the 12-point **Bishkek** Declaration, which pledged to maintain the borders between the states and confirmed the existing agreements on the border issues, mutual respect of their territorial integrity and sover-

eignty, and cooperation against terrorism, illegal **drug-** and arms-traf-
ficking, national separatism, and religious extremism. During this sixth
summit in 2001 the founding members of the "Shanghai Five" reformed
it into the **Shanghai Cooperation Organization** in order to promote
"effective cooperation between member countries in the political, economic, scientific-technological, cultural, and educational spheres."

Kyrgyzstan's relations with Western countries took an uneasy path
in the 1990s. Initially, Akayev's efforts to bring about radical political
and economic changes in the republic received substantial support
from the Western countries as well as from international assisting organizations. Between 1991 and 1997 Kyrgyzstan received sizeable international assistance, one of the highest in the CIS in per capita terms.
However, since 1998 Akayev's administration has been under increasing pressure and criticism from Western governments over its
handling of the opposition and elections. Nevertheless, in 1999 the
North Atlantic Treaty Organization (NATO) and the United States sig-
naled their concern over security problems on the Kyrgyzstani borders
and agreed to provide further political and financial support. It was,
however, the 11 September 2001 terrorist attacks in New York that became a turning point for the relations between the George W. Bush administration and the Kyrgyzstani government. Akayev immediately
expressed his full support for the U.S. actions against "international
terrorism and extremism" and offered Kyrgyzstan's territory and air-
space for American action in **Afghanistan**. In October 2001 Washington officially asked Bishkek for the possible use of Kyrgyzstan's
territory to station U.S. troops. After intensive consultations with the
members of the CIS Security Treaty, Bishkek agreed to host the **U.S.
military airbase** at Manas civil airport. However, Kyrgyzstan did not
join the "alliance of willing" in the U.S.-led war in Iraq in 2003.

During the 1990s Kyrgyzstan made special efforts to increase and
diversify its foreign trade and attract foreign investors. The proportion of trade with countries outside the CIS grew from virtually zero
to almost 55 percent. From 1992 to 1997 Kyrgyzstan managed to attract an estimated US$450 million, with the largest foreign investor
being Canada (45 percent of total investments), followed by Turkey
(20 percent), the United States (12 percent), and China (10 percent).

Despite joining the CAEU and maintaining positive relations with
the CIS members, Kyrgyzstan's trade was affected by a regional

"customs war" and high tariffs imposed by Kazakhstan and Uzbekistan on Kyrgyzstani goods in 1998 and 1999. This originated in disagreement over taxation and other policies and Kazakhstan's and Uzbekistan's anger over Bishkek's unilateral negotiations on entry to the **World Trade Organization**. In an attempt to calm the tensions, in October 2000 Kyrgyzstan joined the **Eurasian Economic Community (EEC)**, which consisted of the CIS Customs Union members (Belarus, Kazakhstan, Kyrgyzstan, Russia, and Tajikistan).

FREE ECONOMIC ZONES (FEZs) (Svobodnaya Ekonomicheskaya Zona in Russian). Areas in Kyrgyzstan where goods, production, and other economic activities are free of taxes and can be landed and reexported freely. The Kyrgyz **government** began establishing Free Economic Zones in 1991 modeled on **China**'s experience in order to attract investments to the most remote and economically depressed parts of the country.

In 1991 the entire **Naryn** *oblast* was declared an FEZ. According to official reports the Naryn FEZ attracted some investments from China, **Russia**, the United States, and some other countries, but many of the registered enterprises never began to work. In 1995 an FEZ "Bishkek" was established near **Bishkek**. In 1996 an FEZ was established in **Karakol (Ysyk Kol** *oblast*). By 2002 there were six FEZs in Kyrgyzstan. However, there were debates within the government about the future of the FEZs in the country, as they failed to attract the anticipated amount of foreign investments.

FRUNZE (CITY). *See* BISHKEK.

FRUNZE POLYTECHNIC INSTITUTE (FPI). The institute was founded in 1954 and it obtained university status in 1992. It is the largest and most prestigious technical university in Kyrgyzstan. Its library collection has about 500,000 holdings, one of the largest collections of technical literature in the republic. The university has four faculties, five specialized institutes, and several specialized centers. There are also a business school, printing center, computer center, sport center, and more than 60 scientific laboratories. Since the 1960s the Printing Center of the FPI has been publishing a university newspaper, the *Collection of Scientific Studies* series, and a series of academic books.

The university also offers degrees by evening and correspondence courses. It also has a postgraduate studies program at its *aspirantura* and *doktorantura*, upon completion of which, students are awarded degrees of **kandidat nauk** and **doktor nauk**, respectively. All students are enrolled in full-time five-year undergraduate degree programs or three-year *aspirantura* programs. In 1992 the FPI was renamed the Kyrgyz Technical University. It teaches mainly in the Kyrgyz and Russian languages, although since the early 1990s the FPI has increasingly moved toward replacing Russian with the **Kyrgyz language** in all faculties and departments. In 2002 the university enrolled about 10,000 students, including around 200 international students, in 15 departments for undergraduate and postgraduate studies. *See also* EDUCATION.

FRUNZE, MIKHAIL (1885–1925). Commander of the Red Army troops in Central Asia and one of the founders of the regular Soviet army. Born in Pishpek (now **Bishkek**) to the family of a Moldavian medical practitioner, Mikhail Frunze graduated from the Vernyi (now Almaty, **Kazakhstan**) Gymnasium in 1904 and joined the Saint Petersburg Polytechnic Institute. While a student he joined the Bolshevik Party and was arrested several times for his revolutionary activities. In 1916 he was recruited to the tsarist army to fight against the Germans in World War I. After the Bolshevik Revolution of 1917 he became one of the prominent Red Army commanders and successfully fought against the Russian White Guards in various campaigns.

In 1919 Frunze was sent to Central Asia to battle the combined troops of the Russian White Guards and native Central Asian military regiments. His troops successfully fought against the large White Guard army of General Alexander Kolchak on the territory of contemporary Kazakhstan and the Russian Urals. In the middle of 1919 Frunze was appointed commander of the Turkistan Front. A combination of his knowledge of local Central Asian traditions and customs, his ability to deal with the native Central Asian commanders, and his personal popularity helped him to organize several successful operations in **Turkistan**, including a series of operations against the **Basmachi movement** in the **Ferghana valley** in 1919. He also defeated the **Bukhara** and Khiva Khanate troops and organized offensive of the sizable Basmachi movement on the territory of contemporary **Uzbekistan**. In the fall of 1920 Frunze was transferred to the Ukraine, where he commanded the Red Army troops in the military campaign against General Petr Vrangel. In 1921–22 he led the Ukrainian delegation to Turkey, which conducted the peace negotiations between the Ukraine and Turkey. Between 1922 and 1925 he held various military positions. He authored several books and articles on tactics and offensive operations in contemporary 20th-century wars, which became textbooks at all military Red Army colleges during the Soviet era. Commander Frunze died in 1925 under suspicious circumstances, allegedly by poisoning at the order of Josef Stalin. Pishpek, the capital of Kyrgyzstan, was named after Frunze from 1926 to 1991.

– G –

GANCI AIRBASE. *See* U.S. MILITARY AIRBASE.

GAP. In traditional Central Asian society a group of friends or neighbors who get together for entertainment or discussion of various political or nonpolitical issues or for mutual support through consultancy or other means. The *gap* traditionally consists of people of the same sex: a female *gap* and a male *gap*, and they always have their parties or meetings separately. Nowadays the tradition of *gap* is more popular in southern Kyrgyzstan.

GOLD. Gold has been mined in Kyrgyzstan since the Soviet era, although in small volumes. In the 1960s and 1970s several geological expeditions explored and mapped around 30 prospective deposits. The proven reserves are believed to be between 500 and 700 tons. However, inadequate technologies and remoteness of most of the gold deposits made gold mining unprofitable during that time. On the eve of Kyrgyzstan's independence only the Makmalsky enterprise was operating mines in **Naryn** *oblast*, extracting about 1.2 tons of gold annually.

In the early 1990s Kyrgyzstan opened its gold mining sector to international investors and after a series of intensive negotiations signed its first contract. The largest joint venture project was established with Cameco International (a Canadian mining company), which received exclusive rights to extract gold in the **Kumtor** area (**Ysyk Kol** *oblast*). By 2002 the Kumtor gold mining enterprise had developed its extracting capacity to 20–22 tons annually, which is expected to rise to 25–28 tons annually between 2005 and 2010 and to begin declining after 2010 or 2012.

The **government** of Kyrgyzstan intends to open an international tender for several new potentially significant gold deposits. However, these plans were delayed due to the volatility of the gold price in the late 1990s.

GORNO-BADAKHSHAN AUTONOMOUS OBLAST. *See* BADAKHSHAN.

GOVERNMENT. The **constitution of Kyrgyzstan** provides that the government bears the executive power and directs the ministries, state committees, administrative agencies, and local state administration. The head of the government is the prime minister (the chairman of the Council of Ministers until 1992). The president of Kyrgyzstan appoints a prime minister with the consent of the **Jogorku Kenesh** (parliament). The parliament has the power to adopt a vote of nonconfidence in the prime minister by not less than two-thirds of the total number of members of parliament. *See also* CONSTITUTION OF KYRGYZSTAN (in Appendix A).

GREAT GAME. A term widely used to describe the bitter 19th-century Anglo-Russian rivalry for influence in Central Asia. British and Russian strategists (mainly young military officers) saw the need for influence over Central Asia from a strategic perspective. They argued that most military campaigns against the Indian subcontinent were undertaken through the territory of Central Asia, which at that time included **Afghanistan** and the eastern part of Iran. Thus, for the British, the primary influence over Central Asia was pivotal for defending their interests in India against Russian encroachment. In the meantime for **Russia** it was crucial to defend its communications lines with Siberia and the Russian Far East, the "soft underbelly" of the **Russian Empire** in Winston Churchill's words.

The British and Russians, joined by the French and Germans, undertook a number of highly adventurous geographic expeditions and espionage/counterespionage operations in search of allies and routes for troops, glorified by such writers as Rudyard Kipling. The Russians conducted the first expedition to Khiva in 1839–40, but the campaign was unsuccessful, and they lost a number of solders and officers in this ill-prepared expedition. Then in 1842 two British officers, Colonel Charles Stuart and Captain Arthur Connolly, were hanged in Bukhara. The Russians collided with the **Kokand Khanate** when they captured Tashkent (1865), an important economic outpost of the khanate, Khodzhent (1866), and later Kokand (1875). The Russian Empire then established its influence over the Bukhara Khanate (1868), advancing all the way to the borders of Afghanistan, the last political barrier before India. Perceiving this as a direct threat to British interests in India, the British advanced northwest in an attempt to establish direct control over Afghanistan.

In the 18th century Ahmad Shah (1747–73), the leader of the Abdali tribe of the Pushtuns, proclaimed Afghan rule as far to the east as Kashmir and Delhi, north to the Amu Darya, and west into northern Persia. In the 19th century, as internal conflicts gradually weakened the Afghan empire, both the British in India and the Russians to the north sought to bring Afghanistan under their control. This resulted in two Anglo-Afghan wars (1838–42 and 1878–80). After a devastating defeat and the loss of an expedition army, the British finally won, establishing their dominance over Afghanistan's foreign relations. Gradually, both sides, British and Russian, accepted Afghanistan as a buffer zone between their respective empires.

The strategic importance of Central Asia was highlighted again in the early 20th century by Sir Halford John Mackinder, the British political geographer, who in 1919–20 went as a British high commissioner to southern Russia in an attempt to unify the White Russian forces against the Bolsheviks. He produced a simple geopolitical formula: "Who rules the Heartland [which included Central Asia] commands the World-Island [Eurasian continent]. Who rules the World-Island commands the World."

Since the Soviet Union's dissolution in 1991 a new competition for political influence and a share in the Central Asian market, especially for its natural resources, has emerged between various actors. This competition has often been described in terms of establishing influence over the newly independent Central Asian republics on a basis strategically similar to the competition between Britain and Russia in the 19th century. In 2001 the fist **U.S. military airbase** was established in

Manas airport in Kyrgyzstan; in response to this move, Russia established the **Russian military base** in Kant in Kyrgyzstan in 2002.

GREAT SILK ROAD (also *Jibek Jolu* in Kyrgyz). An ancient trade route that connected **China** with Western Europe. Over 6,000 kilometers long the road started somewhere in what is now central and northern China, passed through China's western provinces and crossed the **Tian-Shan** and **Pamir mountains** and continued through **Uzbekistan** and **Afghanistan** to the eastern Mediterranean Sea and to Byzantium or Rome. Merchants carried wool, **gold**, silver, and weaponry eastward and brought silk, opium, spices, and luxury goods westward.

The first recorded references to the Great Silk Road could be dated to the second–first centuries B.C. The road had its peaks when there was peace in the vast steppe of Eurasia and its nadirs when there were wars in the region. The Venetian Marco Polo (1254–1324) traveled over the road and reached the court of the grandson of Genghis Khan, Kublai Khan (1215–94), the Mongol emperor, becoming the first European who traveled and described the Great Silk Road. The Great Silk Road contributed immensely to the wealth of Central Asian cities on the trade route, but disappeared in the 18th–19th centuries with the rise of cheaper maritime routes from Europe to India and China.

Frequent military campaigns and changes in political conditions and the climate redrew the routes of the Great Silk Road over time. Several of them passed Kyrgyz land in the medieval era, contributing to the rise of several cities, such as **Balasagun, Uzgen, Osh,** and some others. Numerous remains of *karavan-sarais* can still be found on the territory of present-day Kyrgyzstan. In the 1990s, with the opening of the borders between China and the Central Asian republics, the routes of the Great Silk Road became popular among adventuresome tourists.

GUMBEZ. See KUMBEZ.

GUTNICHENKO, LARISA (1947–). Kyrgyz politician. Born in Frunze (now **Bishkek**), Larisa Gutnichenko graduated from the Faculty of Law of **Kyrgyz State (National) University** in 1972. From 1973 to 1974 she worked as a senior-consultant at the Ministry of

Justice and Department of Justice in **Ysyk Kol** *oblast*. From 1974 to 1983 she held various positions in the Ysyk Kol *oblast* court and from 1983 to 1984 she worked at the Central Committee of the **Communist Party of Kyrgyz SSR**. From 1994 to 1995 Gutnichenko was the deputy chairperson of the High Court of Kyrgyzstan and she held the post of minister of justice 1995–96. From 1996 to 1998 she served as deputy prime minister for social and cultural policy.

In 1999 Gutnichenko was appointed resident representative of the Kyrgyz **government** in the **Jogorku Kenesh** (parliament). Gutnichenko was among the few **women** in post-Soviet Kyrgyzstan who held ministerial positions.

– H –

HAJJ. The sacred pilgrimage to the holy city of Mecca for all practicing Muslims. It is an important religious duty and one of the fundamentals of the Islamic creed. A person who performed the *Hajj* is called *Hajji* or *Hojji*. *See also* ISLAM.

HEALTH CARE SYSTEM. The Soviet state introduced a free mass health care system in the **Kyrgyz Republic**. Between 1917 and 1973 the number of hospitals grew from six (100 beds) to 268 (33,500 beds). There were 10 beds for every 1,000 inhabitants of the republic. In 1971 there were 6,600 doctors for a population of 3.8 million or one doctor per 468 people, and 20,000 intermediate-level personnel. All major operations, care, and prescription drugs at hospitals were provided free of charge. During the Soviet era the majority of specialized clinics and hospitals were concentrated in Frunze (now **Bishkek**) and **Osh**, but medical doctors were also relatively evenly represented in all major towns and cities.

After 1991 Kyrgyzstan experienced difficulties in supporting the free universal health care system and between 1992 and 1999 the **government** deeply cut the expenditure on health care. The health care system and admission to hospitals remains free; however, the patients are required to pay for their medication and care. In the 1990s several hospitals were privatized and doctors were allowed to open private practices. However, there was a significant deterioration in the quality of the health care system, water sanitation, and prevention of infectious diseases, as underfunded hospitals could not provide adequate services. In 2002 Kyrgyzstan spent 1.9 percent of its gross domestic product for the health care system, down from 3.4 percent in 1994. In 2000 the birth rate in Kyrgyzstan stood at 21.53 per 1,000, while the death rate stood at 5.51 per 1,000. Maternal and infant mortality grew significantly, although it remains far below such countries as Pakistan or India. In 2002–03 some international organizations expressed their concern about a possible outbreak of AIDS, tuberculosis, malaria, and sexually transmitted diseases in Kyrgyzstan, and they offered their assistance.

HIZB-UT-TAHRIR. The largest nonmainstream political group based in the **Ferghana valley** and active in **Batken, Jalal Abad,** and **Osh** *oblasts* in southern Kyrgyzstan. Since 1999–2000 it was also increasingly active in some parts of northern Kyrgyzstan, notably in **Bishkek** and **Chui** *oblast.* The organization declared that it would promote the Islamic creed and Islamic awareness in the republic by peaceful means. It also declared that it supported social justice and rule of Islamic Law (**Shariah**) and was opposed to extremes of western capitalism and its immorality. The Hizb-Ut-Tahrir claimed up to 20,000 supporters in various parts of the republic, although the exact number is unknown.

In 2000, 2001, and again in 2002 the Kyrgyz **National Security Service** and *militsia* launched a major crackdown on the group, which was justified mainly by alleged support of and links to the Taliban movement in **Afghanistan** and radical Islamic groups such as the **Islamic Movement of Uzbekistan.** Also, after the 11 September 2001 attacks in New York, there were alleged links to or sympathies toward Osama bin Laden. Kyrgyzstan officials also claimed that they had proof that the organization's ultimate plans were to establish an Islamic state in Central Asia. The Hizb-Ut-Tahrir denied any terrorist links. However, its credentials were undermined by the reports that several Kyrgyz citizens were arrested along with the Taliban fighters between November 2001 and March 2002; they were allegedly recruited through the Hizb-Ut-Tahrir network. *See also* ISLAM; UNOFFICIAL MUSLIM CLERGY.

HOJA (also *Khoja, Khaja*). 1. A title for people or groups of people who claim their descent from the Prophet Muhammad through his daughter Fatima and her husband Ali or from companions of the

Prophet Muhammad who arrived in Central Asia with the first wave of Arabs in the seventh century A.D. There are several extended families in southern Kyrgyzstan and in Namangan (Nomongon) *oblast* of **Uzbekistan** who claim this title. Traditionally *hojas* have a significant influence in the local communities. 2. A title sometimes used to refer to respected members of society (usually scholars of **Islam**) and high-ranking government or religious officials in a **khan's** palace, who are not necessarily descendants of the Prophet.

HOJA NASREDDIN. A popular folk hero in satirical stories and anecdotes. He defended poor people against corrupt government officials or greedy members of communities. During the tsarist and Soviet era the stories about Hoja Nasreddin were widely used to criticize indirectly the shortcomings of the regimes and political practices.

HOKIM. *See AKIM*

HORSE. In the traditional nomadic society horses played an important role not only as means of economic activities but also in everyday life, and the symbol of horse is a part in art and oral traditions. For centuries horse herding was one of the most important pillars of economic activities of the Kyrgyz society, as it provided a means of life, **transportation,** and trade for the **Kyrgyzs.** Horses are also raised for meat used to prepare Kyrgyz national sausages—*kazy*. Mare's milk is used to prepare the national fermented drink—*kymyz* (*kumys*). During the Soviet era several *kolkhozes* and *sovkhozes* in Kyrgyzstan specialized in raising these animals on a large scale. The total number of horses in the collective farms reached approximately 248,000 in 1979. Kyrgyzstan was among the top five producers of horse meat and *kymyz* in the former USSR.

Through centuries of breeding, the Kyrgyz farmers succeeded in producing a local breed of horse, the *Kyrgyz horse*. This horse is raised mainly in Kyrgyzstan, **Kazakhstan, Tajikistan,** and **Uzbekistan** since ancient times. The Kyrgyz horse is small (average height of about 140 centimeters) and solid, and it has strong short legs. It is well adapted to the harsh climate of the mountainous terrains and has a high fertility rate and it is often used for riding and carrying goods to *jayloo*. During the Soviet era, however, Kyrgyzs increasingly turned to raising racehorses.

In the 1990s a combination of lost state subsidies, mismanagement, and difficulties of transition to private farming negatively affected horse herding in Kyrgyzstan. Nevertheless, according to the official statistics the number of horses increased to approximately 353,000 in 2001. *See also* AGRICULTURE.

HUKMAT. 1. Term used in southern Kyrgyzstan in reference to the duty or obligation to the state. 2. Service.

HUKUMAT. 1. Term used in southern Kyrgyzstan in reference to the **government** or to state administration. 2. Supreme power.

HURJUM (also *paranja*). A veil that covered the faces of Muslim women in Central Asia, worn in public until the middle of the 1920s. Kyrgyz **women** traditionally did not wear *hurjum,* although it was compulsory in the major cities and religious centers in the **Ferghana valley.** In the middle of the 1920s the Soviet government launched a campaign against wearing *hurjum,* and by the end of the 1930s most of the women stopped wearing it. A tradition of wearing *hurjum* began to return in the 1990s, as some women started to wear it under pressure from members of devout religious families, mainly in southern Kyrgyzstan.

– I –

IMANALIYEV, MURATBEK (1956–). Kyrgyz politician and diplomat. Born in Frunze (now **Bishkek**), Muratbek Imanaliyev graduated from the Institute of Asia and Africa of Moscow State University in 1978 and the *aspitantura* of the Institute of Vostokovedeniya (Institute of Oriental studies) of the Academy of Sciences of the USSR (Moscow) in 1982. He joined the Soviet Ministry of Foreign Affairs in 1982. From 1982 to 1989 he worked at the Soviet embassy in **China** and also held various positions in the Soviet Ministry of Foreign Affairs (Moscow). In 1991 he moved from **Russia** to Kyrgyzstan.

From 1991 to 1992 Imanaliyev served as the minister of foreign affairs of Kyrgyzstan. From 1993 to 1996 he was ambassador of the **Kyrgyz Republic** in China and from 1996 to 1997 he served as head of the International Department of President **Askar Akayev**'s administration.

In 1998 he was reappointed as minister of foreign affairs. In May 2002 Imanaliyev lost his position due to the fall of the cabinet, but in 2003 he was named one of the 20 most influential politicians in the republic.

Imanaliyev played an important role in the republic's foreign policies, especially in the late 1990s. He took part in various negotiations with the United States and Western governments and international institutions, such as the International Monetary Fund and World Bank. He was considered an architect of the resolution of the territorial disputes and territorial delimitation with China. He has the rank of extraordinary and plenipotentiary ambassador. He has authored more than 40 articles and brochures. *See also* CHINA-KYRGYZSTAN BORDER DELIMITATION.

INDUSTRY. Industrialization arrived in Kyrgyzstan in the 1930s and 1940s with large investments from the central government of the Union of Soviet Socialist Republics (USSR) in the industrial sector, especially military plants, **mining,** and agricultural product processing. Between 1929 and 1959 the industrial sector in Kyrgyzstan grew at annual rate of about 12–28 percent. In the 1970s and 1980s Kyrgyzstan's **government** directed significant investments into hydroelectric production facilities, becoming one of apse of regional cooperation and the traditional Soviet market, in the 1990s Kyrgyzstan's industry underwent considerable downsizing. By 2001 Kyrgyzstan increasingly relied on exports of mineral resources, though there were efforts made to revive the manufacturing sector.

The manufacturing industry was one of the fastest growing sectors of the economy in the 1960s and 1970s, though it was relatively inefficient and production was of low quality due to a quantitative approach and excessive state control. The manufacturing industry was traditionally organized around large military and machinery plants as well as agricultural product processing, leather goods, and carpets. Until 1991, 98 percent of these goods were produced for export to the other republics of the Soviet Union and to Eastern Europe. **Russia** was the main market for the equipment and machinery produced at Kyrgyzstan's plants.

In the 1990s the government introduced a privatization program aimed at stimulating private initiative and increasing productivity. However, Kyrgyzstan's manufacturing industry collapsed in the mid-1990s. The steep decline was attributed to a combination of factors, such as inability to compete internationally due to inefficient technologies and lack of management skills and inadequate domestic and international investments. According to the **National Statistical Committee**, the manufacturing sector accounted for 5.7 percent of GDP in 2000, down from 27.7 percent in 1990. *See also* MINING.

INTERNATIONAL TRADE. During the Soviet era Kyrgyzstan's international trade was limited and tightly controlled by Moscow-based companies and ministries. Since 1991 Kyrgyzstan has been trading directly with the outside world and has significantly increased its international trade, although the trade volumes have fluctuated considerably, experiencing a dramatic decline in the first half of the 1990s but recovering in the early 2000s. In international markets Kyrgyzstan sells its primary natural resources (such as **gold**, electric energy, gemstones, etc.) and agricultural products (such as cotton, leather, tobacco, etc.), as well as products of its manufacturing sector (such as textile, footwear, garments, etc.). It buys mainly manufactured products, machinery, medical supplies, petroleum, gas, and some others.

Russia was traditionally the primary trading partner of Kyrgyzstan, although during the 1990s Kyrgyzstan managed to diversify its markets, and Germany, **China,** and Turkey became fast-growing trade partners. According to the **National Statistical Committee** in 2001 exports to **Russia, Kazakhstan,** and **Uzbekistan** amounted to about 14, 8, and 10 percent of Kyrgyzstan's total exports, respectively, while exports to Germany reached 22 percent, to Switzerland about 27 percent, and to China about 4 percent (excluding border and small-scale retail trade). In terms of imports, in 2001 Russia remained the primary source of imports totaling about 20 percent. Meanwhile imports from Uzbekistan reached 13.5 percent, from Kazakhstan 18 percent, from the United States 6 percent, and from Canada about 3 percent.

IORDAN, ANDREI (1934–). Kyrgyz politician. Born in Klarus village in Saratov *oblast* (**Russia**), Andrei Iordan graduated from the **Frunze Polytechnic Institute** in 1960. From 1964 to 1972 he climbed from the position of a worker and engineer to the position of director of the Kara Suu auto-repairing plant (**Osh** *oblast*). From 1972 to 1979 he held various positions in the Ministry of **Transportation**. From 1979 to 1983 he was deputy minister of transportation and from 1983 to

1987 he worked as chairman of the state committee on petroleum. Iordan was minister of transportation 1987–89. From 1989 to 1991 he served as deputy chairman of the Council of Ministers and from 1992 to 1993 he was minister of trade. From 1993 to 1994 he was the deputy prime minister and minister of trade and **industry**. He was minister for trade and industry 1994–96. In 1996 he was appointed minister of foreign trade and industry.

Iordan played an important role in the republic's **government** during most of the difficult years for Kyrgyzstan's economy. He was considered one of the most experienced government officials and one of the least involved in politics. *See also* INTERNATIONAL TRADE.

ISFARA CONFLICT (also known as Isfara events). In July 1989 a quarrel between local communities of **Kyrgyzs** and Tajiks over land and water usage turned into turmoil and clashes around the town of Isfara, which is situated on the border between **Kyrgyzstan** and **Tajikistan**.

This conflict had a lengthy history, as there were long-standing disputes over the borders, which were arbitrarily established in the 1920s. During the 20th century the Tajik population in the border area had grown rapidly and by the 1980s the district around the Tajik town of Isfara had become one of the most densely populated places in the **Ferghana valley**. In the meantime on Kyrgyzstan's side of the border the population had also grown, especially in the 1970s and 1980s. Low intensity frictions between the two ethnic groups took place in 1982 and 1988, but the conflict in 1989 unfolded on a much larger scale.

In July 1989, at a time when drinking and irrigation water was in high demand, a large crowd gathered on both sides of the border arguing about the water usage. At one point the people overcame the group of *militsia* officers, who stood between the rivals, and clashed. The conflict was based on this communal disagreement, rather than on political or religious differences. The events led to human casualties, as several people were killed and dozens were injured.

The mediation of **government** officials, *aksakals,* and local *mahallya* (neighborhood community) leaders brought the conflict to an end, but tensions between the communities remained for nearly a decade. By the end of 2002 there were reports of new quarrels in the area. *See also* BORDER DELIMITATION IN THE 1990s.

ISHIMOV, BEKSULTAN (1947–). Kyrgyz politician. Born in Charvak village in **Osh** *oblast* (southern Kyrgyzstan), Ishimov graduated from the Kyrgyz Physical (Sport) Education Institute in 1969. From 1969 to 1971 he was conscripted into the Soviet **army**. In 1971 he joined the Ministry of Internal Affairs, as head of a field operation group. From 1975 to 1976 he worked as deputy head of the political department of the ministry and from 1978 to 1980 he was instructor of the administrative department of the Central Committee of the **Communist Party of Kyrgyz SSR.** From 1986 to 1988 Ishimov worked as head of the **Naryn** province office of the Ministry of Internal Affairs. He served as deputy minister of internal affairs 1988–89. From 1989 to 1990 he was head of the Juridical Department of the Central Committee. From 1990 to 1995 Ishimov was chairman of the Parliamentary Commission on Defense, National Security and Law and from 1995 to 1996 he was the president's representative in the **Jogorku Kenesh** (parliament). In 1996 he was appointed as secretary of the **Security Council** and concurrently head of the department of the presidential administration. In 1999 he was appointed rector of the Academy of the Internal Affairs Ministry of the **Kyrgyz Republic**.

Ishimov played a significant role in the development of the republic's defense policy in the post-Soviet era as a strong administrator and head of the parliamentary commission.

ISLAM. One of the major world religions founded by the Prophet Muhammad in Arabia at the beginning of the seventh century A.D. Arab troops reached the territory of contemporary Kyrgyzstan in the middle of the eighth century and established a strong presence in the **Ferghana valley**. In a decisive battle in 751, the Arabs and Chinese fought each other in the **Talas valley,** where both armies suffered huge losses and both retreated, but Islam ultimately established its roots in the region. The Kyrgyz tribes had regular contacts with the Islamic world through traders and dervishes (members of Sufi orders) who traveled in the region and along the **Great Silk Road** between the ninth and 12th centuries. Probably some time between the 12th and 15th centuries a significant number of **Kyrgyzs** began to convert to Islam. Nonetheless, conversion of the Kyrgyzs to Islam was a long process and took several centuries, as even in the 19th century some travelers reported shamanistic traditions among the Kyrgyzs. Most contemporary scholars of religion in Central Asia believe that Islam was introduced to the Kyrgyz through activities of the Sufi orders. The strong influence of **Sufism** can be observed in local traditions and incorporation of some local rituals and beliefs in everyday life.

The Soviet authorities generally tolerated the Islamic creed in the early 1920s. The approach was radically changed under Josef Stalin's leadership in the second half of the 1920s and in the 1930s. Some mosques were destroyed and some **mullahs** were executed, sent to Siberia (**Russia**), or escaped to **Afghanistan**, Xinjiang (**China**), and Turkey. After World War II the Soviet government generally tolerated Islamic practices, insofar as they were private actions and did not interfere with public life. However, it established a strict control over the registration of mosques and mullahs; thus, many Muslims sought the help of **unofficial Muslim clergy** to practice their religion. Kyrgyzstan experienced a major resurgence of Islam in the 1980s and 1990s, as almost 700 mosques were built and a significant number of people turned to practicing the religion. Yet both the Soviet constitution of 1978 and the 1993 **constitution of Kyrgyzstan** declared that the republic is a secular state. Islam traditionally maintains a strong presence and influence in **Jalal Abad** and **Osh** *oblast* and less so in northern Kyrgyzstan.

According to official statistics around 95 percent of Kyrgyz are Sunni Muslims of the Hanafi school, along with their Central Asian neighbors and Turks. According to Kyrgyz **mass media** reports less than 2 percent of the citizens support radical Islamic groups. *See also* HIZB-UT-TAHRIR; ISLAMIC DEMOCRATIC PARTY OF KYRGYZSTAN; KAZI; KAZIAT; MUFTI; MUFTIAT.

ISLAMIC DEMOCRATIC PARTY OF KYRGYZSTAN (IDPK)

(**Kyrgyzstandyn Islam Demokratialyk Partiasy in Kyrgyz**). An Islamic organization established on 20 July 2002. The IDPK claims up to about 100,000 supporters, mainly in **Chui, Jalal Abad,** and **Osh** *oblasts,* though the exact number is unknown and probably is less then 5,000. It was established by Narkas Mulladjanov in order to bring Islamic groups into the mainstream politics of Kyrgyzstan in response to a crackdown against the **Hizb-Ut-Tahrir** and other Islamic groups. However, the IDPK had problems with official registration as the **Constitution of Kyrgyzstan** banned political parties based on a religious ideology. In its political program the party declared that it would promote Islamic awareness among the population and defend the Muslim community from the negative influence of the West. *See also* ISLAM; KAZI; KAZIAT; MUFTI; MUFTIAT; UNOFFICIAL MUSLIM CLERGY.

ISLAMIC MOVEMENT OF UZBEKISTAN (IMU) (Uzbekistandyn Islam Kyimyly—in Kyrgyz). The largest radical Islamic group of Uzbekistan based in the **Ferghana valley**. It is active in the Andijan, Namangan, and **Ferghana** *oblasts* of **Uzbekistan** and in **Osh** *oblast* in southern Kyrgyzstan. The IMU claims up to about 3,000–4,000 active members and about 9,000–12,000 supporters. It has its roots in several Islamic youth groups, which emerged in the Ferghana valley in the early 1990s and attempted to promote and enforce Islamic practices among local communities. IMU members were active during the civil war in **Tajikistan,** fighting alongside the Islamic opposition. Allegedly they received substantial financial assistance from the Middle East and training assistance from **Afghanistan** in the mid-1990s. There were unconfirmed reports that some IMU members were involved in lucrative drugs trafficking from Afghanistan to Europe.

In 1998 and 1999 the Uzbekistan government launched a crackdown campaign blaming the movement of killing police officials in Namangan and masterminding an assassination attempt on President Islam Karimov of Uzbekistan in 1999. A number of active members and supporters of the IMU were arrested and the IMU leaders moved to northeastern Tajikistan where they established their stronghold. In 1999 and 2000 there were **militant incursions,** as the IMU attempted to infiltrate from Tajikistan to Uzbekistan via Kyrgyzstan and to capture several villages and a number of hostages, but in a series of battles the IMU was expelled from both Kyrgyzstan and Uzbekistan. In 2001 it moved to Afghanistan and fought along with Al-Qaida against the U.S. troops and experienced severe losses. *See also* ISLAM; UNOFFICIAL MUSLIM CLERGY.

ISLAMIC UNIVERSITY OF KYRGYZSTAN. A university established in **Bishkek** in 1991. It was sponsored mainly from overseas sources and some donations from local communities. Its curriculum was developed with the help of expatriates from Turkey and the Middle East, and it contains mainly religious disciplines and the Arabic language, although some secular subjects are taught as well. The Kyrgyz *muftiat* is formally in charge of the university and it hopes to establish in-country training for native Islamic scholars and **mullahs** and to reduce the number of students who are educated in various Islamic schools and universities in the Middle East and Turkey. In 2002 there were approximately 400 students enrolled in the five-year programs at the two faculties—Faculty of **Shariah** and Arabic Language and Faculty of Religious Studies.

ISSYK-KUL CITY. *See* BALYKCHI.

ISSYK-KUL FORUM (also Isyk Kol Forum). A public organization founded by writer **Chingiz Aitmatov** in 1986 to discuss important global and regional political, environmental, and cultural issues. The Issyk-Kul Forum was styled as a free-format discussion club for leading intellectuals and held its meetings in various places in Kyrgyzstan, **Russia,** and Switzerland with a regular frequency in the 1980s.

Many **Commonwealth of Independent States** (CIS) and world political leaders, prominent writers, and philosophers participated in the forum, including Peter Ustinov, Arthur Miller, James Baldwin, Suleiman Demirel (Turkish president), Mikhail Gorbachev (former USSR president), President **Askar Akayev,** and others. In the 1990s the forum held its meetings at irregular intervals.

The last congress took place in 1997 in **Bishkek** and it was attended by then Kyrgyz prime minister Apas Joumagulov, Chingiz Aitmatov (the founder of the Forum), Federiko Major (UNESCO director general), Yevgenii Yevtushenko (Russian poet), Mukhtar Shakhanov (Kazakh poet, Kazakh ambassador to the Kyrgyz Republic), and some other prominent figures.

ISSYK-KUL LAKE. *See* YSYK KOL LAKE.

ISSYK-KUL *OBLAST.* *See* YSYK KOL *OBLAST.*

ISSYK-KUL VALLEY. *See* YSYK KOL VALLEY.

– J –

JADIDISM (from Arabic *Jadid* new). A reformist movement in Central Asia and the **Russian Empire,** which emerged in the early 20th century. Its members (Jadidists) called for a reformation of Islamic society and introduction of new approaches to politics, social relations, and especially **education**. The movement originated in a Crimean Tatar reformist circle led by Ismail Gasparaly (Gasparinski). In Central Asia it was particularly influential in **Bukhara** and Tashkent. In the 1910s the Jadidists established a network of schools (reformed or Jadidist schools) with a new curriculum all over Central Asia, including the Kyrgyz land.

JAGATAI. *See* CHAGATAI.

JALAL ABAD CITY (also *Dzhalal Abad*). This is the third largest city in the republic, after **Bishkek** and **Osh**, the fifth largest industrial center, and the capital of **Jalal Abad** *oblast*. The city is located in southern Kyrgyzstan, 300 kilometers southwest of Bishkek. Its population stood at about 71,900 (1999 census), up from about 55,400 (1979 census), consisting mainly of **Kyrgyzs** and Uzbeks, but it also included significant communities of Russians, Ukrainians, Tatars, Germans, and some others. It is an important industrial and **transportation** center in southern Kyrgyzstan. There are light **industry**, machinery production, automobile assembling, cotton and tobacco-processing plants, and an oil refinery. It is also an **education** center of the southern part of the republic with Jalal Abad State University (founded in 1993), University of Peoples' Friendship, Jalal Abad Commercial Institute (founded in 1993), Jalal Abad Technical Institute (founded in 2000), a medical college, an agricultural college, and Jalal Abad Kyrgyz-Turkish high school. The cultural life of the city revolves around its libraries, a theater, philharmonic orchestra, and a museum. As an *oblast* center the city is a transportation hub with its own airport and railway station.

Jalal Abad was founded as a small village in the late 19th century. Most of its growth, however, occurred in the middle of the 20th century, as the Soviet authorities invested in the development of local industries and cotton production and processing. In 1939 the city became the capital of the newly established Jalal Abad *oblast* (the status was abolished in 1959 and reestablished in 1990). As the city was largely expanded in the 1960s and 1970s, its **architecture** reflects the combination of Soviet functionalism and faceless mass construction. Most of the buildings were built of red bricks or concrete, making its central streets similar to all other cities of the republic, although private construction, especially after 1991, added an Oriental flavor to Jalal Abad's architecture. During the post-Soviet era the city's infrastructure experienced visible decay, as many businesses and industries fell into a deep recession or went out of business.

JALAL ABAD *OBLAST* (also *Dzhalal Abad oblast*). The second most populous *oblast* in Kyrgyzstan, located in the southern part of the republic, bordered by **Naryn** *oblast* in the east, **Osh** *oblast* in the south, **Uzbekistan** in the west, **Talas** *oblast* in the north, and the **Chui** *oblast* in the northeast. Jalal Abad *oblast* was formed in 1992 and consists of Aksy, Ala Buka, Bazar Korgon, Nooken, Suzak, Toguz Toro, Toktogul, and Chatkal *raions* (districts). Jalal Abad *oblast* has a total area of about 33,700 square kilometers and is the third largest *oblast* of the republic, with over 16 percent of its territory. Its **population** stood at about 869,300 (1999 census), or about 18 percent of the country's population, up from about 586,700 (1979 census). It is one of the least urbanized *oblast*s in the republic, as nearly 77 percent of the people live in rural areas. Its population is heterogeneous in terms of ethnic composition. **Kyrgyzs** account for 69.8 percent of the population, and Jalal Abad is the home of the second largest Uzbek community (24.4 percent), after Osh *oblast*. Others include Russians (2 percent), Tajiks (0.8 percent), Turks, and Kazakhs.

Jalal Abad *oblast* hosts almost 20 percent of the country's industrial enterprises. **Agriculture**, light **industry**, petrochemicals, and **mining** are the main sectors of its economy. During the Soviet era Jalal Abad received considerable investments for building hydroelectric power plants (the Toktogul groups of hydroelectric powers stations is among the largest in Central Asia) and consumer electrical products.

In 2000 the *oblast* produced nearly 88 percent of the republic's electricity, 100 percent of its electric bulbs, and 100 percent of its oil and gas, and refined 100 percent of its gasoline. The second largest **gold** field is also situated in Jalal Abad.

In the early 1990s the *oblast* experienced economic difficulties due to structural changes and the disruption of communications with **Bishkek** and northern Kyrgyzstan. However, the *oblast* managed to revive its industries and to attract a sizeable share of the foreign direct investments (FDIs) in the mid-1990s. Yet a significant portion of its population, especially in rural areas, lost their jobs and moved to subsistence agriculture, and around 64 percent of the population lived below the poverty line (2001).

JANGARACHEVA, MIRA. *See* DZHANGARACHEVA, MIRA.

JANUZAKOV, BOLOT. *See* DZHANUZAKOV, BOLOT.

JAYLOO **(pronounced as jaylo'o).** 1. A highland summer pasture where Kyrgyz pastoral nomads escape from the summer heat of the low land (or *kyshtoo*—a winter pasture in the lowland valleys) with their herds of **horses** and **sheep**. Traditionally the **Kyrgyzs** took their families, leaving a few relatives to look after their housing and crops in the *kyshtoo*. The life in the *jayloo* was important for teaching critical skills and for passing on essential cultural traditions to younger generations, as several extended families worked together and regularly spent long evenings and nights awake listening to heroic epics and stories about the past and present life of Kyrgyzs from *akyns* and *manaschis*. 2. In present-day Kyrgyzstan the term is often used to refer to a place where people live a simple and pleasant life, equivalent to "Arcadia" in Greek mythology.

JEKSHEYEV, ZHYPAR (1947–). Kyrgyz politician. Born in Taldy Suu village of **Ysyk Kol** *oblast*, Zhypar Jeksheyev graduated from the Art College in Frunze (now **Bishkek**) in 1971 and from the Institute of Art in 1986. From 1971 to 1980 he held various managerial positions in the Ysyk Kol *oblast* Art Fund. From 1980 to 1988 he taught at the art college under the Ministry of Culture. From 1988 to 1989 he was chairman of the art cooperative. In 1989 Jeksheyev organized the Ashar Movement, one of the first opposition political groups in Kyrgyzstan. The Ashar defended rights of the Kyrgyz squatters. In 1990 he became the co-chairman of the newly established **Democratic Movement of Kyrgyzstan (DMK)**, which contributed significantly to the failure of First Secretary **Absamat Masaliyev** in the presidential elections of October 1990. In 1993 Jeksheyev was elected as chairman of the DMK. In 1995 he was elected as member of the **Jogorku Kenesh** (parliament).

Jeksheyev was among the founding members of democratic movements in Kyrgyzstan and contributed to the rise of the political opposition in the republic. He presented and fiercely defended a nationalistic platform, which included the immediate replacement of the Russian language by the **Kyrgyz language** in public life and **education** and various other measures. He also called for changes in the state's social policy in order to fight poverty among the population. He was considered one of the most influential members of the opposition throughout the 1990s.

JENGISH PEAK. *See* POBEDY PEAK.

JETISUU (also *Dzheti-suu* and *Semirechiye* [in Russian]—literally "seven rivers"). The area in northern Kyrgyzstan and southern **Kazakhstan** located between Lake Balkhash in the north, Lakes Sasykol and Alakol in the northeast, the Dhumgal Alatau in the southeast, and the northern **Tian-Shan mountains** in the south. The Jetisuu derives its name from the name of the seven rivers: the Ili, Karatal, Bien, Aksu, Lepsa, Baskan, and Sarkand.

In historical chronicles the Jetisuu also included the area of the **Chui valley.** The Jetisuu was one of the most important centers of Turkic culture, as the medieval centers of the Turkic Khanate (6th–8th centuries), the Turgesh Khanate (8th century), the Karluk Khanate (8th–10th centuries), and the Karakhanid Khanate (10th–12th centuries) were situated here. In the 16th century this area was under control of the Greater Horde (*Uluu Dzus*). In the middle of the 19th century the Jetisuu area was acquired by the Russians and was included in Semirechye *oblast.*

JIBEK JOLU. See GREAT SILK ROAD.

JIENBEKOV, SADRIDDIN. *See* DZHIENBEKOV, SADRIDDIN.

JIGIT **(also *dzhigit*).** 1. A horse rider or warrior. 2. In present-day Kyrgyzstan the term is often used to refer to a brave and energetic young man.

JIHAD (holy battle, campaign). One of the central concepts in **Islam**, which obliges Muslims to spread and strengthen Islam in the world. According to the Islamic scholarly interpretation of the concept, Jihad can be carried in four ways: by heart, by sword, by hand, and by tongue. It should be directed against evil desires, actions, or enemies. There is no clear concept of who can call for Jihad by sword. In the 19th and 20th centuries leaders of Islamic communities in Central Asia frequently called for Jihad against the tsarist authorities. The **Popular Uprising of 1898** in Andijan, the **Popular Uprising of 1916** in the **Jetisuu** (Semirechie) and **Ferghana valleys,** and the **Basmachi movement** in 1918–21 were carried out under the banner of Jihad. In the 1990s the Islamic Movement of Uzbekistan, which had some supporters in **Osh** *oblast*, declared Jihad against the regime of President Islam Karimov in Uzbekistan.

JOGORKU KENESH (Parliament of Kyrgyz Republic). Kyrgyzstan's parliament is a bicameral 105-seat legislative and representative assembly, which replaced the old Soviet-style unicameral 350-seat Jogorku Kenesh by presidential decree in October 1994. The new Jogorku Kenesh consisted of a 35-seat Legislative Assembly, the Myizam Chygaruu Jyiyny, and a 70-seat Assembly of People's Representatives, the El Okuldor Jyiyny. In 1999 several changes were introduced in the structure of the parliament, which included a change in the number of the seats of the Myizam Chygaruu Jyiyny to 60 seats and of El Okuldor Jyiyny to 45.

The current **constitution of Kyrgyzstan** stipulated that all citizens over 18 years of age are eligible to vote and that all citizens over 25 years of age resident in the republic for no fewer than five years before the election are eligible to be elected to the Jogorku Kenesh. The revised election law (1994) stipulated that the nomination of candidates should start from the day of the official publication of the list of constituencies. Candidates could be nominated by registered political parties, public organizations (such as labor collectives), and meetings of voters. Candidates are required to deposit the equivalent of 300 minimum monthly salaries with the Central Election Commission (CEC). On 29 April 1999, however, the Myizam Chygaruu Jyiyny introduced new and controversial changes in the election law, requiring political parties wishing to take part in the elections to register at least 12 months prior to the elections. On 2 February 2003 the Constitutional Referendum reintroduced single chamber Jogorku Kenesh, which "shall consist of 75 deputies elected for the term of five years from single member constituencies." However, the legality of the referendum was disputed by the opposition, opening the door for a new round of political conflict.

Members of each House of the Jogorku Kenesh elect a **toraga** (chairman) from among the members of the House and his deputy, and form committees and commissions. By law all members of the parliament (Jogorku Keneshtyn deputaty, or Muchosu) have immunity from court prosecution.

During the first years following independence in 1991, the contribution of the Jogorku Kenesh to the republic's political life was bigger than that of the legislatures in other Central Asian republics. Its influence has always been crucial for maintaining the balance between two major regional groupings, or **clans**: *Chui, Ysyk Kol, Naryn,* and *Talas* on the one hand, and *Batken, Jalal Abad,* and *Osh* on the other. Kyrgyzstan's legislature has also been an important instrument for checking and balancing the power of the executive and **government**.

Kyrgyzstan has held two parliamentary elections since independence. The first elections were conducted in February 1995 and the second elections were conducted in February–March 2000.

Party Composition of the Jogorku Kenesh after the Parliamentary Elections in Kyrgyzstan, 20 February and 12 March 2000

	No. of seats
Sojuz Demokraticheskikh Sil	12
(Union of Democratic Forces, pro-presidential)	
Partiya Kommunistov Kyrgyzstana	6
(Party of Communists of Kyrgyzstan, communist)*	
Politicheskaya Partiya "Moya Strana"	4
("My Country" Political Party, pro-presidential)	
Demokraticheskaya Partiya Zhenshchin Kyrgyzstana	2
(Democratic Women's Party of Kyrgyzstan)	
Politicheskaya Partiya Veteranov Voiny v Afganistane	2
(Party of Afghanistan's War Veterans)	
Sotsialisticheskaya Partiya Ata Meken	2
(Ata Meken Socialist Party)	
People's Party (*El* Party)	2

Progressivno-Demokraticheskaya Partiya
   "Erkin Kyrgyzstan"   1
   (Erkin Kyrgyzstan Progressive Democratic Party)
Agrarno-Trudovaya Partiya Kyrgyzstana   1
   (Agrarian Labor Party of Kyrgyzstan, agrarian)
Argarnaya Partiya Kyrgyzskoi Respubliki   –
   (Agrarian Party of the Kyrgyz Republic, agrarian)
Izbiratel'nyi Blok Manas (Manas coalition)   –
Partiya Natsional'nogo Vozrozhdeniya "Asaba"
   (Asaba Party)   –
Independent   73

* Not to be confused with Communist Party of Kyrgyzstan (Kommunisticheskaya Partiya Kyrgyzstana) led by **Klara Azhibekova**.

JOLDOSH (also *dzholdosh*). 1. Comrade. A formal title widely used in Kyrgyzstan during the Soviet era, especially with reference to a senior public or Communist Party official. 2. Friend, companion.

JUMAGULOV, APAS. *See* DZHUMAGULOV, APAS.

JUMALIYEV, KUBANYCHBEK. *See* DZHUMALIYEV, KUBANYCHBEK.

JUMHURII TOJIKISTON. *See* TAJIKISTAN.

JUSTICE PARTY (Adylet Partiasy—in Kyrgyz). A progovernment centrist party established in **Bishkek** and first registered on 22 September 1999. Among the founding members were **Chingiz Aitmatov** (chairman of the party), Mirsaid Mirrahimov, and several influential members of the progovernment intelligentsia. In its political program the party declared that it aimed at the social and economic stabilization of society. It claimed that this stabilization could be achieved through harmony in interethnic relations and defending the spiritual and economic interests of the people. The Adylet party was among the groups that endorsed a national program "Kyrgyzstan is our Common Home." The party claims up to 35,000 registered members in various *oblasts* of the republic, though about one-third of this number would probably be more accurate. Most members of the party are representatives of the urban intelligentsia.

The Adylet has been very active since its creation. It initiated several public debates and discussions and organized round tables and meetings among the intelligentsia and with **government** officials. However, it refrained from any direct criticism of the government or President **Askar Akayev** and lacks genuine support among the population. In 2002 its representatives also participated in the discussions of the government-initiated program "Kyrgyzstan is a Home for Human Rights."

– K –

KABAR (Kirgiz Telegraph Agency—KirTAG—until 1992). The largest state-controlled national news agency, which provides official information about the activities and policies of the Kyrgyzstan **government**. It was established in Frunze (now **Bishkek**) in 1937, as a branch of the Telegraph Agency of the Soviet Union (TASS), becoming an important part of the Soviet information and propaganda system.

The agency was transformed into the State Information Agency KyrgyzKabar in 1992. In 1995 it was transformed into the National Agency of Telecommunication and Information Kabar. In 2001 it was renamed the Kyrgyz National Information Agency Kabar.

Kabar prepares and publishes daily news reports and news briefs about the republic and the government. It also publishes official and diplomatic chronicles, daily reviews of national and regional events, analytical briefs, and economic information. The agency maintains its website in the **Kyrgyz language** as well as in English and Russian, though the English section gives information in a smaller format and covers only key topics. Kabar has a branch in **Osh city** and contributing reporters in all major cities of the republic. In 2001 it began to transmit audio and video reports on its website.

Kabar is a member of the Organization of National Agencies of the Asia Pacific Countries and other bodies. *See also* MASS MEDIA.

KADI. See QADI.

KAIRAN EL PARTY (Kairan El partiasy in Kyrgyz). One of the new opposition political organizations. It was registered on 24 September 1999. The party adopted a centrist political platform and called for the creation of a civil society, respect of the constitutional rights of the Kyrgyz citizens, and preservation of the cultural heritage of Kyrgyzstan. The Kairan-El claimed that it has up to 3,000 members and active supporters in **Chui, Jalal Abad,** and **Ysyk Kol** *oblasts* in 2001, although its real electorate comes mainly from **Bishkek.** Its chairperson, Dooronbek Sadyrbayev, an influential writer and movie director, was elected to the **Jogorku Kenesh** (parliament) in 1995 and was an active member of the opposition.

The Kairan-El was particularly active during the opposition campaign for release of **Felix Kulov** in 2001 and 2002. In August 2002 the party joined the "Movement for Askar Akayev's Resignation and Reforms for the People," which united 22 opposition political parties and **nongovernmental organizations** (NGOs) and demanded the immediate resignation of incumbent president **Askar Akayev.**

KALYM. See QALYM.

KANDIDAT NAUK. A postgraduate academic degree in the **Kyrgyz Republic**, equivalent to the Ph.D. degree. To obtain the degree a student has to do three years of coursework at an *aspirantura* (part time and by correspondence it takes five to six years), complete a series of exams (dubbed *kandidatskii minimum*), write an original research dissertation, and publicly defend the dissertation at a university or research institution. In addition, the Specialized (Attestation) State Commission must register and approve it. The degree was introduced in the former Union of Soviet Socialist Republics (USSR) in 1934, and the republic opted to keep the Soviet system of academic qualifications until comprehensive reforms of its **educational** system. *See also DOKTOR NAUK.*

KARA BALTA (literally "black axe" in Kyrgyz). The sixth largest city in the republic, located on the Kara Balta (also known as *Kel Bashi*) River in northern Kyrgyzstan, 62 kilometers west of **Bishkek.** Its population stood at about 47,400 (1999 census), up from about 47,300 (1979 census), consisting of mainly Russians and **Kyrgyzs**, but it also included significant communities of Ukrainians, Kazakhs, Germans (although most of them left the city in the 1990s), and some others. Kara Balta is an important industrial and **transportation** center in **Chui** *oblast*. There are textile and agricultural-processing plants, a carpet factory (largest in the republic), medical colleges, two technical colleges, an agricultural college (founded in 1938), **libraries**, and museums. The Kara Balta Hydro-Metallurgical plant processed uranium from local mines for the Soviet nuclear military and civil projects between 1955 and 1989. In 1989 the extraction of local uranium ore was stopped and the plant began processing tin-tungsten concentrate and **gold**-containing ores and assembling mining drifts, boring machines, antifriction molybdenum composition, and consumer goods. Since 1997 the plant has been processing uranium ore (about 500 tons) for the **Kazakhstan** national company Kazakhatomash.

Kara Balta was built close to the ruins of the ancient city of Shish Debe, one of the oldest known urban centers in northern Kyrgyzstan, which existed probably between the sixth and 12th centuries A.D. Some Kyrgyz historians associate Shish Debe with the ancient city Nuzket. Archeologists discovered one of the largest collections of ancient silver and copper coins on the territory of Kyrgyzstan (more than 8,000 coins dated to the 11th and 12th centuries A.D.) during the excavation of Shish Debe in the 1960s and 1970s. The city disappeared probably between the 15th and 16th centuries.

Kara Balta's importance was enhanced after the completion of the Kara Balta **railway** station in 1924 and opening of several light **industry** enterprises in the 1930s. The city has obtained national prominence because it is situated on the strategically important Bishkek-Tashkent highway and due to the presence of the Kara Balta Hydro-Metallurgical plant. The modern Kara Balta city was established after amalgamation of three villages—Kara Balta, Kosh Tegirmen, and Kalininskoye in 1975.

KARAKOL (literally "black hand" in Kyrgyz; Przhevalsk between 1889 and 1920 and between 1939 and 1991). The fourth largest city in the republic, the capital of **Ysyk Kol** *oblast*. The city is located on the Karakol River located in northeastern Kyrgyzstan, 1,690–1,825 meters above sea level, 386 kilometers east of **Bishkek,** and 150 kilometers from the Kyrgyz-**China** borders. Its population was estimated at about 65,400 (1999 census), up from about 50,800 (1979 census), consisting mainly of **Kyrgyzs**, but it also included Russians, Ukrainians, Dungans, and some others. It is an important **tourism** and commercial center in northeastern Kyrgyzstan. There are light **industries**, agricultural-processing plants, and textile and shoe factories. It also hosts the Ysyk Kol State University (founded in 1940), a campus of the Kyrgyz International Academy of Management (founded in 1991), Karakol Branch of the Moscow Management and Tourism University (founded in 1996), Islamic college (founded in 1992), a medical college, a pedagogical college of early childhood **education**, the Kyrgyz-Turkish lyceum, secondary schools, **libraries**, theaters, museums, and an airport (opened in 1934).

A small village and a trading center existed in the place of Karakol most probably for centuries, as it was situated along one of the passes of the **Great Silk Road** through the **Tian-Shan mountains**. In the early 19th century the **Kokand Khanate** advanced into the Ysyk Kol region and established a fortress at Karakol. The Kyrgyz **tribes**, however, resisted the Kokand intervention, but they were too weak and too divided to challenge the better-equipped troops of the **Khan** of Kokand. Several Kyrgyz tribal leaders tried to find outside aid, including help from the Kazakh tribes, Russians, and Chinese. It took several decades for the tsarist military forces to establish their control in this volatile part of the Kyrgyz land. In 1869 the tsarist authorities established an administrative center in Karakol, housing the Cossack troops here. In 1889 Karakol was renamed Przhevalsk, honoring Nikolai Przhevalskii (1839–88), a Russian explorer, geographer, and military officer.

In the late 19th and early 20th centuries Karakol became an important administrative, military, education, and trade center in Ysyk Kol *oblast*, as it experienced a large influx of settlers from **Russia.** The Russians opened the first library and several primary and secondary schools in the 1910s. After the Revolution of 1917 it took several years for the **Bolsheviks** to establish their full control in the area around the city. The Soviet authorities invested heavily in the development of light and agricultural products processing industries throughout the 1920s and 1930s, making Karakol the *oblast* center of the newly established Ysyk Kol *oblast* in 1939. The importance of the city was further enhanced as **border guard** troops were stationed in the city. Since 1991 Karakol has been a popular destination for tourists traveling along the Great Silk Road and from the city of

Kashgar (China) to Bishkek. In 1996 a **Free Economic Zone** (FEZ) was established in Karakol.

KARA-KYRGYZ AUTONOMOUS *OBLAST* (KKAO). The *oblast* was established on 14 October 1924, after the completion of the **border delimitation in 1924–1926** in Central Asia. It had the status of an autonomous *oblast* under the jurisdiction of the **Russian Federation**. It included parts of former Semirechenskaya, Syrdar'inskaya, Ferghanskaya, and Samarkandskaya provinces (*oblasts*) of the **Turkistan Governor-Generalship** (the **Turkistan ASSR** between 1918 and 1924). The Kara-Kyrgyz Autonomous *Oblast* was renamed the Kyrgyz Autonomous *Oblast* in May 1925. It was upgraded to the status of the **Kyrgyz Autonomous Soviet Socialist Republic** (Kyrgyz ASSR) on 1 February 1926 (also within the Russian Federation).

KARA-KYRGYZS. *See* KYRGYZS.

KARAVAN-SARAI **(also** *Karavan-seray***).** 1. A traditional guest-house or inn in the cities and towns along major routes and mountain passes. They were used as shelters by caravans and travelers in Central Asia and the Middle East. *Karavan-sarais* were usually built as a quadrangular building with small windows, large central court, and storerooms. 2. Ruins of old *Karavan-sarais* and trading outposts on the territory of Kyrgyzstan and other Central Asian republics. 3. In everyday life the term sometimes refers to a motel.

KARYPKULOV, AMANBEK (1939–). Kyrgyz politician. Born in Kara Suu village in **Talas** *oblast* (northern Kyrgyzstan), Amanbek Karypkulov graduated from the Przhevalsk Pedagogical Institute in 1962. From 1962 to 1964 he was a lecturer and concurrently the secretary of the **Komsomol** at the institute. From 1964 to 1967 he was a lecturer at the **Kyrgyz State (National) University** and from 1967 to 1983 he held various positions at the Central Committee of the **Communist Party of Kyrgyz SSR.** From 1983 to 1985 Karypkulov worked as secretary of the Central Committee. He lost his position during Mikhail Gorbachev's **perestroika.** From 1985 to 1986 he was a professor at the **Frunze Polytechnic Institute** and from 1992 to 1994 he was editor-in-chief of the *Kyrgyz Encyclopedia.* He was chairman of the *Akyl* state enterprise 1994–96 and from 1996 to 1999 he was the president of the State Television and Radio Company. From 1999 to 2002 he was the head of the presidential administration. In 2002 he was dismissed from that position and was appointed ambassador to Turkey.

Karypkulov was considered one of the most influential politicians in the late 1990s and early 2000s. He was the key architect of President **Askar Akayev**'s reelection campaign in 2000. He became notorious for taking journalists to court for "violating his honor and dignity" and for advocating harsh measures against the political opposition and **mass media**. Karypkulov resigned under accusations of mishandling the **Aksy conflict.**

KASYMBEKOV, TOLOGON (1931–). Prominent Kyrgyz writer and publicist. Born in the remote village of Akzhol in **Jalal Abad** *oblast* (southern Kyrgyzstan), Tologon Kasymbekov graduated from the faculty of philology of the **Kyrgyz State (National) University** in 1957. From 1957 to 1960 he worked as editor of a small printing house. From 1960 to 1967 he held various administrative positions at the influential *Ala-Too* literary journal. Kasymbekov became editor of the journal in 1967. From 1973 to 1990 he was senior editor in the republic's printing house and from 1990 to 1994 he was a member of the **Jogorku Kenesh** (parliament) and head of the commission on language, culture, and interethnic relations.

Kasymbekov was considered one of the most influential **Kyrgyz language** writers in the republic. In the 1980s and 1990s he played a very important role in debates on the state language, Kyrgyz cultural development, and various other issues, as he supported radical hardliners. His books (*Broken Sword, Kel-Kel,* and others) on the historical past sparked significant controversy during the Soviet era, as he was accused of promoting radical Kyrgyz nationalism. He has authored four books, numerous novels, and articles (mainly fiction stories). Even after retirement Kasymbekov remained an influential figure in the political and cultural life of Kyrgyzstan.

KAZAKHSTAN (official name Qazaqstan Respublikasy or Qazaqstan). The republic is located north of **Kyrgyzstan**, and they share 1,051 kilometers of common borders. Kazakhstan is the largest state in

Central Asia (2,717,300 square kilometers), and with a population estimated at about 16.8 million in July 2002 it is the second most populous country in the region after **Uzbekistan**. The Kazakhs account for 54 percent of the population, Russians about 28 percent, Ukrainians about 3.7 percent, Uzbeks about 2.5 percent, Germans about 2.4 percent, Uigurs about 1.4 percent, Tatars about 1.6 percent, and so on. Some 80,000 **Kyrgyzs** live in Kazakhstan, mainly in Almaty, Zhambyl, and South Kazakhstan *oblasts*.

During the 19th century the Kazakhs actively helped the Kyrgyzs in their resistance and struggle against the **Kokand Khanate**. The activities of Kazakh officers in Russian service convinced the leaders of northern Kyrgyzstan **tribes** to accept the **Russian Empire**'s advancement into the region and suzerainty.

During the Soviet era, Kazakhstan became one of the most industrially developed countries in Central Asia and one of the important destinations for Kyrgyzstan's agricultural and industrial production. Kyrgyzstan also intensively used Kazakhstan's **transportation** network, pipelines, telecommunications, and other infrastructure.

Since 1991 Kazakhstan has remained Kyrgyzstan's fourth largest trading partner. Kyrgyzstan's trade with Kazakhstan was estimated at 9 percent of its total foreign **trade**, or at US$95 million in 2000. Kyrgyzstan exported about US$35 million in goods and services, mainly products of its **agriculture** and **industry**, and imported about US$60 million in goods and services, petroleum, and machinery. Experts reported about smuggling of cheap Kyrgyz products to the southern *oblasts* of Kazakhstan and about immigration of Kyrgyz workers to Kazakhstan in search of temporary jobs. Some of **Kyrgyzstan**'s actions, such as the unilateral introduction of the national currency, the som, in 1993 and joining the **World Trade Organization** in 1998, were negatively perceived by members of Kazakhstan's government. Astana imposed temporary restrictions on imports of Kyrgyzstan's products. The Kyrgyzstan business community also complained about high fees and levies imposed by Kazakhstan customs and transportation officials on Kyrgyzstan's goods. Nevertheless, the relations between the two countries continued to be friendly throughout the 1990s, as they remained strategic partners on economic and security issues to the extent that there was speculation about a possible merger of the two states. Still, between 2000 and 2003 Bishkek demanded from Astana payments for its drinking and irrigation water. Negotiation between the two countries failed to resolve the situation and increased tensions in their relations.

In 1999 and 2000 Kazakhstan provided substantial logistic and political support to Kyrgyzstan when the latter experienced the incursion of militant groups in **Batken** *oblast* from **Tajikistan**. In late 2001 and early 2002 there were intensive security consultations between the two countries, as Kyrgyzstan agreed to host the **U.S. military airbase** at Manas airport, 50 kilometers from Kazakhstan's border and around 100 kilometers from Kazakhstan's Otar military base.

Kazakhstan along with Kyrgyzstan joined the **Central Asian Forum** (formerly Central Asian Economic Union), **Commonwealth of Independent States (CIS), CIS Collective Security Treaty**, the **Economic Cooperation Organization, Eurasian Economic Community, Organization of the Islamic Conference, Organization for Security and Cooperation in Europe, Shanghai Cooperation Organization,** and some other regional and international organizations. By 2001 Kazakhstan had resolved most of its territorial and border disputes with Kyrgyzstan within the framework of the Shanghai Cooperation Organization. *See also* JETISUU.

KAZI. 1. A legal authority in **Islam**, who interprets to the Islamic community the religious teachings and Islamic law (**Shariah**). 2. Until 1991 the highest Islamic authority in Kyrgyzstan, subordinated to the **Muftiat** of Central Asia, which had its headquarters in Tashkent (**Uzbekistan**). *See also* KAZIAT; MUFTI; UNOFFICIAL MUSLIM CLERGY.

KAZIAT. During the Soviet era, the highest Islamic decision-making body in **Kyrgyzstan** based in Frunze (now **Bishkek**). It was established in 1943 after the regime of Josef Stalin lifted some restrictions on religious activities in the Soviet Union. The Kaziat was subordinated to the **Muftiat** of Central Asia—a Tashkent-based Central Asian spiritual body. Traditionally, the Kaziat was led by a prominent local Islamic scholar, the *kazi,* who was approved by both the Muftiat and the State Committee on Religious Affairs. The Kaziat supervised the work of officially registered mosques, *medreses*, and official Muslim clergy on the territory of the republic. In 1991 the status of the Kaziat was upgraded and it became the Muftiat of Kyrgyzstan. *See also* ISLAM; MUFTI; UNOFFICIAL MUSLIM CLERGY.

KELIN ALA KACHUU **(literally "abduct a bride" in Kyrgyz).** A controversial Kyrgyz tradition of abducting a young woman with intention to marry her. In some cases, a young bridegroom runs off with a young woman with her consent, as he and his family cannot pay *qalym* (dowry). In other cases, a young man abducts a young woman without her consent, as he probably met her but could not win her affection or build positive relations. In extreme cases, a man carries off any unmarried woman, even a stranger, if he could not find a bride until a certain age. During the Soviet era, *kelin ala kachuu* was persecuted by law, though in some cases young couples and their parents settled the cases out of court in order to avoid public embarrassment.

KERIMKULOV, MEDETBEK (1949–). Kyrgyz politician. Born in Ken Bulun village in **Chui** *oblast* (northern **Kyrgyzstan**), Medetbek Kerimkulov graduated from the **Frunze Polytechnic Institute** in 1972. From 1972 to 1982 he held various managerial positions at a state-controlled construction enterprise. From 1982 to 1985 he worked as deputy head of the **Communist Party of Kyrgyz SSR** committee in **Tokmak** and then deputy head of the chairman of the Chui district council. He was executive director of the Tokmakstroi division of the Ministry for Construction 1985–90 and from 1990 to 1991 Kerimkulov worked as the first deputy chairman of the Tokmak City Council. From 1992 to 1994 he was chairman of the Tokmak city administration. From 1994 to 1995 he was head of the **Osh city** administration and from 1995 to 1998 he was first deputy head of the local administration in **Bishkek**. From 1998 to 1999 he served as vice-mayor of the Bishkek city administration. In 1999 he was appointed mayor of the Bishkek city administration.

Kerimkulov has played an important and controversial role in the republic's domestic politics since 1999, as he replaced **Felix Kulov**, one of those challenging President **Askar Akayev**, and bore witness against his former superior in court.

KESE. A traditional bowl made of porcelain, clay, or wood, used in Kyrgyzstan to serve the national food or drink, especially *kymyz* (kumys). It is also popular in some other parts of Central Asia.

KHAN. 1. The traditional title of a chief of a **tribe** or a confederation of tribes. 2. The title of a ruler (king) of a state or a principality during the medieval era. 3. Sometimes the term is used as an equivalent of "lord" or "your highness," usually after the first name.

KHANA (also *khona*). 1. A building, hall, or living place. 2. A public building, such as a tea house (***chai-khana***) or restaurant (***ash-khana***).

KHAN-TENGRI MOUNTAIN (also Han Tengri mountain; translated as "the Lord of the sky"). The mountain peak located in the Tengritag mountain range, in the eastern part of the **Tian-Shan** mountains, close to the Kyrgyz-**Kazakhstan**-**China** border. The Khan-Tengri is 6,995 meters high, and it is the second highest mountain peak in Kyrgyzstan, after the **Pobedy Peak**. It has a pyramidal shape, and one of the largest glaciers—the Inylchek glacier—is located in the mountain range. It was considered the highest peak in Kyrgyzstan until the Pobedy Peak was discovered, and it is still regarded as one of the most difficult summits to climb in Central Asia. The Khan-Tengri is a sacred mountain in the Kyrgyz and Central Asian shamanistic mythology. The areas east of Khan-Tengri were in dispute between Kyrgyzstan and China. After completion of the **China-Kyrgyzstan border delimitation** Kyrgyzstan agreed to cede to China around 100,000 hectares of its land east of Khan-Tengri.

KHOJA. *See HOJA.*

KHOZRASCHET (pronounced—*khozras'chet*; literally self-efficiency in Russian). Part of the economic policy introduced by Mikhail Gorbachev in order to achieve economic self-efficiency at the local level and to improve the overall productivity of enterprises.

KIRGIZ TELEGRAPH AGENCY. *See KABAR.*

KIRGIZS. *See KYRGYZS.*

KIRTAG. *See KABAR.*

KISHLAK. *See QISHLAQ.*

KOICHUMANOV, TALAIBEK (1956–). Kyrgyz politician and scholar. Born in **Jalal Abad** city in **Jalal Abad** *oblast* (southern Kyrgzstan), Talaibek Koichumanov graduated from the **Kyrgyz State (National) University** in 1978. He started his career as a junior researcher at the same university in 1978. From 1979 to 1982 he studied at the university's *aspirantura* and obtained the degree of *kandidat nauk*. From 1982 to 1990 he held various positions at the Institute of Mathematics of the **National Academy of Sciences** and from 1990 to 1991 he was at the Institute of Economics of the Academy of Sciences. Koichumanov worked in various positions in the presidential administration 1991–93 and from 1993 to 1994 he was head of the analytical department of the presidential administration. From 1994 to 1995 he was head of a department of the presidential administration and from 1995 to 1996 he served as minister of the economy. He was minister of finance 1996–99. In 1999 he was dismissed from his post under charges of corruption.

In the 1990s Koichumanov played a visible role in the formulation of economic policies as a member of the presidential administration and as minister in the Kyrgyz government. Before being charged with corruption, he was regarded as one of the most promising stars in Kyrgyzstan's politics.

KOICHUYEV, TURAR (1938–). Kyrgyz politician and scholar. Born in Sary Bulak in **Chui** *oblast* (northern Kyrgyzstan), Koichuyev graduated from the **Kyrgyz State (National) University** in 1961. He started his career as an economist in **Osh** *oblast* in 1961. From 1963 to 1966 he studied at the *aspirantura* of the Institute of Economics of the **Academy of Sciences**. From 1966 to 1971 he worked as a researcher in the same institute and from 1971 to 1987 he was head of a section and then head of a department in the Institute of Economics. Koichuyev served as vice president of the Academy of Sciences 1987–90 and from 1990 to 1992 he worked as state secretary of the Kyrgyz Republic. From 1993 to 1994 he was vice-president in the Kyrgyz government and from 1993 to 1998 he also served as president of the Kyrgyz National Academy of Sciences. In 1998 he became the director of the Center for Economic and Social Reform.

In the 1990s Koichuyev played a visible role in the formulation of economic policies as an economic adviser to President **Askar**

Akayev and as a leading Kyrgyz economist. However, due to his criticism of the privatization program in the republic, he lost his position in the **government**. Koichuyev was the head of the team of researchers who produced the first Human Development Reports of the **Kyrgyz Republic** for the United Nations Development Program (UNDP). He has authored around 80 publications, including five monographs, several articles, and brochures on economic reforms and economic policies in Kyrgyzstan.

KOKAND AUTONOMY. A nationalist government and independent state that was declared in Kokand at the fourth Extraordinary Congress of Muslims on 9–12 December 1917. The government intended to overthrow the Soviet authorities, restore the **Kokand Khanate,** and then secede from **Russia,** creating an independent state. It received considerable support from the **Bukhara Khanate**, the British envoy, and Russian White Guards. The Kokand Autonomy's army led by Irgash clashed with the Red Army in January–February 1918, but it was defeated. After taking over Kokand the Soviet authorities abolished the autonomy.

KOKAND KHANATE. A Central Asian feudal state in the **Ferghana valley.** Until the 18th century it was a small principality in the eastern part of the **Bukhara Emirate** (also called Bukhara Khanate). In 1710 Shoukrukh **Bek** of the Uzbek tribal dynasty Ming succeeded in seceding from Bukhara and established the city of Kokand as the capital of the Khanate. The Kokand rulers gradually captured Khojent, **Osh,** **Tokmak,** Tashkent, and some other cities. Between the second half of the 18th century and the beginning of the 19th century Kokand colonized almost all the territories that belonged to the Kyrgyz **tribes,** brutally suppressing their resistance and fuelling intertribal hostilities. The last ruler of Kokand Khudoyar Khan (ruled 1845–75) exhausted his army in continuing wars with his *beks,* Bukhara, and especially the rebellious Kyrgyz tribes during the **popular uprising of 1873–1876.**

    The Russian Empire defeated the Kokand Khanate in a series of battles in the 1860s and 1870s and conquered its territory in 1876. On 19 February 1876 the Kokand Khanate was abolished due to its internal turbulence and inability of the last khan of Kokand to stabilize the Khanate. Its territory was divided between several *oblasts* of the **Turkistan** Governor-Generalship, and later during the **border** delimitation in 1924–1926 between Kyrgyzstan, **Tajikistan,** and **Uzbekistan.**

KOKAND UPRISING. *See* POPULAR UPRISING OF 1873–1876 IN KOKAND.

KOLKHOZ **(plural in Russian** *kolkhozy***).** This stands for the Russian acronym *"kollektivnoye khozyaistvo,"* or collective farm. The *kolkhozes* were established across the Soviet Union in the late 1920s. They were introduced to replace subsistence and semi-pastoral farming and they were thought to boost **agricultural** production. In Kyrgyzstan, the collectivization campaign coincided with the sedentarization campaign. Both campaigns were implemented forcibly and were completed between 1928 and 1936, as all the major arable land and pastures (with the exception of small plots of land for private gardening) were given to the collective farms. In 1940 there were 1,723 *kolkhozes,* which were consolidated into 306 by 1960 and into 180 *kolkhozes* in 1979. In theory, the *kolkhozes* were independent and voluntary associations of the farmers; in practice, however, they were under state control until the 1990s. In 1992 all the *kolkhozes* on the territory of Kyrgyzstan were voluntary dissembled. *See also* SOVKHOZ.

KOMITET GOSUDARSTVENNOI BEZOPASTNOSTI (KGB). Security service in the former Soviet Union and Kyrgyzstan from 1946 until 1991. In 1991 the Kyrgyz **government** took control of the KGB's infrastructure on the territory of the republic and renamed it the **National Security Committee.**

KOMSOMOL (Kommunisticheskii Soyuz Molodezhi). The Communist Union of Youth of Kyrgyzstan (1918–92) was established and functioned as a republican branch of the All-Union Komsomol organization and a youth wing of the **Communist Party of Kyrgyz SSR.** The Komsomol was a powerful ideological instrument in the Soviet political system and an important source of recruitment to the ranks of the Communist Party. Youths joined the Komsomol at the age of 14 and were expected to leave it at the age of 28.

After the creation of the **Kyrgyz Soviet Socialist Republic** in 1937 the Komsomol was renamed the Lenin Communist Union of

Youth of Kyrgyz SSR. It was one of the largest officially approved political organizations in the republic during the Soviet era. Its membership grew from about 30,000 in 1937 to about 572,000 members in 1990, with cells in all public organizations in every district and province of the republic, including schools, universities, police, and ministries. The Komsomol of Kyrgyzstan controlled several popular youth newspapers and magazines published both in the Russian and **Kyrgyz languages,** had its own training institute and recreational centers, and managed the paramilitary-style training of schoolchildren. Following the banning of the Communist Party of the Kyrgyz SSR in 1991, the Komsomol made several unsuccessful attempts to relaunch itself as a nonpolitical youth organization but was finally forced to voluntarily disband and all its property was privatized.

KOMUZ. A Kyrgyz traditional plucked stringed musical instrument with a wooden pear-shaped body and a long neck. The *komuz* resembles the three-stringed lute and is customarily made of wood. The *komuz* is traditionally used by the *Komuzchi* (literally *Komuz*-player— national bard) during various major events and family gatherings. Traditionally during evenings in the *jayloo* (a highland summer pasture) after long working days *Komuzchi* are invited to sing the songs of heroes, especially about **Manas.**

KOSHCHI (read "kosh-chi"; "Herdsman" in Kyrgyz). A farmers' union or league, which played an important role in the Sovietization of Kyrgyz *ails* and in establishing a cooperative movement in the 1920s. The members of the koshchi supervised the expropriation of surplus land from rich landlords—*bais* and *manaps*—and the land's distribution among the poorest members of local communities.

KULOV, FELIX (1948–). Kyrgyz politician. Born in Frunze (now **Bishkek**) city (northern Kyrgyzstan), Felix Kulov graduated from the Omsk High Police School under the Ministry of Internal Affairs of the USSR (**Russia**) in 1971 and from the Academy of the Ministry of Internal Affairs of the USSR (Moscow, Russia) in 1978. He started his career as a field police officer, but he quickly rose in the police ranks to the position of minister of internal affairs of Kyrgyzstan. He sided with President **Askar Akayev** and played a critical role during the August 2001 putsch inspired by the Soviet hard-liners. In 1992 he became vice-president of the Kyrgyz Republic. From 1993 to 1997 he was head of the **Chui** *oblast* administration. From 1997 to 1998 he was the chairman (minister) for the **National Security Committee** (former **Komitet Gosudarstvennoi Bezopastnosti [KGB]**). In 1999 he was dismissed under charges of corruption and brought to court. After the dismissal he joined the opposition and founded the **Ar-Namys party**. He attempted to return to national politics by becoming a member of the **Jogorku Kenesh** (parliament) but lost the parliamentary elections in February 2000. Kulov challenged incumbent President Akayev in the October 2000 presidential elections. He took part in the presidential elections in partnership with **Omurbek Tekebayev,** but together they received only 13.9 percent of the vote. In 2001 Kulov was arrested and sentenced to seven years imprisonment under corruption charges that he persistently denied, yet in 2003 he was named one of the 20 most influential politicians in the republic.

Kulov played a central but highly controversial role in the political process in Kyrgyzstan, first as the second highest-ranking government official and then as the leading figure of the opposition. The **government** brought corruption charges against Kulov accusing him of amassing a fortune through dubious deals and inappropriate actions during his work as chairman for the National Security Committee. Kulov and his supporters vigorously denied the charges and claimed that the case was politically motivated. A series of protest meetings of the opposition, which demanded Kulov's release from prison, continued throughout the country in 2001 and 2002. Kulov has the military rank of lieutenant-general.

KUMBEZ (also *gumbez*). 1. Mausoleum on a burial place of a prominent member of society or a tribal leader (**Manas Gumbezi**). 2. A sacred burial place. 3. A historical monument over a burial place.

KUMYS. *See KYMYZ.*

KURGAN. *See QURGON.*

KURMANBEK. 1. Kyrgyz heroic oral epic set in medieval times. Kurmanbek was a legendary hero who united the previously deeply divided and hostile Kyrgyz **tribes** and led them to defend the Kyrgyz land from foreign aggression. This oral epic existed among the **Kyrgyzs** for several centuries, but was only first fully recorded in 1923 from Moldobasan Musulmankul(ov), an authoritative *akyn*. It was first published in 1928. The second version was recorded from *akyn* Manan Kalandar(ov). The third and most complete version was recorded in the 1930s from *akyn* **Kalyk Akiyev**. The *Kurmanbek* was published in 1938 and in 1957. 2. The name of the legendary Kyrgyz hero, one of the legendary founders of the early united Kyrgyz state.

KURMANJAN-DATKHA (full name Kurmanjan Mamatbai-Kyzy) (1811–1907). An influential leader of Kyrgyz **tribes** in the **Pamiro-Alay** area in the 19th century, who played an important role in the political development in this part of the region in the middle of the 19th century. In 1832 she married Alymbek-Datkha, the leader of the Kyrgyz tribes in the Pamiro-Alay and became one of his most trusted advisers. In 1862 the **Kokand Khanate** troops killed Alymbek-Datkha, and Kurmanjan-Datkha became the leader of the tribes.

In 1864 Kurmanjan-Datkha contacted a commander of the Russian Imperial troops and, after intensive negotiations, she peacefully accepted the **Russian Empire**'s protectorate over the tribes, which she led. The Russian officers in the region often called her "Alay Queen" and she became the only female person in 19th-century Central Asia who was awarded the military rank of colonel.

In post-Soviet Kyrgyzstan she was promoted as a symbol of the liberal attitudes of traditional Kyrgyz society toward **women**. Many streets, schools, and charity organizations were named after her.

KURPACHA **(also *kurpocho*).** A traditional Kyrgyz cotton-filled quilt or mattress. It is usually thrown on the floor of a *yurt* or house. The **Kyrgyzs** use a colorful *kurpacha* to sit around the *dastarkhan* for dinners and other occasions, or to sleep on.

KURULTAI. 1. Gathering of the people for an important event, consultation; meeting, congress. 2. Gathering of the people for election of a **khan** of groups of **tribes** or a military leader for a period of a war. 3. In contemporary Kyrgyzstan it is a gathering of the **Kyrgyzs** from various parts of the world for establishing cultural, educational, and economic ties between members of the Kyrgyz community in different countries. The first *Kurultai* of Kyrgyz people was held in 1994, the second *Kurultai* took place in 1996, and the third *Kurultai* has been planned for 2003.

KUZ-ORDU. *See* BALASAGUN.

KYMYZ **(also** *kumys***).** The national Kyrgyz drink prepared from mare's fermented milk. Traditionally, the milk is poured into a special leather bag for fermentation and is then stirred with a special wooden stick to turn the milk into *kymyz*. In the 1970s and 1980s several processing plants were established to process and bottle *kymyz*.

KYRGYZ AUTONOMOUS SOVIET SOCIALIST REPUBLIC (KYRGYZ ASSR). The Kyrgyz ASSR was established on 1 February 1926, when the status of the **Kara-Kyrgyz Autonomous** *Oblast* was elevated to that of an autonomous republic within the **Russian Federation.** It was upgraded to the **Kyrgyz Soviet Socialist Republic** (Kyrgyz SSR) on 5 December 1936, and it became a full member of the Union of Soviet Socialist Republics (USSR).

In December 1926 the population of the Kyrgyz ASSR stood at about 1 million people (87 percent lived in rural areas) and the total area was around 198,000 square kilometers. The Kyrgyz ASSR was comprised of Dzhalal Abad **(Jalal Abad),** Issyk-Kol **(Ysyk Kol), Naryn, Talas,** and **Osh** *kantons* (provinces).

KYRGYZ ENCYCLOPEDIA (Kyrgyz Entsykopediasy). The *Kyrgyz Encyclopedia* was established in 1968 under the **National Academy of Sciences** and from 1974 to 1999 it was under the State Committee on Publishing and Book Trade. In 1999 it was transformed into the Center of the State Language and Encyclopedia. This is the only institution in the republic that prepares and manages the publication of encyclopedias in the Russian and **Kyrgyz language.** In the 1980s it published a six-volume encyclopedia *Sovettyk Kyrgyzstan* in Kyrgyz, a one-volume encyclopedia *Kirgizskaya Sovetskaya Sotsialisticheskaya Respublika,* and some others. In the 1990s it published *Manas Entsyklopediasy* in two volumes. In 2001 it published *Kyrgyzstan: Entsyklopedia* in both Kyrgyz and Russia.

KYRGYZ FINE-FLEECE BREED SHEEP. *See* SHEEP.

KYRGYZ HORSE. *See* HORSE.

KYRGYZ KHANATE. A medieval empire, which according to the Chinese chronologies, existed somewhere on the **Yenisei River** basin between the eighth and 10th centuries A.D. There are no clear links between the Kyrgyz Khanate and the modern **Kyrgyzs**, although contemporary Kyrgyz historians claim that the medieval Kyrgyz Khanate was a predecessor of modern Kyrgyzstan and that the Khanate was an early Kyrgyz state.

KYRGYZ LANGUAGE. The Kyrgyz language belongs to the northwestern or Kypchak group of the Turkic language family. Traditionally there are three dialects distinguished in Kyrgyzstan: northern, southeastern, and southwestern. The Kyrgyz language is distinguished from other Turkic languages by the presence of the initial *dzh-* (Kyrgyz *dhzakshy*, "good, well," corresponding to Uzbek *yokshi* and to Kazakh *zhah'sy*) and by some other features. Some influences of the Arabic, Farsi, and Russian languages could be traced in the contemporary Kyrgyz language.

The modern literary Kyrgyz language was systematized at the beginning of the 20th century. Until 1926 the Kyrgyz language was based on the Arabic script; from 1926 to 1940 it was based on the Latin script. From 1940 to the present it has been using the Cyrillic (Russian) alphabet, though since 1991 there were widespread debates about a need to convert to the Latin script, as in Turkmenistan or neighboring **Uzbekistan**. Due to the difference in historical developments and cultural and other influences the modern terminology in the Kyrgyz language is significantly different from the terminology used in the Turkish of Turkey or Kyrgyz of Chinese Xinjan. In the 1990s and 2000s the Kyrgyz colloquial language began to experience a significant influx of English words, especially among the youth, who experienced the influence of American culture.

The Kyrgyz language is spoken by about 5 million people in Kyrgyzstan, as well as in some parts of **China, Kazakhstan, Tajikistan,** and Uzbekistan. During the Soviet era the Russian language was introduced to Kyrgyzstan and became a lingua franca, often replacing Kyrgyz in major cities, in **education,** and in public life, especially in the legal and technical areas. According to the Law on Languages (1990) all state and public institutions had to switch from the Russian to Kyrgyz language and to use the Kyrgyz language only by the end of the 1990s. However, at the end of the 1990s the **Jogorku Kenesh** (parliament) initiated some changes in the Law on Languages, adopting the Russian language as the second official language in the republic and pushing for compulsory proficiency tests of the Kyrgyz language in public and state institutions from 2003 to 2010.

KYRGYZ REPUBLIC. Official name of the Kyrgyzstan state. The name was officially established by the **Constitution of Kyrgyzstan** in 1993. *See also* KARA-KYRGYZ AUTONOMOUS OBLAST; KYRGYZ AUTONOMOUS SOVIET SOCIALIST REPUBLIC; KYRGYZ SOVIET SOCIALIST REPUBLIC.

KYRGYZ SOVIET SOCIALIST REPUBLIC (KYRGYZ SSR). The Kyrgyz SSR was established on 5 December 1936 as a full member of the Union of Soviet Socialist Republics (USSR). According to the Soviet Constitution, the republic could maintain significant autonomy in its cultural and domestic affairs, but it was to fully delegate all its **foreign policy**, defense, and security competences to the central Soviet government in Moscow.

In December 1936 the population of the Kyrgyz SSR stood at about 1.5 million people (81 percent living in rural areas) and its total area was around 198,000 square kilometers. The Kyrgyz SSR was comprised of Dzhalal Abad (**Jalal Abad**), Issyk-Kul (**Ysyk Kol**), **Naryn, Talas,** and **Osh** *oblasts* (provinces), although over time the number of provinces fluctuated due to administrative changes.

In 1991 the Kyrgyz SSR was renamed the **Republic of Kyrgyzstan** and on 31 August 1991 it declared its independence from the Soviet Union. *See also* KARA-KYRGYZ AUTONOMOUS OBLAST; KYRGYZ AUTONOMOUS SOVIET SOCIALIST REPUBLIC; KYRGYZ REPUBLIC.

KYRGYZ STATE (NATIONAL) UNIVERSITY (KSNU). The university was founded in 1932 as the Kyrgyz Pedagogical Institute; it obtained university status in 1951 and a status of national university in 1993. It is the largest and one of the oldest universities in Kyrgyzstan. Its library collection has about 1 million holdings, one of the largest in the republic. The university has 16 faculties, seven specialized institutes, and several specialized centers. It also has its own large botanical garden, a printing center, a zoological museum, an ethnographic museum, a computer center, and more than 60 scientific laboratories. Since 1968 the printing center of the KSNU has been publishing a university newspaper, *Collection of Scientific Studies* series, and series of academic books. The university runs degrees by evening and correspondence courses. It also offers postgraduate studies program at its *aspirantura* and *doktorantura,* upon completion of which, degrees of **kandidat nauk** and **doktor nauk** are awarded, respectively. All students are enrolled in full-time five-year undergraduate degree programs, three-year *aspirantura,* or three-year *doktorantura* programs. The education is offered mainly in the **Kyrgyz language** and some subjects are taught in Russian, though since the early 1990s the KSNU has increasingly moved toward replacing Russian with the Kyrgyz language at all faculties and departments. In 2002 the university enrolled about 22,000 students in undergraduate and postgraduate studies. *See also* EDUCATION.

KYRGYZ STATE THEATER OF OPERA AND BALLET. This is the largest and oldest theater in Kyrgyzstan, which played a leading role in establishing national performance traditions. The theater was founded in 1937 as the Theater of Music and Drama in Frunze (now **Bishkek**) and obtained its present name in 1942. In 1955 the theater acquired a new building where it presently gives performances mainly in the **Kyrgyz language**. The first Kyrgyz opera, the *Lunar Beauty* (1939), and the first Kyrgyz national ballet, *Anar* (1940), were performed at this theater.

During the Soviet era the theater's repertoire included Kyrgyz, Russian, and foreign classical plays. This included **Manas** (1946, 1966), *On the Shore of the Isyk Kol* (1951), **Toktogul** (1958), *Dzhamilya* (1961), *Asel* (1967), and some other operas. In the 1960s and 1970s the theater was at the zenith of its popularity and performance, and its singers, such as Saira Kiizbayeva, Artyk Myrzabayev, and others, won all-Union and international recognition. After 1991 the theater experienced a severe decline as many leading singers and artists left the republic and there was a steep reduction in state funding of the theater. Lack of funds seriously undermined the quality of the performances, but with both government and international grants the theater managed to preserve some of its best traditions.

KYRGYZ TECHNICAL UNIVERSITY. *See* FRUNZE POLY-TECHNIC INSTITUTE.

KYRGYZCHYLYK **(translated as kyrgyzness).** Throughout the 1980s and 1990s the term was often used in public life to refer to Kyrgyz national unity, national identity, and resurgence of Kyrgyz culture. It was used as a counter-term to *mankurtism* (loss of cultural roots), introduced by Kyrgyz writer **Chingiz Aitmatov** in his novel *I dolshe veka dlitsia den. Kyrgyzchylyk* was often used by various political groups, ranging from moderate to extremely nationalistic parties, in order to develop a unified national idea and to overcome the deep-seated political polarization of society into southern and northern **clans**.

KYRGYZFILM. A state-controlled movie studio established in 1942 in Frunze (now **Bishkek**). Initially Kyrgyzfilm focused on producing a documentary series about Kyrgyzstan—*Sovetskaya Kigiziya*. In the 1950s the studio produced its first feature movie *Saltanat* (1955). In the 1960s and the 1970s Kyrgyzfilm produced its most acclaimed feature movies, some of which became classics of the Kyrgyz and Soviet cinema and brought the studio to the attention of the Soviet and international publics. In the 1970s and 1980s the studio produced around three feature movies and several documentaries a year and was heavily subsidized from the state budget. In the 1990s Kyrgyzfilm lost most of its subsidies and experienced significant difficulties and by the end of the 1990s it had stopped producing feature-length films. *See also* AITMATOV, CHINGIZ; UNION OF CINEMATOGRAPHERS OF KYRGYZSTAN.

KYRGYZ-RUSSIAN SLAVONIC UNIVERSITY (KRSU). The university was founded in **Bishkek** in 1992 in accordance with the Kyrgyz-Russian Friendship Treaty. Soon it became one of the largest and most prestigious universities in Kyrgyzstan. The university has seven faculties, more than 40 departments, a **library,** and several specialized centers. The university offers degrees by evening and correspondence courses. It also offers postgraduate studies programs at its *aspirantura* and *doktorantura*, upon completion of which degrees of **kandidat nauk** and **doktor nauk** are awarded, respectively. All students are enrolled in full-time five-year undergraduate degree programs, three-year *aspirantura*, or three-year *doktorantura* programs. The language of instruction is mainly Russian, though Kyrgyz and some major international languages are also taught at the KRSU. In 2003 the university enrolled about 4,200 students in undergraduate and postgraduate studies. The university is increasingly moving toward a Western-style tertiary educational establishment and is developing its international relations with foreign, mainly Russian, universities. *See also* EDUCATION.

KYRGYZS (also Kirgizs, Kara-Kyrgyzs). The Kyrgyzs are an ethnic group that make up the majority of the population of the **Kyrgyz Republic**. Until 1926 they were also known as the Kara-Kyrgyzs (black Kyrgyzs), while the Kazakhs were called Kyrgyzs or Kaisak-Kyrgyzs. Traditionally, Kyrgyz society is divided into two major tribal confederations—Sol kanat and Ong Kanat, which historically preserved significant autonomy from each other. The tribal identity is deeply rooted in the psychology of the **Kyrgyzs** and every male is expected to know his ancestors for seven generations. The Kyrgyzs speak the **Kyrgyz language,** one of the languages of the Kypchak linguistic group of the Turkic language family. The Kyrgyzs are differentiated significantly from their neighbors, the Kazakhs and the Uzbeks, by some features of social, political, cultural, and economic organization of their society, though the Kyrgyzs experienced significant influences from both neighbors. The overwhelming majority of the Kyrgyzs are Sunni Muslims, who turned to **Islam** between the 12th and 18th centuries, though their beliefs incorporate significant influences of the pre-Islamic past (devotion to ancestors, belief in mountain spirits and the Universe, and some others). Yet, after 1991 various religious sects, including Protestants, Evangelicals, **Wahhabists,** and some others, began to penetrate into Kyrgyz society. Nevertheless, those groups are still very small in Kyrgyzstan.

There are several competing theories about the origin of the Kyrgyzs and about their links to the legendary Yenisei Kyrgyzs of Siberia (some scholars reject existence of any links). There are also academic disputes about relations of modern Kyrgyzs to the mysterious **Kyrgyz Khanate** and Karakhanid nomadic empires (the latter controlled significant territories of present-day **Kazakhstan**, Russian Siberia, Mongolia, and **Uzbekistan**). Most historians agree that the Kyrgyzs lived on the territory of modern Kyrgyzstan for several centuries or probably longer, though some Chinese and other historical chronicles and Kyrgyz legends claim that the Kyrgyz ancestors probably lived in southern Siberia in the first centuries A.D. During the period of the Turkic Khanates (sixth to 10th centuries A.D.), various Turkic-speaking groups began to form the Kyrgyz ancestor **tribes** and frequently moved between Altai, Xinjan, and eastern **Tian-Shan** due to the political turbulence and instability of the nomadic empires of that era. In the 13th century the Mongols recruited some Kyrgyz tribes through various agreements or by force. By the 16th–17th centuries the Kyrgyzs became distinguished from their neighbors and began to develop the Kyrgyz identity and Kyrgyz language, which increasingly differed from the Turkic languages of their neighbors. In 1924 the **Kara-Kyrgyz Autonomous *Oblast*** (**Kyrgyz Autonomous Soviet Socialist Republic** from 1926) was established in recognition of the consolidating Kyrgyz identity.

During the Soviet era the Kyrgyzs significantly changed their economic activities, as the majority of them abandoned the pastoral nomadic lifestyle and settled in the towns and cities. There was a relatively small number of interethnic marriages and few Kyrgyzs left their native republic for other parts of the Soviet Union, though there was significant immigration of non-Kyrgyz people from all over the Soviet Union and Eastern Europe.

After 1991 more Kyrgyzs began to move between Kyrgyzstan and all neighboring Central Asian republics, **Russia,** and **China**. The proportion of Kyrgyzs in the total population of the republic increased from 53 percent in 1991 to about 68 percent in 2003. At present compact groups of Kyrgyzs live in **Afghanistan**, China, Kazakhstan, Russia, **Tajikistan**, Turkey, and Uzbekistan. *See also* CLANS.

KYRGYZSTAN (translated as "the land of Kyrgyzs"). 1. The conventional name of the land populated by Kyrgyzs, which includes the territory of present-day Kyrgyzstan and some other areas with a Kyrgyz population. 2. The conventional name for the **Kyrgyz Republic**.

KYRGYZSTAN ABA JOLDORU (also Kyrgyzstan Aba Zholdoru; Kyrgyzstan Air Company). A state-controlled airline established in 1991 as the successor of the Kyrgyzstan branch of the Soviet air giant Aeroflot. Aba Joldoru is based at the Manas International Airport, about 40 kilometers from **Bishkek,** but also operates several small airports in major *oblast* centers. It provides connections to all major cities in Kyrgyzstan, though in the 1990s it cut services to numerous unprofitable destinations within the republic and the former Union of Soviet Socialist Republics (USSR).

In the 1990s Aba Joldoru experienced a severe three-fold decline in passenger traffic due to the economic recession, safety concerns, and significant downsizing of private and public spending on air travel. At the end of the 1990s the **government** attempted to revive the national airline in order to boost **tourism** and ease international travel. The Manas airport was renovated with a US$50 million credit from Japan. In 2001 the company employed about 2,000 people and had a fleet of 130 airplanes (some of them not operational) and four helicopters. In 1998 the company leased one A320 airbus and conducted negotiations for purchase of two A319 airbuses in 2002.

In 2001 the **Jogorku Kenesh** (parliament) adopted a deregulation program according to which the company was split into three financially independent units: Kyrgyz Air Navigation, Kyrgyz Airports, and Kyrgyzstan Air Company. The government plans to keep Kyrgyz Air Navigation under state control, and to partially privatize Kyrgyz Airports and Kyrgyzstan Air Company. In 2000 and 2001 Kyrgyzstan Aba Joldoru signed several joint agreements in order to open flights to new destinations in the **Commonwealth of Independent States** and in Asia. The major regular destinations included Beijing, Delhi, Dubai, Frankfurt, Hanover, Istanbul, Karachi, Moscow, Seoul, Saint Petersburg, and some others. In 2001 part of Manas International Airport was leased to the **U.S. military airbase** to conduct operations in **Afghanistan.** *See also* AIRLINES.

KYRGYZSTAN AIR COMPANY. *See* KYRGYZSTAN ABA JOLDORU.

KYSHTOO **(pronounced** *kysh'to'o***).** A winter pasture in the low land valleys, where the **Kyrgyzs** move from the *jayloo* with their herds of

horses and **sheep**. Traditionally the Kyrgyz herdsmen spent the winter season in the *kyshtoo* with their families and relatives. In the 19th and early 20th centuries growing numbers of people spent the entire year in the *kyshtoo,* as they increasingly focused on production of various crops.

– L –

LANGUAGE. *See* KYRGYZ LANGUAGE.

LEVITIN, LEONID (1931–). Kyrgyz politician. Born in Minsk (**Belarus**), Leonid Levitin graduated from the Faculty of Law of the Central Asian State University (**Uzbekistan**) in 1952 specializing in labor and enterprise law. During the Soviet era he was a lawyer and deputy-procurator in Przhevalsk (now **Karakol**), lecturer, senior lecturer, and a professor at the **Kyrgyz State (National) University**.

Levitin started his political career as a legal adviser to President **Askar Akayev** in 1991. In this position he became one of the architects of the legal and constitutional reforms in post-Soviet Kyrgyzstan. He played a key role in drafting the first post-Soviet **constitution of Kyrgyzstan**. In 1994 Levitin left his position and emigrated to Germany when his name was mentioned in several high-profile corruption cases. However, no legal charges were brought against him or his associates. Since the mid-1990s he has frequently visited Kyrgyzstan and other Central Asian republics. Levitin has authored four books and more than 70 articles and papers on legal and constitutional issues.

LIBRARIES. The first public libraries were opened in **Osh** and **Tokmak** in the 1870s, though private and public collections of books existed in *medreses* and in private possession of wealthy feudal lords and *khans* for centuries. By 1917 there were several public libraries in Kyrgyzstan, mainly in the northern provinces. After the establishment of the **Kara-Kyrgyz Autonomous *Oblast*** in 1924, the Kyrgyz **government** adopted a program of cultural revolution. An important part of the program was the eradication of illiteracy and opening of small public libraries in every town and city, as well as having *Kyzyl Yurts* (mobile libraries) in every village or *jayloo*. During the 1920s several dozen libraries and *Kyzyl Yurts* were opened in all parts of the republic. Another significant development came in the 1930s, as the major Soviet libraries from different parts of the USSR donated thousands of books to Kyrgyz libraries. The number of district and city libraries grew from 33 in 1933 to about 150 in 1938. In 1934 the first centralized system of library acquisition was established in the republic. It became responsible for planning library expansions and book orders. Also in 1934 the National Library (named after writer Nikolai Chernyshevskii in 1939) was opened in Frunze (now **Bishkek**); in 1984 it moved into the modern library facility.

In the post–World War II era, libraries in Kyrgyzstan underwent major expansions. There was established a hierarchic system of the libraries: central, *oblast*, district, and city libraries. In addition around 2,000 small libraries were opened at every school or tertiary **education** center. The total number of libraries grew to about 2,500 (2003). Most of the libraries are open to the public for free, with the limited exception of specialized libraries. In 1984 part of the National Library moved to a new larger building. The National Library, the biggest library in the republic, contains more than 6 million books and 900,000 periodical publications. It possesses a collection of rare and specialized books, which are open for scholars and students. In 1991 an electronic library catalog, *Kyrgyzstan,* was established in Bishkek.

In the 1990s the government cut spending significantly on the libraries and the library system in the republic experienced a steep decline. Several international organizations and private foundations (such as the Soros-Foundation Kyrgyzstan) provided assistance to public libraries, especially university libraries, by donating books and computer equipment.

LIQUIDATION OF ILLITERACY. A mass campaign launched by the Soviet authorities in Kyrgyzstan in the 1920s. The campaign targeted lifting the literacy rate from 4.7 percent among the **Kyrgyzs** in 1926 to 70–80 percent within a decade. Small schools and literacy groups were established in all cities and towns of the republic. The "liquidation of illiteracy" campaign was combined with some social initiatives and administrative command actions. By 1939 the **government** announced that the major objectives of the campaign had been achieved as the overall literacy reached 70 percent (82 percent in the age group between 9 and 40). In 2003 the literacy rate stood at about 98 percent. *See also* EDUCATION.

– **M** –

MADAMINBEK (unknown–1921). One of the most successful commanders of the Basmachi **movement** in the **Ferghana valley** between 1918 and 1921. In 1919 the Basmachi groups under his command controlled a number of cities and towns and a significant part of the Ferghana valley, including such cities as **Jalal Abad** and **Osh**. Madaminbek attempted to mobilize broad local support under the banner of *Gazavat* (Jihad) against the Red Army and to attract military and financial support from Russian White Guards, Britain, and Turkey. However, his troops, which were plagued by personal rivalries and lack of discipline, were defeated by the united units of the Red Army and local **militia** in 1920–21.

MADRASAH. See MEDRESE.

MAHALLYA **(also *Mahalla*).** A neighborhood community in Kyrgyzstan and in Central Asia. The institution of the *mahallya* appeared most probably in the medieval era as the smallest administrative unit of a state. It survived during the Soviet era and gained strength after Kyrgyzstan's independence, especially in southern Kyrgyzstan. The *Mahallya* is usually run by a group of *aksakals* (the elderly). Traditionally feasts (weddings, funerals, etc.), community work (building of mosques, repairing irrigation system), or local charities are organized at the *mahallya* level and are managed by *aksakals*.

MALDYBAYEV, ABDYLAS (1906–1978). Prominent Kyrgyz composer, singer, and artist; one of the founders of contemporary Kyrgyz music. Born in Kara Bulak village in **Chui** *oblast* (northern Kyrgyzstan), Maldybayev began composing music at the age of 16. His first songs, such as *Akynai*, *Life*, and others, were written in the 1920s and became classics of Soviet-era music. In the 1930s he continued to experiment with music forms that were new for Kyrgyzstan, such as hymns, marches, and some others. He was awarded the title of People's Artist of **Kyrgyz SSR** in 1937 and People's Artist of the

USSR (official honorary title given to outstanding singers, actors, musicians, and ballet dancers) in 1939. From 1939 to 1967 he worked as chairman of the Union of Composers of Kyrgyzstan. From 1953 to 1954 he was the director of one of the most prestigious music colleges in **Bishkek**.

Maldybayev was considered one of the most influential Kyrgyz composers of his era in the republic. He authored numerous songs, a symphony, and various musical compositions. After his death one of the theaters in Frunze (now Bishkek) was named after him.

MAMYTOV, MUTALIP (1939–). Kyrgyz politician. Born in Kok Jar village in **Osh** *oblast* (southern Kyrgyzstan) in 1950, Mutalip Mamytov graduated from the Kyzyl Kia Medical College in 1960 and the Kyrgyz State Medical Institute in 1966. From 1966 to 1971 he studied and worked in Leningrad (now Saint Petersburg) medical research institute (**Russia**). From 1972 to 1986 he held various teaching and research positions. In 1988 he defended his doctoral dissertation in Kiev (Ukraine). From 1988 to 1997 he held various teaching positions at the Kyrgyz State Medical Institute (**Bishkek**). From 1997 to 1999 he was deputy-rector of the institute. From 1999 to 2002 he was the head of department at the institute. In 2002 Mamytov was appointed minister of health.

Mamytov has authored more than 60 papers, articles, and brochures and three university textbooks. He was considered an important figure in the Osh **clan**.

MANAP. 1. In traditional Kyrgyz society the term refers to a noble tribal leader. 2. The term also refers to a native administrator during the tsarist era. 3. Wealthy and influential person; the term sometimes carries a negative connotation.

MANAS. The most acclaimed and biggest Kyrgyz heroic epic named after Manas, a legendary Kyrgyz hero (*batyr*). This is the story of the life of Manas, who united the Kyrgyz **tribes** and led them to defend the Kyrgyz land from foreign aggression and to establish the first legendary Kyrgyz state. The importance of the *Manas* epic for Kyrgyz society arises from the fact that it serves as an encyclopedia of their history, cultural traditions, relations with other countries, and ideals of social and political ethics. The epic reflects the history of the

Kyrgyz people in the medieval era and their social life and beliefs covering a whole millennium.

The *Manas* consists of three parts. The first part of the trilogy— *Manas*—tells about the life and actions of Manas. The second part— *Semetey*—tells about the life and deeds of Semetey, son of Manas. The third part—*Seitek*—tells about the life and experience of Seitek, son of Semetey and grandson of Manas. The plot was believed to be set between the ninth and 11th centuries.

The *Manas* is the world's biggest epic; it contains 500,553 poetic lines (recorded version of Sayakbay Karalayev)— it's about 30 times longer than the Greek epic *Illiad*, or 2.5 times longer than the ancient Indian *Mahabharata*.

This oral epic existed among the **Kyrgyzs** for several centuries and it was passed from generation to generation by Kyrgyz *manaschis*, national bards who devoted their whole life to memorizing the epic and reciting it to the public. Western scholars, however, discovered it only in the 19th century, when several travelers and orientalists recorded parts of the epic. It was first fully recorded only in the 20th century. At present there are more than 60 versions of the epic, each of them recorded from different prominent *manaschis*. All copies are kept and studied in the **National Academy of Sciences** of Kyrgyzstan. Many of the versions have never been published.

In 1995 Kyrgyzstan celebrated the 1,000th anniversary of the *Manas* epic in an attempt to promote it as a symbol of Kyrgyz national unity and Kyrgyz cultural identity. The Kyrgyz **government** sponsored publication in Kyrgyz and translations in Russian, English, and German of the *Manas* and *Encyclopedia of Manas* in commemoration of the anniversary. *See also* MANAS GUMBEZI.

MANAS GUMBEZI (Manas's mausoleum). A medieval mausoleum built probably in the 14th century in **Talas** *oblast*. The **Kyrgyzs** widely believe that it is the burial place of the legendary Kyrgyz hero **Manas**. There are several opinions about who built the mausoleum. One version is that the mausoleum was built by the wife of Manas, Kanykey, and that she was ordered to inscribe the name of a woman on it to deceive enemies and protect her husband's body from defilement. Another version says that it was built by the son of Manas, Semetey, after his father was killed in a battle. In 1946 archaeologists Mikhael Masson and Galina Pugachenkova carried out a thorough study of the mausoleum and published their findings in the 1950s. In the post-Soviet era the mausoleum has became a major attraction for local and international **tourists**.

MANAS'S MAUSOLEUM. *See* MANAS GUMBEZI.

MANASCHI. A singer who devotes his entire life to memorizing and reciting the **Manas** epic by heart, which is often accompanied by *komuz*. *Manaschi* always enjoyed an honorable and influential position in Kyrgyz society, as they were considered important guardians of the Kyrgyz culture and tradition. They often had great influence over tribal and military leaders and voiced the concerns and grievances of the ordinary people. Since 1991 Kyrgyzstan has organized annual competitions of *Manaschis*.

MASALIYEV, ABSAMAT (1933–). Kyrgyz politician and leader of the **Kyrgyz Soviet Socialist Republic (Kyrgyz SSR)** from 1985 to 1991 as first secretary of the **Communist Party of Kyrgyz SSR**. Born in Alysh village in **Osh** *oblast* (southern Kyrgyzstan) in 1933 Masaliyev spent his entire career in the government and Communist Party apparatus. He graduated from the Kyzyl Kia Technical College (Kyrgyzstan, 1953), Moscow Institute of Mining (Moscow, 1956), and Party School (Moscow, 1964). From 1956 to 1960 he held various managerial positions at the Kyrgyzugol enterprise, and later held various party posts in Osh *oblast* and Frunze (now **Bishkek**) before assuming leadership in the republic. Masaliyev belonged to the cohort of Central Asian leaders who remained unreformed hard-line communists throughout their lives. In 1985, on the wave of the campaign against patronage, corruption, and mismanagement, Masaliyev was appointed first secretary, replacing **Turdakun Usubaliyev.**

Masaliyev remained a hard-line unreformed Communist in the era of Mikhail Gorbachev's *glasnost* and *perestroika*, and he measured development of the republic purely in terms of economic development and state-led industrialization. He fiercely resisted the rise of opposition political groups in the republic in the late 1980s. His refusal to accept the political realities and to recognize growing interethnic tensions led to violent clashes and numerous casualties in the **Osh-Uzgen conflicts**. By the end of 1990 he had become so unpopular that he lost the first contested presidential elections to **Askar Akayev,** then the president of the

Kyrgyz **Academy of Sciences.** This was a particularly hard blow for Masaliyev, as he was the leader of the largest political party and largest faction in the **Jogorku Kenesh** (parliament). In August 1991 the Communist Party of Kyrgyz SSR was banned for its support of the anti-Gorbachev military putsch.

Masaliyev led the reemergence of the Communist Party in 1992, when it was re-registered as the **Party of Communists of Kyrgyzstan (PCK).** In 1995 he returned to the political arena as a member of the Jogorku Kenesh, leading the PCK faction and playing an important role in the Osh **clan.** He remained the most vocal critic of the privatization and market-oriented reforms in the republic in the 1990s. During the 1996 presidential elections Masaliyev attempted to challenge incumbent President Akayev, but obtained only about 20 percent of the votes. Masaliyev regained some of his popularity after the **Aksy conflicts** in 2002, leading the group of opposition parties and organizations that demanded the resignation of President Akayev.

MASS MEDIA. Most of the media outlets were established in Kyrgyzstan during the Soviet era in the 1920s, including the first national newspapers in the **Kyrgyz language**—*Erkin Too* and *Sovettik Kyrgyzstan* ("Free Mountains" and "Soviet Kyrgyzstan"), both established in 1924. All newspapers and other publications were state-owned and were under strict state control. This included extensive censorship and full control over distribution. Sizable support from the state and subsidized **transportation** costs allowed the media to attain large circulations. In the 1980s there were 90 newspapers in the republic with a total annual circulation of about 184.4 million and 46 magazines with total annual circulation of about 21 million copies.

The situation changed radically with independence in 1991. Most of the media enterprises were privatized and they lost the state support and subsidies. Throughout the 1990s many newspapers and other publications were closed or significantly downsized their circulation. The situation worsened even further when, due to the economic recession, people stopped buying newspapers and magazines.

By the end of the 1990s the biggest private and state-controlled newspapers and television stations gradually recovered and recaptured their positions in the market, while smaller, especially *oblast*-level, media outlets still struggled for their survival or disappeared altogether. Television and radio remain the two most important sources of public information, as they can be accessed all over the country. These are followed by newspapers, which are steadily declining in importance due to the population's falling purchasing power and financial constraints. Most national newspapers are based in the capital of **Bishkek** and they often do not reach remote rural districts at all. There are a few weekly and monthly magazines, but they have a very narrow market, as it is very expensive to produce, publish, and distribute quality products in this small and impoverished country. The Internet is gradually becoming a popular source of public information, but it too is limited by financial constraints and rudimentary infrastructure. With monthly Internet subscriptions often equal to the average monthly salary, the Internet is only accessible in major cities and only to a relatively small number of people.

The state-controlled national newspapers, including *Slovo Kyrgyzstana* and *Kyrgyz Tuusu*, and television stations, including KTP and KOORT, have the largest audiences and are accessible all over the republic. In 2002 there were about 50 independent, semi-independent, and privately owned newspapers and magazines, including the popular *Vechernii Bishkek, Delo No, Res Publica, AKI-press,* and others. Many newspapers had a circulation of between 20,000 and 50,000 copies, while *oblast* newspapers often had a circulation below 5,000 copies. There were also 14 independent or privately owned television stations and 11 radio stations, including Piramida Television and Radio, Independent Bishkek Television, Asman Television, Almaz Radio, and so on.

Most of the privately owned newspapers are not financially viable. The main constraints are very limited advertising revenue and a small circulation base. Additionally, the low income of the population does not allow increases in the retail price of newspapers and magazines, and there are few businessmen with the money and experience to establish and run profitable media businesses. According to the law, advertising is limited to about 20 percent of print space and 25 percent of television and radio airtime, although many media outlets engage in hidden advertising.

MAZAR. 1. A sacred burial place of a prominent scholar in **Islam** or of a **Sufi** *sheikh*. 2. A sacred burial place, which is believed to have a magic or healing power. A place where people would usually come to seek a cure from illness, bad luck, or the evil eye.

MEDRESE **(also** *madrasah***).** 1. An Islamic school, which provides post-primary religious **education.** 2. A theological seminary and law school, which provides Islamic religious education and is usually attached to a *masjit* (mosque). 3. A building where the boarding students of Islamic seminaries stay. See *also* ISLAM; SUFISM.

MEERIM FOUNDATION. A major charitable foundation in Kyrgyzstan, founded in 1993 by Meerim Akayeva, the wife of President **Askar Akayev.** Throughout the 1990s it became the largest nongovernmental foundation in the country. It has been involved in fund-raising within the country and overseas, project management, and various social and economic joint programs with major international institutions, such as the International Monetary Fund, World Bank, UNESCO, and UNICEF. In 2003 the Meerim Foundation ran 18 grant projects, including projects on **education,** support of youth talents, computerization of rural schools, and various forms of support for **women,** orphans, and some others.

MEHMANKHANA **(from** *mehmon*—**guest).** 1. A guest room in a house or palace. 2. A traditional name for an inn or hotel (the term is mainly used in southern Kyrgyzstan).

MEKTEB **(also** *maktab***).** 1. A school in prerevolutionary Central Asia. 2. An Islamic school, which provides primary religious education. 3. A primary and secondary school in contemporary Kyrgyzstan, usually a school where schoolchildren are instructed in the native **Kyrgyz language** or Uzbek. See *also* EDUCATION; ISLAM.

MENIM ELKEM PARTIASY. *See* MY COUNTRY PARTY.

MILITANT INCURSIONS. Incursions of members of the **Islamic Movement of Uzbekistan (IMU)** from neighboring **Tajikistan** into **Batken** *raion* (now *oblast*) of **Osh** *oblast* in summer 1999 and 2002. On 6 August 1999 a group of guerrillas entered Kyrgyzstan's southwestern part of the **Ferghana valley,** which is shared among Kyrgyzstan, Tajikistan, and **Uzbekistan,** and captured the small village of Zardaly. They also seized four Kyrgyzstani government officials, who were sent to assess the situation and negotiate with the intruders. It did not take long to establish that the guerrillas belonged to the forces controlled by Jumabai Namangani. Namangani, who led a 1,000-strong religious radical force, opposed to Islam Karimov's regime in Uzbekistan. He was a field commander based in Khodjent *oblast* of Tajikistan. The Kyrgyz authorities also confirmed that the guerrillas demanded safe passage to Uzbekistan, and later they asked for a large sum of money for releasing the hostages. These demands caused a harsh reaction of the Uzbekistani government, which in 1997 persecuted what it called the "Islamic fundamentalist forces" in its part of the Ferghana valley.

The actions of Kyrgyzstan's **army** and **National Security Committee** forces against the guerrillas were largely unsuccessful despite military and intelligence assistance from Uzbekistan and Tajikistan. On 13 August the guerrillas released the hostages in exchange for 2 million Kyrgyz **soms** (US$50,000) while the Uzbekistani airforce bombed the areas controlled by the intruders. On 22 August 1999 another group of guerrillas crossed the border and took around 320 villagers hostage. The next day the group seized the commander of the Kyrgyz Interior Ministry forces, General Anarbek Shamkeyev, and four Japanese geologists. An attempt by Kyrgyzstan forces to push the intruders back into Tajikistan was unsuccessful. Meanwhile, the intruders expanded their control over Kyrgyzstani territory. Only high-level official and unofficial negotiations with the militants and the various political groups in Tajikistan, including the United Tajik Opposition, led to the political resolution of the hostage drama. In the middle of October 1999 all the Kyrgyzstani hostages as well as four Japanese geologists were released, allegedly for US$4 million ransom.

The events highlighted several fundamental problems for the Kyrgyzstan **government**, such as the high vulnerability of its borders. The threat of military incursions and of terrorism imposed an additional burden on the budget for defense and **border guards**. Kyrgyzstan pledged to spend 1.5 billion soms (US$36 million) on strengthening the 400-kilometer Kyrgyz-Tajik border and setting up 15 border troop posts, which would considerably increase the military expenditures of the republic.

MILITARY DOCTRINE. The Kyrgyz **government** has no clearly defined and consistent military doctrine. During the first year of independence the Kyrgyz authorities maintained that they would not build an **army**, would maintain a low military budget, and therefore would develop a military doctrine accordingly. In May 1992 Kyrgyzstan signed the **Commonwealth of Independent States Collective Security Treaty** (extended in 1999), which developed close military cooperation with **Russia**. However, due to the civil war in neighboring **Tajikistan** from 1992 to 1997, and the **militant incursions** into southern Kyrgyzstan in 1999 and 2000, the Kyrgyz government radically changed its approach to the issue. There was another change in late 2001 when the **U.S. military airbase** was established in the Manas International Airport and the United States and its NATO allies established a significant military presence in the republic.

MILITARY FORCE. The Kyrgyzstan Military Force consists of the **Army**, Airforce and Air Defense, Security Forces, and **Border Guards**. According to Central Intelligence Agency (CIA) estimates Kyrgyzstan has military manpower reaching military age annually of about 50,000 conscripts (2003, CIA est.). The republic's annual military expenditure equals about 1.4 percent of its GDP (2003, CIA est.). According to the **Constitution of Kyrgyzstan** the president of the **Kyrgyz Republic** is also the chief commander of the Military Forces and he appoints and dismisses commanders of the Military Forces of the Kyrgyz Republic. During the political crisis in 2002 and 2003 the military forces refrained from intervening in political developments in the country.

MILITSIA (police). A state-controlled agency in charge of public safety, law enforcement, investigation of crimes, and road patrolling. Kyrgyzstan inherited from the Soviet era a well-established militsia (police), which is in charge of internal issues, and the **National Security Committee** (former **Komitet Gosudarstvennoi Bezopastnosti [KGB]**), which is in charge of the major criminal and other problems threatening national security. In 1991 they both came under the jurisdiction of the republic. They assumed the main role in maintaining law and order and preserving the security of the state against any threat of terrorism, organized crime, or any other actions from inside and outside the republic. In August 1992 Kyrgyzstan created its own National

Guards of about 900 men—an elite troop assigned to protect the president and **government** officials and some important state facilities. The militsia in Kyrgyzstan is subordinated to the Ministry of Internal Affairs. It is estimated that the militsia has about 20,000 men and women in service, although since 1991 it has suffered from slack discipline, corruption, poor training, and poor equipment. *See also* ARMY.

MINING. At present, antimony, **gold**, mercury, and uranium are the major natural resources of export significance in Kyrgyzstan. According to the *International Monetary Fund Country Report*, in 2001 Kyrgyzstan extracted around 22,000 kilograms of gold and around 18,000 kilograms of gold in 2002. The gold exports accounted for nearly US$197 million or one-third of Kyrgyzstan's total exports in 2000. In 2000 Kyrgyzstan extracted about 3.3 tons of mercury, down from 1,000 tons in 1990. In 1990 Kyrgyzstan produced 5,400 tons of antimony, becoming the largest producer of antimony in the USSR and the third largest producer in the world (after China and Bolivia); however, this sector experienced difficulties in the late 1990s due to the declining world prices for antimony. Until 1980 Kyrgyzstan extracted and milled uranium ore in the towns of Maili-Sai (Maili Suu), Ming Kush, and some other places. In 1989 it stopped extracting uranium, but the **Kara Balta** Hydro-Metallurgical Plant continued to process uranium ore from Kazakhstan.

Kyrgyzstan's reserves of coal are estimated at approximately 31 billion tons. However, some reserves are located in mountainous areas and economically unviable. The country mines coal mainly for domestic consumption at a level of around 419,000 tons per annum in 2000, down from 3,500,000 tons in 1991. In the late 1990s there were plans to attract foreign investors for coal extraction and to significantly increase coal production for domestic needs and for exports.

In 2001 there were reports of discovery of new large (by Kyrgyzstan's scale) oil reserves, estimated at around 70 million barrels that could be used for domestic consumption. Kyrgyzstan's total oil reserves are estimated at around 700 million barrels in the southern *oblasts* of the republic and 1,500 million barrels of oil reserves in the northern and eastern *oblasts*. In 2000 Kyrgyzstan extracted 77,000 tons of oil, down from 155,000 tons in 1990 and 464,000 tons in 1960. Kyrgyzstan needs to attract international investors to develop its oil reserves fully.

However, international investors expressed their reluctance to invest and frequently criticized the republic for its investment-unfriendly regime, frequently changed regulations, and corruption.

MOLDO. *See* MULLAH.

MOTOR ROADS. Kyrgyzstan is served by a network of 30,300 kilometers of primary and secondary roads; 22,600 kilometers are paved (CIA est., 2002). This includes 140 kilometers of international quality expressways. However, the road **transportation** system is still underdeveloped and of poor quality in eastern, central, and southern Kyrgyzstan (**Batken, Naryn,** and **Jalal Abad** *oblasts*). The **Bishkek-Osh** highway, which connects northern and southern Kyrgyzstan and is usually impassable in winter, is still under reconstruction (as of 2003) to allow year-round transportation. Other strategically important highways connect Bishkek with **Karakol** and with Almaty (**Kazakhstan**). There is a highway, which connects Kyrgyzstan with **China,** over the **Tian-Shan mountains**. In 2001 there was a report of completion of the highway from Osh to Karakorum (Pakistan), though at present the latter part cannot be used for commercial purposes.

After 1991 the Kyrgyzstan **government** faced considerable financial constraints and could not invest in expansion or reconstruction of its road network. In the 1990s due to underinvestment and the rapidly growing number of privately owned cars, the quality of the roads in the capital and other major cities deteriorated significantly. There was a total of around 480,000 motor vehicles registered in Kyrgyzstan in 2000 (up from about 210,000 in 1990), including about 420,000 passenger cars, 3,500 buses and coaches, and 12,000 trucks and vans. More recently, international institutions, such as the Asian Development Bank (ADB), World Bank, and International Monetary Fund, played a significant role in providing loans and assistance for modernizing the network, including a multimillion dollar loan for rehabilitation of the Bishkek-Osh highway and building additional tunnels along it. Within the next decade the Kyrgyzstan government also plans to invest in building new motor roads to China, in order to ease its dependence on the transportation network of neighboring Central Asian countries and to promote **trade** and **tourism** with China and along the ancient **Great Silk Road**. *See also* AIRLINES; RAILWAYS.

MUFTI. The highest Islamic legal authority and the official leader of the Muslim community in the **Kyrgyz Republic**. A *mufti* is elected by the most prominent Islamic scholars of Kyrgyzstan. Until 1991 Kyrgyzstan's Islamic clergy was subordinated to the Central Asian *Muftiat* based in Tashkent and Kyrgyzstan had no *mufti*. Until 1991 the head of the Muslim community in Kyrgyzstan had the title of *kazi*. In 1991 the Congress of Islamic authorities of Kyrgyzstan decided to secede from the *Muftiat* of Tashkent and establish its own position of *mufti*.

A *mufti* overviews the activities of the Islamic clergy in the republic, the work of the mosques, *medrese*, and **Islamic University of Kyrgyzstan**. He has the authority to proclaim a *fatwa*, a binding opinion on religious or public issues. *See also* ISLAM; UNOFFICIAL MUSLIM CLERGY.

MUFTIAT. The highest Islamic decision-making body in Kyrgyzstan based in **Bishkek**. It was established in 1991 after the Kyrgyz Islamic authorities (*Kaziat*) decided to secede from the *Muftiat* of Central Asia–Tashkent-based Central Asian Spiritual Body (SADUM in Russian abbreviation). The *Muftiat* is led by the *mufti*, an Islamic legal authority elected by the most eminent Islamic scholars of Kyrgyzstan. The *Muftiat* has the authority to issue a *fatwa*, a binding opinion on religious or public issues. However, as the **constitution of Kyrgyzstan** declares that the republic is a secular state, the state authorities supervise the work of the *Muftiat*. By law the *Muftiat* cannot take part in political activities, since the constitution prohibits the formation of political organizations on religious principles. *See also* ISLAM; KAZI; UNOFFICIAL MUSLIM CLERGY.

MULLAH. 1. A Muslim clergyman, who leads the prayers and various Islamic rituals and who oversees the work of mosques and *medreses*. 2. A religious instructor.

MURALIYEV, AMANGELDY (1947–). Kyrgyz politician. Born in Kum Aryk village in **Chui** *oblast* (northern Kyrgyzstan), Amangeldy Muraliyev graduated from a technical college in 1967 and from the **Frunze Polytechnic Institute** in 1976 (by correspondence). From 1970 to 1976 he worked in the design section of the "Selkhozmashinostroyeniye" plant in Frunze (now **Bishkek**). From 1976 to

1978 he worked in the Department of **Industry** and **Transportation** in the Frunze City Committee of the **Communist Party of Kyrgyz SSR** and from 1978 to 1982 he was the senior engineer and later the director of the "Tiazhelektromash" plant in Frunze. He worked as the director of the "Kyrgyzavtomash" auto-assembly factory in Frunze 1982–88. From 1988 to 1990 Muraliyev served as chairman of the Frunze City Council. In 1990 he was appointed chairman of the State Committee on Economics. From 1992 to 1994 he was minister of economics and finance and from 1994 to 1996 he was chairman of the State Committee on State Property. In 1996 he served as vice prime minister for industrial policy. From 1996 to 1999 he was the head of the **Osh** *oblast* administration and from 1999 to 2000 he served as prime minister of the republic.

Muraliyev played an important role in the republic's **government** during the most difficult years for Kyrgyzstan's **economy** in the 1990s. He was considered one of the important advocates of implementing market-oriented reforms.

MY COUNTRY PARTY (Menim Elkem partiasy in Kyrgyz). This is one of the new political organizations in Kyrgyzstan. It was established and registered on 19 November 1998. The party adopted a centrist political platform and stated that it supported further political reforms toward democratization and market-oriented economic changes. It also insisted that there was a need for strong government and economic planning. The party claims that it has up to 3,000 members in all parts of the republic, but its real stronghold is in **Bishkek**. Its electorate consists mainly of public sector workers and entrepreneurs. Its chairman, Almazbek Ismankulov, was a successful businessman and the director of a private hospital.

The My Country Party was active in the 2000 parliamentary elections, during which it won four seats. In 2002 Joomart Otorbaev, one of the party's leaders, was appointed deputy prime minister; the move indicated the party's growing influence in Kyrgyzstan. The party remains one of the most important members of the progovernmental coalition in the **Jogorku Kenesh** (parliament).

MYRZA (also *mirza*). 1. Historically, a title used to refer to a senior person or administrator. 2. In contemporary Kyrgyzstan a formal title used with the name of a person, equivalent to mister or sir, (i.e., Myrza Nurbek).

– N –

NANAYEV, KEMELBEK (1945–). Kyrgyz politician. Born in Merke village in **Kazakhstan**, Nanayev graduated from the **Kyrgyz State (National) University** in 1967 and from the *aspirantura* of the Moscow State University in 1970. From 1970 to 1981 he held various teaching positions in the Kyrgyz State (National) University and he worked in the Institute of Economics of the **National Academy of Sciences** 1981–82. From 1982 to 1989 he served as head of department at the Frunze (now **Bishkek**) City Committee of the **Communist Party of Kyrgyz SSR** and from 1989 to 1990 he was deputy director of the Institute of Economics of the Academy of Sciences. He worked as chairman of the *Maksat* commercial bank in Frunze 1990–91 and from 1991 to 1992 Nanayev sat on the State Committee on State Property. From 1992 to 1994 he was the chairman of the National Bank of the Kyrgyzstan. From 1994 to 1996 he served as minister of finance and from 1996 to 1999 he was first deputy prime minister. In 1999 he was appointed ambassador to **Russia**.

Nanayev played an important role in the early stages of the economic reforms in the republic, especially during the introduction of the national currency, the **som**. He was considered one of the important advocates of implementing market-oriented reforms.

NAQSHBANDIYA. One of the mystic fraternities (*tariqats*) in **Sufism** that was established in Central Asia in the 14th century. The founder of this *tariqat* was Baha ad-Din Naqshband (1318–89), renowned for his piety and spirituality. His followers traveled all over Central Asia and spread **Islam** and the teachings of the founder among various communities. By the 15th–16th centuries the *tariqat* had become one of the most influential Sufi orders in Central Asia. *Sheikhs* (scholars and spiritual leaders) and *dervishes* (members of a Sufi brotherhood) of the Naqshbandiya order played an important role in spreading Islam among nomads and pastoral nomads of Central Asia, including Kazakhs and **Kyrgyzs**. Many *sheikhs* and their students (*murids*) were purged or moved to remote areas during the Soviet era. There has been some revival of Naqshbandiya traditions in post-Soviet Kyrgyzstan, especially in **Jalal Abad** and **Osh** *oblasts*. It is widely believed that all the *muftis* of the last 50 years came from the Naqshbandiya *tariqat*.

NARYN CITY. The ninth largest city in the republic; capital of **Naryn** *oblast*. Located on the **Naryn River** in central Kyrgyzstan, about 250 kilometers southeast of **Bishkek**. It is situated 2,050 meters above sea level. Its population stood at about 40,500 (1999 census), up from about 30,400 (1979 census); this is the only *oblast* center in the republic populated almost exclusively by **Kyrgyzs** (about 97 percent). It is the only industrial and commercial center in Naryn *oblast*. It hosts light **industries, agriculture** products processing plants, Naryn State University (founded in 1996), a campus of the Central Asian University, a college of early childhood **education**, secondary schools, **libraries**, a theater, a museum, and an airport.

A small village and an inn (*karavan-sarai*) existed on the site of Naryn city most probably for centuries, as it was situated along the Torugart pass through this inhospitable part of the **Tian-Shan mountains**. The tsarist administration established a small garrison there in 1868, after acquiring this part of the Kyrgyz land. The Soviet authorities struggled for several years to establish full control in this remote area. They invested in development of the **transportation** infrastructure throughout the 1920s and 1930s and made considerable efforts to settle the local pastoral-nomad population and bring them into the state-controlled *kolhhozes*. Naryn's importance was enhanced due to its proximity to the border with **China**, with which the Soviet authorities had border disputes throughout the 1960s. In 1939 the city became the center of the newly established *oblast* (then called Tian-Shan *oblast*, abolished in 1962, and reestablished in 1970 as Naryn *oblast*). In the 1970s the government invested heavily in building hydroelectric power stations on the Naryn River, which brought considerable investments into the city as well. Since 1991 the city has been experiencing a steep decline, as the state subsidies to support local industry and agriculture were eliminated and many local enterprises were closed or downsized. Naryn city became one of the poorest cities in the republic, although the local government was making considerable efforts to attract trekker and adventure **tourism** companies.

NARYN *OBLAST*. Located in the central part of the Kyrgyz Republic, bordered by **China** in the southeast, **Jalal Abad** *oblast* in the southwest, **Osh** *oblast* in the west, **Chui** *oblast* in the north, and **Ysyk Kol** *oblast* in the northeast. It was formed in 1939 under the name of **Tian-Shan** *oblast*, abolished in 1962, but reestablished in 1970 under the name of Naryn *oblast*. It consists of Akta Alaa, At Bashy, Jumgal, Kochkor, and Naryn *raions* (districts) and **Naryn city**. It is the largest province in Kyrgyzstan, with a total area of about 45,200 square kilometers, or around 25 percent of the country's territory. It has the second smallest population in the republic, which stood at about 248,700 (1999 census), or 5 percent of the country's population, up from about 214,500 (1979 census). It has the lowest population density in the republic and one of the lowest in Central Asia. Naryn *oblast* is the country's most homogeneous *oblast* in terms of ethnic composition, as the **Kyrgyzs** make up about 99 percent of its inhabitants.

   Agriculture, food processing, and coal **mining** are the main sectors of the *oblast's* economy. During the Soviet era the *oblast* was underdeveloped due to its remote location, high elevation above sea level of the entire *oblast* (more than 1,500 meters above sea level), extremely harsh climate (Central Asia's coldest temperature of −50°C was registered there), and exceptionally high cost of **transportation**. The *oblast* specializes in animal husbandry, mainly **sheep, horses**, and **yaks**.

   Economic changes after independence in 1991 hit Naryn *oblast* hard, as it became the republic's poorest *oblast* with the highest unemployment rate. In 1991, in order to reverse the negative effect of the market-oriented reforms in the *oblast*, Kyrgyzstan's government declared the entire *oblast* a **Free Economic Zone (FEZ)**. According to official reports the Naryn FEZ attracted investments from China, **Russia**, the United States, and some other countries, but many of the registered enterprises never began work. Since the late 1990s the *oblast's* administration has been developing the **tourism** sector, especially mountain trekking and adventure tourism along one of the secret passes of the **Great Silk Road** from Kashgar (China) to the Torugart pass and further to the **Ferghana** and **Chui valleys**.

NARYN RIVER. This river is 807 kilometers long (535 kilometers within Kyrgyzstan) with a basin area of around 59,100 square kilometers (53,700 square kilometers within the republic). The river flows from the Petrova and Chymchyk glaciers of eastern Kyrgyzstan through the Middle-Naryn, Toguz Toro, and Ketmen Tube gorges into the **Ferghana valley**. It flows further to **Uzbekistan** and then joins the Kara Darya River, becoming the Syrdarya River, the second largest river in Central Asia. The highest flow of the Naryn River is from May to September, as snow melts in the high **Tian-Shan** glaciers, and its lowest flow is in November and December.

The river is one of the most important sources of drinking and irrigation water for southern Kyrgyzstan. During the Soviet era several reservoirs were built on Kyrgyzstan's part of the river along with five hydroelectric power stations and its water was used excessively for irrigation. During the droughts of the 1990s the water supply of the Naryn River to Uzbekistan became a bone of contention between the two countries. Kyrgyzstan's **government** demanded payment for the water, claiming that it needed substantial resources to maintain the water reservoirs on the Naryn River.

NATIONAL ACADEMY OF SCIENCES OF KYRGYZSTAN. After establishing the **Kyrgyz Autonomous Oblast** in 1924 (**Kyrgyz Autonomous Soviet Socialist Republic** from 1926 and **Kyrgyz Soviet Socialist Republic** [Kyrgyz SSR] from 1936) Kyrgyzstan's government made considerable efforts to create a modern academic research center on its territory. In 1924 an Academic Center was established in Pishpek (now **Bishkek**). During the next two decades, however, Kyrgyzstan's institutes of tertiary **education** became centers for most of the academic research projects. In 1943 the Academy of Sciences of the USSR established its branch in Bishkek, utilizing existing research facilities of the republic. The Kyrgyz branch of the Academy of Sciences operated eight sections, 17 laboratories, the Botanical Garden, the Museum of National Culture, and a **library**.

In 1954 the Kyrgyz Branch of the Academy of Sciences of the USSR was transformed into the Academy of Sciences of Kyrgyz SSR. It consisted of eight research institutes that covered geology, botany, chemistry, water resources and energy, zoology, medicine, history, and language and literature. Dr. Isa Akhunbayev, a medical doctor and surgeon, was elected as the first president of the Academy of Sciences.

Not only was the academy the most important research institution in the republic, it also held a great political importance. It exclusively provided the academic expertise to Kyrgyzstan's **government**, and it often had the final say in evaluating various construction projects, important ideological issues, and economic planning during the Soviet era. **Askar Akayev**, the former president of the academy, was elected the first president of Kyrgyzstan in 1990.

Since 1991 the role of the academy has declined significantly due to extensive budget cuts and political changes in the republic. In addition, the research activities were gradually dispersed among major national universities and institutions of tertiary education, though the academy preserved its status of major research institution in the republic. In December 1993 the Kyrgyz Academy of Sciences was transformed into the National Academy of Sciences of the Kyrgyz Republic and a branch was established in the southern *oblast* of the country—the city of **Osh**. The National Academy is an independent nongovernmental research institution with a budget funded both by the government and by independent sources, including the private sector. An assembly of academicians elects the president of the academy. At the beginning of 2001 the National Academy consisted of 27 institutes and centers with 1,502 specialists, including 45 academicians, 63 correspondent-members, 117 doctors, and 315 *kandidat nauk*.

In 2002 the academy included the following institutions: Institute of History, Institute of Linguistics, Institute of Philosophy and Law, Institute of Biochemistry and Physiology, Institute of Biology and Soil Studies, Institute of Chemistry and Chemical Technologies, Institute of Forestry and Nut Studies, Institute of High Altitudes Physiology and Experimental Pathology, Institute of Automatics, Institute of Geology, Institute of Machinery Sciences, Institute of Mathematics, Institute of Physics, Institute of Minerals, Institute of Seismology, Institute of Water Problems, Institute of Complex Use of Natural Resources, Institute of Public (Social) Sciences, Institute of Biosphere, Institute of Engineering and Electronics, Institute of Medical Problems, Institute of New Technologies, Center for Economics, Center for Manasology (*Manas* epic studies), Center for Social Research, and Department of Dungan Studies and Botanical Garden. The academy maintains its own library collection and **archive**, which are open to the public, and publishes several scholarly journals.

NATIONAL HOLIDAYS. The government of the Kyrgyz Republic declared the following eight days as public holidays: 1 January—New Year's; 8 March—International Women's Day; 21 March—**Nawruz**; 1 May—International Workers' Solidarity Day; 5 May—Constitution Day; 9 May—Day of the Victory; 31 August—Independence Day; 2 December—National Day. In addition, Kyrgyzstan celebrates *Ramazan-ait* (*Aid-al-Fitr* in Arabic) and *Qurban-ait* (*Aid-al-Adha* in Arabic); the dates of the religious celebrations move from year to year according to the Islamic lunar calendar.

NATIONAL SECURITY COMMITTEE (NSC) (Komitet Natsionalnoi Bezopastnosti in Russian). A state-controlled agency in charge of public safety and national security. Kyrgyzstan inherited from the Soviet era the Security infrastructure of the former **Komitet Gosudarstvennoi Bezopastnosti (KGB)**. In 1991 it came under the jurisdiction of Kyrgyzstan. The NSC together with the **militsia** assume a key role in maintaining law and order and in preserving the security of the state against any threat of terrorism, organized crime, or any other actions from inside and outside the republic. The head of the NSC is appointed by the president and he is accountable to the **Jogorku Kenesh** (parliament). It is estimated that the committee has about 2,000 people under its command, though since 1991 it has suffered from falling discipline, corruption, poor training, and poor equipment. In addition, there is a specially trained unit of commandos, which could be used against terrorist threats and organized crime groups.

The NSC could be mobilized to support the army in case of emergency. It is also responsible for carrying out border controls with **Kazakhstan, Tajikistan,** and **Uzbekistan**, and it checks on **Commonwealth of Independent States's** flights in Kyrgyzstan's airports. One of the tests for reliability of Kyrgyzstan's security forces came in 1999 and 2000, when guerrillas from Tajikistan crossed over into **Batken** *oblast* (then *raion*) and took several hostages. The NSC agents were deployed to conduct major intelligence-gathering operations and supported the **army** units. In 2001 and 2002 there were reports that the United States pledged anti-terrorist equipment and special training for the NSC. *See also* MILITANT INCURSIONS.

NATIONAL STATISTICAL COMMITTEE (NATSTATCOM). The National Statistical Agency of Kyrgyzstan responsible for conducting censuses and gathering and publishing statistical data. The Natstatcom has its own publishing center and a large **archive**, which is open to the public with some restrictions. It regularly publishes statistical data, which is open to the public, as well as classified statistical data for government officials only (called in Russian *Dlia sluzhebnogo polzovaniya*).

NAWRUZ (also *Nouruz*). A traditional spring festival celebrated among the **Kyrgyzs** since ancient pre-Islamic times. The *Nawruz* starts on the first day of spring according to the solar calendar or 21 March. The *Nawruz* was not celebrated during the Soviet era, but it was reestablished after 1991.

NONGOVERNMENTAL ORGANIZATIONS (NGOs). Since 1991, more than 3,000 NGOs have been established and registered in the **Kyrgyz Republic**, though many of them disappeared or become inactive. At present, only between 600 and 1,000 NGOs, or between 20 and 30 percent of those registered, are actually active. They focus on providing various social services not only in the capital of **Bishkek** and surrounding areas but also, most important, in remote mountain villages. Most of the NGOs are led by local activists, who try to increase awareness of the importance of volunteerism and philanthropy. A significant number of the NGOs are led by **women** who were very active in public life during the Soviet era (when informal quotas required government to reserve 30 to 40 percent of public positions for women), but who lost their jobs and political presence due to the economic recession and political changes in the 1990s. In the late 1990s several NGOs introduced micro-credit programs to farmers with the assistance of the Asian Development Bank (ADB).

The NGOs provide permanent and temporary employment to a considerable number of people. Although precise figures are not available, up to 5 percent of the working adult population, or approximately 100,000 people, are engaged in various voluntary activities. This figure does not take into account the *ashar*, an old tradition of assistance to community members in need through gathering donations locally or organizing community work for single mothers, elderly people, the disabled, and so on.

– O –

OBLAST. Province, a territorial-administrative unit in Kyrgyzstan established during the Soviet era. There were several changes in administrative division during the Soviet and post-Soviet eras, including a discussion of the possibility of abolishing *oblasts* altogether in order to save on administrative expenditures. As of 2003 Kyrgyzstan is divided into seven *oblasts* (**Batken, Chui, Ysyk Kol, Jalal Abad, Naryn, Osh,** and **Talas**). Each *oblast* is in turn divided into *raions* (districts). *See also* ADMINISTRATIVE STRUCTURE.

OFFICIAL MUSLIM CLERGY. Until 1991 the official Muslim clergy in Central Asia was represented by those practicing Muslim scholars and *mullahs* who formally registered with and were supervised by the Central Asian *Muftiat* (Russian abbreviation SADUM) in accordance with the Soviet-era regulation. Their activities were also regulated by the state through the Department of Religious Affairs. This registration requirement remained in place after 1991, when Kyrgyzstan's *Kaziat* seceded from the SADUM and established its own *Muftiat*. Traditionally, the official Muslim clergy were loyal to the government, held moderate views on current affairs, and stayed away from politics; this was in a sharp contrast to the **unofficial Muslim clergy**, who were always critical of the secular government and sought to be involved in politics.

OKEYEV, TOLOMUSH (1936–). Prominent Kyrgyz film producer. Born in Ton village in **Ysyk Kol** *oblast* (eastern Kyrgyzstan), Tolomush Okeyev graduated from Leningrad (now Saint Petersburg) Institute of Film Engineers in 1958 and the Moscow High Courses for Film Producers in 1966. From 1956 to 1964 he worked as a sound operator at the *Kyrgzfilm* studio. From 1965 to 1993 he worked as a film producer at the studio. Concurrently, from 1988 to 1990 he served as first secretary of the **Union of Cinematographers of Kyrgyzstan**. In 1993 he was appointed ambassador to Turkey and Israel.

Okeyev was considered one of the first and most prominent Kyrgyz film producers, whose works were widely acclaimed as classics of Central Asian cinematography during the Soviet era. His movies *Nebo nashego detstva* (1967), *Poklonis' ognyu* (1972), *Krasnoye Yabloko* (1975), *Ulan* (1977), and others, which were produced mainly in Russian but praised the natural philosophy of the **Kyrgyz** people and culture, won numerous awards at all-Soviet and international festivals. During the post-Soviet era Okeyev, unlike many of his other colleagues, chose to abstain from politics and focused on the promotion of Kyrgyz culture.

ORDERS OF KYRGYZSTAN. The **Jogorku Kenesh** (parliament) adopted the law on State Awards of the **Kyrgyz Republic** in 1996 and established the following state orders: *Kyrgyz Respublikasynyn Baatyry* (Hero of the Kyrgyz Republic); *Manas* Order; *Danaker* Order; *Baatyr Ene* Order (Order of Mother-Hero); *Erdik* Medal (Medal of Courage); *Dank* Medal (Medal of Honor); *Kyzhyrmon Kyzmat Otogondugu Uchun* Medal (Medal for Excellent Service); and *Ene Danky* Medal (Medal of Honorable Mother).

In addition there are several state awards established in Kyrgyzstan, including the **Toktogul** State Premium of the Kyrgyz Republic (in the fields of literature, art, and **architecture**) and the State Premium of the Kyrgyz Republic for Sciences and Technology. There are honorary titles for achievements in various fields such as People's Artist of the Kyrgyz Republic (People's Writer, People's Poet, People's Painter, People's Teacher). Also citizens are awarded distinguished titles such as Renowned Jurist of the Kyrgyz Republic, Renowned (Medical) Doctor, Renowned Educator, and so on.

ORGANIZATION FOR SECURITY AND COOPERATION IN EUROPE (OSCE). The organization was previously known as the Conference on Security and Cooperation in Europe (CSCE). It was established in 1972. In 1990 the Charter of Paris changed the CSCE status from an international forum to a permanent international organization. In 1995 the CSCE changed its name to the present one.

Kyrgyzstan joined the organization in 1992 along with other states of the **Commonwealth of Independent States (CIS)** and cooperated with it on a number of issues. The OSCE partnership was essential in arranging various negotiations at the regional level and especially in negotiating the peace process in **Tajikistan**. The OSCE also played a significant role in promoting human rights, civil society, and conflict prevention issues and monitoring parliamentary and presidential elections in Kyrgyzstan in 1995 and 2000.

ORGANIZATION OF THE ISLAMIC CONFERENCE (OIC) (Munazamat Al-Mutamir Al-Islami in Arabic). An organization established in 1969 to promote cooperation and solidarity between Muslim countries. The **Kyrgyz Republic** joined the organization in 1992 along with other Central Asian states in hopes of attracting investments from Middle Eastern countries. In the mid-1990s Kyrgyzstan obtained some assistance from the Islamic Development Bank and cooperated with the OIC on a number of issues. However, Kyrgyzstan played a very minor role in the activities of the OIC and did not support its stand on several issues. The partnership between Kyrgyzstan and the OIC was strained, as Kyrgyzstan established diplomatic relations with Israel and was less critical of Israeli policy toward Palestine in 2001–02.

ORMON NIYAZBEK-UULU (Ormon Khan) (1791–1854). An influential *manap* and leader of **Kyrgyz tribes** in the **Chui valley** in the 19th century. Ormon Niyazbek-Uulu played a notable role in political and military developments in northern Kyrgyzstan in the second half of the 19th century. In 1841 he managed to organize a *kurultai* (congress) and to bring together several influential Kyrgyz tribes of northern Kyrgyzstan into a confederation. The *kurultai* elected Ormon Niyazbek-Uulu as the **khan** of the Kyrgyzs. He attempted to establish an independent principality and destroyed several of the **Kokand Khanate**'s fortresses in northern Kyrgyzstan. He also attempted to establish a working administration and systematize taxation and organize the judiciary system. He invited several influential scholars from the cities of Andijan and Namangan to open schools. Ormon Niyazbek-Uulu also ordered the writing of one of the first histories of the Kyrgyz tribes—*Zho'op-Name*. In the late 1840s he successfully fought against the intervention of the Kazakh tribes led by Kenesary Kasym-Uulu (Kenesary Khan) and in a decisive battle his troops defeated the Kazakhs. However, the war significantly undermined the military potential of Ormon Niyazbek-Uulu and in the 1850s several Kyrgyz tribes left the confederation. He launched several expeditions against these tribes, but he was killed in one of the battles in 1854.

OSH CITY. This is the second largest city in the republic, after **Bishkek**, the second largest industrial center, and the capital of **Osh**

oblast. The city is located in southern Kyrgyzstan, 360 kilometers southwest of Bishkek. Its population stood at about 211,900 (1999 census), up from about 169,200 (1979 census), consisting mainly of **Kyrgyz** and Uzbeks, but also including significant communities of Russians, Ukrainians, Tatars, Tajiks, and some others. It is an important industrial and **transportation** center in southern Kyrgyzstan: light **industries**, machinery production, textiles (90 percent of the republic's cotton fabric), natural silk (100 percent), and cotton-processing plants. It also hosts the Osh State University (founded in 1951), Osh Technological University (founded in 1991), Kyrgyz-Uzbek University (founded in 1997), **libraries**, two theaters, museums, several medieval mosques, the second largest airport in the country, and a railway station.

Osh is the oldest city in the republic and probably one of the oldest cities in Central Asia. Kyrgyz archeologists claim that the city's history could be dated as far back as 2,000 years B.C. Alexander the Great is said to have passed Osh in his conquest of the ancient Central Asian states of Bactria and Sogdiana. Historical chronicles mentioned that for centuries Osh was an important entrepot on one of the routes of the **Great Silk Road** and it was a significant silk production center itself. The history of the city is also connected with **Zaheriddin Muhammad Babur** (1483–1530), one of the greatest descendants of Tamerlane (Timur). Osh had been part of Babur's fiefdom and his summer capital before he moved to India and established the great Mogul Empire. In addition, Osh was considered one of the major religious centers in Central Asia and a site for pilgrimages to the Sulayman Tash (Solomon's throne). However, in the 16th–17th centuries the city started to lose its significance, as the Great Silk Road and regional trade dwindled due to the discovery of the maritime route from Europe to India and further to **China**, and due to the never-ending feuds between Central Asian *khans*. Gradually the city became part of the **Kokand Khanate,** but it never recovered its past glory.

Russian imperial troops clashed with the Kokand Khanate and in 1876 the Khanate was conquered and abolished. Yet several Kyrgyz **tribes** in **Alay** and **Pamir** (the southern part of present-day Kyrgyzstan) continued to struggle against the Russian advance, despite the fact that many Kyrgyz tribes in northern Kyrgyzstan had already voluntarily accepted the **Russian Empire**'s protection. During the tsarist era

Osh became the center of Osh district in **Ferghana** *oblast* and grew rapidly, hosting new industries and businesses. After the Revolution of 1917, many **Kyrgyzs** joined the **Basmachi** resistance movement, and it took the Bolsheviks nearly a decade to establish Soviet control over this portion of the Kyrgyz land. After the national delimitation of 1924 Osh became part of Kyrgyzstan, and in 1939 it became the center of the newly established Osh *oblast*. The Soviet authorities invested significantly in the development of heavy and light industries, especially large textile and silk factories, throughout the 1930s and 1940s, making Osh a major powerhouse of the republic.

Representatives of the Osh elite became leading powerbrokers in the political life of the republic, as the *oblast*'s economy grew extensively during the Soviet era. Yet behind the façade of economic and political success there were growing tensions between the two major ethnic groups—Kyrgyzs and Uzbeks—in the city throughout the 1980s. These tensions culminated in the **Osh-Uzgen conflicts** in June 1990, when representatives of the two communities clashed over land distribution. In the post-Soviet era the political and economic importance of Osh declined significantly, as its economy experienced a severe recession and industries downsized their activities.

The city was greatly expanded between the 1950s and 1970s, and its **architecture** reflected a combination of the traditional Central Asian style and Soviet functionalism. Many **government** and cultural buildings were constructed in the semi-classic style, while apartment buildings in the central part of the city were built of red brick or concrete. Yet Osh retained its oriental flavor, especially in its large bazaars, mosques, and private housing zones. During the post-Soviet era the city's infrastructure experienced visible decay, although the city still remains very green and livable.

OSH *OBLAST*. The most populous province in the **Kyrgyz Republic**, located in the southern part of the republic, bordered by **Tajikistan** in the south, **Batken** *oblast* in the southwest, **Uzbekistan** in the west, **Jalal Abad** *oblast* in the north, and **Naryn** *oblast* in the northeast. Osh *oblast* was established in 1939. It was reorganized in 1980, 1990, and 1999, as the **Talas**, Jalal Abad, and later Batken areas of Osh *oblast* were established as separate *oblasts*. At the beginning of 2003 it consisted of Alay, Aravan, Kara Kulja, Kara Suu, Nookat, **Uzgen**, and Chong Alay *raions* (districts) and **Osh city**. Osh *oblast* has an area of 29,200 square kilometers, or just over 16 percent of Kyrgyz territory, and it is the fourth largest *oblast* in the republic. Its **population** was estimated at about 1,176,700 (1999 census), up from about 733,700 (1979 census), or 20 percent of the country's population. The population almost doubled since 1970, due to improved health and medical facilities and longer life expectancy. In 2000 the birth rate stood at 26 per 1,000. Osh *oblast*'s population is young, with 43.4 percent below the age of 14 and just 7 percent older than 65. If the current demographic trend remains unchanged, the population is expected to double once more within the next 25–30 years. The **Kyrgyzs** account for 63.8 percent of the population. The *oblast* is home to the largest Uzbek community (31.1 percent) in the republic. Others include Russians (1.2 percent), Uygurs (0.9 percent), Tajiks (0.5 percent), Tatars (0.5), Turks, and Azerbaijanis.

Osh *oblast* is the third largest powerhouse in the republic after **Bishkek** and **Chui** *oblast*. **Agriculture**, machinery, light **industry**, and mining are the main sectors of its economy. Since the Soviet era the *oblast* has specialized in producing consumer products and agricultural products. The *oblast* produces 90 percent of the republic's cotton fabric and 90 percent of cotton yarn, 100 percent of natural silk fabric, 40 percent of vegetable oil, 16 percent of cotton, and 31 percent of tobacco.

In the early 1990s the *oblast* experienced a severe economic recession and struggled to attract foreign direct investments (FDIs) in order to revive its economy. In 2002 Osh *oblast* had the second highest unemployment rate in Kyrgyzstan, after Naryn *oblast*, and it became a major entrepot on the illicit **drugs** route from **Afghanistan** to **Russia** and eastern and western Europe.

OSH-KHONA. *See* ASH-KHANA.

OSH-UZGEN CONFLICTS (also known as Osh-Uzgen events). In May–June 1990, a quarrel between local communities of **Kyrgyzs** and Uzbeks turned into disastrous riots in the *oblast*'s administrative center of **Osh**, and spread to the Kyrgyz provincial town of **Uzgen** (both are very close to the border with **Uzbekistan**). The immediate cause for the violence was the news that, in response to the demands of the Kyrgyz movement "Osh-Aimagy," the local administration was going to distribute plots of land to the landless Kyrgyzs at the expense of the Uzbek community. The conflict was based on this communal disagreement, rather than any political or religious differences. The security service and **militsia** could not deal with such a crisis effectively. The events became the bloodiest ones that occurred at that time with official calculations of 220 dead and a thousand hospitalized (unofficial estimates gave from 600 to 1,200 killed during the turmoil). These events had a shocking effect, as they destabilized the political situation in the whole **Ferghana valley,** shared by Kyrgyzstan, **Tajikistan,** and Uzbekistan.

Some radical participants demanded redrawing of the national borders between Kyrgyzstan and Uzbekistan in order to accommodate the ethnic composition. The curfew and mediation of several **non-governmental organizations** (NGOs), *aksakals,* and leaders of the local communities brought the conflict to an end, but the tensions between communities remained for nearly a decade. *See also* MASALIYEV, ABSAMAT.

OTUNBAYEVA, ROZA (1950–). Kyrgyz politician and diplomat. Born in Frunze (now **Bishkek**), Roza Otunbayeva graduated from the Moscow State University in 1972. From 1975 to 1981 she was a lecturer at **Kyrgyz State (National) University** and from 1981 to 1986 she was secretary of the Frunze City Committee of the **Communist Party of Kyrgyz SSR.** From 1986 to 1988 she worked as deputy chairman of the Council of Ministers and concurrently minister of foreign affairs of Kyrgyzstan. She was invited by Foreign Minister Edward Shevardnadze to join the Soviet Ministry of Foreign Affairs in 1988. From 1989 to 1991 she served as general secretary to the chairman of the Ministerial Committee on the United Nations Educational, Scientific, and Cultural Organization (UNESCO) and member of the collegiums of the Soviet Ministry of Foreign Affairs. In 1991 she was the Soviet Union's representative to UNESCO.

In 1992 Otunbayeva returned to Kyrgyzstan and was appointed vice prime minister and minister of foreign affairs. From 1992 to 1994 she served as the first Kyrgyz ambassador extraordinary and plenipotentiary to the United States and Canada. From 1994 to 1997 she was minister of foreign affairs and from 1997 to 2002 she was ambassador extraordinary and plenipotentiary to the United Kingdom and Northern Ireland. In 2002 she became deputy special representative of the United Nations Observer Mission in Georgia (UNOMIG).

Otunbayeva played a key role in the formulation of the republic's **foreign policies,** especially in the early 1990s and in building close relations with the U.S. and other Western governments. She contributed extensively to promoting the democratic image of the country in the Western world. Otunbayeva was considered one of the potential candidates to the post of prime minister, but she fell out of favor due to her criticism of the Kyrgyz **government**'s policies.

OZGEN. *See* UZGEN.

– P –

PAMIR-ALAY MOUNTAINS. A mountain range located south of the **Ferghana valley**, which forms part of Kyrgyzstan's southern border with **Tajikistan**. Most of these mountains are located in northeastern Tajikistan and their northern part is in southern Kyrgyzstan (**Alay mountain range**). In the 18th and 19th centuries the valleys in the Pamir-Alay mountains were controlled by various Kyrgyz **tribes**, who vigorously resisted the expansion of the **Kokand Khanate** in the first half of the 19th century. The population of the Alay valley also offered the most resistance to the **Russian Empire** advance in the 19th century and opposed the Soviet government in the 1920s.

The Pamir-Alay mountains have a very harsh climate with winter temperatures falling below −20°C. Several of its valleys are located more than 1,500 meters above sea level and therefore they were sparsely populated and economically underdeveloped. After the **militant incursions** in 1999 and 2000 the Kyrgyz **government** made significant investments to strengthen the borders between Kyrgyzstan and Tajikistan in the Pamir-Alay mountains.

PAMIRS (from ancient Iranian *pai-mir*—foot of Mitra [god of sun]). A mountainous land bounded by the Trans-Alay range in the north, Sarykol range in the east, Lake Zorkul, the Pamir River, and the upstream part of the Pianzh River in the south. The Pamir highlands are divided between **Afghanistan, Tajikistan,** and Kyrgyzstan (**Pamir-Alay mountains**). The Pamirs have an average elevation of about 3,960 meters. Several of the highest peaks in the **Commonwealth of Independent States (CIS)** can be found in the Pamir area, with an altitude of more than 7,000 meters above sea level. Historically the Pamirs are subdivided into the western Pamirs and eastern Pamirs. Large glaciers in the eastern Pamirs conserved significant reserves of clear water, which is becoming particularly important due to the growing water shortages in Central Asia.

In the 1990s the Kyrgyz **government** initiated the construction of the **Osh**-Karakorum (Pakistan) highway through the Pamir mountains, while the Tajikistan government initiated the building of a road from Tajikistan to **China**. Both projects require significant investments to be completed, because of the difficult terrain of the Pamir mountains.

PARANJA. See HURJUM.

PARLIAMENT OF THE KYRGYZ REPUBLIC. *See* JOGORKU KENESH.

PARTY OF AFGHANISTAN'S WAR VETERANS (Afgan sogushunun ardagerlerin sayasii partiasy in Kyrgyz). A party established as the Democratic Party of Economic Unity and first registered on 14 October 1994. It was re-registered on 13 September 1999 under the current name. The party demands wider social guarantees to the citizens of the republic combined with a free market economy and private entrepreneurship. It also insists that there is a need for a balanced **foreign policy**, which should follow the international principles of the United Nations. The party claims that it has up to 11,000 members in **Bishkek, Ysyk Kol, Osh,** and **Talas** *oblasts* of the republic. Its chairman, Akbokon Tashtanbekov, has been a successful businessman and a member of the commission on changes to the **constitution of Kyrgyzstan**.

The party was active in the 2000 parliamentary elections, during which it won four seats, becoming one of the most visible groups on the country's political landscape. The party remains one of the prominent members of the progovernmental coalition in the **Jogorku Kenesh** (parliament).

PARTY OF COMMUNISTS OF KYRGYZSTAN (PCK) (Kyrgyzstan Kommunisterdin partiasy in Kyrgyz). This is the official political successor of the Soviet-era **Communist Party of Kyrgyz SSR** and one of the most influential left-wing political organizations in Kyrgyzstan. It was established and registered on 17 September 1992, after the **government** lifted the ban on the Communist Party. The ban was introduced in August 1991 after an alleged attempt to launch a coup d'etat against President **Askar Akayev**. Throughout the 1990s the party significantly moderated its political program. The PCK calls for the restoration of centralized economic planning, though it accepts private entrepreneurship. It also demands state control over foreign **trade** and state support for domestic **industry** and **agriculture**, state guarantees of jobs, pensions, and free medical services and **education**, and eradication of mass poverty. The party further demands that the **Kyrgyz Republic** should join the Belarus-Russia Union and work toward "restoration of its political and economic ties" with the **Commonwealth of Independent States (CIS)** partners.

The PCK claims that it has up to 25,000 members, mainly among the older Soviet-era generation of Communist Party members. Its chairman, **Absamat Masaliyev**, who led the Communist Party during the last years of the Soviet Union, is regarded as one of the most experienced opposition figures, although he is deeply unpopular among the moderate intelligentsia, members of the democratic parties, and hardline nationalists for his role in the **Osh-Uzgen conflicts** in 1990. In 1995 the party leader challenged the incumbent president and came in second in the presidential election, receiving 24.4 percent of the votes.

The PCK experienced a steep decline of its support base and in its influence throughout the 1990s, despite the fact that it significantly moderated its political platform and attempted to relaunch itself as the major mainstream political organization in the republic. In the 2000 parliamentary elections the party won six seats, becoming the second largest political group in the **Jogorku Kenesh** (parliament). The party received another boost in 2002 on the wave of the opposition attempt to force the resignation of the government and President Akayev for mishandling the **Aksy conflict,** as support from the party was seen to be important in forming a united opposition front against the regime.

PASTORAL NOMADISM (also pastoralism). An economy based on animal herding (**sheep, horses,** cattle) and movement of herders and their families in search of pasture. Traditionally, the **Kyrgyzs** were engaged in a subsistence semi-pastoral nomadic animal husbandry, raising Kyrgyz horses, sheep, goats, cattle, and **yaks** in the ecologically fragile mountain valleys of the **Tian-Shan** and **Pamir-Alay mountains.** Their technique, developed through hundreds of years, utilized the unique climate and land resources in their mountainous homeland without damaging them. The economy of so-called vertical pastoral nomadism was based on seasonal migration to the valleys in the lower reaches of mountains during the winter (what they called the *kyshtoo*), when deep snow covered the tops of mountain ranges and the temperature often fell below 20°C. In summer they migrated to the *jayloo* (summer camps), the valleys in the higher reaches of the mountains, as water of melting glaciers and rains helped the grass to grow in the rich pasture-lands of the *jayloo*. The *jayloo* provided enough grass for animals and an escape for people and animals from the summer heat.

This pastoral nomadism in the Tian-Shan mountains provided a unique economic niche for the Kyrgyz **tribes,** as the Uzbek and Tajik settlers controlled oases in the west and the Kazakh tribes controlled vast grasslands in the north. The Kyrgyzs often bought wheat, barley, and oats from their settled neighbors, though they also cultivated some crops. Hunting in the mountain forests was another source of livelihood for people, especially when diseases, conflicts, or *barymta* (animal theft, often as revenge) damaged their animal stock. This animal husbandry provided the Kyrgyz tribes with both staple food and products for trade or exchange with settled neighbors or with traders from other countries, who continued to travel and trade on what once was the **Great Silk Road.** *See also* AGRICULTURE; COLLECTIVIZATION.

PERESTROIKA **(restructuring).** A program of political reforms introduced by the last Soviet leader, Mikhail Gorbachev, between 1985 and 1991 in order to reform the Soviet system. This included political and economic liberalization and decentralization, abandoning the strict ideological approach to international relations and domestic policies, and fighting corruption. In the case of Kyrgyzstan, *pere-*

stroika led to the removal of the old leadership under accusation of corruption, significant changes in nationality policy, introduction of competitive elections, and private entrepreneurship.

PIATILETKA. *See* FIVE-YEAR PLAN FOR THE DEVELOPMENT OF THE NATIONAL ECONOMY.

PISHPEK. The name of a small town and a fortress of the **Kokand Khanate** in the **Chui valley**, which became the capital of Kyrgyzstan in 1924. In 1926 it was renamed Frunze and in 1991 **Bishkek**.

POBEDY PEAK (also Jengish peak in Kyrgyz, translation of Victory Peak). The mountain peak located in the Kokshaltay mountain range, the eastern part of the **Tian-Shan mountains**, close to the Kyrgyz-**China** border. The height of Pobedy Peak is 7,439 meters, and it is the highest peak in Kyrgyzstan and the second highest mountain peak in Central Asia. The peak was only identified in 1943, and it is regarded as one of the most difficult summits to climb in Central Asia. Its name commemorates the Soviet victory in World War II. After 1991 Kyrgyz maps often refer to it as **Jengish** peak, which is the Kyrgyz translation of the original name.

POLICE. *See* MILITSIA.

POPULAR UPRISING OF 1873–1876 IN KOKAND (also known as Kokand uprising). A popular uprising against the ruler of the **Kokand Khanate**—Khudoyar **Khan**—that brought down the Khanate and led to its abolishment. The uprising started in 1873 in response to the repression of the Kyrgyz **tribes** in the **Ferghana valley** and a sharp increase in taxes. It was led by Iskhak Mullah Hasan-ogly, who adopted the name of Pulat-bek. The rebels successfully fought against Khudoyar Khan's troops and seized several important towns. Some influential Kyrgyz tribal leaders, and the children of the **khan**, the *beks* of Andijan and Margelan, joined the uprising in 1874. Khudoyar Khan was defeated and escaped to Tashkent, seeking the protection of **Russian Empire** troops in 1875. Nasreddin Bek, a son of the former ruler, inherited the throne, and he recognized Russian suzerainty; however, he was overthrown by Pulat Bek. General Michael Skobelev, who arrived with a large Russian army from Tashkent, defeated the rioters in Andijan and Uchkurgan in January–February 1876. Pulat-Bek escaped and found refuge in the mountains, but he was captured and executed in 1876. After defeating the rebels, the Russian authorities abolished the Khanate on 19 February 1876.

POPULAR UPRISING OF 1898 (also known as Andijan uprising). One of Central Asia's largest popular uprisings against the **Russian Empire**, led by Madali-Ishan and widely supported by various Kyrgyz **tribes**. It started in a small town close to Andijan city (now in **Uzbekistan**, around 50 kilometers northwest of **Osh city**) in 1898 as a result of popular discontent fueled by religious zeal. Between 10,000 and 20,000 people organized in large groups seized the city and destroyed various properties associated with the Russian administration, but they were quickly dispersed. They also intended to seize Osh, but failed. Several influential Kyrgyz tribal leaders joined the uprising and confiscated properties belonging to those who collaborated with the Russian authorities. The Russian troops, who arrived soon from Tashkent, clashed with the armed groups of rioters and captured the riot leaders. Several rebel groups escaped and found refuge in the mountains in the **Ferghana valley**. For a year or two after its suppression small armed groups of **Kyrgyzs** continued to ambush Russian settlements and administrative offices.

POPULAR UPRISING OF 1916. One of Central Asia's largest popular uprisings against the tsarist regime and the largest on the territory of present-day Kyrgyzstan. This mass uprising of Kazakhs, **Kyrgyzs**, and Uzbeks was triggered by the June 1916 decree on mobilization of 250,000 people (who were traditionally exempted from military services) to carry out war-related duties in the unpopular war of the **Russian Empire** against Germany and its ally Turkey, the guardian of the Holy Places and culturally close to the Turkic people. However, the uprising had much deeper roots, as it was also a reaction to economic depression, seizure of arable land from the local population by Russian settlers, war taxes, and skyrocketing food prices.

The local rioters attacked Russian settlements, administrative centers, and gendarmerie headquarters, destroying property and killing settlers and local administrators mainly in Semirechiye *oblast*

(**Jetisuu**) and **Ferghana** *oblast*. In retaliation the tsarist administration mobilized its armed forces and Cossack regiments fought back against rioters, killing thousands, and driving tens of thousands of civilians out of their land and homes. In late 1916 many Kyrgyz families were forced to escape to Chinese Kashgar through high mountain passes, often covered with impassable snow at this time of the year. Various estimates indicate that up to 140,000 Kyrgyzs were either killed, died frozen or of starvation, disappeared in the war calamities, or migrated to **China**. Some rioters later joined the **Basmachi movement**. *See also* SEMIRECHIYE COSSACKS.

POPULATION. The population of the **Kyrgyz Republic** was estimated at 5 million in August 2002, up from 663,000 in 1897. During the 20th century, Kyrgyzstan's population experienced not only a significant increase in size but also considerable changes in literacy rate, life expectancy, ethnic composition, and reproduction behavior. It almost doubled since the 1960s due to high reproduction rate (45.5 percent of Kyrgyz families had five and more children in 1979), improved health, and longer life expectancy (up from an average 43.4 years in 1938 to 69.1 years in 1979). Immigration of people from other parts of the Union of Soviet Socialist Republics (USSR) also contributed to the rapid growth of the population in the 1960s and 1970s.

Since 1991 the republic has experienced a major change in population movements. There are serious difficulties in assessing current changes, as existing statistical data is quite unreliable and incomplete. Around 600,000–650,000 of the Russian-speaking population emigrated, either permanently or temporarily from 1989 to 2003. The major destinations for migrants from Kyrgyzstan are **Russia**, Ukraine, Germany, **Kazakhstan,** and some other countries. In addition between 100,000 and 250,000 Kyrgyz citizens arrived as temporary workers in those countries (many of them unregistered). They are mainly employed in the low-skill and low-wage construction and services sectors and in agricultural plantations in neighboring Kazakhstan and Russia. According to the *CIA World Factbook,* the emigration rate stood at about 2.66 migrants per 1,000 population in 2002, or approximately 15,000 a year, though it is significantly lower than the emigration peak of about 120,000 people in 1993. In the meantime, a significant number of ethnic **Kyrgyzs** moved to Kyrgyzstan from

Tajikistan, Uzbekistan, and other parts of the former USSR. In 2002 the birth rate stood at 26.11 births per 1,000 while the death rate stood at 9.1 deaths per 1,000 (CIA est.). The population growth rate in Kyrgyzstan is 1.45 percent (2002), and if the current trend in fertility rate remains unchanged it is estimated that the population of the country would double by 2050.

Kyrgyzstan's population is unevenly distributed, with almost three-fourths, or 3.5 million, living in **Jalal Abad, Osh,** and **Chui** *oblasts*. The average population density is about 25 people per square kilometer (65 people per square mile); however, it ranges between 40 people per square kilometer (103 people per square mile) in Osh and Chui *oblasts* to 5.5 people per square kilometer (14.2 people per square mile) in **Naryn** *oblast*. Some parts of northeastern Kyrgyzstan are uninhabited due to the high mountain altitude and harsh climate.

Kyrgyzstan is a multinational country with a very diverse population. The Kyrgyzs (singular Kyrgyz) make up 64.9 percent of the population. Ethnic Uzbeks, the second largest ethnic group, make up 13.8 percent of the population, Russians comprise 12.5 percent, and other various groups make up the remaining 8.8 percent of the population. The current ethnic structure was mainly formed during the 20th century, when the tsarist and then the Soviet administrations encouraged migration from central Russia, Ukraine, and Caucasus. Kyrgyzstan's population is very young, with 34.4 percent (male 838,224; female 821,230) below the age of 14 and just about 6.2 percent of the population (male 113,861; female 185,609) above 65 (CIA 2002 est.).

Urbanization did not penetrate Kyrgyzstani society very far. In 1999 just over 34.8 percent of the population lived in urban areas, up from 33.5 percent in 1959, but down from 38.3 percent in 1979. Kyrgyzstan along with Tajikistan are the only countries in the **Commonwealth of Independent States (CIS)** that experienced a decline of population in urban areas. This was mainly attributed to the emigration of the Slavic population from major urban areas of the republic. The country's capital city, **Bishkek** (known as Frunze between 1926 and 1991), is home to 720,000 people (2002) or 14 percent of the population. However, independent experts estimated the actual figure at between 1.0 and 1.3 million people, including temporary and seasonal workers and migrants.

PRESIDENCY IN KYRGYZSTAN. The office of the president was introduced in 1990 according to the amendments to the Soviet Constitution. Initially the first president was elected by the **Supreme Soviet** (parliament) and fully accountable to it. According to the new changes in 1991 the president was elected by popular vote. The first post-Soviet **constitution of Kyrgyzstan** (May 1993) provided that the president should be a Kyrgyzstan citizen, aged between 35 and 65, with a good command of the **Kyrgyz language** (according to the new amendments since 2000 candidates should sit for a written exam), and reside in the republic for no fewer than 15 years before nomination. The president can be elected to the post for only two consecutive terms of five years each.

According to the constitution the president has broad authority including the following powers: to determine the structure of the **government**; to appoint and dismiss (with the consent of the **Jogorku Kenesh**) the prime minister; to appoint and remove (with the advice of the prime minister) heads of administrative agencies; to accept the resignation of the prime minister, the government, or an individual member of the government; to appoint the state secretary; to constitute and head the National Security Council of the Kyrgyz Republic and other coordinating bodies; to nominate, for selection by the Jogorku Kenesh, candidates for the offices of chairman of the Constitutional Court of the Kyrgyz Republic, his deputy, and judges of the Constitutional Court of the Kyrgyz Republic; to nominate, for selection by the Jogorku Kenesh, candidates for the offices of chairman of the Supreme Court, his deputies, and judges of the Supreme Court; to appoint (with the consent of the Jogorku Kenesh) the procurator-general of the Kyrgyz Republic, chairman of the Board of the National Bank; judges of local courts, diplomatic representatives of the Kyrgyz Republic in foreign states, and in international organizations; chairman of the Central Commission of the Kyrgyz Republic on Elections and Referendums; to appoint half of the membership of the Central Commission of the Kyrgyz Republic on Elections and Referendums; to appoint (with the consent of the Jogorku Kenesh) chairman of the Auditing Chamber of the Kyrgyz Republic; and to appoint half of the auditors of the Auditing Chamber. The president also can sign and promulgate laws, call a referendum on his own initiative, dissolve the Jogorku Kenesh, introduce a state of emergency, declare a general or partial mobilization, declare a state of war and impose martial law. Askar Akayev was the first president of the republic. He was elected in 1990, and reelected in 1995 and again in 2000.

– Q –

QADI **(also *Kadi*).** A judge, legal interpreter of Islamic canon law in Muslim countries. In the prerevolutionary Kyrgyz land, the **Russian Empire** administration left common criminal cases, crimes and disputes between communities, under the jurisdiction of the *qadi*. The Soviet authorities banned the *qadi* from practicing in the mid-1920s.

QALYM **(also *Kalym*).** A dowry in the form of money or gift, which the parents of the bridegroom send to the parents of the bride before the marriage. The *qalym* may be in the form of various household goods, livestock, or cash, but is usually a combination of these. Traditionally, the amount is decided by the parents on both sides and often depends on the income and social status of the families. The *qalym* played a central part in prearranged or forced marriages among **Kyrgyzs** and Uzbeks and was officially banned during the Soviet era. In post-Soviet Kyrgyzstan, the tradition of *qalym* has strengthened, particularly in **Batken, Jalal Abad, and Osh** *oblast*s.

QARATEGIN. An area in the remote **Pamirs** in Gharm, Jirgatal, and Darband districts of northern **Tajikistan** populated by the Kyrgyz **tribes** since the 17th century. In the early 1920s this area was a stronghold of the **Basmachi movement**. During the 20th century the number of the **Kyrgyzs** who lived in the area significantly decreased, and in the 1990s many Kyrgyz families chose to move from Qarategin to Kyrgyzstan due to the devastating effect of the civil war in Tajikistan.

QARATEGIN BEKLIK. A semi-independent principality located in a strategically important area in the **Pamirs** and contested by the **Bukhara** and **Kokand Khanates** in the 19th century. The conflicts over the Qarategin Beklik continued between the two khanates for decades and only after abolishment of the Kokand Khanate in 1876 did the Bukhara Khanate acquire the Qarategin. After the **border de-**

limitation in 1924–1926 most of the territory of the *beklik* was transferred to **Tajikistan**.

QARNAI. A traditional musical instrument that resembles a long wind pipe. It is often used at public celebrations, such as weddings, performances of the Central Asian circus, celebration of *Nawruz,* or commemoration of the end of the harvest season. It is more common in southern Kyrgyzstan and among the Uzbek communities.

QAZAQSTAN (also Qazaqstan Respublikasy). *See* KAZAKHSTAN.

QISHLAQ **(also *kishlak*).** A term used for a village or small town in southern Kyrgyzstan and in **Uzbekistan**.

QURGON **(also *kurgan*).** 1. A man-made hill on a burial place of ancient warriors or *khans*. 2. A city wall or protective wall made of mud.

– R –

RAILWAYS. Kyrgyzstan has a railway network of only about 370 kilometers. It is extremely expensive to build railways in this mountainous republic where nearly 60 percent of the territory is elevated higher than 2,500 meters above sea level. The major railway track runs from **Kazakhstan** to Lugovaya station and then to **Bishkek**, and further to **Tokmak**; the other one runs via **Uzbekistan** to **Jalal Abad** and **Osh**. The railways are relatively well established in northern and southern Kyrgyzstan, but practically none exist in the eastern and central parts of the republic due to the difficult terrain. Several industrial railways were constructed in the 1930s and in the 1950s to serve Kyrgyzstan's coal and metallurgy **industries**, but by 2002 they were in a poor state.

Kyrgyzstan intends to invest heavily in development of the railway connection to **China** in order to boost its **trade** and **tourism** with this country and to ease Kyrgyzstan's dependence on the railways systems of neighboring Kazakhstan and Uzbekistan. These states frequently interrupt Kyrgyzstan's goods transit for nonpayment of the transit fees or due to various disagreements on fees and tariffs.

Several multi-multimillion dollar railway projects were initiated and discussed by the Kyrgyz **government** and international donor organizations and individual countries. In 2001 and 2002 China and Kyrgyzstan discussed the possibility of building a railway that would connect Kyrgyzstan with Xinjang. However, practically all of these projects were put on hold due to financial difficulties caused by the effect of Kyrgyzstan's economic recession in the 1990s and due to the regional instability caused by the **militant incursions** and the U.S.-led war in **Afghanistan**. *See also* TRANSPORTATION.

RAMAZAN (also Ramadan). The holy month in **Islam**, which commemorates the revelation of the Quran to the Prophet Muhammad. During Ramazan all devoted Muslims should refrain from eating and drinking during daylight hours, and devote their bodies and souls to purification. The dates of Ramazan move from year to year, as they are determined by the lunar calendar.

REPUBLIC OF KYRGYZSTAN. The official name of Kyrgyzstan between 1991 and 1993. With adoption of the first post-Soviet **Constitution of Kyrgyzstan** in May 1993 the official name was changed to the **Kyrgyz Republic**.

RUSSIA (official name the Russian Federation). This country is located north of the **Kyrgyz Republic** and separated from Kyrgyzstan by **Kazakhstan**'s territory. Russia's population was estimated at about 145.6 million in July 2001. Russians account for 81.5 percent of the population, Tatars about 3.8 percent, Ukrainians about 3 percent, Chuvash about 0.8 percent, and others about 10.8 percent. According to official estimates about 150,000–200,000 ethnic **Kyrgyzs** (including temporary workers and students) chose to temporarily move to Russia, mainly in Russia's central regions and in western Siberia (2002 est.). In addition about 600,000 people (mainly Russians and Ukrainians) have moved from Kyrgyzstan to the Russian Federation since 1991. The ethnic Russian population in Kyrgyzstan was estimated at about 570,000 in 2002.

Russia and Kyrgyzstan have maintained close political relations since 1991, as President **Askar Akayev** joined the Russia-led **Commonwealth of Independent States (CIS)**, **CIS Collective Security**

Treaty, Customs Union, Eurasian Economic Community, and some other organizations. Nevertheless, Russia expressed its concern about the treatment of the Russian population in Kyrgyzstan in the early 1990s. Since 1991 Russia has remained Kyrgyzstan's largest trading partner. Kyrgyzstan's **trade** with Russia was estimated at 20 percent of its total foreign trade, or at about US$140 million in 2001, down from about US$210 million in 2000. Kyrgyzstan exported about US$70 million in goods and services, mainly products of its **agriculture** and light **industry**, natural resources, and machinery, and imported about US$170 million in goods and services, including petroleum, machinery, and consumer goods. In 1999 and 2000 Russia provided substantial military and financial assistance and political support to Kyrgyzstan, when the latter experienced the **militant incursions** from **Tajikistan** into **Batken** *oblast*.

In 2001 and 2002 Kyrgyz-Russian relations were strained, as Kyrgyzstan agreed to lease its territory for the **U.S. military airbase**. In order to reduce the tensions, in June 2002 the **government** agreed to host the **Russian military base** and leased to Russia the facilities of the former Soviet airbase in the city of Kant and several other military installations on its territory. In 2003 Kyrgyz government supported the Russian criticism of the U.S.-led war in Iraq.

RUSSIAN EMPIRE (also called the Tsarist Empire). The name of the Russian state from 1721 to 1917, as the Russian tsar accepted the title of emperor. *See also* RUSSIA.

RUSSIAN MILITARY BASE. The **Kyrgyz Republic** agreed to host the Russian military base in June 2002. This military base was established in the city of Kant in **Chui** *oblast* (40 kilometers from **Bishkek**) in response to the opening of the **U.S. military airbase** at Manas airport in 2001. **Russia** leased the land and facilities of the former Soviet military base on the territory of the republic. Officially, the base hosts the **Commonwealth of Independent States's** Collective Forces of Rapid Deployment (CFRD), which were established to assist Kyrgyzstan and other Central Asian republics against **militant incursions** or activities of any hostile forces. The military base will operate within the mandate and framework of the **Commonwealth of Independent States Collective Security Treaty**, signed in 1992 between

Russia, Kyrgyzstan, and several other former Soviet states. It was agreed that the annual cost of the base (around US$50 million) would be funded by the Security Treaty members and that the base would host Russian military aircraft and military personnel. In January 2003 the Russian military base consisted of about 20 military airplanes, including five Su-25 attack jets, two Il-76 cargo aircraft, five L-39 planes, five Su-27, and two MI-8 helicopters, and it was supported by about 700 servicemen.

RYBACHIYE. *See* BALYKCHI.

– S –

SAJARE. See *SHAZHERE.*

SART. 1. A term used in Central Asia until the 1920s to identify both the Turkic- and Persian-speaking sedentary population. The classification "Sart" was used in the prerevolutionary censuses; however, this term disappeared from official references after the **border delimitation in 1924–1926**. 2. A term used in southern Kyrgyzstan to identify Uzbeks, with a negative connotation.

SATYLGANOV, TOKTOGUL. *See* TOKTOGUL.

SECURITY COUNCIL. A state agency established in 1994 by President **Askar Akayev**'s decree. Initially it was called the Council on Security Issues, and it was renamed the Security Council of the **Kyrgyz Republic** in April 1996. The Security Council focuses on most important strategic issues, covering not only security matters but also, most important, **foreign policy** and some domestic issues (such as long-term economic planning, privatization strategies, etc.).

According to the **constitution of Kyrgyzstan**, the president "forms and heads the Security Council" and there is no mention about any needs for approval from the legislature. The Security Council is a "consultative and coordinating body" headed by the president. Its tasks include "elaboration of the strategy of national security," "coordination of activities of the state institutions on guaranteeing national security," and "preparation of suggestions on internal, external and defense policies in area of the national security." Its functions include: "consideration of strategic issues in the state, economic, social, defense, information, environment and other types of security," "fighting crime and corruption," "protection of public health, and prevention and recovery from emergency situations." In the area of foreign policy it is expected to coordinate the foreign policy activities of various state institutions.

The Security Council consists of 16 members and includes four representatives of the presidential administration (the president, who is the chairman of the Security Council, the state-secretary, the head of the presidential administration, and the secretary of the Security Council) and 11 ministers (including the prime minister, minister of foreign affairs, minister of defense, minister of internal affairs, minister for the **National Security Committee,** and others). According to the statute on the Security Council, the Council does not have its own executive staff and its activities are "assured" by the presidential administration. The secretary of the Security Council is directly subordinated to the president and may be appointed and dismissed by a special presidential decree.

The Security Council kept a relatively low profile until 1999. It played a crucial role during the **militant incursions** in the summer of 1999, when insurgents from **Tajikistan** attacked several villages in southern Kyrgyzstan and took hostages, including high-ranking Kyrgyzstani defense officials and Japanese engineers. During the crisis the Security Council took control of the day-to-day activities of all ministries and local administration. The plenary sessions of the Security Council were widely publicized in the official **mass media.**

SEMIRECHIYE. *See* JETISUU.

SEMIRECHIYE COSSACKS (also known as Semirechenskoye kazach'ye voisko in Russian). Between 1847 and 1867 the **Russian Empire** promoted migration of the Cossacks from different parts of **Russia** to **Semirechiye** (at present the territory of northern Kyrgyzstan and southern **Kazakhstan**). In 1867 the Russian tsar agreed to grant the local Cossacks the status of Semirechye Cossack territorial army with their center in the city of Vernyi (now Almaty, Kazakhstan). General Gerasim Kolpakovskyi was appointed as the first head of the unit. The Cossacks played a central role in the Russian colonization of the region and they owned about 744,000 hectares of land in Semirechye *oblast*. By 1916 there were approximately 45,000 Cossacks and the Cossack Host was made up of three cavalry regiments and 12 detached troops. In April 1920 the Cossacks' territorial army was officially dissolved. Since 1991 several activists have been trying to revive the Cossack tradition in Kyrgyzstan and Kazakhstan. They created and registered the Semirechenskie Kazaki (Semirechiye Cossacks) Society. *See also* TOKMAK.

SERVICES. Kyrgyzstan's service sector was tightly controlled by the state during the Soviet era, and it was significantly underdeveloped. In the early 1990s Kyrgyzstan's government made considerable efforts to deregulate this sector, focusing on privatization of retail and hospitality businesses and on reforming financial services. In 2002 the service sector generated up to 34 percent of the gross domestic product (GDP).

The most significant changes were introduced in finance and **banking** services. The monopoly of the state bank was broken and commercial banks were allowed in. A new banking law was introduced in 1992 and the government conducted financial restructuring with assistance from the World Bank and International Monetary Fund (IMF). By the 2000s most of the private banks began to offer basic services to the local population, expatriates, and private businesses, such as currency exchange, money transfer, introduced debit and credit cards, and the like. However, banking services are mainly available in the capital of Bishkek, while outside the metropolitan most of trade and business is conducted in cash.

According to Western standards, the retail sector is relatively well-developed in Bishkek and in the major cities and consists of numerous small oriental-style shops and restaurants complimented by several large Western-style department stores. The sector is significantly underdeveloped outside **Chui** and **Ysyk Kol** *oblasts*, especially in the rural areas. The notorious deficit of consumer goods and long queues, which plagued the country in the late 1980s and early 1990s, has practically disappeared. At present, virtually all imported or locally produced consumer goods are offered at traditional bazaars or numerous stores across the country, although these products are often of dubious quality and origin. *See also* TOURISM.

SHABDAN ZHANTAI-UULU (1840–1912). An influential *manap* and leader of Kyrgyz **tribes** in the **Chui valley** in the 19th century. Shabdan Zhantai-Uulu played an important role in the political development of this part of the republic in the second half of the 19th century. In 1860 he fought fiercely against Kudoyar Khan of the **Kokand Khanate**. In 1862 he was imprisoned in Pishpek (now **Bishkek**), but escaped. He continued the pro-Russian policy of his father, **Zhantai Karabek-Uulu** (Zhantai Khan). Between 1868 and 1876 he played an important role in assisting the **Russian Empire**'s administration in establishing control over northern and southern Kyrgyzstan. In recognition of his service Shabdan Zhantai-Uulu was invited to the coronation of Russian tsar Alexander III and was awarded the rank of colonel. He also received several Russian imperial orders and medals for his role in the war against the Kokand Khanate.

In 1884 Shabdan Zhantai-Uulu retired but remained an important and influential public figure in the Kyrgyz land and in Turkistan. Another contribution of Shabdan Zhantai-Uulu to the social development of the region was his decisive role in opening modern schools in the town of Chon-Kemin (**Chui region**).

SHANGHAI COOPERATION ORGANIZATION (SCO) (also known as Shanghai-Five and Shanghai Forum). Five countries, **China, Kazakhstan, Kyrgyz Republic, Russia,** and **Tajikistan,** established the Shanghai Cooperation Organization during a gathering of the heads of the states in Shanghai in April 1996. It was the first large-scale cooperation initiative since the China-Soviet split in the 1960s. Its main purpose was the resolution of disputed territorial issues, demilitarization of the borders, and removal of the last vestiges of the Cold War era confrontation. Additionally, the members sought to boost their regional economic cooperation and the movement of investment between these neighboring countries and encourage trade, especially border trade.

During their first meetings in 1996 and 1997 the Shanghai Five members signed agreements on borders and on demilitarization and agreed to draw back their armed forces 100 kilometers from their borders. These fundamentally important documents endorsed the resolution of the long-standing disputes that existed between the Union of Soviet Socialist Republics (USSR) and later the **Commonwealth** of Independent States (CIS), on the one hand, and the People's Republic of China on the other, which had led to several military conflicts in the past.

After the **borders delimitation in the 1990s** and resolving the disputed territorial issues, the Shanghai Five turned to other problems of mutual importance such as terrorism, the growing militancy of opposition groups, and separatism. During the meeting in Almaty in July 1998, the members decided to initiate annual summits. In August 1999, during the summit in **Bishkek**, the Shanghai Five issued the Bishkek Statement, expressing their desire to tackle "international terrorism, illegal dealing in **drugs** and narcotics trafficking, arm smuggling, illegal immigration and other forms of cross-border crimes." The summit set up a joint consultative group and launched military cooperation among the members of the organization. Another outcome was the establishment of an **Anti-Terrorist Center in Bishkek.** In 2000 the members decided to rename the organization the Shanghai Forum.

In June 2001 the Shanghai Forum decided to relaunch the organization as the Shanghai Cooperation Organization (SCO) in response to the increasing marginalization of Russia in the international arena and China's worries about the prospects of the United States's domination in the unilateral world order. The SCO members emphasized military cooperation against terrorism and promotion of regional economic development, **transportation,** and **international trade**. In addition, China and Russia stressed their support for a "multipolar world" and a new world order based on "democratic, fair, and rational" principles. The SCO members also agreed to extend their cooperation into new fields, such as cultural issues, ecological problems, and disaster relief. They also declared the organization open to new members. During the 2001 summit **Uzbekistan** officially joined as the sixth full member. During the 2002 summit the member states signed the charter (the basic regulations of the Shanghai Cooperation Organization activities), which declared the need for joint efforts to maintain peace, security and stability in the region. *See also* CHINA-KYRGYZSTAN BORDER DELIMITATION.

SHARIAH (also Sharia, Shariat). The Islamic law practiced in Muslim societies. It is based on four fundamentals: the Quran; the Hadith (Sunna), that is, the recorded story of the life and deeds of the Prophet

Muhammad; the Ijma, that is, the universal decisions agreed by Islamic scholars; and the Qiya, or legal precedent. The Shariah imposes a strict regulation of public and private aspects of life according to divine revelation. It was practiced among Central Asians, including the **Kyrgyzs**, until 1924–26 and it was guided by the *qadis* and *sheikhs*. The Soviet authorities banned the Shariah courts in Kyrgyzstan in the mid-1920s. *See also* ISLAM; OFFICIAL MULSIM CLERGY.

SHAZHERE (Sajare, Shejere). 1. A genealogical tree of a family, which every male Kyrgyz must know by heart. A traditional requirement is to know ancestors up to seven generations. 2. A genealogy of the tribal composition among **Kyrgyzs**, Kazakhs, and other nomadic groups. After 1991 research on *Shazhere* of the Kyrgyzs became very popular and a number of books, posters, and leaflets on this issue was published in Kyrgyzstan.

SHEEP. For centuries sheep herding was one of the most important pillars of economic activities for Kyrgyz society. During the Soviet era many *kolkhozes* and *sovkhozes* in Kyrgyzstan specialized in raising these animals on a large scale. The total number of sheep reached approximately 9.9 million in 1980, but declined to about 9.1 million in 1991. Kyrgyzstan was the third largest producer of wool and it was among the top five producers of lamb meat in the former USSR.

The Kyrgyz farmers were successful in producing a local breed of sheep, *Kyrgyz fine-fleece breed sheep.* This sheep was produced through crossing a local coarse-wool *kurduk* sheep with rams of various fine-wool breeds at the Juan Tyube pedigree stock farm in Kyrgyzstan. The animals are large (55–60 kilograms) with compact rounded trunks and one or two folds of skin on the neck. They yield between 8 to 16 kilograms of wool and their fleece is about 7.5–8.5 centimeters long. The sheep are adapted to the mountain pasture and are raised mainly for wool and meat in Kyrgyzstan and **Tajikistan**.

In the late 1980s scientists and local farmers raised their concern about large-scale animal herding in the fragile mountainous pastures in Kyrgyzstan, claiming that this form of sheep herding is unsustainable for the republic. In the 1990s the combination of lost state subsidies, loss of the ex-Soviet and Central Asian markets, mismanagement, and difficulties of transition into private farming led to a considerable decline of this sector of the national economy. The number of sheep, for example, declined to approximately 3.2 million in 2001, although independent experts claim that the real number most probably was close to 4 million. *See also* AGRICULTURE.

SNOW LEOPARD. A large, cat-like animal, which can grow up to two meters long (including 0.8 meters tail). The animal lives in the high mountains of Central Asia. Since ancient time Kyrgyzs, Kazakhs, and other Central Asian nations regarded leopards as a symbol of wealth and power. Leopards were hunted for their beautiful skin and for cubs, which were raised as pets for palaces of medieval **khans**.

Snow leopards live in the **Tian-Shan mountains** in Kyrgyzstan and are under protection. There were between 800 and 900 snow leopards in Kyrgyzstan in the 1980s; however, the number has dramatically fallen since 1991 due to illegal hunting for their skins and for their cubs. Cubs are often sold to wealthy owners and to foreign zoos in the black market. According to experts estimates there were just 200 snow leopards left in the wild in Kyrgyzstan in 2003.

SOCIAL DEMOCRATIC PARTY OF KYRGYZSTAN (SDPK) (Kyrgyzstan Social Democrattyk partiasy in Kyrgyz). A progovernment centrist party established by a group of **Jogorku Kenesh** (parliament) members and **government** officials in 1993. It was first registered on 19 October 1993 and re-registered on 16 December 1994. The political platform of the party called for pragmatic and centrist domestic and **foreign policies** and for rejection of any political dogmas. The SDPK supported stabilization of interethnic relations and civil society in the republic, selective intervention of the state in economic development, and development of greater cooperation with **Commonwealth of Independent States (CIS)** partners. The party claimed up to 4,500 members in all parts of the republic. Its electorate consists mainly of public sector workers, center and center-right intellectuals, and entrepreneurs. Its chairman, Abdygany Erkebayev, has been a state-secretary and a member of the several commissions in the parliament.

The SDPK was particularly active in the 2000 parliamentary elections, during which it won several seats as one of the principal members of the progovernment coalition. The party remains one of the important and influential political forces in the Kyrgyz parliament.

SOM. National currency of Kyrgyzstan. It was introduced in May 1993 to replace the **Russian** ruble. One Kyrgyz som equals 100 tiin (pronounced ti'in). Due to the high cost of the production of metal coins, the republic opted to also produce paper tiins of 1, 5, 10, 20, and 50 tiin denomination. However, the circulation of these tiins was gradually phased out due to rising inflation and the high cost of producing the tiins.

The exchange rate of the Kyrgyz som (KS) per US$1 is as follows: 46.7 (January 2003); 47.7 (2000); 39.0 (1999); 20.8 (1998); 17.42 (1997); 12.8 (1996); and 8.0 (1993).

SOVKHOZ **(plural in Russian** *sovkhozy*)**.** This stands for the Russian acronym *sovetskoye khozyaistvo*, or Soviet farm. The first *sovkhozes* were established across the Soviet Union in the 1920s. In 1925 there were six *sovkhozes* in Kyrgyzstan, 36 in 1940, 103 in 1970, and 222 in 1979. They were established to complement the *kolkhozes* in agricultural production. The major difference between *kolkhozes* and *sovkhozes* was that the property of *sovkhozes*, equipment, and land, belonged to the state and not to the farm's members. The *sovkhozes* were often established to produce agricultural products in large quantities. In 1992 most of the *sovkhozes* in Kyrgyzstan were reorganized into commercial agricultural firms. *See also* AGRICULTURE; COLLECTIVIZATION.

SUBANBEKOV, BAKIRDIN (1952–). Kyrgyz politician. Born in Kyzyl Oktyabr village in **Chui** *oblast* (northern Kyrgyzstan), Bakirdin Subanbekov graduated from **Kyrgyz State (National) University** by correspondence in 1979. He joined the ranks of the **militsia** in 1973. From 1974 to 1976 he worked as senior-inspector on the Frunze (now **Bishkek**)-**Osh** road. From 1976 to 1985 Subanbekov held various district level positions in the Ministry of Internal Affairs and from 1985 to 1988 he worked as a police investigator at district level in Chui *oblast*. From 1988 to 1994 he was deputy head and then head of the police administration at the district and city levels in Chui *oblast*. He was head of the Osh *oblast* administration of the Ministry of Internal Affairs 1994–96 and from 1996 to 2001 he was head of the Chui *oblast* administration of the Ministry of Internal Affairs. From 2001 to 2002 he held various senior positions in the Ministry of Internal Affairs. In 2002 Subanbekov became the minister of internal affairs as his predecessor was dismissed under accusations of mishandling the **Aksy conflict.**

SUFISM (also known as tasawwuf). Mystical movement in **Islam,** which emphasizes development of a personal spirituality and an internal comprehension of divinity. Most scholars trace the beginning of Sufism to the seventh-eighth centuries A.D., though there are some disagreements about the precise dating. Through the first five centuries after its establishment, Sufism developed into several distinctive orders or *tariqats*. Some of the influential *tariqats* originated in Central Asia. Sufi *sheikhs* (scholars and spiritual leaders) and dervishes (members of a Sufi fraternity) played an important role in spreading Islam among nomads and pastoral nomads of Central Asia, including Kazakhs and **Kyrgyzs.** The biggest school in Sufism, **Nakhshbandyah,** has been influential in the **Ferghana valley,** especially around the **Osh** area, since medieval times.

SUPREME SOVIET (1936–1994). A unicameral 350-seat parliament elected for a five-year term during the Soviet era. Conventionally, the Supreme Soviet had two sessions a year. There was some ambiguity in the usage of this term: the Russian language **mass media** used the term in Russian—Verkhovnyi Sovet, while the **Kyrgyz language** mass media used the Kyrgyz translation—**Jogorku Kenesh.** The last Soviet-era Supreme Soviet was elected in 1990 and it was dissolved by President **Askar Akayev**'s decree in October 1994. A bicameral parliament replaced the Supreme Soviet in 1995 under the name of the Jogorku Kenesh, which is presently used in both the Kyrgyz and Russian languages.

SYDYKOVA, ZAMIRA (1960–). Kyrgyz politician and journalist. Born in **Naryn city** (in a remote eastern province of the republic), Zamira Sydykova graduated from the Faculty of Journalism of the Moscow State University in 1984. From 1986 to 1987 she worked as a correspondent for the *Komsomolets Kirgizii* newspaper and from 1988 to 1990 she was the executive secretary of the *Uchitel Kyrgyzstana* newspaper. From 1990 to 1991 she was the deputy editor of the *Komsomolets Kyrgyzstana* newspaper. In 1992 she founded the *Res Publica* newspaper and became its editor-in-chief.

Sydykova is best known as one of the most vocal critics of the political regime and corruption in the republic throughout the 1990s and 2000s. Her sharp and highly critical articles caused a number of political scandals and consequently political reprisals. In 1995 she was charged with insulting President **Askar Akayev** by publishing an article about his foreign bank accounts and was banned from working as a journalist for 18 months. She was sentenced to a lengthy term of imprisonment in 1997, but she was soon released under intense international and local pressure. She transformed the *Res Publica* newspaper into one of the influential opposition media, though it was closed several times under **government** pressure, but was reopened again. She has authored numerous articles and investigative papers. In 1997 and 1999 critical articles published in the newspaper led to a number of resignations among government officials. Sydykova was awarded the Lifetime Achievement: Flora Lewis (New York Times Syndicate) in 2000 and the International Women's Media Foundation's Courage in Journalism Award in 2001. *See also* MASS MEDIA

– T –

TAJIKISTAN (official name Jumhurii Tojikiston or Tojikiston). The republic is located southwest of the **Kyrgyz Republic**, and these two countries share about 870 kilometers of common borders. Tajikistan's territory is 143,100 square kilometers and its **population** was estimated at about 6.6 million in July 2001, making Tajikistan the third most populous state in Central Asia. The Tajiks account for 68 percent of the population, Uzbeks about 25 percent, Russians about 2.5 percent, and others about 4.5 percent. About 200,000 **Kyrgyzs** live in Tajikistan, mainly in Leninabod and Garm *veloyats* (provinces) and in Kuhistoni Badakhson (Gornyi-Badakhshan).

During the 19th century the territory of modern Tajikistan, especially its eastern portion, was probably one of the most underdeveloped regions on the continent. Between the 1930s and 1970s Tajikistan together with Kyrgyzstan received substantial investments for development of their **transportation**, pipelines, telecommunications, and other infrastructure. However, in the late 1970s and early 1980s the inflow of investments decreased, despite the fact that between

1960 and 1980 the population of both republics had nearly doubled. This demographic change led to a rise in social tensions in both countries and to frequent conflicts on the borders over water and pasture issues.

After 1991 Tajikistan's **trade** with Kyrgyzstan was insignificant, because both republics have similar economic structures and produce similar products. However, illicit **drug** smuggling ballooned, as the porous borders between the two countries in the **Ferghana valley** were used by drug dealers for a large-scale transit of cheap drugs from **Afghanistan**. Tajikistan frequently received complaints from Kyrgyzstan's authorities about the drug smuggling and trade.

During the civil war (1992–97) in Tajikistan, **Bishkek** sent a peace-keeping battalion to Tajikistan, which along with troops from **Russia** and **Kazakhstan** backed maintenance of the secular government in Dushanbe. During the civil war almost 60,000 Tajiks sought refuge in Kyrgyzstan in addition to several thousand ethnic Kyrgyzs who migrated from Tajikistan to Kyrgyzstan. As of 2003 a significant number of Tajik refugees still remained in Kyrgyzstan.

In 1999 the **Islamic Movement of Uzbekistan (IMU)**, a militant Uzbek opposition group, entered Kyrgyzstan from the territory of Tajikistan. The IMU captured several villages and took hostages in **Batken** *oblast*, sparking protests from Kyrgyzstan's **government**. In 2000 and 2001 the two governments actively cooperated in fighting the militant groups that found protection in the remote areas of Kyrgyzstan along the Tajikistan-Kyrgyzstan borders.

Tajikistan along with Kyrgyzstan joined the **Commonwealth of Independent States (CIS), Commonwealth of Independent States Collective Security Treaty, Economic Cooperation Organization, Organization of the Islamic Conference, Organization for Security and Cooperation in Europe, Shanghai Cooperation Organization (SCO),** and some other regional and international organizations. By 2003 Tajikistan had resolved most of its territorial disputes with Kyrgyzstan within the framework of the SCO, although some disputes over water and pasture usage remained unsettled. *See also* ISFARA CONFLICTS.

TALAS CITY (Ak Chii from 1877 to 1913; Dmitrievskoye from 1913 to 1944). The 10th largest city in the republic, capital of **Talas** *oblast*.

A city on the **Talas River** located in northwestern Kyrgyzstan, about 200 kilometers west of **Bishkek**. Its **population** stood at about 33,000 (1999 census), up from about 23,000 (1979 census), consisting mainly of **Kyrgyzs**; it also included Russians, Ukrainians, Uzbeks, Germans, and some others. It is an important industrial and commercial center in northwestern Kyrgyzstan. There are light **industries**, agricultural-processing plants, Talas State University (founded in 2000), a medical college, nine secondary schools, **libraries**, and a theater.

The city was founded in the 1870s as a Russian settlement for peasants from the Russian Voronezh province, after the **Russian Empire** acquired the land from local Kyrgyz **tribes**. In 1877 it was named Ak Chii village, renamed to Dmitrievskoye in 1913, and it was part of **Syrdarya** *oblast*. After the delimitation of borders between **Kazakhstan** and Kyrgyzstan in 1925, the city became an administrative center in Kyrgyzstan. In 1944 the city received its current name, Talas, becoming an administrative center of the newly established **Talas** *oblast* (abolished in 1956, but reestablished in 1980). Its importance was enhanced due to its proximity to Zhambyl (Dzhambul), a large railway entrepot in southern Kazakhstan. After 1991, however, Talas city decayed, as its major industrial enterprises were closed or significantly downsized due to the economic recession and the market was lost to cheaper products from **China** and other countries.

TALAS *OBLAST*. A province in northern Kyrgyzstan, bordered by **Jalal Abad** *oblast* in the south, **Kazakhstan** in the north and northwest, and **Chui** *oblast* in the east. Talas *oblast* has a total area of about 11,400 square kilometers, or just over 5 percent of Kyrgyzstan's territory; it is the smallest *oblast* in the republic. Its **population** was estimated at about 200,300 (1999 census), or 4 percent of the country's population, up from about 163,500 (1979 census). Talas's population consisted mainly of the **Kyrgyzs**—88.5 percent (2000, est.)—but also included Russians, Ukrainians, Germans, Koreans, Turks, Uzbeks, Kazakhs, and others. During the 1990s a significant share of the non-Kyrgyz population emigrated from Talas to **Russia** and Germany and in the early 2000s many Kyrgyzs moved to the **Chui valley** and **Bishkek**. Talas *oblast* was originally formed in 1944; it was abolished in 1956 but was reestablished in 1980. It consists of Bakai Ata, Kara Buura, Manas, and Talas *raions* (districts) with the city of Talas as the capital.

Agriculture (animal husbandry, tobacco production, etc.), food processing, **tourism,** and **services** are the main sectors of the economy of Talas *oblast*. During the Soviet era it specialized in producing and processing agricultural products, including tobacco for local consumption and for export, tourism, and services.

Since the early 1990s Talas *oblast* has experienced a severe economic recession due to structural changes, abolishment of state subsidies, and loss of the former Soviet market for its goods and services. It attempted to attract foreign direct investments (FDIs) by establishing a **Free Economic Zone** (FEZ) near the Zhon-Debe railway station, on the border with Kazakhstan, in 1997. The importance of Talas *oblast* was enhanced by the fact that according to the Kyrgyz historical narratives it was home of the legendary Kyrgyz hero, **Manas.** Manas's burial place—**Manas Gumbezi** (Manas' mausoleum)—is located there. The mausoleum was built between the 14th and 15th centuries A.D. and it is one of the attractions for tourists traveling on Kyrgyzstan's part of the **Great Silk Road.** The Talas clan played an important role in the political life of the republic forming one of the most influential political **clans** in the post-Soviet era.

TALAS RIVER. This river is 661 kilometers long with a basin area of around 52,700 square kilometers. The river originates in the **Ala-Too mountain** range of northern Kyrgyzstan and continues through the **Talas valley** to **Kazakhstan.** It disappears in the sands of the Moun Kum desert. The river's highest flow is from March to July, and its lowest flow is in November and December.

The Talas River is one of the most important sources of drinking and irrigation water for northeastern Kyrgyzstan. During the Soviet era the Kirovsk water reservoir was built on Kyrgyzstan's part of the river. Its water has been used for irrigation.

TALAS VALLEY. This valley is located in northern Kyrgyzstan and its area is about 3,600 square kilometers, divided between Kyrgyzstan and **Kazakhstan.** The valley is bordered by the Kyrgyz **Ala-Too mountain** range in the south and northeast and it opens in the west to the Kazakh steppe. Most of the valley is elevated between 600 and 2,000 meters above sea level. The valley often experiences extremes of cold continental weather, as winter temperatures range between

−14° (7°F) to +7°C (45°F) in January, and the average daily temperature is between 20°C (70°F) and 26°C (78°F) in July.

Talas played a special role in Central Asian history, as numerous armies crossed this area throughout the last two thousand years. In a decisive battle in 751, the Arabs and Chinese met in the Talas valley in the struggle for control over the region. There were contradictory reports about the outcome of the battle, but the fact is that both the Chinese and Arab armies suffered huge losses at the battle of Talas.

In addition the Talas valley has special meaning for the **Kyrgyzs** and Kyrgyz history, as much of the life and activities of the legendary hero **Manas** took place in the Talas valley. His burial place, **Manas Gumbezi**, is also situated in the valley, and it inspired many Kyrgyz *akyns* and *manaschis* to create songs and heroic epics.

TANAYEV, NIKOLAI (1945–). Kyrgyz politician. Born in Mikhailovka village in Penza oblast (**Russia**), Tanayev graduated from Dzhambul Hydro-Melioration and Construction Institute (**Kazakhstan**) in 1969. From 1969 to 1979 he worked at the "Osh-stroi" company and rose from foreman to senior engineer. From 1979 to 1984 he was first deputy of the chairman of the **Osh city** administration and from 1984 to 1985 he worked as head of the Osh regional division of the Vodokanal agency. From 1985 to 1995 he was deputy director of the "Chuipromstroi" company. He was president of the company Kyrgyzkurulush 1995–2000. From 2000 to 2001 he served as chairman of the State Commission on **Architecture** and Construction. In 2001 he was appointed first vice prime minister. In 2002, at the height of the political crisis in the republic due to the **Aksy conflict**, he was appointed prime minister. In 2003 Tanayev was named one of the 20 most influential politicians in the republic.

Tanayev, an ethnic Russian, was selected for the position of prime minister as a temporary compromise figure because of his qualities as a sound economic manager and government administrator who had no affiliation with any political **clans** in the republic.

TASAWWUF. *See* SUFISM.

TEKEBAYEV, OMURBEK (1958–). Kyrgyz politician. Born in Akmal village in **Osh** *oblast*, Omurbek Tekebayev graduated from **Kyrgyz State (National) University** in 1984 (by correspondence). From

1981 to 1991 he held various teaching and supervisory positions in his native region. In 1991 he served as head of the **Jalal Abad** *oblast* committee for support of private entrepreneurship. From 1992 to 1994 he was deputy head of the Jalal Abad *oblast* administration. In 1990 he was elected as a member of the **Jogorku Kenesh** (parliament). Tekebayev was also chairman of the Parliamentary Committee on State Structure and Judicial and Legal Reform. In 1994 he headed the **Ata Meken** political party. He challenged incumbent president **Askar Akayev** in the 2000 presidential elections and took part in the presidential election in partnership with **Felix Kulov**. Together they obtained only 13.9 percent of the vote, but claimed that the elections were highly rigged and full of irregularities. In 2000 he was elected as deputy speaker of the parliament.

Tekebayev is best known as one of the leading and most experienced opposition figures, who adopted a relatively moderate political stand and promoted the center-left populist democratic platform. Throughout the 1990s he was also considered to be one of the leading figures in parliament, and a prominent person in the southern Kyrgyzstan regional grouping (**clan**). He played a significant role in stabilizing the political situation in the 2002 political crisis ensuing from the **Aksy conflict**.

TIAN-SHAN MOUNTAINS (Tian Shan mountains, also Tien Shan mountains—translated "Heavenly Mountains"). The mountain system located in the eastern part of Central Asia, between 40 and 45 degrees northern latitude, and between 67 and 95 degrees eastern longitude. It stretches from east to west and is up to 2,400 kilometers in length, starting in **China** and expanding into Kyrgyzstan and then running further into **Uzbekistan** and **Tajikistan**. Its width is about 500 kilometers. The Tian-Shan has an area of about 1 million square kilometers. It is the highest mountain system north of Tibet. The **Pobedy Peak** (7,439 meters) is also the highest point in the republic. Kyrgyzstan's **population** often refers to Kyrgyzstan's part of the Tian-Shan as **Ala-Too**.

The Tian-Shan mountains consist of several mountain ranges, which stretch from east to west, with the exception of the Central Tian-Shan, which stretches from north to southwest. The Tian-Shan is bounded by the Dzungarian plain and southern **Kazakhstan** plains in the north, by the Tarim Basin in the southeast, and by the Alay, Surkhandarya, and Gissar valleys in the southwest, which are the boundaries of the system with the **Pamir** mountain ranges.

Tian-Shan's glaciers, lakes, and rivers provide drinking and irrigation water for most of the population in Kyrgyzstan. Some of the largest glaciers in the Central Asian region—Yuzhnyi Inelchek (59 kilometers) and Severnyi Inelchek (38 kilometers)—are located in these mountains. The mountainous areas also include waterways: the **Naryn River**, the longest river in the country, begins in the Tian-Shan mountains. Some rivers flow westward, providing drinking and irrigation water for the **Ferghana valley**; the others flow northward, providing water for the **Chui** and **Talas valleys**. Some parts of the Tian-Shan mountains were heavily forested in the past, and the timber resources of Kyrgyzstan were extensively exploited. However, by the beginning of the 21st century deforestation had become a real problem, though the Kyrgyzstan **government** established several national parks in the republic. These parks were created to preserve the unique forests of the mountains.

Some of Kyrgyzstan's least populated areas are located in these mountains, at about 2,000 meters above sea level. The climate in this area is very harsh, with long, cold winters lasting from November to March and a summer season from May to September. However, those valleys up to 1,500 meters above sea level are the most densely populated areas in Kyrgyzstan. In the 1990s the Kyrgyzstan government invested considerable resources in rebuilding the mountain roads **Bishkek-Osh**, Bishkek-Kashgar (**China**), and Bishkek-Karakorum (Pakistan) and reconstructing the existing **motor roads** that were built mainly in the 1950s and 1960s.

TOKMAK. The fifth largest city in the republic, and the third largest industrial center, after **Bishkek** and **Osh**. It is located on the **Chui River** in northern Kyrgyzstan, 60 kilometers east of Bishkek. Its **population** stood at about 59,300 (1999 census), up from about 58,700 (1979 census), consisting mainly of Russians and **Kyrgyzs**, but also including significant communities of Ukrainians, Uzbeks, Dungans (Chinese descendants), Germans, Koreans, and some others. It is an important industrial and **transportation** center in the north of Kyrgyzstan. There are light **industries**, machinery production, automobile assembly, consumer electronics (joint ventures with Korean and Turkish companies), agricultural-processing plants, a campus of **Kyrgyz Technological University** (founded in 1991), one of the oldest medical colleges in the republic (founded in 1938), a technical college, an agricultural college (founded in 1938), **libraries**, a theater, and a museum.

The area occupied by Tokmak is known for its proximity to the ruins of ancient **Balasagun** (also known as Kuz Ordu), one of the oldest known urban centers in northern Kyrgyzstan and a notable entrepot on the **Great Silk Road**. The city was described by the Arab traveler Al-Mukandisi (10th century A.D.) and Turkic geographer Makhmud Kashgari (12th century A.D.). It was captured by the Mongols led by Genghis Khan and gradually disappeared in the 15th–16th centuries, leaving behind only mud ruins of the buildings, palaces, and a huge 11th-century minaret—**Burana** (originally 45 meters high).

Modern Tokmak was founded in the early 19th century as a Kokand military fortress, after the **Kokand Khanate** conquered the **Chui valley**. Gradually it became an important trade center for Kyrgyz, Kazakh, and Uzbek merchants. In 1862 Russian troops led by Colonel Gerasim Kolpakovskii captured the fortress and destroyed it. Very soon after, however, the Russians rebuilt Tokmak as the center for Tokmak *uyezd* (district). In 1878 Tokmak was nearly destroyed by a flood on the Chui River and the Russians moved the administrative center to Pishpek (now **Bishkek**). Yet, Tokmak remained an important trade and business center, as the first hospital on the Kyrgyz land, and one of the first schools, libraries, and telegraph posts were opened here. The city survived the **popular uprising of 1916**, though many villages and properties around Tokmak were burned down or destroyed during the events. After the Revolution of 1917 Tokmak became a Bolshevik stronghold. The Soviet authorities invested heavily in the development of light and heavy **industries** in the city throughout the 1920s and 1930s, making Tokmak a leading powerhouse of the republic. Its importance was further enhanced after completion of the Bishkek-**Balykchi railway**. In the 1970s and 1980s the city was significantly expanded through intensive public housing construction. In the 1990s many businesses were closed due to economic restructuring and the city experienced a significant decay of its infrastructure. *See also* SEMIRECHIYE COSSACKS.

TOKONBAYEV, AALY (1904–1988). Prominent Kyrgyz writer; one of the founders of contemporary Kyrgyz literature. Born in Chon Kayndy village in **Chui** *oblast* (northern Kyrgyzstan), Tokonbayev began writing his first stories, poems, and essays in the 1920s. From 1927 to 1969 he worked as editor of *Kyzyl Kyrgyzstan*, the largest **Kyrgyz language** newspaper. From 1930 to 1931 he served as editor of the Kyrgyz section of Tsentrizdat (one of the largest publishers in the USSR) in Moscow and from 1931 to 1934 he was senior editor of Kyrgyzgosizdat (state-controlled national publishing house) in Frunze (now **Bishkek**). From 1934 to 1949 he served as chair of the **Union of Writers of Kyrgyzstan**. He was chief-editor of the *Chalkan* magazine 1955–56. He was awarded the title of People's Poet of Kyrgyz SSR in 1945, became a member of the **Kyrgyz Academy of Sciences** in 1964, and was awarded the highest Soviet honorary title of the Hero of Socialist Labor in 1974.

Tokonbayev was considered one of the most acclaimed Kyrgyz writers of his era in the republic. He authored numerous poems and several books of poetry, which were published in Kyrgyz, Russian, and some other languages of the Union of Soviet Socialist Republics (USSR).

TOKTOGUL (full name Toktogul Satylganov) (1864–1933). Prominent Kyrgyz poet, *akyn*; one of the founders of modern Kyrgyz poetry. Born in the remote village of Kysh'chu in **Jalal Abad** *oblast* (southern Kyrgyzstan), Toktogul Satylganov had no formal education. However, at the age of 12 he mastered playing the *komuz*, acquired a comprehensive knowledge of the Kyrgyz national oral epics, and began to compose his own music. He became a famous master of *aitysh*, an improvised epic accompanied by the *komuz*. His songs (*Alymkan* and others) became popular not only in his native region but also among all the **Kyrgyzs**. He also created several satiric works, in which he talked about social injustice and ignorance. Under pressure from the local administrators and *manaps*, the tsarist administration exiled Toktogul to Siberia, but he managed to escape and return to his native land.

Toktogul supported the Revolution of 1917 and composed several songs expressing his perception of the needs for social changes and a new life. He became one of the most influential *akyns* in the early 20th century, and his acceptance of the Bolshevik Revolution and social changes played an important part in pacifying the Kyrgyz population between 1918 and 1922. After the creation of the **Kyrgyz Autonomous Oblast** in 1924 (**Kyrgyz ASSR** from 1926) he became one of the most acclaimed *akyns* in the republic. His songs, such as *Toguz kairyk, Min kyal, Myrza kerbez,* and others, were recorded and became classics of 20th-century Kyrgyz music. Many of his songs and epics were translated into other languages of Central Asia and the Union of Soviet Socialist Republics (USSR). In 1965 the Kyrgyz **government** established the Toktogul State Prize for high achievements in art and music.

TOKTOGUL WATER RESERVOIR. The Toktogul water reservoir is situated in **Jalal Abad** *oblast* and is one of the largest and most important man-made water reserves in Kyrgyzstan. It provides drinking and irrigation water for up to 400,000 hectares of irrigated land in the **Ferghana valley.** The Toktogul reservoir was created after the completion of the 215-meter-high concrete dam for the Toktogul hydroelectric station (HES) on the **Naryn River** in 1975. The hydroelectric station produces about 1,200 megawatts of electricity annually.

The reservoir has a surface area of about 284 square kilometers, stretching up to 65 kilometers in length, and about 61 kilometers in width. Its average depth is about 69 meters; it contains up to 19.5 cubic kilometers of high quality drinkable water. According to the Kyrgyz authorities 20 percent of the water from the reservoir is used for irrigation of Kyrgyzstan's part of the Ferghana valley and 80 percent of the water goes to neighboring **Uzbekistan.** In the 1990s disputes over the usage of the water sparked tensions between Kyrgyzstan and Uzbekistan, as Kyrgyzstan's **government** demanded payment for the water, claiming that it needs substantial resources to maintain the water reservoirs on the Naryn River, and especially for the aging Toktogul reservoir.

TOPOYEV, ESEN (1952–). Kyrgyz military official. Born in the town of Kyzyl Kia in **Osh** *oblast* (southern Kyrgyzstan), Esen Topoyev graduated from the Tashkent Military College (**Uzbekistan**) in 1973, Moscow Military Academy in 1985, and Moscow Military Academy under General Staff in 1995. From 1973 to 1982 he commanded various units of the Soviet army in Central Asia and the Caucasus and from 1985 to 1992 he held various command positions in the Far East region of the **Russian Federation.** In 1992 he served as the senior officer for public relations in the Russian Far East Military District. From 1992 to 1995 he worked as deputy commander of division. He was the first deputy minister for defense of the **Kyrgyz Republic** 1995–99. In 1999 he served as head of the presidential security troops and concurrently secretary of the **Security Council** of the Kyrgyz Republic.

In 1999 Topoyev was appointed the minister of defense. He supervised the reform of the defense forces with the aim of facing the threats from external **militant incursions** in 1999 and 2000, and cooperation of the Kyrgyz defense forces with the military command of the **U.S. military airbase** in Kyrgyzstan in 2001 and 2002. Although he kept a relatively low profile in Kyrgyz politics, he made a significant contribution to the reform of the Kyrgyz defense forces in the early 2000s.

TORAGA. Chairman of the **Jogorku Kenesh** (parliament). Each of the two houses of the Jogorku Kenesh elects its chairman from among the members of the house. According to the **constitution of Kyrgyzstan,** the Toraga chairs sessions of the Jogorku Kenesh, signs acts adopted by the Jogorku Kenesh, represents the Jogorku Kenesh abroad, and conducts other duties.

TOURISM. Tourism is an underdeveloped sector of the **economy**, severely limited by lack of transportation infrastructure, management skills, and accommodation facilities. Only in 1991 was the tourism sector significantly liberalized, as the government privatized state monopolies—Intourist, Sputnik, and Restursovet—and allowed the opening of new privately run tourists companies. Tourism has significant potential, especially adventure tourism, due to Kyrgyzstan's beautiful and rugged landscape, and the number of cultural sites on the **Great Silk Road**, which connected **China** with western Europe in medieval times. Kyrgyzstan's government declared 2001 as the year of tourism, hoping to boost this sector of the economy. According to a Radio Free Europe report, almost 500,000 tourists visited Kyrgyzstan in 2001, up from 400,000 in 2000. However, the tourism sector was in steep decline in 2002 and 2003 due to several factors. They included proximity to **Afghanistan**, war in Iraq, political instability in the region, and crime and terrorist activities in the region and in the republic.

TRADE UNIONS. The first trade unions were established in Kyrgyz-stan in 1917 in Pishpek (now **Bishkek**) and the trade union move-ment had 14 branches with 10,000 members in 1920. On 31 March 1925 the First Constituent Congress of the Trade Unions of **Kara-Kyrgyz Autonomous** *Oblast* was held. In November 1926, at the Second Congress the Trade Unions of **Kyrgyz Soviet Socialist Re-public** was transformed into the republic's Council of Trade Unions (CTU). During the Soviet era the trade unions enjoyed significant support from the state. They were practically integrated in the Soviet political and economic system. They represented the largest public organization in the republic during the Soviet era with a membership reaching 1.6 million people.

The situation changed radically in 1991, as the trade unions lost their generous state financial subsidies and special relations with the **government**. The Law on Labor regulates the activities of trade unions in Kyrgyzstan and guarantees the rights of the workers to join independent trade unions or remain non-unionized. The government generally does not restrict workers' membership in trade unions be-cause in the post-Soviet era the role and power of the trade unions has largely diminished and they do not confront the government on any key economic policy issues.

The Federation of Trade Unions of Kyrgyzstan (FTUK) is a direct successor of the Council of Trade Unions. However, the influence and financial viability of the FTUK diminished significantly after 1991, as most of the trade unions' property was privatized, and at the same time most of the enterprises collapsed. The FTUK had little to say about this, and was largely silent when hundreds of thousands of workers were laid off or forced to do unpaid work in the 1990s. It claimed that it showed only a small decrease in its membership and has around 1 million members; though the scale of the economic re-cession makes it likely that membership was decreasing at a much higher rate. Among the new trade unions that emerged since 1991 is the Union of Entrepreneurs and Small Business Workers, which at-tempted to package itself as a Western-style trade union and to defend the rights of small business workers.

Despite all the difficulties and setbacks, the FTUK was vocal dur-ing the process of changing some local labor regulations and advised the government on such issues as the status of child labor practices and the minimum age for employment, minimum wages, and health and safety in the workplace. In practice, however, these regulations are often ignored and the trade unions rarely protest against violations of workers rights.

TRANSPORTATION. Transportation is an important sector of Kyrgyzstan's **economy** accounting for about 4.7 percent of GDP (2001, IMF est.). The country's transportation system consists of a network of 30,300 kilometers of primary and secondary **motor roads** and around 370 kilometers of **railways** (the figure does not include industrial lines). The country is also served by 50 airports, only four of them paved (CIA est., 2002); there are also 200 kilometers of natural gas pipelines. Due to its landlocked situation Kyrgyzstan depends heavily on the transportation network of the neighboring countries, especially **China, Kazakhstan, Russia,** and **Uzbekistan,** in accessing the international market. In 2001 28 million tons of freight were transported in Kyrgyzstan. Motor vehicles carried nearly 26 million tons of the freight within the republic, and the rest was sent or arrived via railways. In 2001 total annual passenger traffic was about 466 million people, down from 656 million people in 1990: 398 million of them or about 85 percent were carried by autobuses; 63 million people or about 13 percent by trolley-buses; and 630,000 by railways. About 197,000 people were transported by **Kyrgyzstan Aba Joldoru** and other airlines.

From the Soviet era Kyrgyzstan inherited a relatively well developed but unevenly distributed transportation network. However, the national transportation system was seriously disrupted by the introduction of passport and customs controls and various restrictions on the borders with the neighboring Central Asian states. Between 2002 and 2012 the republic needs from US$400 million to US$1.5 billion to be able to reconstruct its transportation system according to international standards. The Ministry of Transportation regulates and controls most of the transportation network, though the **airlines,** some **services** in the airports, and railways were privatized in the 1990s.

TRIBES. Kyrgyz society is traditionally divided into tribes—social groups defined by a tradition or perception of common descent. In fact, one of the translations of the name "Kyrgyz" derives from the Turkic "qyrq" and "yz," which means 40 tribes (clans). The Kyrgyz tribes were subdivided into three groups. The Ong Kanat (right wing) united those **Kyrgyzs** who lived in what is now northern Kyrgyzstan, to the north of the Ala-Too, the **Tian-Shan mountain** range. The Sol Kanat (left wing) united those Kyrgyzs who lived to the south of the **Ala-Too mountains**, in what is now southern Kyrgyzstan. The third group is Ichkilik.

A major consolidation of the Kyrgyz tribes took place between the 15th and 17th centuries, when the Kyrgyzs began to form a distinct language, identity, and culture. This process was at an advanced stage by the beginning of the 19th century. The major tribes (in alphabetical order) are as follows:

Ong Kanat	Sol Kanat	Ichkilik
Adygene	Basyz	Avat
Kara Bagysh	Chon Bagysh	Boston
Mongoldor	Kush'chu	Deeles
Munkush	Kytai	Kandy
Tagai	Munduz	Kesek
	Saruu	Kydyrsha
Bugu	Tebei	Kypchak
Deeles	Zhetigen	Noigut
Sayak		Orgu
Sary Bagysh		Teyit
Solto		Zhoo Kesek
Zhediger		
Azyk		
Baaryn		
Bagysh		
Cherik		
Kara Choro		
Keldike		
Kongurat		
Suu Murun		

Source: *Kirgizskaia SSR Entsyklopedia* [*Kyrgyz SSR Encyclopedia*]. Frunze, 1982, p. 115

During the 20th century the importance of tribal identity and tribal politics eroded significantly. After independence in 1991, however, there was a significant growth of interest in tribal identities and histories as well as the role of tribalism in political life. In the 1990s Kyrgyz historians published several researches on evolution of tribal relations in Kyrgyzstan. *See also* CLANS.

TURGUNALIYEV, TOPCHUBEK (1941–). Kyrgyz politician. Born in the remote village of Temirgen-Sai in **Osh** *oblast*, Topchubek Turgunaliyev graduated from the Moscow State Institute of Culture and the *aspirantura* in 1975. From 1966 to 1969 he held various teaching positions at the Kyrgyz Women's Pedagogical Institute in Frunze (now **Bishkek**). From 1969 to 1975 he was head of the department of culture of the Central Committee of the **Communist Party of Kyrgyz SSR** and from 1975 to 1980 he was director of the **Kyrgyz State Theater of Opera and Ballet.** He was head of the philosophy department of the Kyrgyz Women Pedagogical Institute 1980–92.

In 1990 Turgunalyev was among the founding members of the first mass opposition organization, the **Democratic Movement of Kyrgyzstan** (DMK), and he was elected as chairman of the movement. In 1991 he became chairman of the **Erkin Kyrgyzstan** political party. The support from the DMK played a vital role in defeating **Absamat Masalyev**, the Communist Party leader, and in the election of **Askar Akayev** as the president. However, very soon Turgunaliyev began to criticize the president for shortcomings in his economic policy and for growing corruption. In 1997 Turgunaliyev was sentenced to seven years imprisonment on corruption charges, which he vigorously denied. Turgunaliyev's supporters claimed that the case was politically motivated and the charges were fabricated. He was released from prison in August 2001 under intense international and local pressure. After the release he took up the position of chairman of the Institute of Human Rights and Liberties in Bishkek.

Turgunaliyev is best known as one of the leading opposition figures in the republic, who held relatively moderate political views and promoted a populist democratic platform. However, his influence was undermined by the internal political split in the ranks of the DMK and absence of a sound political platform. He played a significant role during the political tensions in the 2002 political crisis ensuing from the **Aksy conflict**.

TURKISTAN. A geographic area, which historically comprised what is now the five Central Asian republics and the Xinjan Autonomous

Region in **China**. In the 19th century **Russia** established its control over the western parts of Turkistan (sometimes called Western Turkistan), while China maintained its control over the eastern parts of Turkistan. Some sources also called the Turkic-populated parts of northern **Afghanistan** Afghan Turkistan.

In 1867 the **Russian Empire** established the **Turkistan Governor-Generalship** with its center in Tashkent. This administrative entity covered most of Russian-controlled Turkistan, except the **Bukhara** and **Khiva Khanates**, which nominally remained independent. In 1886 the Turkistan Governor-Generalship was renamed the Turkistanskii Krai (Turkistan region). In April 1918 the Fifth All-Turkistan Congress of Soviets established the **Turkistan Autonomous Soviet Socialist Republic** to replace the tsarist-era administrative entity Turkistanskii Krai. In 1920 it was renamed the **Turkistan Soviet Socialist Republic**. In October 1924 it was abolished due to the **border delimitation in 1924–1926** in Central Asia. *See also* KARA-KYRGYZ AUTONOMOUS OBLAST; TURKISTAN COMMUNIST PARTY.

TURKISTAN AUTONOMOUS SOVIET SOCIALIST REPUBLIC (TASSR). The republic existed between 1918 and 1924 as part of the **Russian Federation**. The TASSR was established in Tashkent on 30 April 1918 at the Fifth All-Turkistan Congress of Soviets. Its first constitution was adopted on 5–14 October 1918 at the Sixth Extraordinary Congress of Soviets. The republic included territories of present-day **Kazakhstan** (its southern *oblasts*), Kyrgyzstan, **Tajikistan,** and **Uzbekistan** with a total population of about 5.2 million people (1920 census). Between 1918 and 1919 the TASSR was cut off from the Russian government by anti-Bolshevik forces and it functioned as a semi-independent state. The TASSR government and **Turkistan Communist Party** played an important role in establishing the Soviet administration and control over the territory of the Central Asian region from 1918 to 1920. In 1920 the new constitution was approved and the TASSR became the **Turkistan Soviet Socialist Republic** (TSSR).

The TSSR was officially abolished on 27 October 1924 due to the **border delimitation in 1924–1926** in Central Asia, when it was divided into the Central Asian Soviet Republics. The territories of the four eastern *oblasts* of the TSSR were consolidated into the **Kyrgyz Autonomous *Oblast*** in 1924.

TURKISTAN COMMUNIST PARTY (TCP). A political organization that existed between 1918 and 1924 with headquarters in Tashkent. It was inaugurated at the First Congress of the TCP in June 1918 and was formalized at the Second Congress of the TCP in December 1918. The party played a central role in consolidating various Communist and leftist groups on the territory of Central Asia into a disciplined political organization in 1918. It also played a key role in establishing and mobilizing support for the Soviet system in 1918–19. In 1919 Vladimir Lenin suggested to send the Turkistan Commission (Turkomissiya), in order to strengthen the TCP's political stand and institutional structure. The Turkomissiya supervised the establishment of the regional and district structures of the TCP in Central Asia. In 1924 the TCP ceased to exist after the **border delimitation in 1924–1926** in Central Asia. *See also* COMMUNIST PARTY OF KYRGYZ SSR.

TURKISTAN GOVERNOR-GENERALSHIP. An administrative entity that existed between 1867 and 1886 and was administered by the governor-general—usually a military general in Russian service. The first governor-general, Konstantin Petrovich von Kaufman, served from 1867 until 1882, supervising the acquisition of the new lands, abolishment of the **Kokand Khanate,** and administrative delimitation of **Turkistan** into *oblasts* (provinces). In 1886 the Turkistan Governor-Generalship was renamed the Turkistanskii Krai (Turkistan region). *See also* TURKISTAN; TURKISTAN AUTONOMOUS SOVIET SOCIALIST REPUBLIC.

TURKISTAN SOVIET SOCIALIST REPUBLIC (TSSR). The republic was established on 24 September 1920 as a successor of the **Turkistan Autonomous Soviet Socialist Republic (TASSR)** and abolished on 27 October 1924 due to the **border delimitation in 1924–1926** in Central Asia. *See also* TURKISTAN AUTONOMOUS SOVIET SOCIALIST REPUBLIC; TURKISTAN COMMUNIST PARTY.

TURKSIB (full name Turkestansko-Sibirskaya Zheleznaya Doroga in Russian). A major 1,452-kilometer-long railroad built between 1927 and 1932 as one of the first **transportation** projects of the Soviet government. It runs from Semipalatinks and Almaty (**Kazakhstan**) to Lugovaya and **Bishkek** (Kyrgyzstan). At the Lugovaya station the railroad connects with the Central Asian railroad. At present the Turksib is a part of the Kazakh railroad and an important transportation link between Kyrgyzstan and **Russia** via Kazakhstan. *See also* RAILWAYS.

–U–

UCHKUN PUBLISHING HOUSE. The largest state-controlled publishing house in Kyrgyzstan established in Frunze (now **Bishkek**) in 1926. Between 1926 and 2000 it published more than 100 million copies of books, brochures, and pamphlets. In the 1990s it had the only publishing capacity with modern printing facilities and was able to publish newspapers and magazines in large commercial volumes. Between 2000 and 2002 the Uchkun regularly caused political scandals when it refused, as the monopolist in the market, to publish opposition newspapers. *See also* MASS MEDIA.

ULUT. The term refers to a Kyrgyz **tribe**. Traditionally it is customary among the **Kyrgyz** to remember all ancestors of their *ulut* up to seven generations.

UNION OF CINEMATOGRAPHERS OF KYRGYZSTAN. The public organization established in 1962 as a professional union of the cinematographers of Kyrgyzstan. The first Congress of the Union was held in 1962, which elected **Chingiz Aitmatov** as chairman of the union and adopted the major principles and conditions for membership in the organization. The union provided various social benefits and training sessions, assisted young cinematographers and cinema critics in their professional growth, and supervised the distribution of state subsidies for movie productions. It gradually became a rigid corporate-style organization. Until 1991 the Union of Cinematographers of Kyrgyzstan was part of the Union of Cinematographers of the USSR. The union experienced decay in the 1990s, as it lost most of the state grants and subsidies. The union claimed up to 200 members in 2001.

UNION OF JOURNALISTS OF KYRGYZSTAN. The public organization established in 1959 that united the professional journalists in

Kyrgyzstan. The union held its first Congress in 1959 and adopted the major principles and conditions for membership in the organization. The union provided various social, professional, and educational benefits; organized training sessions; and assisted young journalists in developing their professional skills. During the Soviet era the union functioned under the strict control of the **Communist Party of Kyrgyz SSR** and gradually became an exclusive corporate-style organization. It played an important role in the Soviet propaganda machinery. After 1991 the union was transformed into an independent nongovernmental and nonpolitical organization open for professional and independent journalists. The union claimed up to 2,000 members in 2001. In 1991 journalist Abdukadir Sultanbayev was elected as chairman of the organization. *See also* MASS MEDIA.

UNION OF WRITERS OF KYRGYZSTAN. The public organization established in 1932 that united the writers in Kyrgyzstan. The first Congress of the Union was held in 1934, which adopted the major principles and conditions for membership in the organization. The union brought together writers and poets in the republic and provided various social benefits and training sessions, arranged translations of the works written by the Kyrgyz writers in **Kyrgyz language** into Russian and other major languages of the USSR, and assisted young writers in preparation of their manuscripts for publications. The union functioned under the strict control of the **Communist Party of Kyrgyz SSR** and gradually became an exclusive corporate-style organization. The Union of Writers of Kyrgyzstan published *Ala-Too* literary journal (in Kyrgyz) and *Literaturnyi Kyrgyzstan* (in Russian) as well as the newspaper *Kyrgyzstan Madani'aty.* The union experienced decay in the 1990s, as it lost most of its state grants and subsidies. The union claimed up to 400 members in 2001. In 1996 Kyrgyz poet Nadyrbek Alymbekov was elected chairman of the organization.

UNOFFICIAL MUSLIM CLERGY. The Soviet-era restrictions on the number of registered mosques and **official Muslim clergy** led to the emergence of a large group of **mullahs** (*moldos*), who performed various religious rituals and led prayers, but who were not registered with the state authorities. Representatives of the unofficial Muslim clergy often received informal Islamic **education** from old *sheikhs* or mullahs at underground *medreses*, and they often brought in some local traditions and practices, including those learned from **Sufism**. These mullahs often had more radical views and were critical of the official Muslim clergy. The Soviet authorities largely tolerated the existence of the unofficial Muslim clergy as long as they refrained from public actions or interference in politics. After 1991 some representatives of this group were registered with the state authorities. Many of those who did not register joined various grass-root Sufi orders or Islamic groups, including **Hizb-Ut-Tahrir**. *See also* ISLAM; ISLAMIC DEMOCRATIC PARTY OF KYRGYZSTAN.

URAZBEKOV, ABDUKADYR (1889–1938). Kyrgyz politician and the first chairman of the Central Executive Committee. Abdukadyr Urazbekov received little formal education. He became a political activist during the civil war in Kyrgyzstan (1918–20). In March 1927 he was elected as the first chairman of the Central Executive Committee, thereby becoming the first head of state. He served in this position from 1927 to 1937. In 1937 he was dismissed and accused of anti-Soviet activities. Urazbekov was executed in 1938, but he was rehabilitated posthumously after the death of Josef Stalin.

U.S. MILITARY AIRBASE (also called Ganci Airbase). A military base established at the Manas International Airport (40 kilometers from **Bishkek**) in November 2001. It hosts the U.S. and North Atlantic Treaty Organization (NATO) aircraft and personnel deployed for military actions in **Afghanistan**. The United States leased 37 acres and built housing for up to 3,000 military personnel and facilities for servicing fighter jets, C-130 cargo planes, and KC-135 refueling planes. By the beginning of 2002 military personnel from more than 12 countries were deployed in the base. The base is located about 50–60 minutes flying time from Kabul and was especially intensively used in the winter and spring 2002 campaign in Afghanistan. The total budget for building and running the airbase was estimated at about US$500 million in 2001 and 2002.

The negotiations for establishing the base began in October 2001. Immediately after the 11 September 2001 terrorist attacks on the World Trade Center President **Askar Akayev** expressed his condolences to the American people and his full support of U.S. actions against "international terrorism and extremism." In October 2001 the United States's government officially asked the **government** of Kyrgyzstan about the possible use of Kyrgyzstan's territory to station U.S. troops. After intensive consultations with the members of the **Commonwealth of Independent States Collective Security Treaty**, officials in Bishkek agreed to host the U.S. military personnel and U.S. aircraft. In June 2002 the agreement was extended for another year with an option to extend the lease on an annual basis.

USENOV, DANIYAR (1960–). Kyrgyz politician. Born in Frunze (now **Bishkek**), Daniyar Usenov graduated from the **Frunze Polytechnic Institute** in 1982 and from the Faculty of Law of **Kyrgyz State (National) University** in 1992 (by correspondence). From 1984 to 1990 he worked as an engineer at the Mining-Metallurgical Combine. From 1990 to 1992 he was first deputy chairman of the **Kara Balta** city administration and from 1992 to 1994 he worked as assistant to the head of the **Chui** *oblast* administration and concurrently as executive director of the Kyrgyz-British joint venture enterprise. From 1994 to 1995 he was director-general of the Eridan financial and industrial corporation. In 1995 he was elected to the **Jogorku Kenesh** (parliament), becoming one of the most active parliamentarians and a vocal critic of the **government**. He attempted to challenge incumbent president **Askar Akayev** in the 2000 presidential elections but was barred from registration due to legal irregularities, though he was regarded as one of the strongest candidates in these elections.

Usenov is best known for his active role in the opposition and for his vocal criticism of the government. However, his political career came to an abrupt halt in 2000 when he was brought to trial and sentenced to three years imprisonment in a case that the opposition viewed as politically motivated persecution.

USTOZ **(also** *ustaz* **or** *usta***).** 1. A master, teacher, or highly qualified expert in his field. 2. The head of a craftsman shop or a craftsman order in Central Asia. 3. A term used in present-day Kyrgyzstan to refer to an expert, lecturer, or head of a working group.

USUBALIYEV, TURDAKUN (1919–). Kyrgyz politician, academician, and publicist. Turdakun Usubaliyev led the **Kyrgyz Soviet Socialist**

Republic (Kyrgyz SSR) from 1961 to 1985 as first secretary of the **Communist Party of Kyrgyz SSR**. Born in Kochkorka village in **Naryn** *oblast* (a remote eastern province of the republic) in 1919, he spent his entire career in the Communist Party apparatus, becoming one of the republic's most influential politicians for almost three decades in the late Soviet era. He graduated from the Kyrgyz Pedagogical Institute (Frunze, 1941), Party School (Moscow, 1945), and Moscow Pedagogical Institute (Moscow, 1965). From 1955 to 1956 he worked as the editor of the leading national newspaper, *Sovettyk Kyrgyzstan,* and later he held various party posts before assuming the leadership of the republic. He viewed the Soviet policy (reflected in his writing) as an important mode of modernization of a traditional "backward" country, and measured it purely in terms of economic development and state-led industrialization. These views largely shaped Kyrgyzstan's political and economic trajectory in the 1960s and 1970s.

Usubaliyev belonged to the cohort of Central Asian leaders who were the most loyal to the Soviet political system and to Moscow's leadership. As the country leader he contributed to the vigorous implementation of Russification and "internationalism" policies. However, it was his success in attracting huge investments in the industrialization of the republic that won him nationwide recognition.

In 1985, with the introduction of Mikhail Gorbachev's policy of *glasnost,* Usubaliyev was forced to leave his post and was charged with patronage, corruption, and mismanagement. However, these accusations were never brought to court. In 1992 he returned to the political arena as a member of the **Jogorku Kenesh** (parliament), supporting moderate nationalism and remaining highly critical of the Westernization of Kyrgyz society. In the 1990s Usubaliyev remained one of the most influential politicians in the republic and a prolific writer (mainly memoirs), but in the 2000s he largely retired from politics. He has authored seven books and more than 70 brochures and articles, including his memoirs, published after 1992.

UZBEKISTAN (official name Uzbekiston Respublikasi or Uzbekiston). The republic is located west of Kyrgyzstan, with which it shares its longest border—1,099 kilometers. Uzbekistan is the second largest state in Central Asia (447,000 square kilometers). It is the most populous country in the region with a **population** estimated at about 25.2 million in 2003, or nearly 45 percent of the total Central Asian population. The Uzbeks account for 80 percent of the population, Russians about 5.5 percent, Tajiks about 5.1 percent, Kazakhs about 3.0 percent, Karakalpaks about 2.5 percent, Tatars about 1.1 percent, and others about 2.5 percent. About 200,000 **Kyrgyz** live in Uzbekistan, mainly in Namangan, Andijon, **Ferghana,** and Kashkadarya *veloyats* (provinces).

During the Soviet era Uzbekistan together with Kyrgyzstan and other Central Asian republics was part of the Central Asian economic region and shared most of its **transportation**, pipeline, telecommunications, and other infrastructure, as it was built during the Soviet era to serve the whole region as a single entity. After 1991 Tashkent inherited the most vital parts of this infrastructure network, and there were considerable disagreements over transportation fees, border **trade,** and border control issues between the two states. In 2000 Uzbekistan was Kyrgyzstan's second largest trading partner, after the **Russian Federation.** Kyrgyzstan's trade with Uzbekistan was estimated at 15 percent of its total foreign trade, or at about US$200 million. Kyrgyzstan exported about US$110 million in goods and **services**, mainly **agricultural** products and machinery, and imported about US$90 million in goods and services, mainly natural gas, machinery, and consumer goods. Experts reported about large-scale smuggling of cheap Uzbek gasoline to **Batken, Jalal Abad,** and **Osh** *oblasts* and about unrecorded border trade in the **Ferghana valley**. Kyrgyzstan's delays with payments for natural gas delivered from Uzbekistan and disputes over water issues and transportation fees in the Ferghana valley remained major bones of contention in economic disputes between the two countries throughout the 1990s. Additionally, Tashkent established restrictions on the transit of Kyrgyzstan's goods through its territory in 1993, 1998, and 1999. Between 2000 and 2002 **Bishkek** demanded from Tashkent payments for drinking and irrigation water from rivers originating in Kyrgyzstan's mountains and that continued to Uzbekistan. The negotiations reached an impasse and produced considerable tension between the two countries.

In 1999 and 2000 the **Islamic Movement of Uzbekistan** (IMU), a militant Uzbek opposition group, which was formed in exile in **Tajikistan** and **Afghanistan**, attempted to enter Uzbekistan through Kyrgyzstan's territory. The IMU entered Batken *oblast* from Tajikistan.

The Kyrgyz defense and security forces battled the IMU for weeks without success. Tashkent provided logistic and political support to Bishkek. Uzbekistan's airforce bombed the areas controlled by the intruders, but a lack of coordination led to substantial casualties among the civilian population. Uzbekistan also mined the borders between the two countries, leading to numerous casualties among the local citizens. Both actions provoked anger among Kyrgyzstan's public. The mining of the borders as well as territorial claims from both sides, since the borders were never formally endorsed during the 20th century, created much of the friction in political relations between the two neighboring countries. In December 2000 Uzbekistan imposed an entry visa regime for citizens of Kyrgyzstan, creating a huge obstacle for travel and business between the two republics.

Both Uzbekistan and Kyrgyzstan are members the **Central Asian Forum** (formerly Central Asian Economic Union), **Commonwealth of Independent States (CIS)**, **Commonwealth of Independent States Collective Security Treaty** (Uzbekistan left it in 1999), **Economic Cooperation Organization, Organization of the Islamic Conference, Organization for Security and Cooperation in Europe (OSCE), Shanghai Cooperation Organization,** and some other regional and international organizations.

UZGEN (also Ozgen). This city is located in southern Kyrgyzstan, around 300 kilometers southwest of **Bishkek** and 30 kilometers east of **Osh city**. It is one of the oldest cities in the republic and the second largest city in **Osh** *oblast*. Its **population** was estimated at about 41,700 (1999 census), up from about 30,200 (1979 census), consisting mainly of **Kyrgyzs** and Uzbeks, but also including Russians, Tatars, Tajiks, and some others. It is an important agricultural, trading, and **tourist** center in southern Kyrgyzstan. Its **agriculture** is built around producing rice, which is considered the best in Central Asia, tobacco, fruits, and sunflower kernels for oil. The city also hosts a college, eight schools, **libraries**, a museum, and several medieval mosques and a *medrese*.

Kyrgyz historians claim that the city was established in the first century B.C. as a small fortress. For centuries it was an outpost on the **Great Silk Road** and a bazaar (market place) of regional importance. It was destroyed several times, but was rebuilt again. There are remains of the 11th-century minarets and towers, the 12th-century's Karakhanids-built mausoleums, and some others historical sites. During the Soviet era it became an administrative center of Uzgen *rayon* (district) and a tourist attraction of regional importance. Several small agricultural-processing plants were built there. In 1990 Uzgen became the site of one of the bloodiest interethnic conflicts in modern Kyrgyzstan, known as the **Osh-Uzgen conflicts.** Clashes between neighboring Uzbek and Kyrgyz communities led to numerous deaths, as several dozens people were killed and injured and many houses were burned to the ground. After 1991 peace was restored and in the post-Soviet era the Uzgen authorities tried to reinvent the city as a major attraction for the modern adventure tourists traveling on the Great Silk Road.

–V–

VAQF. Religious endowment, properties, and land donated to mosques and *medreses* (*madrasah*). During medieval times the Islamic religious institutions controlled significant areas of arable land in Central Asia, including the **Ferghana valley.** In the 1920s the Soviet government confiscated the *Vaqf* properties and land, and distributed it among the local people. In the late 1990s some religious leaders suggested reestablishing the institute of the *Vaqf* in Kyrgyzstan.

VATAN (from Persian "Fatherland"). A term used among people of some Central Asian republics. It is widely used among the Uzbek and Tajik population in the **Ferghana valley,** although the **Kyrgyz** traditionally use the Turkic term, Ata Meken.

VAZIR **(from Arabic** *wazir***).** 1. A chief minister and adviser to *khans* or sultans in Central Asian and Middle Eastern states in the medieval era. 2. A minister and a representative of a sultan in the Ottoman Caliphate.

VELOYAT. Province. The term *veloyat* replaced the term *oblast* in **Tajikistan** and **Uzbekistan** and is frequently used among the Tajik and Uzbek population of Kyrgyzstan.

VICTORY PEAK. *See* POBEDY PEAK.

–W–

WAHHABISM (also wahabi, wahabiyah). A radical puritanical Islamic movement established by Abd-Al-Wahhab (1703–1787) on the Arabian Peninsula. Abd-Al-Wahhab called for a return to the original practices of **Islam** and to the strict following of the Islamic norm **(Shariah).** During the Soviet era, Wahhabism was practically unknown in Kyrgyzstan as the Soviet authorities kept strict control over the religious practices among Muslim communities in the republic. In the 1990s a significant amount of literature on Wahhabism was allegedly brought to Kyrgyzstan from Middle Eastern countries and distributed among the Muslim population of **Jalal Abad** and **Osh** *oblasts.* In addition several hundred students received **education** or training in religious institutions in the Middle East. Wahabism received no significant support among the **population** of Kyrgyzstan, though there were reports that it found some appeal among radical Islamic groups in the republic. In 2002 and 2003 the Kyrgyz **National Security Committee** claimed that it had confiscated several hundred books on Wahhabism.

WAHHABIST. 1. A follower of **Wahhabism**, who usually strictly follows the religious duties of **Islam** as interpreted by Abd-Al-Wahhab. 2. A term often used in Kyrgyzstan in reference to any person who strictly follows the pillars of Islamic belief, though not necessarily a follower of the Wahhabism movement.

WOMEN. Women always held prominent position in Kyrgyz society, although some patriarchal traditions affected their social and political status. However, there is a significant difference in the traditional view of the role and status of women in northern and southern Kyrgyzstan. In northern and in some mountains part of southern Kyrgyzstan, where people were engaged in **pastoral nomadism** until the 20th century, the traditional role of women went far beyond being just housewife. Women played an important part in economic activities and often accompanied and fought alongside their husbands in numerous wars. Meanwhile, in southern Kyrgyzstan, where the influence of the settled societies and Islamic traditions was stronger, women were often perceived in their traditional role of housekeepers.

They often played a secondary role in public life and were often compelled into forced marriages to men who were able to pay *qalym* (dowry). One of the symbols of these differences was the fact that many women in southern Kyrgyzstan wore a *paranja* (veil) every time they went outside their houses; in contrast, in northern Kyrgyzstan this tradition was not followed at all.

The Soviet authorities enforced the policy of equality for women and men in the 1920s. The **liquidation of illiteracy** campaign eliminated mass illiteracy among women by the end of the 1930s and *qalym* was outlawed. There was an unofficial but strictly followed policy of quotas for women in all state institutions and public organizations. During the Soviet era women held up to 20–30 percent of important public positions in the ruling **Communist Party of Kyrgyz SSR** and in the **government**, including ministerial positions. At the same time, however, the public views of the position of women in family life remained quite conservative, as divorces were strongly discouraged and any relations outside wedlock were strongly disapproved.

The situation changed significantly after independence in 1991. The **constitution of Kyrgyzstan** guarantees equal rights of men and women. However, the state abandoned the quota system and women quickly lost most of their positions in the public sector and in government. Yet Kyrgyz women established several women's organizations in order to maintain more prominent position in public life and defend the rights of women. Some of them, like **Roza Otunbayeva**, **Mira Dzhangaracheva,** and **Rakhat Achylova,** obtained ministerial positions and became influential politicians at the national level. However, some pre-Soviet traditions, such as forced marriages, *qalym,* wearing the *paranja,* and others, found their way back, especially in southern Kyrgyzstan.

At present, women constitute about 52 percent of the total population of Kyrgyzstan. The proportion of women among students at tertiary level was about 58 percent in 2000. Due to the steep economic recession many women lost their jobs and they constitute between 60 and 70 percent of the unemployed people in the republic. Their average wages were about 70 percent of the average wages of men. Some women's organizations reported that many women tried to find work overseas and were often trapped into prostitution rings.

WORLD TRADE ORGANIZATION (WTO). An international organization established in 1994 by the members of the General Agreement on Tariffs and Trade (GATT) in order to promote **international trade** and free movement of capital. Its rules are legally binding for its member states. The **Kyrgyz Republic** joined the WTO in 1998 through unilateral negotiations, despite the fact that there was an informal agreement with the members of the **Central Asian Economic Union** and **Customs Union** that such a step should be made through mutual consultations among the members. Kyrgyzstan's joining the WTO sparked the regional customs and tariff war between the republic and neighboring **Kazakhstan** and **Uzbekistan**, which continued in 1998 and 1999 and was only settled in 2000.

–Y–

YAK. A large domesticated ox (*Bos grunniens mutus*), which could be found in high mountain altitudes in the **Pamirs, Tian-Shan,** and Tibet. The wild yaks live in small herds and they nearly disappeared in Central Asia. Most of the yaks in Kyrgyzstan are domesticated. Large bulls have long black hair, a hairy tail, and up to 0.5 meter-long horns, which are spread outward. The yaks grow up to 1.8 meters tall and weigh as much as 400–500 kilograms. They graze on grass in the mountains and can easily sustain themselves through the cold winters of the Pamirs or Tian-Shan. The yaks are valued for their exceptionally durable skin, milk, and meat. They are often the only mode of **transportation** during the winter for high mountain villagers.

The **Kyrgyzs** raised yaks in the high mountains for centuries mainly on small subsistence family-owned farms. During the Soviet era approximately 120 *kolkhozes* in Kyrgyzstan specialized in raising these animals on a relatively large scale. The total number of yaks reached 66,500 in 1979, but declined to about 55,000 in 1991 and to 16,500 in 2001. The Kyrgyzs also raised a hybrid between female yaks and domestic cattle. Yak herding has significant potentials, as a considerable proportion of the Kyrgyz territory is located at an altitude over 3,000 meters above sea level. These pastures have very low productivity and are economically unviable for raising **sheep** or **horses**, but appropriate for raising yaks.

YAK-40. Designed in the Soviet era by Alexander Yakovlev (1906–89), the Yak-40 is a multifunctional 24- to 28-seat civil aviation jet plane intended to act as an airliner for secondary domestic routes. It was introduced and widely used in Kyrgyzstan in the 1980s. These short-range airplanes are still extensively exploited by the **Kyrgyzstan Aba Joldoru** (Kyrgyz Airline) for domestic flights.

YENISEI RIVER (also Yenisai or Enesai, the mother river in Kyrgyz). A river in **Russia**'s Siberia. According to traditional beliefs, the Kyrgyz **tribes** originated from the Yenisei River delta, where they lived during their golden age. Around the fourth to sixth centuries A.D. the **Kyrgyzs** were forced to leave for Central Asia due to various political, economic, and military circumstances.

YSYK KOL LAKE (also ozero Issyk-Kul in Russian; literally "hot lake" in Kyrgyz). A drainless lake located in **Ysyk Kol** *oblast* (northeastern Kyrgyzstan). Its surface area is about 6,236 square kilometers, stretching from east to west, up to 178 kilometers in length, its width is up to 61 kilometers, and its depth is about 700 meters. It contains up to 1,738 cubic kilometers of salted (nondrinkable) water. The lake is one of the world's largest, although its water level fell by about 8.5 meters between 1856 (year of the first official records) and 2002. The **Ysyk Kol valley**, where the lake is located, is bordered by the Kungey-Alatau Range in the north and the Terskey-Alatau Range in the south.

The northern sandy beaches of the lake have been used for recreational **tourism** since the 1950s. The lake is also noted for clear water, which gives life to more than 20 kinds of fish. The naked osman, the chebak, and the carp are fished for commercial purposes. Kyrgyz archaeologists claim that they discovered large underwater settlements, which disappeared most probably due to a large earthquake or water rise in the Middle Ages.

YSYK KOL *OBLAST* (also Issyk-Kulskaya oblast in Russian). An *oblast* in northern Kyrgyzstan, bordered by **Kazakhstan** in the north, **Chui** *oblast* in the east, **Naryn** *oblast* in the southwest, and **China** in the southeast. Ysyk Kol *oblast* has an area of about 43,400 square kilometers, or over 23 percent of Kyrgyzstan's territory; it is the second largest *oblast* in Kyrgyzstan. Its population was estimated at about 415,600 (1999 census), or about 8 percent of the country's population, up from about 350,700 (1979 census). Ysyk Kol's population consists mainly of the **Kyrgyzs**—79.4 percent in 1999—but also included Russians (13.2 percent), Kazakhs (1.7 percent), Uzbeks (0.8 percent), Tatars (0.7 percent), Dungans (0.7 percent), and others. Yssyk Kol *oblast* was originally formed in 1939; it was abolished in 1959, but was reestablished in 1970. It consists of the Jeti Oguz, Ysyk Kol, Tong and Tup *raions* (districts), and the town of **Karakol** as the capital.

Agriculture (animal husbandry, fruits and vegetables, etc.), food processing, **tourism**, **industry**, and services are the main sectors of its economy. During the Soviet era Ysyk Kol was the primary recreational destination for Central Asians and tourists from western Siberia (**Russia**). It also specialized in producing and processing agricultural products, for local consumption and for export. In the 1970s and 1980s some areas of the *oblast* were used as military testing facilities by the Soviet navy, air defense, and air force.

Between 1991 and 1998 Ysyk Kol *oblast* experienced economic difficulties as its industrial enterprises could not compete with cheap foreign imports while the number of tourists declined significantly. In 1996 a **Free Economic Zone** (FEZ) was established near Karakol, but during the first five years it largely failed to revive the *oblast's* industries. In 1997 the **Kumtor** Operating Company, a joint Kyrgyz Canadian enterprise, began **gold** mining in the *oblast*, extracting almost 85,000 kilograms or 3 million ounces of gold between 1997 and 2002. This was the largest foreign investment project since Kyrgyzstan's independence. In an attempt to revive tourism Kyrgyzstan declared 2001 the year of tourism and managed to attract almost 100,000 foreign tourists and visitors, mainly to Ysyk Kol *oblast*, but in 2002 there was a significant decline in arrivals.

The Ysyk Kol elite played an important role in the intellectual life of the republic and is well represented among artists and academics.

YSYK KOL VALLEY (also Issyk-Kul in Russian; literally "hot lake" in Kyrgyz). Valley located in northern **Kyrgyzstan**. Its area is about 12,000 square kilometers. With a length of about 275 kilometers and a width of about 65 kilometers, most of the valley is elevated 1,500 meters above sea level. The Ysyk Kol valley is bordered by the

Kungey-Alatau Range (maximum height of 4,771 meters) in the north and the Terskey-Alatau Range (maximum height is up to 5,216 meters) in the south. Kyrgyzstan's largest lake, **Ysyk Kol Lake**, is located in the central part of the valley.

The mountains protect the valley from the extremes of cold continental weather. Mild and dry summers make this area one of the most popular destinations for summer retreats in the republic. The nearby mountains are also popular destinations for nonprofessional trekkers.

The valley is located on one of the routes of the **Great Silk Road**, and it was used be traders and travelers as a place to rest during their lengthy travels between **China** and Eastern Europe. In the 19th century support from the local Kyrgyz tribes was crucial to the troops of the **Russian Empire** in defeating the **Kokand Khanate**.

During the 20th century the population of the Ysyk Kol valley grew rapidly, making the valley the fourth most densely populated area in the republic. In the 1990s environmental issues, such as water pollution and soil erosion, became a serious problem in the *oblast*.

YURT (also *Yurta, Boz-ui, Kyrgyz-ui*). A traditional felt tent in Kyrgyzstan, **Kazakhstan,** and Mongolia, which is used for dwelling, especially in the *jayloo* and during military expeditions. It consists of a light collapsible wooden lattice frame (*kerege*), which creates a circular-shaped wall and a cone-shaped roof with a smoke ring (*tyundyuk*) on the top. The structure of an assembled *yurt* is covered by felt rugs (traditionally made of **sheep** fleece). The exterior of the *yurt* is often white, although the color of the exterior may vary or may have some nomadic patterns over the exterior walls. The interior of the *yurt* is divided into a man's part (*er zhak*) and a woman's part (*aial zhak*), and the center is reserved for a fireplace. The floor is often covered by carpets and by a *kurpacha* (a traditional Kyrgyz cotton-filled quilt or mattress). The whole *yurt* can be assembled within a few hours and is light enough to be transported on **horses**.

In contemporary Kyrgyzstan *yurts* are often used as a place for family or public celebration or for a country escape and it is an important cultural symbol in Kyrgyz society. The popularity of the *yurt* surged after independence in 1991, as *yurts* began to be produced in various sizes and with various internal decorations.

–Z–

ZARZAMAN (literally "bitter time" in Kyrgyz). 1. Period of tragic events or social catastrophes, which affected the whole society. 2. Among the **Kyrgyzs** and Kazakhs the term is often used in reference to the disaster of the **popular uprising of 1916** and the war with the Jungar **tribes** in the early 19th century, both of which brought enormous human losses.

ZHANTAI KARABEK-UULU (Zhantai Khan) (1794–1868). An influential *manap* and leader of Kyrgyz **tribes** in the **Chui valley** in the 19th century. Zhantai Karabek-Uulu played an important role in the political development in this part of the region in the middle of the 19th century. In the 1840s he supported the **Kokand Khanate** in opposition to **Ormon-Khan**, who tried to unite the **Kyrgyzs** of northern Kyrgyzstan. In the 1850s Zhantai Karabek-Uulu was involved in intertribal conflicts with neighboring Kyrgyz tribes. In 1862 he accepted the **Russian Empire** protectorate, and he assisted various Russian expeditions in their activities in northern Kyrgyzstan.

ZINDAN. 1. A prison during medieval times. 2. A harsh place where people experience extreme discomfort.

ZNANIYE SOCIETY OF KYRGYZSTAN. A public organization established in 1948 in Kyrgyzstan. The society conducted public lectures on cultural, political, social, and other issues in various parts of the republic, inviting prominent experts in the field, though political topics were heavily censored by the state and Communist Party officials. Initially it played an important role in the cultural development of the republic, as most of its members lectured in all parts of the republic, including the most remote areas. However, in the 1970s the organization was largely reduced to a propaganda machine of the **Communist Party of Kyrgyz SSR**. During the Mikhail Gorbachev era (1985–91) it became one of the few organizations in the republic, which in line with the *perestroika* policy initiated public discussions of political and economic changes in Kyrgyzstan. After 1991 the society lost most of its state subsidies and was turned into an independent public organization. It focused on organizing short training and retraining nondegree courses in the capital of **Bishkek** and major cities. The Znaniye Society claimed up to 9,500 members (2003).

Appendix A: Constitution of the Kyrgyz Republic

Adopted on the twelfth session of the Supreme Council
of the Kyrgyz Republic of the twelfth convocation on May 5, 1993,
changed and amended by the Law of the Kyrgyz Republic on Changes
and Amendments to the Constitution of the Kyrgyz Republic of February
17, 1996 passed by the Referendum of February 10, 1996,
and
changed and amended by the Law of the Kyrgyz Republic on Changes
and Amendments to the Constitution of the Kyrgyz Republic of October
21, 1998 passed by the Referendum of October 17, 1998
and
changed by the Law of the Kyrgyz Republic on Changes to Article 5 of
the Constitution of the Kyrgyz Republic of December 24, 2001

IN THE NEW WORDING
AS SUBMITTED TO THE REFERENDUM OF FEBRUARY 2, 2003
(in bold)[1]

Translated[2] for NDI
by Irina Krapivina
on January 19, 2003

---

[1] *Translator's note*: In this English version of the constitution, the text is used in bold whenever it is enboldened in the Russian version of the proposed constitution as submitted to the referendum of 2 February 2003. Please note that, as has been noticed, the fact that this or that text is used in bold does not necessarily mean that it differs from the current wording of the constitution; and, vice versa, some proposed changes in the wording of the current constitution have not been marked in bold by the authors of the Russian version.

[2] A translation of the 1996 constitution (see the website of IFES Central Asia) has been used as the basis for the current text of the Kyrgyz Constitution although largely edited by Irina Krapivina.

CONSTITUTION OF THE KYRGYZ REPUBLIC

We, the People of Kyrgyzstan,

striving to ensure the national revival of the Kyrgyz [nation], the protection and development of interests of all nationalities, which—together with the Kyrgyz—constitute the people of Kyrgyzstan, on the strength of the ancestors' behest to live in unity, peace and concordance;

confirming our devotion to human rights and freedoms and to the idea of the national statehood;

full of resolution to develop the [country's] economy, political and legal institutes, and culture for providing a decent level of life for everyone;

proclaiming our devotion to common human moral principles and values of national traditions; and

wishing to establish ourselves among the peoples of the world as a free and democratic civil society;

in the person of our authorized representatives, hereby adopt this Constitution.

CHAPTER I.
THE KYRGYZ REPUBLIC

SECTION ONE
GENERAL PRINCIPLES

Article 1

1. The Kyrgyz Republic (Kyrgyzstan) shall be a sovereign, unitary, democratic Republic, and it shall be founded as a rule of law and secular state.
2. The sovereignty of the Kyrgyz Republic shall in no way be restricted, and it shall extend throughout its entire territory.
3. The People of Kyrgyzstan shall bear the sovereignty, and they shall be the only source of state power in the Kyrgyz Republic.
4. The People of Kyrgyzstan shall exercise their power directly [and] through the system of state bodies **and bodies of local self-government** on the basis of this Constitution and the laws of the Kyrgyz Republic. Only **the President of the Kyrgyz Republic and the Jogorku Kenesh of the Kyrgyz Republic**, which will be

elected by the people of Kyrgyzstan, shall be entitled to act on behalf of the People of the Kyrgyz Republic.

5. Changes in and amendments to the Constitution of the Kyrgyz Republic, laws of the Kyrgyz Republic, and other important state matters may be put to referendum (nationwide vote). Procedural rules of holding referendums shall be ascertained by constitutional law.

6. The citizens of the Kyrgyz Republic shall elect a President **of the Kyrgyz Republic**, deputies of **the Jogorku Kenesh of the Kyrgyz Republic**, and their representatives to bodies of local self-government. **Elections shall be free and shall be held on the basis of the equal and direct universal suffrage by secret ballot. Citizens of the Kyrgyz Republic** who have attained to the age of 18 years may cast their votes.

Article 2

1. The state and its bodies shall serve the whole society, and not any particular group.
2. No group of people, no organization, and no individual person shall be entitled to assume power of the state. Usurpation of state power shall be the gravest crime.

Article 3

1. The territory of the Kyrgyz Republic, within its current boundaries, shall be inviolable and indivisible.
2. For the purposes of organizing state government **and local self-government**, the territory of the Kyrgyz Republic shall be divided by law into administrative territorial units.
3. **The cities of Bishkek and Osh shall be cities of the national significance, and their status shall be determined by law.**

Article 4

1. The Kyrgyz Republic shall recognize and protect **private, state, municipal, and other forms of ownership**.

The Kyrgyz Republic shall guarantee the diversity of the forms of ownership and equal legal protection thereof.

2. Land, minerals, air space, water, forests, flora and fauna, and all other natural resources shall be **the property of the Kyrgyz Republic,** and they shall be used as a basis for life and functioning of the People of Kyrgyzstan, and shall be under the special protection of the state.

3. Land may **also** be owned privately, **municipally** and otherwise.

   Limits to and procedures for the execution of their rights by landowners and guarantees of the protection [of such rights] shall be ascertained by law.

4. The Kyrgyz Republic shall protect her citizens' and legal entities' title to property, and it shall protect their property, as well as state-owned property, located in other states.

Article 5

1. The Kyrgyz language shall be a state language of the Kyrgyz Republic.

2. The Russian language shall be used in the Kyrgyz Republic as an official language.

3. The Kyrgyz Republic shall guarantee that representatives of all the nationalities which constitute the People of Kyrgyzstan may enjoy the right to preserve their native languages, and the state shall provide [favorable] conditions for learning and developing them.

4. Rights and freedoms of citizens shall not be abridged on account of ignorance of the state or official languages.

Article 6

1. The Kyrgyz Republic shall have state symbols—the Flag, Emblem, and Anthem, **which description and the way they may be used shall be specified by law.**

2. The City of Bishkek shall be the capital of the Kyrgyz Republic.

3. The Som shall be a currency unit of the Kyrgyz Republic.

SECTION TWO
STATE STRUCTURE AND FUNCTIONING OF THE STATE

Article 7

1. State power in the Kyrgyz Republic shall be based on the following principles:
   - supremacy of the power of the People, where such power shall be represented and ensured by the nationally elected head of the state—the President of the Kyrgyz Republic;
   - division of the state power into legislative, executive, and judicial branches, and their coordinated functioning and interaction;
   - responsibility of state bodies to the people and the exercise of their powers in the interests of the people; and
   - separation of functions between state power and local self-government.
2. In the Kyrgyz Republic, state power shall be represented and exercised, within the bounds of authority ascertained by this Constitution, by:
   - President of the Kyrgyz Republic;
   - Jogorku Kenesh of the Kyrgyz Republic;
   - Government of the Kyrgyz Republic and **executive bodies subordinate to the Government**; and
   - Constitutional Court of the Kyrgyz Republic, Supreme Court of the Kyrgyz Republic and local courts and judges of the Kyrgyz Republic.

Article 8

1. Political parties, trade unions, and other public associations may be formed in the Kyrgyz Republic on the bases of free will and common interests. The state shall secure the rights and lawful interests of public associations.
2. Political parties may participate in state affairs only in the following forms:
   - by nominating their candidates in elections to the Jogorku Kenesh **of the Kyrgyz Republic**, [as well as by nominating

their candidates] for public offices, and for offices of local self-government;

- by forming groups and factions in representative bodies.

3. Religions and all cults shall be separated from the state.
4. The following [activities] shall not be permitted in the Kyrgyz Republic:
    - amalgamation of state and party institutions, as well as subordination of state activities to any party programs or decisions;
    - formation and functioning of party organizations in state establishments and organizations. State officers may engage in party activities outside of discharging the powers and duties of their offices;
    - membership in parties and public support of any political party by the military and officers of the interior, national security, justice, procurator's office, and of courts;
    - formation of political parties on religious **and ethnic** grounds. No religious organizations shall pursue political goals and objectives;
    - interference by members of religious organizations and cults with the functioning of state bodies; and
    - activities of **foreign** political parties, **nongovernmental and religious organizations, [including] their representative offices and branches, which pursue political goals; formation and functioning of political parties, nongovernmental organizations, religious and other organizations, which jeopardize the constitutional system [or] state and national safety.**

Article 9

1. The Kyrgyz Republic shall not pursue the policy of expansion, aggression and territorial claims to be resolved by military force. It shall in no way militarize public life, subordinate the state [and] its activities to the purposes of conducting a war. The Armed Forces of Kyrgyzstan shall be organized under the principles of self-defense and defensive sufficiency.
2. The right to conduct a war shall not be acknowledged unless there is any aggression against Kyrgyzstan or other states which will be bound by the obligations of joint defense. In any event, no mili-

tary unit shall cross the borders of the Kyrgyz Republic unless with such permission of the **Jogorku Kenesh of the Kyrgyz Republic** provided that a two-thirds majority of the whole number of the deputies of the Jogorku Kenesh shall concur.

3. The Armed Forces shall not be used in order to resolve internal political matters of the state. The military may be called upon in case of natural disasters, as well as in other similar circumstances, where such cases shall be directly envisaged by law.

4. The Kyrgyz Republic shall seek universal and just peace, mutually beneficial cooperation, [and] resolution of global and regional problems in a peaceful manner, [and she shall] observe universally recognized principles of international law.

Actions that may disturb peaceful coexistence of peoples, as well as propaganda and incitement of **ethnic or religious** clashes, shall be deemed unconstitutional.

Article 10

1. No state of emergency shall be proclaimed in Kyrgyzstan unless in cases of natural calamities, direct threat to the constitutional system, mass riots involving violence or threat to lives of people, or unless under such circumstances and within such time-limits as constitutional law may prescribe.

2. Only the **Jogorku Kenesh of the Kyrgyz Republic** may proclaim a state of emergency throughout the territory of the Kyrgyz Republic; while in particular localities, where circumstances may require urgent measures, a state of emergency may be proclaimed by the President of the Kyrgyz Republic, of which [he shall], on the same day, promptly notify the Jogorku Kenesh of the Kyrgyz Republic, [and the latter] shall, within three days, approve [or disapprove] such act of the President of **the Kyrgyz Republic**. If no such approval shall have been made within the said term, the state of emergency shall be rescinded.

3. The **Jogorku Kenesh of the Kyrgyz Republic** may impose martial law in the Kyrgyz Republic only in the event of an aggression against the Kyrgyz Republic.

4. No adjournment of a session of the Jogorku Kenesh **of the Kyrgyz Republic** shall be permitted when [the country may be] in a state of emergency or in a state of martial law. In those cases where the

Jogorku Kenesh **of the Kyrgyz Republic** shall be not in session when the President **of the Kyrgyz Republic** shall have proclaimed a state of emergency, the **Jogorku Kenesh of the Kyrgyz Republic** shall convene, without an announcement of the convocation, by no later than the next day after the introduction of the state of emergency.

5. No referendums, no elections, **and no changes in the structure, functions, or authorities of state bodies ordained by the Constitution of the Kyrgyz Republic** shall be permitted during a state of emergency or martial law.

Article 11

1. The state budget of the Kyrgyz Republic shall consist of the national and local budgets, [and it shall be] comprised of all expenditures and revenues of the state. The national budget shall be approved by the **Jogorku Kenesh of the Kyrgyz Republic** on the proposal of the Government **of the Kyrgyz Republic**.

2. Revenues of the national budget shall be generated out of the proceeds of taxes [and] other mandatory charges, provided for by law, as well as out of the incomes by state property and other receipts.

3. A single system of taxation shall operate in the territory of the Kyrgyz Republic. The right to impose taxes shall be vested in the Jogorku Kenesh of the Kyrgyz Republic. Laws which impose new taxes or aggravate the taxpayer's status shall have no retroactive effect.

4. **In exceptional cases [when such measures may be required] to protect economic interests of the Kyrgyz Republic, the Government of the Kyrgyz Republic may take temporal measures with respect to taxation by changing rates of particular taxes or other mandatory budgetary charges, [and it shall] promptly notify the Jogorku Kenesh of the Kyrgyz Republic [of any such changes].**

5. Reports on the implementation of the national budget shall be approved by the Jogorku Kenesh **of the Kyrgyz Republic**.

Article 12

1. The Constitution shall have an ultimate legal force and direct application in the Kyrgyz Republic.

2. Laws and other legal acts shall be adopted on the basis of the Constitution.

3. **International treaties and agreements, which shall have taken effect in accordance with a procedure prescribed by law, to which the Kyrgyz Republic is a party and generally accepted principles and norms of international law shall be a constituent part of the legislation of the Kyrgyz Republic.**

CHAPTER II.
CITIZENS

SECTION ONE
CITIZENSHIP

Article 13

1. Belonging of a person to the Kyrgyz Republic and his status shall be determined by citizenship. A citizen of the Kyrgyz Republic shall be obliged to observe the Constitution and laws **of the Kyrgyz Republic**, respect rights, freedoms, honor, and dignity of other persons.

2. Persons, who shall be citizens of the Kyrgyz Republic, shall not be recognized as citizens of other states.

3. No citizen of the Kyrgyz Republic shall be deprived of citizenship, and of the right to change his citizenship.

4. **No citizen of the Kyrgyz Republic may be extradited to another state.**

5. The Kyrgyz Republic shall guarantee its citizens protection and patronage outside its borders.

Article 14

1. Every citizen of the Kyrgyz Republic, by virtue of his citizenship, shall enjoy rights and bear obligations.

2. In the Kyrgyz Republic, foreigners and stateless persons shall enjoy the rights and freedoms of the citizens and shall bear obligations on the grounds, under conditions, and in compliance with the procedural rules provided for by laws and interstate treaties and agreements of the Kyrgyz Republic.

SECTION TWO
HUMAN RIGHTS AND FREEDOMS

Article 15

1. The human dignity shall be absolute and inviolable in the Kyrgyz Republic.
2. Every person shall enjoy basic human rights and freedoms from birth. Those rights shall be recognized as absolute, inalienable, and [they shall be] protected, by law and by the court, from encroachments of others.
3. All persons in the Kyrgyz Republic shall be equal before the law and the court. No one may be subjected to any discrimination, [and] rights and freedoms of persons shall not be abridged on account of origin, gender, race, nationality, language, creed, political and religious convictions, or on any other account of personal or public nature.
4. Human rights and freedoms shall be in [direct] effect in the Kyrgyz Republic. They shall determine, as such, the meaning, content, and way of application of the laws; shall be obligatory for the legislative, executive, and judicial powers and local self-government; and shall be protected by justice.
5. In the Kyrgyz Republic, the state shall support those folk customs and traditions that shall not contradict human rights and freedoms.

Article 16

1. In the Kyrgyz Republic, fundamental human rights and freedoms shall be recognized and guaranteed pursuant to universally accepted principles and norms of international law, as well as **international** treaties and agreements concerning human rights provided that they have taken legal effect.
2. **Every person in the Kyrgyz Republic has an inalienable right to life. No one shall be deprived of his life intentionally. Everyone may defend his life and health and lives and health of others against unlawful violations.**
3. **Everyone has the right to liberty and security of person. Detention, arrest and committal may be appealed to a court. Everyone who is arrested or detained shall be informed promptly of**

the reasons for his arrest or detention, and of his rights, and he shall be entitled, at the time of his detention, to defend himself in person or through legal assistance of an advocate.

4. Everyone who has been the victim of unlawful acts on the part of state bodies or their officers, committed in furtherance of their duties, shall have the right to compensation by the state.

5. Everyone has the right to confidentiality of correspondence, and of telephone, telegraph, postal, and other communication. This right may be interfered only in accordance with law.

6. Everyone has the right to respect of his private life and to respect and protection of his honor and dignity. No gathering, storing, use, or dissemination of confidential information on a person shall be permitted without his permission except in cases prescribed by law. Everyone has the right to get acquainted with his personal information at state bodies, bodies of local self-government, establishments, and organizations unless such information is a state or other secret protected by law. Everyone shall be guaranteed the right to the protection of the court against untrue information about his own or about members of his family and the right to compensation of actual losses and moral damage caused by any such gathering, storing, or dissemination of untrue information.

7. [The Kyrgyz Republic recognizes] the sanctity of the home. No one may enter a person's home without permission of those who live there. Search or other acts that require entering a person's home may be permitted only in cases prescribed by law, and [in any such instance] the person shall be entitled to appeal such acts in court.

8. Everyone has the right to liberty of movement and freedom to choose his residence and place for staying within the territory of the Kyrgyz Republic. Every citizen of the Kyrgyz Republic has the right to leave the Kyrgyz Republic, and to return without obstruction. The [above-mentioned] rights shall not be subject to any restrictions except those which are provided by law.

9. Everyone has the right to freedom of thought, speech, as well as to freedom of expression of his ideas and opinions. No one may be compelled to impart his ideas and opinions. Everyone has freedom to gather, store, use, and communicate information by

word, in writing or otherwise. No propaganda or advocacy that constitutes incitement to social, racial, ethnic or religious hatred or hostility shall be permitted. Any propaganda for the superiority on social, racial, ethnic, religious, or linguistic distinction shall be prohibited.

10. Censorship shall be prohibited in the Kyrgyz Republic.

11. Everyone shall be guaranteed freedom of conscience, belief, and of religious or atheistic activities. Everyone shall have freedom to profess religion of his choice or not to profess any religion, and to choose, possess, and impart one's religious or atheistic beliefs.

12. Everyone shall have freedom to choose his ethnic belonging. No one may be compelled to choose or indicate his ethnic belonging. Insulting one's ethnic dignity shall be prosecuted in accordance with law.

13. Citizens of the Kyrgyz Republic have the right to freedom of association. All associations shall be equal before the law. No one may be compelled to belong to an association, or restricted in his rights on the distinction of belonging or not belonging to an association. Citizens may not form militarized organizations. No secret associations shall be permitted.

14. Citizens of the Kyrgyz Republic have the right to freedom of peaceful assembly, without weapons, and of holding gatherings, meetings, rallies, demonstrations, and pickets subject to a prior notification of executive bodies or bodies of local self-government.

15. Everyone has the right to launch personal or group inquiries with state bodies, bodies of local self-government, and their officers, and [the latter] shall, within their jurisdiction, consider such inquiries and make rational replies within a term prescribed by law.

16. Everyone shall be guaranteed the right to freedom of literary, artistic, scientific, and technical creative activities, [and] to the protection of intellectual property.

17. Everyone has the right to possess, use, and dispose of his property, products of his intellectual and creative work. By using his property, no one may hurt the rights, freedoms, and lawful interests of others, [or to harm] public interests, [or to damage] land, environment, or natural resources.

18. Everyone has the right to economic freedom, and to free use of his abilities and property for any economic activities except for activities restricted by law.
19. Everyone has the right to freedom of labor, as well as the right to freely use his skills, and to freely choose his profession and occupation.
20. The enumeration in the Constitution of rights and freedoms is not exclusive and shall not be construed to deny or disparage other universally recognized human rights and freedoms.
21. In realizing his rights and freedoms, a person may not violate the rights and freedoms of others.
22. No rights and freedoms may be used to force any change of the constitutional system, to incite to racial, ethnic, social or religious hatred, [or] to propagandize violence or war.

Article 17

1. No laws abolishing or abridging human rights and freedoms shall be enacted in the Kyrgyz Republic.
2. The exercise of rights and freedoms may be restricted by the Constitution or laws of the Kyrgyz Republic only as may be necessary to protect the rights and freedoms of other persons, public safety **and order, territorial integrity**, and the constitutional system. In such cases, the essence of constitutional rights and freedoms shall not be affected.

Article 18

1. Physical and moral inviolability of a person may be limited only under the law by a guilty verdict of a court as the punishment for a committed crime. No one may be exposed to torment, torture, or inhuman and humiliating punishments.
2. No medical, biological, and psychological experiments on persons shall be permitted unless there shall be such voluntary consent of the examinee, properly expressed and certified.
3. No one may be arrested, detained or held in custody unless under law. No actions that tend to impose liability for a crime on a person before the verdict shall have been passed by court shall be allowed, and such actions shall be grounds for compensation to the victim through the court for the material and moral harm suffered.

4. **The death penalty may be envisaged by law, and it may be imposed only by a court as an exceptional penalty for most serious offenses.** Any person sentenced to death shall have the right to seek pardon.

Article 19

1. The right to private property shall be recognized and guaranteed in the Kyrgyz Republic as an inalienable human right, as a natural source of one's welfare, [as a basis for] business and creative activity, and as a security of one's economic and personal independence.
2. **[The Kyrgyz Republic recognizes] the sanctity of property. No person may be deprived of his property arbitrarily, and no seizure of a person's property may occur against the owner's will unless when so shall be decided by court.**
3. **Property may be expropriated for the needs of the state in exceptional cases prescribed by law, [and any such expropriation shall be] subject to the prior and equivalent compensation.**
4. **The right of inheritance shall be guaranteed and protected in the Kyrgyz Republic by law.**

Article 20

The Kyrgyz Republic may grant political asylum to foreign citizens and stateless persons on account of violation of human rights.

SECTION THREE
CITIZEN'S RIGHTS AND DUTIES

Article 21

1. Citizens of the Kyrgyz Republic [and] their associations shall be allowed to engage in any actions or activities, except for those prohibited or restricted by this Constitution and laws of the Kyrgyz Republic.
2. Enjoyment of rights and freedoms by a citizen of the Kyrgyz Republic shall be inseparable from his duties, which shall be necessary to secure private and public interests.

Article 22

1. Laws of the Kyrgyz Republic concerning rights and duties of citizens shall be equally applied to all citizens and shall not bestow on anyone privileges and preferences, except those provided for by the Constitution **of the Kyrgyz Republic** and laws in order to ensure social security of citizens.
2. The state, its bodies, bodies of local self-government, and their officers shall not exceed authority envisaged in the Constitution and laws of the Kyrgyz Republic.

Article 23

1. **Citizens of the Kyrgyz Republic may participate in the governance of the state both directly and through their representatives.**
2. **Citizens of the Kyrgyz Republic may participate in the discussion and adoption of laws and decisions of national and local significance.**
3. **Citizens of the Kyrgyz Republic may elect and be elected to state bodies and bodies of local self-government, as well as take part in referendums.**
4. **Citizens of the Kyrgyz Republic shall have equal access to the state and municipal service.**

Article 24

1. **Citizens of the Kyrgyz Republic shall have the right and bear the duty to defend the Motherland.**
2. **Citizens shall be bound to military service within such limits, and in such forms as shall be ascertained by law.**

   A citizen may be released from military duty or he may choose to substitute military service for alternative service on the grounds, and following the procedure prescribed by law.

Article 25

Citizens of the Kyrgyz Republic shall pay taxes and charges as prescribed by the law **of the Kyrgyz Republic**.

Article 26

1. The family is a fundamental unit of society; family, fatherhood, maternity, and childhood shall be an object of concern to the whole society and [a matter of] the preferential protection by law[;] care [and] upbringing of children shall be a natural right and civil duty of the parents. Able-bodied adult children shall take care of their parents.
2. The state shall provide for care, upbringing, and education of orphans and parentless children.
3. Respect for old people [and] caring for one's own kin and relatives shall be a sacred tradition of the people of Kyrgyzstan.

Article 27

1. In the Kyrgyz Republic, social protection shall be guaranteed at the expense of the state in old age, in sickness, in disability, and in the event of a loss of the breadwinner.
2. Depending on economic resources of the society, pensions and social protection shall provide a standard of living not below the subsistence level established by law.
3. Voluntary social insurance, establishment of additional forms of security, and charity shall be encouraged.

Article 28

1. A citizen of the Kyrgyz Republic shall have the right to protection of labor in all its forms and displays, to working conditions that comply with safety and hygiene requirements, and to social protection against unemployment
2. The state shall take care of professional training and further education of citizens, [and it shall] encourage and promote international treaties and international organizations that aim at securing and establishing the right to work.
3. No forced labor of citizens shall be permitted except in cases of war, natural disaster, epidemic, or other extraordinary circumstances, and when [it shall be enforced] as a way of serving out a sentence imposed by court.

Article 29

Citizens of the Kyrgyz Republic who work for hire by labor agreements (contracts) shall have the right to remuneration in the amount of no less than a subsistence level established by the state.

Article 30

1. Citizens of the Kyrgyz Republic shall have the right to strike.
2. Procedural rules and terms of holding strikes shall be ascertained by law.

Article 31

1. Citizens of the Kyrgyz Republic shall have the right to rest [and leisure].
2. The maximum duration of working hours, the minimum weekly rest and yearly paid leave, as well as other basic terms of exercising the right to rest shall be determined by law.

Article 32

1. Every citizen of the Kyrgyz Republic shall have the right to education.
2. Basic education shall be compulsory and free, [and] everyone shall be entitled to receive it in public **or municipal** educational institutions.

   Every citizen shall have the right to receive free **general secondary** education in public **or municipal** educational institutions.
3. The state shall make vocational, specialized secondary, and higher education equally accessible to all on the basis of individual capacity.
4. Paid education in public and other educational institutions may be permitted on the basis and in accordance with the rules established by the law of the Kyrgyz Republic.
5. **The state shall exercise control over educational institutions and establishments in such forms as specified by law.**

Article 33

Citizens of the Kyrgyz Republic shall have the right to housing. This right shall be ensured by developing the state, municipal, and individual housing stock, [and by] helping citizens with purchasing accommodations on such conditions, and following such procedure as law of the Kyrgyz Republic may provide.

Article 34

1. Citizens of the Kyrgyz Republic shall have the right to health protection and to benefit freely from the network of public **and municipal** health care establishments.
2. Paid medical service shall be permitted on the basis and in accordance with the rules established by law.

Article 35

1. Citizens of the Kyrgyz Republic shall have the right to a healthy and safe environment, and to indemnification of damage caused to one's health or property by **misuse of natural resources**.
2. Protection of the environment, natural resources, and historical monuments shall be a sacred duty of every citizen.

Article 36

1. Culture, art, literature, science, and mass media shall be unrestricted.
2. The state shall protect historical monuments, take care of and provide necessary conditions for development of literature, art, science, mass media, and sports.
3. Citizens shall have the right of access to cultural values, [and the right] to engage in arts and science.

Article 37

Social protection by the state shall not lead to the substitution of state patronage for economic freedom and for business activity and the ability of a citizen to achieve on his own the economic welfare for himself and his family.

Article 38

1. The state, all its bodies, **bodies of local self-government, and their officers** shall be obliged to provide for the full, absolute, and immediate protection of the rights and freedoms of citizens, for the prevention of violations in this field, and for subsequent restitution [of such].
2. The Kyrgyz Republic shall guarantee the protection of the court for citizens' rights and freedoms accorded by the Constitution and laws **of the Kyrgyz Republic.**
3. **Courts of arbitration may be constituted for the purposes of the extrajudiciary resolution of disputes arising from civil relationships. Powers, foundation, and procedures of courts of arbitration shall be ascertained by law.**

Article 39

1. Everyone charged with a criminal offense shall have the right to be presumed innocent until found guilty by a court's verdict provided that it shall have come into effect.
2. The state shall guarantee everyone protection from arbitrary and unlawful interference with one's personal and family privacy, attacks on one's honor and dignity, and breach of privacy of correspondence and telephone conversations.
3. No one shall have the right to enter another's home except in cases when it may be required for conducting a warranted search or seizure, [for] maintaining public order, arresting a criminal, [or for] saving the life, health, or property of a person.

Article 40

1. **Every citizen in the Kyrgyz Republic shall be provided with qualified legal assistance, and with the protection of the rights and freedoms guaranteed by the Constitution of the Kyrgyz Republic. Legal assistance shall be provided for free at such times as law may provide.**
2. **Control after the observance of human and citizen's rights in the Kyrgyz Republic shall be vested with an Ombudsman of the Kyrgyz Republic.**

3. **Procedure for selection, and powers of the Ombudsman of the Kyrgyz Republic, as well as the way they may be realized shall be ascertained by law.**

Article 41

Promulgation of laws and other legal acts concerning rights, freedoms, and duties of a person or citizen shall be recognized as a sine qua non for enforcement thereof.

CHAPTER III.
THE PRESIDENT OF THE KYRGYZ REPUBLIC

Article 42

1. The President of the Kyrgyz Republic shall be the head of the state [and] the highest official person of the Kyrgyz Republic.
2. The President of the Kyrgyz Republic shall be a symbol of the unity of the people and state power, [and he shall be] the guarantor of the Constitution of the Kyrgyz Republic [and] of rights of a person and citizen.
3. The President of the Kyrgyz Republic shall determine major directions of internal and external policy of the state, represent the Kyrgyz Republic within the country and in international relations, take measures to guard the sovereignty and territorial integrity of the Kyrgyz Republic, [and] shall ensure the integrity and continuity of the state power and coordinated functioning and interaction of state bodies, [and] their responsibility to the people.

SECTION ONE
ELECTIONS OF THE PRESIDENT OF THE KYRGYZ REPUBLIC

Article 43

1. A President of the Kyrgyz Republic shall be elected for the term of five years.
2. No person shall hold the office of President of the Kyrgyz Republic for more than two consecutive terms.

3. Any citizen of the Kyrgyz Republic, no younger than 35 years of age and no older than 65 years of age, who shall have command of the state language and who shall have been 15 years a resident within the Kyrgyz Republic at the time of his nomination for the presidency, may be elected a President of the Kyrgyz Republic.
4. The President of the Kyrgyz Republic shall not be a deputy of the Jogorku Kenesh **of the Kyrgyz Republic**, [he shall not] occupy other posts [and] engage in business activities.
5. The President of the Kyrgyz Republic shall suspend his activity in political parties and organizations for the term of his office until the next presidential election shall begin in the Kyrgyz Republic.

Article 44

1. **Regular elections of the President of the Kyrgyz Republic shall be held on the last Sunday of October in the fifth year of the term of the President of the Kyrgyz Republic.**

   Early elections of the President of the Kyrgyz Republic shall be held on the last Sunday before the last day of the three-month period dating from the end of the term of the President of the Kyrgyz Republic.
2. The President of the Kyrgyz Republic shall be elected by citizens of the Kyrgyz Republic **on the basis of universal, equal and direct suffrage by secret ballot.**
3. The number of nominees for the presidency shall not be limited. Any person, who shall have gathered no less than 50,000 signatures of voters, may be registered as a candidate for the presidency of the Kyrgyz Republic.
4. Elections of the President **of the Kyrgyz Republic** shall be considered valid if more than fifty per cent of voters of the [Kyrgyz] Republic shall have cast their ballots in the election.

   A candidate who shall have won more than half of all votes cast in the first ballot shall be considered elected to the office of the President of the Kyrgyz Republic.

   If none of the candidates shall win more than half of the votes cast in the first ballot, then only those two candidates, who shall have won the largest numbers of votes, shall participate in the second ballot. A candidate who shall have won more than half of the votes cast in the second ballot shall be considered elected to the presidency provided that no less than 50 per cent of all voters [of the Kyrgyz Republic] shall have cast their votes in the second ballot.

Article 45

1. Returns of a presidential election shall be validated by the Constitutional Court of the Kyrgyz Republic not later than within 7 days from the date of the election.
2. Within thirty days after the announcement of the returns of the election by the Chairman of the Constitutional Court of the Kyrgyz Republic, the President **of the Kyrgyz Republic** shall take his oath before the **Jogorku Kenesh of the Kyrgyz Republic.**
3. On entering the office, the President of the Kyrgyz Republic shall bring the oath to the people of Kyrgyzstan as follows:

   "I, . . ., while entering the office of President of the Kyrgyz Republic, do swear before my people and the sacred Motherland of Ala-Too:

   that I will rigorously observe and protect the Constitution of the Kyrgyz Republic; guard the sovereignty and independence of the Kyrgyz State; respect and guarantee rights and freedoms of all citizens of the Kyrgyz Republic; faithfully and diligently execute the high duties of the President of the Kyrgyz Republic entrusted to me by the confidence of all the People!"
4. The term of the President **of the Kyrgyz Republic** shall begin at the moment of taking the oath. The powers of the President shall terminate at the moment when the term of a newly elected President **of the Kyrgyz Republic** shall begin.

SECTION TWO
POWERS OF THE PRESIDENT OF THE KYRGYZ REPUBLIC

Article 46

1. The President of the Kyrgyz Republic shall have power:
   1) to determine a structure of the Government of the Kyrgyz Republic, **and to introduce it to the Jogorku Kenesh of the Kyrgyz Republic for consideration;**

2) to appoint, with the consent of the **Jogorku Kenesh of the Kyrgyz Republic, the Prime Minister of the Kyrgyz Republic**;

3) to appoint, by the advice of the Prime Minister of the Kyrgyz Republic, and with the consent of the Jogorku Kenesh of the Kyrgyz Republic, members of the Government of the Kyrgyz Republic; **appoint, by the advice of the Prime Minister of the Kyrgyz Republic, heads of administrative agencies;** and to remove them from office;

4) to accept resignations of the Prime Minister **of the Kyrgyz Republic,** the Government **of the Kyrgyz Republic,** or an individual member of the Government; **dismiss the Prime Minister of the Kyrgyz Republic or [dissolve] the Government of the Kyrgyz Republic; and to dismiss, on his own initiative or on such advice of the Prime Minister of the Kyrgyz Republic, a head of an administrative agency;**

5) to appoint, **by the advice of the Prime Minister,** and with the consent of appropriate local keneshes, heads of local state administrations; remove them from office;

6) to appoint the State Secretary of the Kyrgyz Republic, determine his status and authorities; form the Administration of the President of the Kyrgyz Republic **which shall provide for his activities;**

7) to **constitute and abolish the National Security Service**;

8) to constitute and head the Security Council of the Kyrgyz Republic and other coordinating bodies;

9) to form state security services and the National Guard subordinate to him;

10) **to constitute and abolish such executive bodies that will not be included into the structure of the Government;**

11) to approve, in consultation with the Prime Minister of the Kyrgyz Republic, a single system for the training of personnel of and the selection of personnel to bodies funded from the national budget, [as well as a single system] for financing state bodies, and of remuneration for state employees.

2. The President of the Kyrgyz Republic shall have power:

1) to nominate, for the selection by **the Jogorku Kenesh of the Kyrgyz Republic**, candidates for the offices of Chairman of

the Constitutional Court of the Kyrgyz Republic, his deputy, and judges of the Constitutional Court of the Kyrgyz Republic;

2) to nominate, for the selection by **the Jogorku Kenesh of the Kyrgyz Republic**, candidates for the offices of Chairman of the Supreme Court of the Kyrgyz Republic, his deputies, and judges of the Supreme Court of the Kyrgyz Republic;

3) to appoint, **with the consent of the Jogorku Kenesh of the Kyrgyz Republic**, the Procurator-General of the Kyrgyz Republic; appoint, by the advice of the Procurator-General, deputies of the Procurator-General [and] the Military Procurator of the Kyrgyz Republic; remove them from office;

4) to appoint, **with the consent of the Jogorku Kenesh of the Kyrgyz Republic**, the Chairman of the Board of the National Bank of the Kyrgyz Republic; remove him from office; **appoint, by the advice of the Chairman of the National Bank of the Kyrgyz Republic, deputies of the Chairman and members of the Board of the National Bank of the Kyrgyz Republic; and remove them from office;**

5) **to appoint, with the consent of the Jogorku Kenesh of the Kyrgyz Republic, chairmen, their deputies, and judges of local courts of the Kyrgyz Republic; discharge them in the cases envisaged in the Constitution and constitutional laws of the Kyrgyz Republic.**

3. The President of the Kyrgyz Republic shall have power:

1) to **direct the foreign policy of the Kyrgyz Republic;**

2) to conduct negotiations and sign international treaties of the Kyrgyz Republic;

3) to sign instruments of ratification;

4) to appoint, **in consultation with an appropriate committee of the Jogorku Kenesh of the Kyrgyz Republic,** diplomatic representatives of the Kyrgyz Republic in foreign states, and in international organizations; recall them; accept credentials and letters of recall of heads of diplomatic missions of foreign states, and of representatives of international organizations accredited to the President of the Kyrgyz Republic;

5) to decide on granting and renouncing the citizenship of the Kyrgyz Republic, and on granting political asylum.

4. The President of the Kyrgyz Republic may:
   1) grant state awards of the Kyrgyz Republic;
   2) confer honorary titles of the Kyrgyz Republic,
   3) confer higher military ranks, diplomatic ranks, class categories, and other special titles;
   4) grant pardons.
5. The President of the Kyrgyz Republic shall have power:
   1) to introduce bills to the Jogorku Kenesh of the Kyrgyz Republic;
   2) **to sign and promulgate laws; return them with his objections to the Jogorku Kenesh of the Kyrgyz Republic for reconsideration, or decline them;**
   3) to address the people **of Kyrgyzstan** with his annual messages concerning the state of affairs in the country, which shall be delivered at a session of the Jogorku Kenesh of the Kyrgyz Republic;
   4) to suspend and invalidate **legal acts** of the Government of the Kyrgyz Republic, and of other executive bodies;
   5) to decide on the financing of measures of great urgency at the expense of the state;
   6) to exercise legislative powers at such times, and in such manner as stipulated in Article 68 of this Constitution.
6. The President of the Kyrgyz Republic shall have power:
   1) to convene an early **sitting of the Jogorku Kenesh of the Kyrgyz Republic,** and to determine matters to be considered [at such sitting];
   2) to call a referendum on his own initiative; decide on calling a referendum on the initiative of no less than 300,000 voters, or a majority of the whole number of the deputies of the Jogorku Kenesh **of the Kyrgyz Republic;**
   3) to call elections to the **Jogorku Kenesh of the Kyrgyz Republic**, to dissolve the Jogorku Kenesh of the Kyrgyz Republic in the cases provided for by this Constitution;
   4) to call elections to local keneshes and, in the cases provided for by law of the Kyrgyz Republic, dissolve them;
   5) **to appoint, with the consent of the Jogorku Kenesh of the Kyrgyz Republic, Chairman of the Central Commission of the Kyrgyz Republic on Elections and Referendums;**

appoint half of the membership of the Central Commission of the Kyrgyz Republic on Elections and Referendums; and remove them from office;

6) **to appoint, with the consent of the Jogorku Kenesh, Chairman of the Auditing Chamber of the Kyrgyz Republic; appoint half of the auditors of the Auditing Chamber of the Kyrgyz Republic; and remove them from office.**

7. Should there be grounds envisaged by law, the President of the Kyrgyz Republic may warn of a possibility to introduce a state of emergency, and, if necessary, may proclaim a state of emergency in particular localities without a prior warning, of which action he shall promptly notify the **Jogorku Kenesh of the Kyrgyz Republic.**

8. The President of the Kyrgyz Republic may declare general or partial mobilization; and may declare a state of war in an event of aggression or direct threat of aggression against the Kyrgyz Republic, in which case he or she shall promptly submit this matter to the **Jogorku Kenesh of the Kyrgyz Republic** for consideration; and may impose martial law, in which case he or she shall promptly submit this matter to the **Jogorku Kenesh of the Kyrgyz Republic** for consideration.

9. The President of the Kyrgyz Republic shall be Commander-in-Chief of the Armed Forces, [and he or she shall] appoint and discharge commanders of the Armed Forces of the Kyrgyz Republic.

Article 47

1. The President of the Kyrgyz Republic may issue decrees and orders.
2. Decrees and orders of the President of the Kyrgyz Republic shall be binding for the execution throughout the Kyrgyz Republic.
3. Decrees issued by the President of the Kyrgyz Republic by way of exercising legislative powers under Article 46.5.6 of the Constitution **of the Kyrgyz Republic**, shall have the force of law.

Article 48

The President of the Kyrgyz Republic may delegate his/her powers, stipulated in Article 46.3.2 of this Constitution, to the Prime Minister **of** the **Kyrgyz Republic**, members of the Government **of the Kyrgyz Republic**, or other officials; and he may also ratify international financial instruments and loan agreements signed by them.

Article 49

1. The President of the Kyrgyz Republic shall enjoy immunity. The honor and dignity [reputation] of the President of the Kyrgyz Republic shall be protected by law.
2. Provision, maintenance, and protection of the President of the Kyrgyz Republic and his/her family, shall be provided at the expense of the state.

Article 50

1. Powers of the President may be terminated as a result of his resignation declared **at a sitting of the Jogorku Kenesh of the Kyrgyz Republic**, his removal from office in such manner as provided by the Constitution, inability to discharge the powers due to illness, or in case of his death.
2. Should the President of the Kyrgyz Republic be unable to discharge his/her duties due to illness, **the Jogorku Kenesh of the Kyrgyz Republic**, on the strength of findings of a state medical commission created by [the Parliament], shall decide on an early dismissal of the President of the Kyrgyz Republic provided that no less than two-thirds of the whole number of the deputies **of the Jogorku Kenesh of the Kyrgyz Republic** concur.

Article 51

1. The President of the Kyrgyz Republic may be removed from office only on the basis of a charge of treason or other serious offense brought by the **Jogorku Kenesh of the Kyrgyz Republic** and confirmed by the opinion of the Constitutional Court of the Kyrgyz Republic.
2. A decision of the **Jogorku Kenesh of the Kyrgyz Republic** to bring in a charge against the President of the Kyrgyz Republic in order to remove him or her from office may be initiated by a

majority vote of the whole number of its deputies, and it shall be adopted if no less than two-thirds of the whole number of the deputies of the **Jogorku Kenesh of the Kyrgyz Republic** concur provided that there shall have been obtained findings of a special commission constituted by the **Jogorku Kenesh of the Kyrgyz Republic.**

3. Should the Constitutional Court of the Kyrgyz Republic hand down an unfavorable opinion on a charge brought in by the **Jogorku Kenesh of the Kyrgyz Republic**, it shall entail the dissolution of the **Jogorku Kenesh of the Kyrgyz Republic**.

4. **Provided that the Constitutional Court of the Kyrgyz Republic shall have confirmed a charge brought in by the Jogorku Kenesh of the Kyrgyz Republic, the Jogorku Kenesh of the Kyrgyz Republic shall decide, by no later than within two months after the bringing of the charge by the Jogorku Kenesh of the Kyrgyz Republic, on the removal of the President of the Kyrgyz Republic from office, which decision shall be adopted by a majority vote of no less than four-fifths of the whole number of the deputies of the Jogorku Kenesh of the Kyrgyz Republic. Should the Jogorku Kenesh of the Kyrgyz Republic fail to reach a decision within the specified time limits, the charge shall be considered refuted.**

Article 52

1. In case of inability, due to reasons envisaged in Article 50 hereof, of the President of the Kyrgyz Republic to discharge his or her duties, the same shall devolve on the Prime Minister **of the Kyrgyz Republic** until a new President of the Kyrgyz Republic shall be elected. If this is the case, an election of a new President of the Kyrgyz Republic shall be held within three months after the termination of the powers of the President of the Kyrgyz Republic.

2. As an Acting President of the Kyrgyz Republic, the Prime Minister **of the Kyrgyz Republic** shall not have the right to dissolve the **Jogorku Kenesh of the Kyrgyz Republic**, to call a referendum, to terminate the powers of the Government **of the Kyrgyz Republic**, and to make proposals on changes and amendments to the Constitution of the Kyrgyz Republic.

Article 53

1. All former Presidents of the Kyrgyz Republic, except for those who shall have been removed from office under the terms of Article 51 hereof, shall have the title of an ex-president of the Kyrgyz Republic.
2. **The Ex-President of the Kyrgyz Republic shall enjoy immunity. He or she shall not be subjected to criminal or administrative liability for his or her act or omission committed in furtherance of his or her duties during the term as President of the Kyrgyz Republic, and he or she may not be detained, arrested, subjected to search, interrogation, or body search.**
3. **Immunity of the Ex-President of the Kyrgyz Republic shall extend to housing and offices that he or she may occupy; vehicles and means of communication that he or she may use; archives, other property, and documents that belong to him or her; and to his/her luggage and correspondence.**
4. Provision, maintenance, and protection of the Ex-President of the Kyrgyz Republic, **his spouse, underage children, and other members of his/her household dependent on him/her** shall be provided at the expense of the state in such manner as stipulated by law.

CHAPTER IV.
THE JOGORKU KENESH OF THE KYRGYZ REPUBLIC

Article 54

1. The Jogorku Kenesh—the parliament of the Kyrgyz Republic— shall be a representative body, which shall exercise the legislative power **and controlling functions within the bounds of its authority.**
2. **The Jogorku Kenesh shall consist of 75 deputies elected for the term of five years from single-member constituencies.**

   Candidates to the Jogorku Kenesh of the Kyrgyz Republic may be nominated by political parties, and by citizens—self-nomination.
3. **Deputies of the Jogorku Kenesh of the Kyrgyz Republic shall be elected on the basis of universal, equal, and direct suffrage by**

secret ballot. Procedure for election of deputies of the Jogorku Kenesh **of the Kyrgyz Republic** shall be ascertained by law.

4. **Regular elections to the Jogorku Kenesh of the Kyrgyz Republic shall be held on the last Sunday of February in the fifth year of the term of the Jogorku Kenesh of the Kyrgyz Republic.**

Article 55

1. **A Jogorku Kenesh of the Kyrgyz Republic shall assemble for its first session** when no less than two-thirds **of the constitutional body of the members** shall have been elected, [but] no later than within 30 days from the date of the publication of election returns.
2. The eldest, by age, deputy of the Jogorku Kenesh of the Kyrgyz Republic shall open the first meeting of **the Jogorku Kenesh of the Kyrgyz Republic.**
3. **On entering the office, deputies of the Jogorku Kenesh of the Kyrgyz Republic shall bring the oath before the Jogorku Kenesh of the Kyrgyz Republic:**

   "I, ..., while entering the office of Deputy of the Jogorku Kenesh of the Kyrgyz Republic, do swear allegiance to the Kyrgyz Republic and vow:

   that I will observe the Constitution and laws of the Kyrgyz Republic, execute my duties in the interests of the people, protect the sovereignty and independence of the Kyrgyz State."

   The term of deputies of the Jogorku Kenesh of the Kyrgyz Republic shall begin on the day of taking the oath.
2. The powers of the Jogorku Kenesh of a previous convocation shall end on the day when the Jogorku Kenesh of a new convocation shall assemble for their first session.

Article 56

1. A citizen of the Kyrgyz Republic, who shall have attained to the age of 25 years by the election day, and been a permanent resident within the Kyrgyz Republic during five last years prior to his or her nomination as a candidate for the parliament, may be elected a deputy of the Jogorku Kenesh provided that he or she shall have the suffrage right.

2. No person with a criminal record may be elected a deputy of the Jogorku Kenesh of the Kyrgyz Republic unless such record shall have been expunged and canceled in such manner as the law may provide.

3. A deputy of the Jogorku Kenesh of the Kyrgyz Republic shall be a representative of the people of Kyrgyzstan [and] shall abide by the Constitution and laws of the Kyrgyz Republic.

4. A deputy of the Jogorku Kenesh of the Kyrgyz Republic shall enjoy immunity. He or she shall not be subjected to persecution for any opinion expressed within his or her responsibilities of the deputy, or for results of the voting in the Jogorku Kenesh of the Kyrgyz Republic. A deputy shall not be detained, arrested, subjected to search unless when in cases of being caught in the act of committing a crime. A deputy may be prosecuted or subjected to administrative liability imposed by a court only with the consent of the Jogorku Kenesh of the Kyrgyz Republic.

5. A deputy of the Jogorku Kenesh of the Kyrgyz Republic shall not at the same time be a member of the Government of the Kyrgyz Republic, or a deputy of a local kenesh.

   A deputy of the Jogorku Kenesh of the Kyrgyz Republic shall not be holding an office of judge, procurator, or any other public office. He or she shall not engage in business activities, be a member of any governing body or supervisory board of a commercial organization.

   A deputy of the Jogorku Kenesh of the Kyrgyz Republic may engage in scientific, teaching, or other creative activities provided that such activities shall not interfere with his or her duties as a deputy.

6. The term of a deputy of the Jogorku Kenesh of the Kyrgyz Republic shall end on the expiration of the term of the Jogorku Kenesh of the Kyrgyz Republic.

7. The term of a deputy of the Jogorku Kenesh of the Kyrgyz Republic shall end early in the cases of resignation by submitting a written declaration of abdication, dissolution of the Jogorku Kenesh of the Kyrgyz Republic, adjudication of his or her incompetence, adjudication of his or her death or that he or she is missing by a court decision in legal force, or death of the deputy.

In case of the entry into legal force of a guilty verdict rendered against a deputy **of the Kyrgyz Republic** by court, **taking up another job** or failing to quit a job not compatible with the exercise of his duties of a deputy, invalidation of the election, leaving abroad for the purpose of taking up a permanent residence, renunciation of citizenship of the Kyrgyz Republic, or loss of citizenship of the Kyrgyz Republic, the deputy of the Jogorku Kenesh shall forfeit his or her powers in such manner as may be prescribed by law.

8. Powers of a deputy of the Jogorku Kenesh **of the Kyrgyz Republic** may be terminated or he or she may be divested of his or her powers of the deputy by such resolution of the Central Commission **of the Kyrgyz Republic** on Elections and Referendums.

9. **A deputy of the Kyrgyz Republic may be divested of his or her powers of the deputy for systematic absences, without due cause, at meetings of the Jogorku Kenesh of the Kyrgyz Republic during any one session if such decision shall have been taken by a majority of the whole number of the deputies of the Jogorku Kenesh of the Kyrgyz Republic.**

10. **Procedure for filling a vacancy due to the early expiration of a deputy's term shall be ascertained by law.**

Article 57

A deputy of the **Jogorku Kenesh of the Kyrgyz Republic** shall have the right of inquiry to executive bodies **and bodies of local self-government,** and to their officers, [and] the latter shall be obliged to answer his or her inquiries within one month.

SECTION ONE
POWERS OF THE JOGORKU KENESH OF THE KYRGYZ REPUBLIC

Article 58

1. Powers of **the Jogorku Kenesh of the Kyrgyz Republic** shall be as follows:

    1) to amend the Constitution of the Kyrgyz Republic following the procedure stipulated herein;

    2) to adopt laws of the Kyrgyz Republic;

    3) to make official interpretations of the Constitution, and of the laws adopted by the Jogorku Kenesh;

4) to alter state borders of the Kyrgyz Republic;

5) **to approve the national budget, reports on its implementation, and national programs for the [country's] socio-economic development to be introduced by the Government of the Kyrgyz Republic;**

6) **to decide on matters of the administrative and territorial structure of the Kyrgyz Republic;**

7) **to call presidential elections of the Kyrgyz Republic;**

8) **to approve the structure of the Government of the Kyrgyz Republic proposed by the President of the Kyrgyz Republic;**

9) **to accept appointments to the office of Prime Minister of the Kyrgyz Republic and Member of the Government of the Kyrgyz Republic;**

10) **to cast a vote of no confidence in the Government of the Kyrgyz Republic by a majority vote of the whole number of the deputies at such times as may be provided for by the Constitution;**

11) **to select and recall, by the advice of the President of the Kyrgyz Republic, the Chairperson of the Constitutional Court, his/her deputy, and judges of the Constitutional Court of the Kyrgyz Republic;**

12) **to select and recall, by the advice of the President of the Kyrgyz Republic, the Chairperson of the Supreme Court, his/her deputies, and judges of the Supreme Court of the Kyrgyz Republic;**

13) **to accept appointments to the office of Judge of a local court;**

14) **to accept appointments to the office of Procurator-General of the Kyrgyz Republic;**

15) **to accept appointments to the office of Chairperson of the National Bank of the Kyrgyz Republic;**

16) **to accept appointments to the office of Chairperson of the Central Commission of the Kyrgyz Republic on Elections and Referendums;**

17) **to elect a half of the membership of the Central Commission of the Kyrgyz Republic on Elections and Referendums;**

18) **to accept appointments to the office of Chairperson of the Auditing Chamber of the Kyrgyz Republic;**

19) to appoint a half of the auditors of the Auditing Chamber of the Kyrgyz Republic;

20) to select and recall the Ombudsman of the Kyrgyz Republic and his/her deputies;

21) to ratify and denounce international treaties except in the cases provided by Article 48 of this Constitution of the Kyrgyz Republic;

22) to proclaim a state of emergency, affirm or invalidate decrees of the President of the Kyrgyz Republic on the issue;

23) to decide matters of war and peace; to impose martial law, declare a state of war, [and] affirm or invalidate decrees of the President of the Kyrgyz Republic on those issues;

24) to decide on a possible use of the Armed Forces of the Kyrgyz Republic outside of the country's borders when it may be necessary in order to fulfill obligations under interstate covenants for support of peace and safety;

25) to introduce military ranks, diplomatic ranks, class categories, and other special titles of the Kyrgyz Republic;

26) to introduce state awards and honorary titles of the Kyrgyz Republic;

27) to pass acts of amnesty;

28) to hear messages of, and statements by the President of the Kyrgyz Republic, speeches by heads and representatives of foreign states, international organizations;

29) to hear annual reports of the Constitutional Court of the Kyrgyz Republic as to the state of the constitutional legality in the country, of the Ombudsman of the Kyrgyz Republic as to the state of the observance and protection of human and citizen's rights and freedoms in the country;

30) to hear annual reports of the Prime Minister of the Kyrgyz Republic, Procurator-General of the Kyrgyz Republic, Chairperson of the National Bank of the Kyrgyz Republic, Chairperson of the Auditing Chamber of the Kyrgyz Republic;

Provisions of this Constitution and laws of the Kyrgyz Republic regarding the autonomy and independence of such state bodies and their officers shall be taken into consideration in the hearing of annual reports of the officers mentioned herein;

31) **to remove the President of the Kyrgyz Republic from office.**

2. **When deciding on issues mentioned in paragraphs 2, 7, 9-20, 28-31 hereof, and on issues pertaining to the exercise of control over the enforcement of laws, the Jogorku Kenesh of the Kyrgyz Republic shall pass resolutions.**

3. **Unless otherwise stipulated in this Constitution, no laws and resolutions of the Jogorku Kenesh of the Kyrgyz Republic shall be adopted unless a majority of the whole number of the deputies of the Jogorku Kenesh of the Kyrgyz Republic shall concur.**

Article 59

1. **Issues other than those mentioned in Article 58.2, as well as other significant issues of state and public life, shall be regulated by laws.**

2. **No law shall take effect and promulgated unless signed by the President of the Kyrgyz Republic.**

3. **At such request of the Government of the Kyrgyz Republic, the Jogorku Kenesh of the Kyrgyz Republic may permit the Government of the Kyrgyz Republic to adopt resolutions on issues within the jurisdiction of the Jogorku Kenesh of the Kyrgyz Republic.**

Article 60

1. **The Jogorku Kenesh of the Kyrgyz Republic shall choose, out of the deputies, the Toraga of the Jogorku Kenesh of the Kyrgyz Republic [Speaker], his/her deputies, and recall them.**

2. **The Toraga of the Jogorku Kenesh of the Kyrgyz Republic shall:**

   1) **conduct sessions of the Jogorku Kenesh;**

   2) **preside over the preparation of issues to be considered at sessions of the Jogorku Kenesh of the Kyrgyz Republic;**

   3) **sign acts adopted by the Jogorku Kenesh;**

4) represent the Jogorku Kenesh in the Kyrgyz Republic and abroad, provide for interaction between the Jogorku Kenesh and the President of the Kyrgyz Republic, Government of the Kyrgyz Republic, executive and judicial bodies, bodies of local self-government;

5) control the staff of the Jogorku Kenesh;

6) perform other functions as the Law on the Rules of Procedure of the Jogorku Kenesh of the Kyrgyz Republic may vest in him or her.

3. A Toraga of the Jogorku Kenesh shall be selected by secret ballot provided that a majority of the whole number of the deputies of the Jogorku Kenesh of the Kyrgyz Republic shall concur.

4. Deputies of the Toraga of the Jogorku Kenesh shall be elected by secret ballot, [and they] shall exercise, by order of the Toraga, some of his/her functions, and shall act for the Toraga in his/her absence. Deputies of the Toraga of the Jogorku Kenesh of the Kyrgyz Republic may be recalled in such manner as the Law on the Rules of Procedure of the Jogorku Kenesh of the Kyrgyz Republic may prescribe.

Article 61

1. The Jogorku Kenesh of the Kyrgyz Republic may constitute committees—no more than seven, and ad hoc commissions, and may elect their chairs.

    A deputy of the Jogorku Kenesh of the Kyrgyz Republic may be a member of one committee or one commission only.

2. Committees of the Jogorku Kenesh of the Kyrgyz Republic shall prepare and preliminary consider matters within the jurisdiction of the Jogorku Kenesh of the Kyrgyz Republic, oversight the enforcement of laws and decisions adopted by the Jogorku Kenesh of the Kyrgyz Republic.

3. No laws and other legal acts of the Jogorku Kenesh of the Kyrgyz Republic shall be adopted unless their drafts shall have been preliminary considered by appropriate committees of the Jogorku Kenesh of the Kyrgyz Republic.

4. Any appointment or selection of officers, [if such appointment or selection is] within the jurisdiction of the Jogorku Kenesh

of the Kyrgyz Republic, and any consent of the Jogorku Kenesh to appointments to public offices, and to removal from office require an opinion of an appropriate committee of the Jogorku Kenesh of the Kyrgyz Republic.

Article 62

1. The **Jogorku Kenesh** shall work in sessions. The **Jogorku Kenesh** shall assemble once in every year, and such session shall begin on the first working day of September and shall end on the last working day of June.
2. **Procedures of the Jogorku Kenesh shall be regulated by the Rules of Procedure.**
3. **The Jogorku Kenesh shall have power to do business provided that no less than two-thirds of the whole number of the deputies of the Jogorku Kenesh shall be present at a sitting.**

Article 63

1. **The Jogorku Kenesh of the Kyrgyz Republic may be dissolved early** with the concurrence of no less than two-thirds of the whole number of the deputies **of the Jogorku Kenesh of the Kyrgyz Republic.**
2. The Jogorku Kenesh of the Kyrgyz Republic may be dissolved early by the President of the Kyrgyz Republic: if so decided by a referendum; in the event of three [subsequent] refusals [by the Jogorku Kenesh] to accept a nominee to the office of Prime Minister of the Kyrgyz Republic; or in the event of another crisis caused by an insurmountable disagreement between the Jogorku Kenesh **of the Kyrgyz Republic** and other branches of the state power.
3. In the case provided for in Article 51.3 of this Constitution, the dissolution of the **Jogorku Kenesh of the Kyrgyz Republic** shall become valid from the pronouncement of the resolution by the Constitutional Court of the Kyrgyz Republic.
4. **The Jogorku Kenesh may not be dissolved**: in time of a state of emergency or martial law; during the consideration by the **Jogorku Kenesh** of the Kyrgyz Republic of a possible removal of the President of the Kyrgyz Republic from office; [or] whenever

fewer than six months remain until the end of the term of the President of the Kyrgyz Republic.

5. **In the event of the dissolution of the Jogorku Kenesh of the Kyrgyz Republic, the President of the Kyrgyz Republic shall appoint a day of elections to the Jogorku Kenesh of the Kyrgyz Republic so that a newly elected Jogorku Kenesh of the Kyrgyz Republic shall convene for its first session by no later than within six months after the dissolution.**

SECTION TWO
LEGISLATIVE ACTIVITIES

Article 64

The right of legislative initiative [to initiate bills] shall belong to:
- 30,000 voters (a popular initiative);
- the President of the Kyrgyz Republic;
- deputies of the **Jogorku Kenesh of the Kyrgyz Republic**;
- the Government of the Kyrgyz Republic.

Article 65

1. **Bills shall be introduced in the Jogorku Kenesh of the Kyrgyz Republic.**
2. **Bills shall be considered by the Jogorku Kenesh of the Kyrgyz Republic out of turn if identified as urgent by the President of the Kyrgyz Republic or the Government of the Kyrgyz Republic.**
3. **The Toraga of the Jogorku Kenesh of the Kyrgyz Republic shall direct a bill, introduced in the Jogorku Kenesh of the Kyrgyz Republic, along with the opinion of the Government of the Kyrgyz Republic to an appropriate committee of the Jogorku Kenesh of the Kyrgyz Republic.**

   Within one month, the [responsible] committee shall submit the bill to the Jogorku Kenesh of the Kyrgyz Republic along with a Committee's opinion.
4. No changes to bills on the national budget shall be introduced without the consent of the Government **of the Kyrgyz Republic.**

5. No amendments to national budget laws, to bills imposing or rescinding taxes, altering financial obligations of the state, and to other bills that entail an increase of expenditures at the expense of the state budget or reduction of state revenues shall be **introduced in the Jogorku Kenesh of the Kyrgyz Republic and adopted without the consent of the Government of the Kyrgyz Republic.**

6. **No bills to amend the Constitution of the Kyrgyz Republic, draft constitutional laws, bills to interpret the Constitution of the Kyrgyz Republic or constitutional laws, bills to amend constitutional laws, and bills to alter borders of the Kyrgyz Republic shall be passed by the Jogorku Kenesh of the Kyrgyz Republic unless two-thirds of the whole number of the deputies of the Jogorku Kenesh of the Kyrgyz Republic concur provided that no less than two readings shall have been held.**

7. **No changes and amendments shall be made to the Constitution of the Kyrgyz Republic and constitutional laws in time of emergency or martial law.**

8. No laws abridging freedom of speech, or of the press shall be made.

Article 66

1. **A law passed by the Jogorku Kenesh of the Kyrgyz Republic shall be presented, within one month, to the President of the Kyrgyz Republic for the signing.**

2. The President of the Kyrgyz Republic, no later than within one month from the day when the law shall have been thus presented, shall sign it or shall return it with objections **to the Jogorku Kenesh of the Kyrgyz Republic for reconsideration.**

   If after such reconsideration a majority of two-thirds of the whole number of the deputies of the Jogorku Kenesh of the Kyrgyz Republic shall repass the law in the earlier approved wording, it may be signed by the President of the Kyrgyz Republic within one month dating from the submission.

3. **Should the President of the Kyrgyz Republic [choose] not to sign a law, or [should he or she not] return it [to the Jogorku Kenesh] for reconsideration within the established term, the law shall be deemed declined by the President of the Kyrgyz**

Republic, of which the Jogorku Kenesh of the Kyrgyz Republic shall be notified.

4. A law which shall have been returned [to the Jogorku Kenesh] by the President of the Kyrgyz Republic for reconsideration **shall be considered by the Jogorku Kenesh of the Kyrgyz Republic within one month dating from the submission. Should the Jogorku Kenesh of the Kyrgyz Republic fail to consider thus returned law within one month, the law shall be deemed adopted in the wording of the objections by the President of the Kyrgyz Republic, and shall be subject to the signing.**

5. **A law, specified in Article 65.6 of this Constitution, if returned [to the Jogorku Kenesh] by the President of the Kyrgyz Republic for reconsideration, shall be subject to signing by the President of the Kyrgyz Republic within one month provided that at reconsideration of the law a majority of four-fifths of the whole number of the deputies of the Jogorku Kenesh of the Kyrgyz Republic shall repass the law in the earlier approved wording. At this, the President of the Kyrgyz Republic may choose to resort to provisions of Article 66.3.**

Article 67

A law shall take effect at the expiration of the tenth day following its promulgation unless otherwise provided by the law itself or by the Law regarding the taking of effect.

Article 68

1. The **Jogorku Kenesh of the Kyrgyz Republic** may delegate its legislative powers to the President of the Kyrgyz Republic for a period of up to one year.

2. The legislative powers shall devolve on the President of the Kyrgyz Republic in the case of the dissolution of the Jogorku Kenesh of the Kyrgyz Republic.

3. The President of the Kyrgyz Republic shall exercise legislative powers by way of issuing decrees with the force of law.

CHAPTER V.
EXECUTIVE POWER OF THE KYRGYZ REPUBLIC

Article 69

In the Kyrgyz Republic, the executive power shall be vested in the Government of the Kyrgyz Republic, subordinate ministries, state committees, administrative agencies, **other executive bodies,** and local state administrations.

SECTION ONE
THE GOVERNMENT OF THE KYRGYZ REPUBLIC

Article 70

1. The Government of the Kyrgyz Republic shall be the highest body of the executive power in the Kyrgyz Republic.
2. The Government of the Kyrgyz Republic shall be headed by the Prime Minister of the Kyrgyz Republic. The Government shall consist of Prime Minister of the Kyrgyz Republic, Vice-Prime Ministers, ministers, and chairmen of state committees of the Kyrgyz Republic.
   Structure of the Government of the Kyrgyz Republic shall be determined by the President of the Kyrgyz Republic on advice of the Prime Minister of the Kyrgyz Republic, and subject to approval by the Jogorku Kenesh of the Kyrgyz Republic.
3. When a new President **of the Kyrgyz Republic** shall enter into office, the powers of the Government of the Kyrgyz Republic shall cease.
4. Prime Minister of the Kyrgyz Republic, Government of the Kyrgyz Republic, or an individual member of the Government may submit their resignations, which the President of the Kyrgyz Republic shall accept or decline.
5. **Resignation of the Prime Minister of the Kyrgyz Republic, if accepted [by the President], shall entail resignation of the Government, and of heads of administrative agencies. In case of the acceptance of [the Prime Minister's] resignation, the Government of the Kyrgyz Republic and heads of administrative**

agencies may continue to act upon such authorization from the President of the Kyrgyz Republic until a new Government of the Kyrgyz Republic shall be formed, and heads of administrative agencies shall be appointed.

Article 71

1. The Prime Minister **of the Kyrgyz Republic** shall be appointed by the President of the Kyrgyz Republic with the consent of **a majority of the whole number of the deputies of the Jogorku Kenesh of the Kyrgyz Republic.**

2. The President shall nominate a Prime Minister of the Kyrgyz Republic and shall propose his/her candidacy to the Jogorku Kenesh of the Kyrgyz Republic by no later than two weeks after the new President of the Kyrgyz Republic shall have entered on the execution of his/her office or after the Prime Minister **of the Kyrgyz Republic** or the Government of the Kyrgyz Republic may have resigned, or within one week from the day of rejection of a [previous] nominee to the office of Prime Minister of the Kyrgyz Republic by the Jogorku Kenesh **of the Kyrgyz Republic.**

3. The **Jogorku Kenesh of the Kyrgyz Republic** shall take a decision on accepting the appointment of a [nominated] Prime Minister of the Kyrgyz Republic by no later than within seven days after the nominee shall have been proposed [to it].

4. After the **Jogorku Kenesh of the Kyrgyz Republic** may have thrice rejected candidates for the office of Prime Minister **of the Kyrgyz Republic,** the President of the Kyrgyz Republic shall appoint the Prime Minister of the Kyrgyz Republic and shall dissolve the Jogorku Kenesh of the Kyrgyz Republic.

5. The Prime Minister **of the Kyrgyz Republic** shall, **as provided by the Constitution, laws of the Kyrgyz Republic,** and decrees of the President of the Kyrgyz Republic, determine guidelines for the activities of the Government **of the Kyrgyz Republic,** organize its work, and shall be personally responsible for its activities.

Article 72

1. **In its functioning, the Government of the Kyrgyz Republic shall be responsible to the President of the Kyrgyz Republic and ac-**

countable to the Jogorku Kenesh of the Kyrgyz Republic within the limits prescribed by this article of the Constitution.

The President of the Kyrgyz Republic may chair any sitting of the Government of the Kyrgyz Republic.

2. The Prime Minister of the Kyrgyz Republic shall present annul reports on the work of the Government of the Kyrgyz Republic to the Jogorku Kenesh of the Kyrgyz Republic.

3. **Following the consideration of an annual report of the Prime Minister of the Kyrgyz Republic, the Jogorku Kenesh of the Kyrgyz Republic may, if so initiated by no less than a majority of the whole number of the deputies of the Kyrgyz Republic, cast a vote of no confidence in the Government of the Kyrgyz Republic.**

4. **Any such resolution to vote no confidence in the Government of the Kyrgyz Republic shall require the concurrence of no less than two-thirds of the whole number of the deputies of the Jogorku Kenesh of the Kyrgyz Republic.**

5. **No issue of delivering a vote of no confidence in the Government of the Kyrgyz Republic may be considered by the Jogorku Kenesh of the Kyrgyz Republic: more than once during any one session; during one year since a Work Program of the Government of the Kyrgyz Republic may have been approved; [or] whenever fewer than six months remain until the end of the term of the President of the Kyrgyz Republic.**

6. **After the Jogorku Kenesh may have passed a vote of no confidence in the Government of the Kyrgyz Republic, the President of the Kyrgyz Republic shall either decide to dissolve the Government of the Kyrgyz Republic or disagree with the decision of the Jogorku Kenesh of the Kyrgyz Republic.**

7. **Should the Jogorku Kenesh of the Kyrgyz Republic within three months choose to again deliver the vote of no confidence in the Government of the Kyrgyz Republic, the President of the Kyrgyz Republic shall either announce the dissolution of the Government of the Kyrgyz Republic or dissolve the Jogorku Kenesh of the Kyrgyz Republic.**

Article 73

1. The Government of the Kyrgyz Republic shall decide all matters of state management except for the authorities vested, by the

Constitution of the Kyrgyz Republic, in the President of the Kyrgyz Republic and the Jogorku Kenesh of the Kyrgyz Republic.

2. **The Government of the Kyrgyz Republic shall:**
   1) **provide for the enforcement of the Constitution and laws of the Kyrgyz Republic, legal acts of the President of the Kyrgyz Republic, and of the Government of the Kyrgyz Republic; [and provide for] the realization of internal and foreign policy of the state;**
   2) **take measure to ensure rule of law, citizen's rights and freedoms, the protection of public order, [and] crime prevention;**
   3) **provide for the implementation of fiscal, pricing, tariff, investment, and tax policies;**
   4) **draw up and submit national budget to the Jogorku Kenesh, and provide for its implementation; present reports on the implementation of the national budget to the Jogorku Kenesh of the Kyrgyz Republic;**
   5) **provide for the realization of single state policy with regard to culture, science, education, health care, labor and employment, social security, environmental protection, ecological safety, and use of the nature;**
   6) **draw up and implement nationwide programs for economic, social, scientific and technical, and cultural development;**
   7) **take measures to ensure equal conditions for the development of all forms of ownership, and for their protection, and to manage state-owned facilities;**
   8) **take measures to ensure the sovereignty of the state, defense potential, and national security;**
   9) **organize and realize foreign trade, customs regulation;**
   10) **direct and coordinate activities of ministries, state committees, administrative agencies, state commissions and funds, local state administrations, and other executive bodies;**
   11) **provide for cooperation with civil society;**
   12) **carry out other functions as the Constitution of the Kyrgyz Republic, laws of the Kyrgyz Republic, or decrees of the President of the Kyrgyz Republic may provide.**

3. The Government of the Kyrgyz Republic and the National Bank of Kyrgyzstan shall provide for implementation of uniform monetary, credit, and currency policies.
4. Organization of the work and procedures of the Government of the Kyrgyz Republic shall be ascertained by **constitutional law.**

Article 74

1. **In accordance with, and in pursuance of the Constitution and laws of the Kyrgyz Republic, the Government of the Kyrgyz Republic shall issue resolutions and ordinances, and shall organize, supervise, and provide for their enforcement.**
2. **Resolutions and ordinances of the Government of the Kyrgyz Republic shall be binding throughout the territory of the Kyrgyz Republic. Noncompliance with or undue enforcement of legal acts of the Government of the Kyrgyz Republic shall result in liability as may be envisaged by law.**

Article 75

1. The Government of the Kyrgyz Republic shall direct the work of ministries, state committees, administrative agencies, and of bodies of local state administration.
2. Ministries, state committees, and administrative agencies, **[and] other executive bodies** shall issue, within their powers, orders and ordinances on the basis and in pursuance of the Constitution, laws of the Kyrgyz Republic, resolutions of the Jogorku Kenesh of the Kyrgyz Republic, acts of the President, resolutions and ordinances of the Government of the Kyrgyz Republic, [and] shall organize, supervise, and provide for their enforcement.
3. The Government of the Kyrgyz Republic shall hear reports of heads of ministries, state committees, administrative agencies, **other executive agencies,** and of local state administrations, and shall invalidate their acts that contradict the laws of the Kyrgyz Republic.

SECTION TWO
LOCAL STATE ADMINISTRATION

Article 76

1. **In respective administrative territories, the executive power shall be exercised by local state administration.**
2. **Powers of local state administration, organization of the work and procedures shall be ascertained by law.**

Article 77

1. Local state administrations shall act on the basis of the Constitution of the Kyrgyz Republic, laws of the Kyrgyz Republic, [and] legal acts of the President of the Kyrgyz Republic and of the Government of the Kyrgyz Republic.
2. Decisions of a local state administration, adopted within its powers, shall be binding for implementation within the given territory.

SECTION THREE
PROCURATOR'S OFFICE

Article 78

The Procurator's Office shall supervise, within the bounds of its powers, accurate and uniform execution of legislative acts. The procurator's offices shall conduct prosecutions [and] participate in trials of cases at such times, and in such manner as law may provide.

CHAPTER VI.
COURTS AND JUSTICE IN THE KYRGYZ REPUBLIC

Article 79

1. **Justice shall be administered in the Kyrgyz Republic only by courts.**

   Citizens of the Kyrgyz Republic shall have the right to participate in administration of justice at such times, and in such manner as the law may stipulate.

2. Judicial power shall be exercised through constitutional, civil, criminal, administrative, and other forms of judicial proceedings.
3. The judicial system of the Kyrgyz Republic shall be established in the Constitution of the Kyrgyz Republic and laws of the Kyrgyz Republic, and shall consist of the Constitutional Court of the Kyrgyz Republic, Supreme Court of the Kyrgyz Republic, and of local courts. Specialized courts may be constituted by constitutional laws.

No extraordinary courts shall be constituted.
4. Organization of the work of courts and their procedures shall be ascertained by law.

Article 80

1. The judiciary shall be independent, and shall be subject to the Constitution of the Kyrgyz Republic and laws of the Kyrgyz Republic only.
2. A judge shall enjoy immunity, and may not be detained or arrested, subjected to search, including body search, unless when in cases of being caught in the act of committing a crime.

   A judge of the Constitutional Court of the Kyrgyz Republic, of the Supreme Court of the Kyrgyz Republic may be prosecuted or subjected to administrative liability imposed by court only with the consent of the Jogorku Kenesh of the Kyrgyz Republic.

   The privilege of a judge shall also apply to his/her housing, office, vehicles and means of communication that he/she may use, his/her correspondence, property and documents that belong to him/her.
3. No one shall require of a judge to account for a case.
4. Social, material, and other guarantees of his/her independence shall be ensured to a judge according to his/her status.
5. A judge of the Constitutional Court, or of the Supreme Court of the Kyrgyz Republic shall be a citizen of the Kyrgyz Republic of no younger than 35 years and of no older than 70 years of age, who shall have a degree in law, and who shall have no less than 10 years of work experience in the legal profession.

   The Jogorku Kenesh of the Kyrgyz Republic shall select, on advice of the President of the Kyrgyz Republic, judges of the Constitutional Court, and of the Supreme Court who will serve the term of ten years.

6. A judge of a local court shall be a citizen of the Kyrgyz Republic of no younger than 25 years, and of no older than 65 years, who shall have a degree in law, and who shall have no less than 5 years of work experience in the legal profession.

   The President of the Kyrgyz Republic shall appoint, with the consent of the Jogorku Kenesh, judges of local courts for the term of seven years.

7. Status of judges of the Kyrgyz Republic shall be specified by constitutional law.

Article 81

1. A judge may be relieved of office on resignation, due to the state of his or her health, for the commission of a crime where the judgment of conviction shall have taken legal effect, and on other grounds specified by constitutional law.

2. A judge of the Constitutional Court of the Kyrgyz Republic [and] a judge of the Supreme Court of the Kyrgyz Republic may be removed from office by the advice of the President of the Kyrgyz Republic by a majority vote of no less than two-thirds of the whole number of the deputies of the Jogorku Kenesh of the Kyrgyz Republic.

3. A constitutional law may stipulate other procedures for discharging a judge of the Constitutional Court and a judge of the Supreme Court of the Kyrgyz Republic on resignation or due to the state of his/her health.

4. Procedures for nomination of candidates to the office of judge, appointment of judges, rotation, discharge of judges of local courts, and other matters concerning judges of local courts and their work shall be ascertained by constitutional law.

Article 82

1. The Constitutional Court shall be the highest body of the judicial power for the protection of the Constitution of the Kyrgyz Republic.

2. The Constitutional Court shall consist of the Chairman, Deputy Chairman, and seven judges of the Constitutional Court.

3. On such inquiries of the President of the Kyrgyz Republic, Jogorku Kenesh of the Kyrgyz Republic, Government of the

Kyrgyz Republic, [or] Central Commission of the Kyrgyz Republic on Elections and Referendums, the Constitutional Court shall:

1) find laws and other legal acts unconstitutional provided they contradict the Constitution;
2) resolve disputes, arising from the effect, application, and interpretation of the Constitution,
3) hand down an opinion on validity of elections of the President of the Kyrgyz Republic,
4) hand down an opinion on the removal of the President of the Kyrgyz Republic from office, as well as on the discharge of judges of the Constitutional Court, [and of] the Supreme Court of the Kyrgyz Republic;
5) consent to prosecution of judges of local courts;
6) hand down an opinion on proposed amendments to the Constitution of the Kyrgyz Republic **within one month** in accordance with the requirements of **Article 96.2 of this Constitution;**
7) annul decisions of bodies of local self-government provided that they contradict the Constitution of the Kyrgyz Republic;
8) **determine the constitutionality of activities by political parties, nongovernmental and religious organizations.**

4. A decision of the Constitutional Court shall be final and shall not be appealed.

If a law or another act, **mentioned herein,** shall be found unconstitutional by the Constitutional Court, the effect of such law or act shall terminate throughout the territory of the Kyrgyz Republic, along with the effect of other legal acts which shall have been based on the act recognized unconstitutional **except for judicial acts. Terms of and procedure for repealing judicial acts and [terms of and procedure for] resolving matters in consequence of the repeal shall be regulated by an appropriate law to be made by the Jogorku Kenesh of the Kyrgyz Republic with regard to any one case when a law or other act shall have been found unconstitutional.**

5. **Procedures for administration of constitutional justice and other related issues shall be regulated by law.**

Article 83

1. The Supreme Court of the Kyrgyz Republic shall be the highest body of the judicial power in regard with civil, criminal, and administrative judicial proceedings, as well as in regard to commercial disputes and other matters as law may envisage.
2. Chambers and benches of judges, and the Presidium shall be constituted within the Supreme Court of the Kyrgyz Republic, of which the powers shall be ascertained by law.

   The court instances, thus established within the Supreme Court, shall review judicial acts of lower courts and shall render final decisions in such manner as law may prescribe.
3. The Supreme Court shall overview judicial activities of local courts by way of reviewing judicial acts on appeals by participants of the judicial proceedings. The law shall ascertain powers of the Supreme Court of the Kyrgyz Republic with regard to sustaining acts of local courts, revoking or reversing them.
4. At full sessions [of the court], where all judges of the Supreme Court shall be present,—the Plenum of the Supreme Court of the Kyrgyz Republic, the Supreme Court of the Kyrgyz Republic may adopt guidelines in regard to matters of judicial practice, which will be binding on all lower courts.

Article 84

The state shall provide funding and adequate conditions for courts to function, and for judges to work.

Courts shall be funded from the national budget, and [such funding] shall be adequate to provide for an absolute and independent administration of justice by law.

Article 85

1. Judicial proceedings in all courts shall be open. A court hearing may be held in camera only in cases envisaged by law. Judgment shall be pronounced publicly.
2. No one may be tried, on a criminal or other case, in his absence unless at such times as law may provide.
3. Judicial proceedings shall be based on the principles of adversary process and equality of the parties.

4. Judicial acts may be repealed, reviewed, or suspended only by court in such manner as law may provide.
5. No one charged with a criminal offense shall bear the burden of proof.
6. No one may be convicted of a crime on the account of his confession only.
7. Everyone convicted of a crime shall have the right to his conviction being reviewed by a higher court according to law, and shall have the right to ask for a pardon or for commuting the sentence.
8. No one shall be held liable twice for one offense.
9. Criminal law shall not be applied by analogy.
10. No law which may impose a penalty or provide for a heavier penalty shall have retroactive effect. No one shall be held liable for any act which did not constitute an offense at the time when it was committed. If, subsequent to the commission of the offense, provision is made by law for the revocation of liability for the offense or imposition of a lighter penalty, the new law shall apply.
11. No one shall be compelled to testify against himself, his spouse, or close relatives—the circle of close relatives to be specified by law. Law may also provide for other cases when a person shall not be compelled to testify.
12. Everyone detained, arrested, or charged with a crime shall have the right to enjoy legal assistance of an advocate (defender) from the time of detention, arrest or from the time when the charge was brought accordingly.
13. The rights of victims of crime and of abuse of power shall be protected by law. The state shall provide for their access to justice and compensation for the damage or harm caused.

Article 86

1. Decisions of the courts of the Kyrgyz Republic that shall have come into legal force, shall be binding on all state bodies, business entities, public associations, officials, and persons throughout the territory of the Republic.
2. **Failure to execute, improper execution, or hindrance to the execution of judgments,** as well as interference with courts shall incur liability provided for by law.

Article 87

1. A court shall not apply a legal act that shall contradict the Constitution of the Kyrgyz Republic.
2. Where, in the course of the hearing of a case in any court instance, the constitutionality of a law or other legal act which may effect outcome of the case, shall have been questioned, the court shall send an inquiry to the Constitutional Court of the Kyrgyz Republic.

Article 88

1. A person, charged publicly or otherwise, shall have the right to protect his honor, dignity, and business reputation, and his right in the court; in no circumstances a person may be denied of such court protection.
2. The defense shall be an inalienable right of a person in any stage of the trial of the case.

   If a person shall not have funds, the legal aid and defense shall be provided to him at the expense of the state.
3. **Procedural rights of participants of judicial proceedings, including the right to appeal against rulings, judgments, and other court decisions, and the manner in which they may exercise such rights shall be ascertained by law.**

Article 89

1 In criminal and administrative cases, the burden of proof shall lie with the accuser.
2. Evidence, wrongfully obtained, shall be void, and inadmissible.

Article 90

If not established by this Constitution, principles of justice [which will be binding on] all courts and judges of the Kyrgyz Republic shall be provided by laws of the Kyrgyz Republic.

CHAPTER VII.
LOCAL SELF-GOVERNMENT

Article 91

In the Kyrgyz Republic, local self-government shall be exercised by local communities, which shall, within the bounds of the law, administer local affairs on their own responsibility.

Article 92

1. **Local affairs shall be administered by local keneshes and other bodies, which shall be constituted, in such manner as the law may provide, by the communities themselves.**

   Bodies of local self-government may possess, use, and dispose of municipal (communal) property.
2. **Public gatherings and local keneshes, or other representative bodies of local self-government may decide to constitute—in villages, settlements, and towns—courts of aksakal [courts of elders] which shall consist of elders or other citizens who may enjoy respect and authority.**
3. **Courts of aksakal shall consider torts, family disputes, and other matters which, under the law, shall fall within their jurisdiction, provided that the parties to disputes shall agree to have their disputes considered by courts of elders for the purpose of reaching reconciliation among the parties and rendering a just decision which shall not contradict laws.**
4. **Decisions of courts of aksakal may be appealed in such manner as laws of the Kyrgyz Republic may provide.**

Article 93

Laws of the Kyrgyz Republic shall ascertain the bases for the organization and functioning of bodies of local self-government, and shall regulate their relationships with state bodies.

Article 94

Certain state powers may be vested in bodies of local self-government and, for such purpose, they shall be vested with necessary material, financial, and other means. Bodies of local self-government shall be accountable to state bodies in regard to thus delegated powers.

Article 95

1. Local keneshes shall:
   - approve and monitor programs of social and economic development of the [respective] territories and social protection of the [respective] communities;
   - approve the local budget and reports on its implementation, and shall also hear information of the use of extrabudgetary funds.
2. A local kenesh may pass a vote of no confidence in a head of the local state administration of a respective territorial unit by a two-thirds majority of the whole number of the deputies.
3. Local keneshes shall function independently from the local state administration.
4. Local keneshes **and their executive bodies shall, within the bounds of authorities envisaged by the Constitutions and laws of the Kyrgyz Republic,** adopt acts, which shall be binding for execution throughout their respective territories.
5. Local keneshes and other bodies of local self-government shall be liable, before the state, for the compliance with and implementation of laws, and, before local communities, for their performance.
6. **The deputy of local kenesh shall be elected for four years, and he shall not be subjected to persecution for opinions expressed, and for results of voting in the local kenesh.**

CHAPTER VIII.
CHANGING AND AMENDING
THE CONSTITUTION OF THE KYRGYZ REPUBLIC

Article 96

1. Changes and amendments to this Constitution shall be adopted by a referendum called by the President of the Kyrgyz Republic.

2. [Constitutional] changes and amendments may be adopted by **the Jogorku Kenesh of the Kyrgyz Republic** on the initiation of the President of the Kyrgyz Republic, of a majority of the whole number of the deputies of **the Jogorku Kenesh of the Kyrgyz Republic**, or of no fewer than 300,000 voters.

3. In considering a proposal to change or amend the Constitution of the Kyrgyz Republic, **the Jogorku Kenesh of the Kyrgyz Republic** shall take into account an opinion of the Constitutional Court of the Kyrgyz Republic [on the proposal], and such proposal shall be considered no earlier than in three months, but prior to the expiration of six months dating from the submission of the proposal to **the Jogorku Kenesh of the Kyrgyz Republic**.

4. A proposed wording of changes and amendments to the Constitution of the Kyrgyz Republic shall not be altered while they shall be discussed in the Jogorku Kenesh of the Kyrgyz Republic.

Article 97

1. This Constitution shall be amended by the Jogorku Kenesh **of the Kyrgyz Republic** when two-thirds of the whole number of the deputies **of the Jogorku Kenesh of the Kyrgyz Republic** concur.

2. A proposal, which shall have failed to be adopted, may be resubmitted to the Jogorku Kenesh no earlier than after the expiration of one year.

President of the Kyrgyz Republic   A. Akayev

Appendix B: Tables

Table 1. Kyrgyz Republic: Main Economic Indicators (1993–2004)

	1993	1994	1995	1996	1997	1998	1999	2000	2001	2002	2003	2004
GDP at current prices (Som bn)	5.4	12.0	16.1	22.5	30.7	34.2	48.7	65.4	73.9	73.9	n/a	n/a
GDP at exchange rate ($ bn)	0.7	2.2	1.5	1.8	1.8	1.6	1.2	1.4	1.5	1.6	n/a	n/a
GDP at PPP (a) ($ bn)	8.3	6.3	6.0	6.5	7.3	8.3	7.9	8.5	10.0	9.9	n/a	n/a
Real GDP growth (b) (%)	-16.3	-20.1	-5.4	5.6	9.9	2.1	3.6	5.0	5.3	-2.1	1.0	3.0
Consumer price inflation (av; %)	1,208.70	278.1	53.0	30.3	23.4	10.5	35.9	18.7	6.9	2.1	3.0	6.0
Population (mid-year, m)	4.5	4.6	4.7	4.7	4.6	4.7	4.8	4.9	4.9	5.0	5.0	5.1
Exports ($ m)	340.0	340.0	409.0	506.0	630.0	535.1	462.6	510.9	480.0	489.0	590.0	650.0
Imports ($ m)	506.0	317.0	522.0	890.0	646.0	756.0	546.0	502.0	440.0	512.0	580.0	650.0
Trade balance ($ m)	-166.0	23.0	-113.0	-384.0	-16.0	-221.0	-84.0	8.9	40.0	-23.0	10.0	0.0
Current-account balance ($ m)	-267.0	-201.0	-391.0	-510.0	-138.0	-364.0	-180.0	-77.0	-19.0	-128.0	-80.0	-60.0
Foreign debt ($ bn)	294.0	450.0	610.0	1.1	1.3	1.5	1.7	1.8	1.8	1.5		
Exchange rate (av; som:$)	8.0	10.8	10.8	14.0	17.4	20.8	39.0	47.7	48.4	46.9	49.0	50.0
Reserves excl gold						164.0	230.0	239.0	232.0	233.0		
Labor (in thousands) (c)	1,681.0	1,645.0	1,642.0	1,652.0	1,689.0	1,705.0	1,764.0	1,768.0	1,774.0	1,775.0	1,779.0	1,786.0
Foreign investments ($ m) (c)	n/a	n/a	96.1	46.8	83.0	109.0	44.4	-2.4	5.0	n/a	n/a	n/a

Origins of gross domestic product 2001	% of total	Components of gross domestic product 2001 (c)	% of total
Agriculture and forestry	35.2	Private consumption	66.3
Machinery	21.3	Public consumption	17.3
Construction	4.1	Gross fixed investments	14.5
Other	39.3	Change in stocks	1.7
Total	100.0	Net exports	−0.2

Source: Kyrgyz Republic. EIU Country Report. 1st quarter 1998, pp. 1–5.

Kyrgyz Republic. EIU Country Report. 1st quarter 2003, pp. 5, 12.
(a) Data for 2002, 2003, 2004 EIU estimates.
(b) Trade balance—author estimates
(c) International Monetary Fund. Kyrgyz Republic. Selected Issues and Statistical Appendix. February 5, 2003. Washington, D.C.: IMF, 2003.

Table 2. Kyrgyz Republic: Export of Goods to CIS and non-CIS Countries 1995–2002 (In millions of U.S. dollars)

Export	1995	1996	1997	1998	1999	2000	2001	2002 first half
Total exports	408.9	505.4	603.8	513.6	453.8	504.5	476.2	236.8
Export to CIS countries	269.2	393	319.3	230.6	183.3	207	168.5	70.6
Industry	231.1	345.7	285.7	187.7	135.6	171.8	137.8	53.9
Electric energy	41.0	73.6	83.2	25.6	52.0	79.8	46.8	3.5
Oil and gas industry	1.5	1.9	1.5	2.2	0.9	1.9	4.4	2.0
Coal industry	3.1	2.0	1.8	0.5	0.2	0.3	0.3	0.2
Ferrous metallurgy	3.0	4.5	1.3	1.7	0.3	0.5	0.7	0.2
Nonferrous metallurgy	11.9	22.6	10.4	6.6	2.5	1.3	2.3	0.9
Chemical and petrochemical	9.1	7.9	9.6	5.2	5.5	8.3	5.4	3.8
Machine building	39.5	48.6	49.8	53.7	33.5	39.6	36.4	15.3
Lumber and paper	1.3	2.2	2.8	4.0	0.5	0.6	0.4	0.2
Industrial construction materials	11.4	21.5	26.7	24.0	8.1	8.4	8.3	5.2
Light industry	28.2	38.4	22.7	14.8	14.0	18.8	18.3	15.3
Food industry	74.2	117.7	72.1	45.3	15.6	8.6	10.5	6.1
Other industries	7.0	4.9	3.9	4.2	2.5	3.8	4.0	1.3
Agriculture	38.2	47.7	33.5	42.9	47.5	35.7	30.7	16.7
Others	0.0	0.0	0.0	0.0	0.2	0.0	0.0	0.0

Exports to non-CIS countries	139.7	112.0	284.5	283.1	270.5	297.1	307.6	166.2
Industry	135.0	96.4	272.9	273.4	261.3	285.8	293.0	152.5
Ferrous metallurgy	7.4	2.4	1.7	1.2	1.3	4.9	5.3	2.4
Nonferrous metallurgy	50.7	34.1	205.9	214.4	214.8	232.6	243.7	105.1
Chemical and petrochemical	11.2	5.8	5.2	3.4	1.4	4.1	1.4	4.6
Machine building	5.0	7.6	11.8	16.4	13.3	11.1	20.9	8.8
Lumber and paper	0.6	0.2	0.7	0.6	0.3	0.4	0.2	0.1
Industrial construction materials	0.2	0.3	0.2	0.0	0.1	0.1	0.0	0.0
Light industry	54.3	36.1	38.0	26.0	18.3	25.1	13.8	12.4
Food industry	4.9	9.4	7.5	9.2	3.5	5.0	2.0	1.8
Other industries	0.6	0.6	2.0	2.1	8.4	2.5	5.8	17.2
Agriculture	4.7	15.0	11.7	9.7	9.3	11.2	14.5	13.7
Others	0.0	0.0	0.0	0.0	0.0	0.1	0.1	0.1
Memorandum items:								
Export associated with "shuttle trade"	—	—	58.4	42.2	21.9	20.3	28.3	11.5
Included in official statistics	—	—	31.4	20.8	13.2	13.9	24.0	10.4
Estimated (added to oficial statistics)	—	—	27.0	21.4	8.7	6.4	4.1	1.1

Source: International Monetary Fund. *Kyrgyz Republic. Selected Issues and Statistical Appendix. February 5, 2003.* Washington D.C.: IMF, 2003, p. 76.

(a) EIU estimates. (b) Real GDP growth rates for 1993–1995 are based on series from the World Bank's Statistical Handbook: States of the Former USSR. Data for 1996 are from the Kyrgyz Republic State Statistical Committee. (c) World Bank estimates.

Table 3. Kyrgyz Republic: Import of Goods to CIS and non-CIS Countries 1995–2002 (In millions of U.S. dollars)

Export	1995	1996	1997	1998	1999	2000	2001	2002 first half
Total imports	522.3	837.7	709.3	841.5	599.7	554.6	467.2	270.5
Imports to CIS countries	353.6	486.9	435.8	440.7	259.3	299.0	257.0	153.1
Industry	349.9	473.6	423.0	428.6	248.8	283.9	245.2	143.1
Electric energy	8.6	26.7	23.8	7.9	2.8	7.6	9.8	4.9
Oil and gas industry	160.0	183.1	172.1	176.1	96.8	107.0	102.4	60.6
Coal industry	17.0	25.1	6.9	17.4	19.6	10.8	6.2	9.6
Ferrous metallurgy	16.3	14.3	9.1	17.0	6.0	10.2	8.5	5.2
Nonferrous metallurgy	10.1	7.1	16.9	25.7	12.8	5.4	11.2	8.9
Chemical and petrochemical	22.7	40.3	41.3	46.8	19.0	27.0	18.6	10.1
Machine building	46.6	69.3	58.0	56.9	39.4	46.8	30.8	16.0
Lumber and paper	15.8	18.6	18.8	21.2	10.0	15.3	12.1	5.1
Industrial construction materials	8.2	10.9	10.6	11.5	7.6	6.5	7.6	3.3
Light industry	16.0	10.7	11.7	5.6	3.0	2.0	1.6	0.6
Food industry	22.2	57.3	41.9	21.2	25.6	30.0	29.2	15.2
Other industries	6.4	10.1	11.2	21.3	6.1	15.3	7.2	3.7
Agriculture	3.7	13.2	12.8	12.0	10.5	15.2	11.8	10.0
Others	0.0	0.0	0.0	0.0	0.0	0.0	0.0	0.0

Imports to non-CIS countries	168.8	350.8	273.5	400.8	340.5	255.6	210.3	117.4
Industry	155.5	336.3	251.7	394.2	319.5	229.9	207.9	115.5
Electric energy	0.0	0.0	0.0	0.0	0.0	0.0	0.0	0.0
Oil and gas industry	2.6	4.5	3.2	5.4	2.3	3.8	3.1	1.5
Coal industry	0.0	0.0	0.0	0.0	0.0	0.0	0.0	0.0
Ferrous metallurgy	1.5	0.7	0.8	4.6	3.5	0.8	1.1	0.8
Nonferrous metallurgy	1.1	1.6	5.5	4.9	10.1	7.1	12.8	4.0
Chemical and petrochemical	7.3	10.7	18.6	28.7	19.7	21.1	25.8	12.0
Machine building	57.01	161.21	95.97	162.4	163.02	98.17	67.35	45.75
Lumber and paper	4.0	7.6	10.4	14.1	9.1	11.5	8.9	4.5
Industrial construction materials	1.9	5.0	2.7	4.5	3.4	2.3	2.4	1.6
Light industry	7.2	5.9	36.6	54.7	35.7	36.8	30.8	19.3
Food industry	62.0	104.7	41.4	85.4	28.7	16.9	25.6	14.8
Other industries	10.9	34.5	36.5	29.4	44.1	31.4	30.2	11.2
Agriculture	13.3	14.5	21.8	6.6	21.0	25.7	2.4	1.9
Memorandum items:								
Export associated with "shuttle trade"	—	—	82.4	100.5	58.3	56.7	50.9	26.5
Included in official statistics	—	—	59.4	72.7	44.8	52.7	46.6	24.4
Estimated (added to oficial statistics)	—	—	23.0	27.8	13.5	3.9	4.3	2.1

Source: International Monetary Fund. *Kyrgyz Republic. Selected Issues and Statistical Appendix. February 5, 2003.* Washington D.C.: IMF, 2003, p. 77.

(a) EIU estimates. (b) Real GDP growth rates for 1993–1995 are based on series from the World Bank's Statistical Handbook: States of the Former USSR. Data for 1996 are from the Kyrgyz Republic State Statistical Committee. (c) World Bank estimates.

Table 4. Kyrgyz Republic: Summary Monetary Accounts, 1995–1997. In millions of soms

	1995 1/				1996 1/				1997 2/		
	March	June	Sep.	Dec.	March	June	Sep.	Dec.	March	June	Sep.
					National Bank						
Net foreign assets	−505.2	−433.5	−455.3	−497.8	−692.7	−503.1	−309.0	−303.8	−441.6	48.7	−244.5
Net international reserves	−41.6	−68.4	−87.3	−111.1	−291.2	−75.6	125.6	−191.9	−329.6	160.7	−132.6
Claims on other CIS countries 3/	−463.6	−365.0	−368.0	−386.7	−401.5	−427.5	−434.6	111.9	−111.9	−112.0	−112.0
Medium-term NBKR obligations	−287.1	−289.8	−345.2	−436.4	−415.1	−499.6	−567.8	−748.0	−850.0	−832.4	−854.8
Net domestic assets	1,977.4	2,176.4	2,534.7	2,978.4	3,053.9	2,962.7	3,242.0	3,606.9	3,795.3	3,577.1	3,857.0
Credit to government, net	984.6	1,304.5	1,643.5	2,033.9	2,148.4	1,969.9	2,226.3	3,785.2	4,005.8	3,786.7	4,107.0
Direct credits, a)	962.7	1,077.0	1,433.7	1,601.0	1,742.0	1,839.7	1,940.5	2,059.0	2,250.1	2,206.3	1,925.4
Counterpart funds	−265.1	−62.2	−141.7	−0.8	−4.6	−362.4	−267.5	−0.1	−49.4	−271.1	−0.8
Government bonds 4/	0.0	0.0	0.0	0.0	0.0	0.0	0.0	985.5	1,002.0	1,017.8	1,003.4
Treasury bills (actual value)	0.0	0.0	0.0	0.0	0.0	0.0	0.0	0.0	0.0	69.1	414.4
Turkish loan	287.1	289.8	351.5	433.6	211.0	492.6	533.3	740.7	803.2	764.6	764.6
Credit to other government, net	−2.1	−2.5	−2.9	−2.0	−2.7	−0.6	−3.0	−6.5	−2.1	0.0	0.0
Credit to banks	1,271.5	1,217.6	1,200.1	1,178.7	1,107.4	1,105.3	1,084.4	123.7	123.5	108.5	120.9
Other items, net	−276.6	−343.2	−305.9	−232.2	−199.1	−306.4	−65.8	−295.4	−331.9	−318.1	−370.9
Liabilities	1,185.2	1,453.1	1,725.2	2,044.2	1,946.0	1,960.0	2,365.3	2,555.1	2,503.7	2,793.4	2,757.7
Currency in circulation	1,035.8	1,312.6	1,595.5	1,963.2	1,834.3	1,862.8	2,271.7	2,439.0	2,361.8	2,541.4	2,506.5
Reserves	149.4	140.5	129.7	81.0	111.7	97.2	93.6	116.1	141.9	252.0	251.2

Banking System

Net foreign assets	-303.4	-297.8	-265.2	-329.5	-481.2	-357.9	-147.0	-41.4	-260.8	253.9	-23.1
Medium-term NBKR obligations	-287.1	-289.8	-354.2	-436.4	-415.1	-499.6	-567.8	-748.0	-850.0	-832.4	-854.8
Net domestic assets	2,290.2	2,579.0	2,988.0	3,484.4	3,527.1	3,496.8	3,707.8	4,117.9	4,352.5	4,229.5	4,547.2
Credit to government, net	1,075.8	1,422.3	1,771.6	2,174.1	2,264.2	2,116.0	2,397.6	3,974.6	4,230.8	4,083.8	4,336.1
Credit from NBKR 4/	984.6	1,304.5	1,643.5	2,033.9	2,148.4	1,969.9	2,226.3	3,785.2	4,005.8	3,786.7	4,107.0
Credit from commercial banks	91.2	117.8	128.0	140.2	115.8	146.1	171.3	189.4	225.0	297.1	229.1
Credit to other government, net	-56.3	-74.5	-69.9	-60.7	-54.4	-57.7	-58.8	-47.9	38.2	-55.5	0.0
Credit to rest of economy 4/	2,049.4	2,139.8	2,180.8	1,949.7	1,915.1	1,940.2	1,896.9	862.5	765.2	852.9	858.8
Other items, net	-778.6	-908.6	-894.5	-578.7	-597.8	-501.8	-527.9	-671.3	-605.3	-951.7	-647.7
Liabilities	1,699.7	1,991.5	2,368.6	2,718.5	2,630.7	2,639.4	2,993.0	3,328.5	3,241.7	3,650.9	3,669.3
Currency outside banks	1,014.8	1,292.3	1,573.3	1,937.6	1,791.8	1,837.2	2,233.1	2,398.0	2,300.7	2,494.9	2,433.2
Deposits	684.9	699.2	795.2	780.8	838.8	802.1	759.9	930.5	941.1	1,156.1	1,236.1
Memorandum items:											
Velocity	10.0	9.0	8.5	7.8	7.3	7.1	7.3	7.5	7.7	7.4	7.5
Quarterly CPI inflation (in percent)	16.2	3.2	2.6	7.4	11.8	8.4	-1.1	12.7	7.2	6.0	-1.2
Quarterly growth rate of:											
Broad money	11.1	17.2	18.9	14.8	-3.2	0.3	13.4	11.2	-3.2	12.6	0.5
Contribution from NFA 5/	-9.4	0.2	-1.6	-6.2	-4.8	1.5	5.4	-2.5	-11.8	16.4	-0.1
Contribution from NDA 5/	20.5	17.0	20.5	21.0	1.6	-1.2	8.0	13.7	8.6	-3.1	0.6

Continued

Table 4. *Continued*

	1995 1/				1996 1/				1997 2/		
	March	June	Sep.	Dec.	March	June	Sep.	Dec.	March	June	Sep.
Reserve money	11.0	22.6	18.7	18.5	-4.8	0.7	20.7	8.0	-1.2	11.6	-1.3
Contribution from NFA 5/	-21.9	5.8	-5.9	-7.2	-8.5	5.4	6.4	-7.4	-5.5	20.3	0.5
Contribution from NDA 5/	32.9	16.8	24.7	25.7	3.7	-4.7	14.2	15.4	4.3	-8.7	-1.8
Currency outside banks	1.3	27.3	21.7	23.2	-7.5	2.5	21.5	7.4	-4.1	8.4	-2.5
Yearly growth rate of:											
Broad money	—	—	—	76.7	—	—	—	22.4	—	—	—
Reserve money	—	—	—	91.4	—	—	—	25.0	—	—	—
Currency outside banks	—	—	—	32.0	—	—	—	23.8	—	—	—

Source: National Bank of the Kyrgyz Republic, and International Monetary Fund staff estimates and projections.

1/ Current exchange rate.
2/ Foreign exchange assets and liabilities are valued at 17.0 soms per US dollar, and gold at US$ 350 per Troy ounce.
3/ From December 1996 onwards, incorporates a revaluation of claims and liabilities vis-à-vis other CIS countries.
4/ From December 1996 onwards, reflects the acquisition of government bonds by the NBKR as part of the restructuring of the financial sector, leading to a corresponding reduction in credit to the economy.
5/ In percent of beginning of period money stock.
a) net of budget account deposits.

Table 5. Kyrgyz Republic: Agricultural Production, 1990–1991, 1995–2001 (in thousand of tons, except when otherwise noted)

	1990	1991	1995	1996	1997	1998	1999	2000	2001
Grains	1,572.9	1,445.0	913.0	1,329.0	1,619.0	1,619.0	1,630.0	1,569.0	1,824.0
Wheat	510.0	464,9	626.0	964.0	1,274.0	1,204.0	1,109.0	1,039.0	1,191.0
Barley	631.0	596.0	159.0	166.0	152.0	162.0	180.0	150.0	140.0
Corn	406.0	364.0	116.0	182.0	171.0	228.0	308.0	338.0	443.0
Rice	2.2	2,7	7.0	9.0	12.0	11.0	15.0	19.0	17.0
Cotton	80.0	62.0	75.0	73.0	62.0	78.0	87.0	88.0	98.0
Sugarbeet	1.7	12.7	107.0	190.0	206.0	429.0	536.0	450.0	287.0
Tobacco	53.0	49.0	18.0	18.0	26.0	28.0	30.0	35.0	24.0
Vegetable oil crops	10.0	4.8	20.0	35.0	38.0	44.0	58.0	53.0	59.0
Potatoes	365.0	326.0	432.0	562.0	678.0	774.0	957.0	1,046.0	1,168.0
Vegetables	487.0	398.0	318.0	369.0	479.0	556.0	719.0	747.0	815.0
Melons	71.0	54.0	23.0	41.0	38.0	47.0	63.0	65.0	84.0
Fruits and berries	140.0	85.0	67.0	83.0	111.0	103.0	101.0	161.0	159.0
Grapes	43.0	29.0	20.0	14.0	23.0	17.0	18.0	27.0	27.0
Forage	3,588.0	3,262.0	1,009.0	734.0					
Hay	1,097.0	986.0	907.0	956.0	899.0	905.0	908.0	961.0	—
Meat (slaughtered)	254.0	229.0	180.0	186.0	186.0	191.0	196.0	196.0	197.0
Milk	1,185.0	1,131.0	864.0	885.0	912.0	973.0	1,064.0	1,105.0	1,142.0
Eggs (million)	713.0	649.0	147.0	160.0	164.0	176.0	193.0	207.0	228.0
Wool	39.0	36.0	15.0	12.0	11.0	12.0	12.0	12.0	12.0

Continued

Table 5. *Continued*

(Percentage change from previous year)

	1990	1991	1995	1996	1997	1998	1999	2000	2001
Grains		−8.1	−8.1	45.0	21.0	0.0	7.0	−3.8	16.0
Wheat		−8.9	10.0	54.0	32.0	−5.5	−7.9	−6.3	14.0
Barley		−5.6	−44.0	4.7	−8.9	6.7	11.0	16.0	−6.8
Corn		−10.0	−10.0	56.0	−6.4	33.0	35.0	9.7	30.0
Rice		22.0	71.0	37.0	27.0	−6.0	37.0	25.0	−10.0
Cotton		−22.0	39.0	−1.9	−14.0	24.0	11.0	1.2	11.0
Sugarbeet		647.0	−5.9	76.0	8.0	108.0	24.0	−16.0	−36.0
Tobacco		−8.5	−51.0	1.7	43.0	9.0	6.0	16.0	−30.0
Vegetable oil crops		−53.0	41.0	73.0	8.0	15.0	32.0	−7.8	10.0
Potatoes		−10.0	38.8	30.0	20.0	14.0	23.0	9.0	11.0
Vegetables		−18.0	20.0	16.0	30.0	16.0	29.0	3.8	9.0
Melons		−24.0	23.0	73.0	−5.0	21.0	34.0	4.0	28.0
Fruits and berries		−39.0	−15.0	22.0	33.0	−7.3	−1.7	59.0	−1.4
Grapes		−32.0	12.0	−27.0	59.0	−24.0	5.2	46.0	2.0
Forage		−9.6							
Hay		−10.0	5.8	5.4	−5.9	0.7	0.2	5.9	—
Meat (slaughtered)		−4.5	−8.8	3.1	0.2	2.8	2.3	0.3	0.3
Milk		−9.0	−0.8	2.4	3.0	6.7	9.4	3.8	3.3
Eggs (million)		−9.0	−27.0	8.8	2.7	7.3	9.8	7.5	9.8
Wool		−6.4	−30.0	−17.0	−6.6	0.9	1.7	0.0	0.0

Sources: International Monetary Fund. *Kyrgyz Republic. Selected Issues and Statistical Appendix. February 5, 2003.* Washington D.C.: IMF, 2003, p. 63. Kyrgyz Republic. Recent Economic Development, Washington D.C.: IMF, 1998, p. 93. *Sorsialno-ekonomicheskoe razvitie Kyrgyzskoi Respubliki* [Social-Economic Development of the Kyrgyz Republic]. Bishkek, 2002, p.70.
Note: Data for 1990 and 1991 given for comparison with the Soviet-era production.

Table 6. Kyrgyz Republic: Direction of Trade with CIS Countires, 1993–2002 (In millions of U.S. dollars)

	1993			1994			1995			1996		
	Imports	Exports	Trade balance	Imports	Exports	Trade balance	Imports	Exports	Trade balance	Imports	Exports	Trade balance
Total	316.6	217.5	−89.1	208.3	222.8	14.5	353.5	269.2	−84.3	484.9	393.9	−91.0
Armenia	0.3	0.1	−0.2	0.0	0.1	0.1	0.6	—	−0.6	5.6	0.2	−5.4
Azerbaijan	2.0	3.3	1.3	0.6	1.6	1.0	3.3	2.1	−1.2	3.2	2.0	−1.2
Belarus	2.9	4.5	1.6	2.5	3.8	1.2	5.0	5.0	—	8.9	8.6	−0.3
Georgia	0.6	0.3	−0.4	0.2	0.2	−0.1	0.3	0.7	0.4	1.1	1.4	0.3
Kazakhstan	90.4	67.0	−23.4	57.8	96.4	38.6	112.5	66.8	−45.7	125.7	87.9	−37.8
Moldova	0.5	1.0	0.5	0.1	0.5	0.4	0.2	1.0	0.8	0.4	1.1	0.7
Russia	147.5	105.9	−46.1	69.2	58.2	−11.0	114.3	104.8	−9.5	178.2	161.8	−16.4
Tajikistan	1.4	5.8	4.4	1.1	3.0	2.0	4.8	8.3	3.5	10.2	16.5	6.3
Turkmenistan	6.7	8.1	1.5	9.9	8.4	−1.6	18.6	2.2	−16.4	25.5	8.9	−16.6
Ukraine	6.4	13.1	6.7	3.0	9.0	6.0	4.9	8.3	3.4	7.5	10.4	2.9
Uzbekistan	54.2	22.1	−32.1	62.4	44.8	−17.6	88.9	70.0	−18.9	118.6	95.1	−23.5

Continued

Table 6. *Continued*

	1997			1998			1999			2000		
	Imports	*Exports*	*Trade balance*	*Imports*	*Exports*	*Trade balance*	*Imports*	*Exports*	*Trade balance*	*Imports*	*Exports*	*Trade balance*
Total	435.8	319.3	−116.5	440.0	230.6	−209.4	259.3	183.3	−76.0	255.6	207.4	−48.2
Armenia	0.3	0.0	−0.3	0.4	0.0	−0.4	0.0	60.1	60.1	0.0	0.9	0.9
Azerbaijan	2.5	2.8	0.3	7.2	2.6	−4.6	3.4	1.5	−1.9	2.4	4.0	1.6
Belarus	10.3	8.6	−1.7	9.6	5.3	−4.3	5.5	4.9	−0.6	3.9	3.0	−0.9
Georgia	3.1	0.6	−2.5	0.3	0.5	0.2	0.2	0.4	0.2	0.1	0.2	0.1
Kazakhstan	69.6	87.1	17.5	75.3	85.5	10.2	72.7	45.0	−27.7	57.4	33.4	−24.0
Moldova	0.4	0.0	−0.4	0.0	0.2	0.2	0.2	0.5	0.3	0.1	0.0	−0.1
Russia	174.3	98.8	−75.5	204.0	83.7	−120.3	109.4	70.7	−38.7	132.6	65.1	−67.5
Tajikistan	4.8	12.7	7.9	6.4	8.3	1.9	4.0	9.5	5.5	1.9	7.5	5.6
Turkmenistan	18.6	2.6	−16.0	8.2	1.2	−7.0	7.8	2.8	−5.0	18.7	2.7	−16.0
Ukraine	4.9	4.6	−0.3	6.9	4.7	−2.2	6.3	1.5	−4.8	7.0	1.1	−5.9
Uzbekistan	88.9	101.5	12.6	122.2	38.5	−83.7	50.0	46.6	−3.4	75.1	89.4	14.3

Source: International Monetary Fund. *Kyrgyz Republic. Selected Issues and Statistical Appendix. February 5, 2003.* Washington D.C.: IMF, 2003, p. 78

Table 7. Kyrgyz Republic: Direction of Trade with non-CIS Countries, 1994–1996 (In millions of U.S. dollars)

	1994	1995	1996	1997	1998	1999	2000	2001	2002
Exports									
Total	117.1	139.7	112.0	284.5	283.5	270.5	297.1	307.6	166.2
China	56.7	68.5	36.4	31.6	15.7	25.3	44.1	19.4	19.6
United Kingdom	29.3	27.4	5.3	1.4	1.6	12.4	18.8	14.1	0.8
United States	0.6	4.0	17.6	17.9	7.6	11.2	2.8	7.1	19.1
France	2.2	3.6	1.8	0.3	7.0	8.2	3.3	1.8	2.5
Turkey	4.0	3.2	5.3	8.0	7.4	4.6	7.2	13.8	8.0
Italy	1.8	2.9	2.5	2.6	2.6	0.3	1.0	1.4	0.7
Germany	6.4	2.1	2.9	18.1	192.2	148.2	144.6	94.4	0.9
Poland	0.6	1.3	0.5	1.4	1.0	0.5	0.9	0.4	0.1
Switzerland		1.8	0.9	162.3	1.1	18.1	34.1	124.2	82.5
Other	15.5	24.9	38.8	40.9	47.0	41.7	40.3	31.1	32.1
Imports									
Total	107.5	168.8	350.8	273.5	400.8	340.5	255.6	210.3	117.4
Turkey	14.4	38.3	47.6	43.7	37.4	23.1	26.8	15.8	8.2
Cuba	11.4	22.7	22.1	0.0	12.1	4.1	0.0	0.1	0.0
United States	3.5	19.1	35.7	39.6	40.9	54.2	53.8	26.8	16.8
Germany	6.8	18.7	31.8	38.4	53.1	47.3	25.2	24.3	12.2
Japan	2.8	7.2	12.5	2.7	4.3	12.0	10.3	5.8	2.6
China	10.8	6.3	7.8	32.5	44.4	36.9	36.9	48.5	30.1
Canada	1.6	5.9	42.5	5.2	14.4	25.4	11.3	10.9	4.2
Other	56.2	50.6	150.8	111.4	194.3	137.4	91.3	78.1	43.2

Source: International Monetary Fund. *Kyrgyz Republic. Selected Issues and Statistical Appendix. February 5, 2003.* Washington D.C.: IMF, 2003, p. 78

Table 8. Kyrgyz Republic: External Public Debt, 1994–2000 (In millions of U.S. dollars)

	1994	1995	1996	1997	1998	1999	2000	2001
Debt outstanding	413.8	584.7	752.6	904.9	1,177.5	1,358.6	1,520.3	1,441.5
Multilateral	161.5	300.9	447.5	584.3	743.2	848.2	942.8	947.1
Concessional	70.8	234.0	348.1	487.4	654.4	748.4	848.2	873.0
IDA	57.2	139.6	204.0	951.2	328.4	342.5	406.8	388.4
PRGF	13.6	60.4	83.9	127.2	139.1	159.7	163.6	167.5
Others	0.0	34.0	60.2	109.0	186.9	246.2	277.8	317.1
Non-Concessional	90.7	66.9	99.4	96.9	88.8	99.8	94.7	74.1
IMF	62.9	66.6	62.7	49.2	37.8	37.0	24.4	11.8
Others	27.8	0.3	36.7	47.7	51.0	69.1	70.3	62.3
Bilateral	253.3	283.8	305.1	320.7	434.3	510.4	577.5	494.4
CIS (non-concessional)	181.0	176.9	150.0	180.5	208.2	207.8	160.9	178.1
Non-CIS	71.3	116.3	165.4	140.2	226.0	302.6	416.6	316.0
Concessional	41.0	78.9	113.6	96.8	133.3	211.1	247.6	255.3
Non-Concessional	30.3	37.4	51.8	43.4	92.7	91.5	169.0	61.0

Disbursements	122.8	207.7	180.0	175.6	170.2	232.3	148.0	125.1
Multilateral	50.2	162.7	134.2	164.4	137.8	159.1	88.4	105.1
Concessional	50.2	162.7	117.4	162.6	130.7	136.8	80.7	104.7
IDA	36.6	82.4	57.5	65.4	68.1	21.2	34.4	26.1
PRGF	13.6	46.3	23.5	43.8	14.2	26.7	18.7	14.9
Others	0.0	34.0	36.0	53.5	48.0	88.9	27.6	63.7
Non-Concessional	0.0	0.0	16.8	1.7	7.1	22.2	7.7	0.5
IBRD	0.0	0.0	0.0	0.0	0.0	0.0	0.0	0.0
IMF	0.0	0.0	0.0	0.0	0.0	0.0	0.0	0.0
Others	0.0	0.0	16.8	1.7	7.1	22.2	7.7	0.5
Bilateral	72.6	45.0	45.8	11.2	32.5	73.3	59.5	20.0
CIS (non-concessional)	10.5	0.0	0.0	6.0	6.3	2.7	21.2	0.0
Non-CIS	62.1	45.0	31.9	45.0	45.8	5.2	26.2	70.6
Concessional	41.0	37.9	31.2	5.2	26.2	70.6	38.4	16.6
Non-Concessional	21.1	7.1	14.6	0.0	0.0	0.0	0.0	3.3
Interest payments due	17.4	22.2	18.5	20.8	24.9	19.3	23.6	23.8

Sources: Kyrgyz authorities, and Fund staff calculations.
Note: Includes only public and publicly guaranteed debt.
Source: International Monetary Fund. Kyrgyz Republic. *Selected Issues and Statistical Appendix. February 5, 2003* Washington D.C.: IMF, 2003, p. 81. Kyrgyz Republic. *Recent Economic Development.* Washington D.C.: IMF, 1998, p. 124.

Table 9. Kyrgyz Republic: Privatization by Type of Property, 1991–1999 (End-of-periods; number of enterprises)

	Initial stock	1991	1992	1993	1994	1995	1996	1997	1998	1999
Industry	602	9	118	264	324	462	484	523	527	532
Competitive bidding		0	0	0	5	9	12	12		
Sale to individual		0	0	4	10	18	18	19		
Lease with option to buy		3	7	7	7	7	8	8		
Formation of joint-stock company		5	96	201	235	339	354	360		
Auction sales		0	0	0	6	15	16	16		
Sale to labor collectives		1	10	32	38	48	49	49		
Formation of limited liability comp.		0	5	20	23	25	26	27		
Other methods		0	0	0	0	1	1	1		
Consumer services	1,919	94	1344	1840	1877	1897	1912	1918	1933	1933
Competitive bidding		7	489	524	524	526	529	529		
Sale to individual		1	408	674	696	707	712	718		
Lease with option to buy		3	13	13	14	14	16	17		
Formation of joint-stock company		1	12	33	35	36	36	36		
Auction sales		82	160	160	161	167	171	171		
Formation of limited liability comp.		0	1	7	8	8	8	8		
Sale to labor collectives		1	262	430	440	440	440	440		
Other methods		0	0	0	0	0	0	0		
Nonproductive sphere	1,253	2	5	27	225	444	463	433	453	496
Competitive bidding		0	0	0	4	5	8	8		
Sale to individual		0	0	5	18	30	37	41		
Lease with option to buy		1	1	1	1	1	2	2		
Formation of joint-stock company		1	1	2	122	311	313	313		
Auction sales		0	0	0	11	25	29	30		
Formation of limited liability comp.		0	0	3	48	48	48	48		
Sale to labor collectives		0	3	16	21	24	26	28		
Other methods		0	0	0	0	0	0	0		

									1891	1896
Trade and catering — 1,945	60	905	1631	1750	1799	1880	1882		1891	1896
Competitive bidding	4	342	513	537	542	577	582			
Sale to individual	0	110	242	272	289	300	307			
Lease with option to buy	0	38	38	38	38	41	41			
Formation of joint-stock company	2	75	202	210	212	213	213			
Formation of limited liability comp.	0	5	45	51	52	52	52			
Auction sales	54	94	94	101	120	149	151			
Sale to labor collectives	0	241	497	541	546	548	549			
Other methods	0	0	0	0	0	0	0			
Agriculture — 855.0	0	59	233	320	343	353	354		359	362
Competitive bidding	0	1	1	1	1	1	1			
Sale to individual	0	5	12	23	28	30	30			
Lease with option to buy	0	3	3	3	3	3	3			
Formation of joint-stock company	0	16	66	113	122	125	126			
Formation of limited liability comp.	0	1	4	7	8	8	8			
Auction sales	0	0	0	1	3	6	6			
Sale to labor collectives	0	33	147	172	178	180	180			
Other methods	0	0	0	0	0	0	0			
Construction — 730.0	10	80	233	318	391	413	417		420	425
Competitive bidding	5	0	1	1	3	3	3			
Sale to individual	0	1	5	7	10	13	13			
Lease with option to buy	0	2	2	2	2	2	2			
Formation of joint-stock company	5	55	166	226	282	294	298			
Formation of limited liability comp.	0	1	9	18	21	22	22			
Auction sales	0	0	0	2	7	11	11			
Sale to labor collectives	0	21	50	62	66	68	68			
Other methods	0	0	0	0	0	0	0			

Continued

Table 9. *Continued*

Transport	295.0	0	18	30	101	134	141	159	163	165
Competitive bidding		0	0	0	0	0	0	0		
Sale to individual		0	0	0	2	2	3	3		
Lease with option to buy		0	0	0	0	0	0	0		
Formation of joint-stock company		0	18	70	88	120	125	136		
Formation of limited liability comp.		0	0	4	4	4	4	4		
Sale to labor collectives		0	0	6	7	8	9	10		
Other methods		0	0	0	0	0	0	0		
Other branches	2,390	4	31	149	269	451	589	665	780	867
Competitive bidding		2	6	17	16	22	28	28		
Sale to individual		0	0	18	53	133	165	169		
Lease with option to buy		1	2	2	2	9	24	25		
Formation of joint-stock company		0	1	9	15	17	24	24		
Formation of limited liability comp.		1	16	38	48	55	90	91		
Auction sales		0	0	0	8	51	75	77		
Sale to labor collectives		0	6	65	124	164	183	191		
Other methods		0	0	0	0	0	0	1		
Total 1/	9,989	174	2560	4457	5,184	5,921	6,235	6,305	6,526	6,676

Source: Kyrgyz authorities
International Monetary Fund. *Kyrgyz Republic. Selected Issues and Statistical Appendix. February 5, 2003.* Washington, D.C.: IMF, 2003, p. 72.
1/ Excluding privatized housing.

Table 10. Kyrgyz Republic: Output of Selected Industrial and Manufacturing Production, 1989–2002

	1989	1990	1991	1995	1996	1997	1998	1999	2000	2001
Coal	3,997.0	3,742.0	3,473.0	463.0	410.0	522.0	433.0	417.0	425.0	475.0
Oil (thousands tons)	165.0	155.0	143.0	89.0	84.0	85.0	77.0	77.0	77.0	76.0
Natural gas (million m3)	105.0	96.0	83.0	36.0	26.0	24.0	18.0	25.0	32.0	33.0
Electric engines (thousands)	327.0	275.0	235.0	49.0	44.0	27.0	14.0	1.0	0.8	1.0
Steel cutting machines	1,311	1,342	1,142	27	17	44	12	—	3	0
Stamping machines	335	317	324	—	2	10	35	14	6	0
Centrifugal pumps (thousands)	51	49	45	12	7	5	2	0.7	0.7	1
Trucks (,000)	24	25	24	8	1	12	0	0	0	0
Hay-compacting machines (thousands)	25	23	20	—	17	—	13	6	0	0
Cement (thousands tons)	1,408.0	1,387.0	1,320.0	310.0	546.0	658.0	709.0	386.0	453.0	469.0
Window glass (millon m2)	8.0	1.0	—	2.0	3.0	2.0	2.0	1.0	0.0	0.0
Roofing sheets (million pieces)	174.0	178.0	175.0	66.0	102.0	129.0	150.0	132.0	138.0	168.0
Rugs (thousands m2)	1,955.0	2,004.0	1,661.0	979.0	768.0	326.0	121.0	33.0	22.0	18.0
Textile (million m2)	—	134.6	142.0	23.1	29.2	25.1	16.7	14.0	8.7	8.0
Knitted fabrics (million pieces)	—	19.0	19.0	1.4	1.0	—	—	—	—	—
Shoes (millions)	—	11.1	9.5	0.7	0.6	0.4	0.2	0.1	0.1	0.19
Stockings and socks (millions)	—	33.5	26.5	8.8	12.6	7.4	5.4	4.1	3.6	4.1
Washing machines (thousands)	234.0	234.0	209.0	4.0	3.0	2.0	0.1	0.0	0.0	0.0
Light bulbs (millions)		320.0	299.0	138.0	157.0	180.0	200.0	213.0	232.0	253.0

Source: International Monetary Fund. Kyrgyz Republic. Selected Issues and Statistical Appendix. February 5, 2003. Washington D.C.: IMF, 2003, p. 63. Kyrgyz Republic. Recent Economic Development, Washington D.C.: IMF, 1998, p. 93.

Table 11. Ethnic Trends in Kyrgyzstan (in thousands)

Ethnic group	1926 No. and %	1959 No. and %	1970 No. and %	1989 No. and %	1998* No. and %	2001 No. and %
Kyrgyzs	661.1 (66.7%)	836.8 (40.5%)	1284.7 (43.8%)	2229.6 (52.3%)	2836.8 (61.2%)	3278.8 (66.3%)
Russians	116.4 (11.7%)	623.5 (30.1%)	855.9 (29.2%)	916.5 (21.5%)	690.9 (14.9%)	552.7 (11.2%)
Ukrainians	64.1 (6.4%)	137.0 (6.6%)	120.0 (4.1%)	108.0 (2.5%)	69.0 (1.5%)	41.6 (0.8%)
Uzbeks	109.7 (11.1%)	218.8 (10.5%)	332.9 (11.3%)	550.0 (12.9%)	666.3 (14.4%)	694.0 (14.0%)
Kazakhs	1.7 (0.2%)	20.0 (0.9%)	21.9 (0.7%)	37.3 (0.9%)	42.8 (0.92%)	42.4 (0.9%)
Tatars	4.9 (0.5%)	56.2 (2.7%)	68.8 (2.3%)	70.0 (1.6%)	58.2 (1.3%)	41.9 (0.9%)
Germans	4.2 (0.4%)	39.9 (1.9%)	89.8 (3.0%)	101.3 (2.3%)	15.3 (0.3%)	16.7 (0.3%)
Others	(3.0%)	(6.8%)	(5.6%)	(6.0%)	(5.7%)	(5.6%)
Total	989.9 (100%)	2066.1 (100%)	2933.2 (100%)	4257.7 (100%)	4634.9 (100%)	4946.5 (100%)

* As of 1 January 1998.

Table 12. The Kyrgyz Republic: Employment of Population by Sector. (In thousands)

	1987	1988	1989	1990	1991	1992	1993	1994	1995	1996	1997	1998	1999
TOTAL	1702.7	1716.1	1738.9	1747.9	1754.1	1835.9	1680.6	1645.4	1641.7	1650	1,689	1,705	1,764
Agriculture	577.2	577.2	577.2	577.2	622.7	700.6	655.4	690.8	776.4	811.8	816	837	924
Mining	21.5	22.7	22.8	23.4	15.4	15.8	14.9	13.5	10.2	10.0	—	—	—
Manufacturing	266.4	262.5	256.3	254.7	215.9	203.6	178.6	158.2	128.4	126.5			
Electricity, gas & water supply	7.3	7.0	7.6	9.3	11.1	13.6	14.0	14.4	15.2	14.2			
Construction	123.8	126.5	151.5	152.8	147.0	114.2	89.4	77.0	65.7	63.7	57	51	45
Wholesale and Retail trade	57.0	58.0	58.1	59.1	59.2	70.6	55.9	—	—	—			
Wholesale & hotels	—	—	—	—	—	—	—	113.0	103.8	109.4	—	—	—
Hotels and restaurants	27.5	28.0	27.3	28.0	27.6	16.2	13.4						
Transport & communication	117.8	110.8	95.2	94.0	93.4	94.0	86.3	85.0	76.4	74.0	79	75	66
Financial intermediation	6.6	6.4	7.0	7.0	7.2	7.9	8.5	8.0	7.0	6.7			
Real estate & business activity	29.4	28.6	28.8	29.4	22.0	17.2	12.8	9.0	8.2	8.0			
Public administration & defense	46.2	44.8	41.5	42.5	36.6	54.2	56.0	58.0	56.9	53.1			
Education	185.6	194.8	204.6	215.5	212.5	216.5	198.9	169.0	155.9	151.0			
Health & Social work	91.1	95.4	101.3	104.6	107.4	142.4	124.7	102.0	101.3	98.1			
Other social activities	43.8	45.2	47.8	45.3	43.8	42.1	35.8	33.0	27.7	26.9			
Not classified by economic activities	101.5	107.9	112.5	112.0	132.3	127.0	135.9	113.6	105.9	96.6	—	—	—

Source: International Labour Organisation. *ILO Yearbook of Labour Statistics 1997.* Geneva: IOL. 1997. pp. 131–132.

Table 13.   Kyrgyz AO, Kyrgyz ASSR, and Kyrgyz SSR

Government

1 Feb 1926	Kyrgyz ASSR formed within Russian SFSR
5 Dec 1936	becomes Kyrgyz SSR

In Power	Name	Born and Died
First Secretaries of the Communist Party		
23 Apr 1937–7 Nov 1937	Maksim Kirovich Ammosov	1897–1938
	(acting to 16/17 Jun 1937)	
20 Feb 1938–Jul 1945	Aleksey Vlasovich Vagov	1905–1971
	(acting to 16 Jul 1938)	
Jul 1945–7 Jul 1950	Nikolay Semyonovich Bogolyubov	
7 Jul 1950–9 May 1961	Izkhak Razzakovich Razzakov	1910–1979
9 May 1961–2 Nov 1985	Turdakun Usubaliyevich Usubaliyev	b. 1919
2 Nov 1985–6 Apr 1991	Absamat Masaliyevich Masaliyev	b. 1933
6 Apr 1991–	Jumgalbek Beksultanovich Amanbayev	b. 1945

Chairmen of the Central Executive Committee

12 Mar 1927–16 Sep 1937	Abdukadyr Urazbekov	1889–1938
16 Sep 1937– 4 Oct 1937	Mikhail Ivanovich Us (acting)	
4 Oct 1937–16 Dec 1937	Sultankul Shamurzin (acting)	1906–1938
16 Dec 1937–15 Feb 1938	Ivan Fyodorovich Sokolov (acting)	
15 Feb 1938–15 May 1938	Murat Salikhov (acting)	1905–1938
15 May 1938–18 Jul 1938	Kalima Amankulova (f) (acting)	

Chairman of the Supreme Soviet

18 Jul 1938–19 Jul 1938	L. P. Boryak

Chairmen of the Presidium of the Supreme Soviet

19 Jul 1938–22 Mar 1943	Asanaly Tolubayev	
22 Mar 1943–14 Nov 1945	Moldogazy Tokobayev	1905–1974
14 Nov 1945–25 Aug 1978	Turabay Kulatovich Kulatov	1908–1984
25 Aug 1978–22 Dec 1978	Sultan Ibraimovich Ibraimov	1927–1980
22 Dec 1978–10 Jan 1979	Andrey Andreyevich Buss (acting)	1911–1980
10 Jan 1979–14 Jan 1981	Arslanbek Duysheyevich Duysheyev	b. 1933
14 Jan 1981– 8 Aug 1987	Temirbek Khudaybergenovich Koshoyev	b.1931
8 Aug 1987–10 Apr 1990	Tashtanbek Akmatovich Akmatov	b. 1938

Chairman of the Supreme Soviet

10 Apr 1990–27 Oct 1990	Absamat Masaliyevich Masaliyev (s.a.)

Chairmen of the Council of People's Commissars
(from 29 Mar 1946, Chairmen of the Council of Ministers)

12 Mar 1927–Sep 1933	Yusup Abdrakhmanov	1901/04–1938
27 Sep 1933–8 Sep 1937	Bayaly Dekombayevich Isakeyev	1897–1938
8 Sep 1937–15 Feb 1938	Murat Salikhov (s.a.)	
Fe/Mr 1938–27 Apr 1938	Ismail Khasyanovich Abuzyarov (acting)	
27 Apr 1938–19 Jul 1938	Ivan Pavlovich Rebrov (acting)	

In Power	Name	Born and Died
20 Jul 1938–14 Nov 1945	Turabay Kulatovich Kulatov (s.a.)	
14 Nov 1945–10 Jul 1950	Izkhak Razzakovich Razzakov (s.a.)	
10 Jul 1950– 6 Mar 1958	Abdy Suyerkulovich Suyerkulov	b. 1912
6 Mar 1958–10 May 1961	Kazy Dikambayevich Dikambayev	b. 1913
10 May 1961–23 Jan 1968	Bolot Mambetovich Mambetov	1907–1990
23 Jan 1968–22 Dec 1978	Akhmatbek Suttubayevich Suyumbayev	1920–1993
22 Dec 1978– 4 Dec 1980	Sultan Ibraimovich Ibraimov (s.a.)	
4 Dec 1980–14 Jan 1981	Pyotr M. Khodos (acting)	
14 Jan 1981–20 May 1986	Arslanbek Duysheyevich Duysheyev (s.a.)	
20 May 1986–21 Jan 1991	Apas Jumagulovich Jumagulov	b. 1934

Kyrgyzstan Prime Ministers (all non-party)

21 Jan 1991–29 Nov 1991	Nasirdin Isanov	1943–1991
29 Nov 1991–10 Feb 1992	State Secretaries of the Cabinet of Ministers:	
	Andrey Andreyevich Yordan	b. 1934
	(signed most documents on behalf	
	of government)	
	Turar Koychuyevich Koychuyev	
	Esenbek Duysheyevich Duysheyev	
	Yan Yefimovich Fisher	
	Amangeldy Mursadykovich Muraliyev	
	(acting)	b. 1947
10 Feb 1992–13 Dec 1993	Tursunbek Chyngyshevich Chyngyshev	b. 1942
	(acting to 26 Feb 1992)	
13 Dec 1993–14 Dec 1994	Almanbet Matubraimov (acting)	b. 1952
14 Dec 1993–24 Mar 1998	Apas Jumagulovich Jumagulov	b. 1934
24 Mar 1998–23 Dec 1998	Kubanychbek Myrzabekovich Jumaliyev	b. 1956
	(acting to 25 Mar 1998)	
23 Dec 1998–25 Dec 1998	Boris Ivanovich Silayev (first time) (acting)	b. 1945
25 Dec 1998– 4 Apr 1999	Jumabek Ibraimovich Ibraimov	1944–1999
4 Apr 1999–12 Apr 1999	Boris Ivanovich Silayev (second time)	
	(s.a.) (acting)	
12 Apr 1999–21 Dec 2000	Amangeldy Mursadykovich Muraliyev (s.a.)	
	(acting to 21 Apr 1999; and from	
	11 Dec 2000)	
21 Dec 2000–22 May 2002	Kurmanbek Saliyevich Bakiyev	b. 1949
22 May 2002–	Nikolay Timofeyevich Tanayev	b. 1945
	(acting to 30 May 2002)	

Bibliography

This is a selected bibliography of major modern writing on Kyrgyzstan and the Kyrgyzs. The fascinating history of this land attracted a number of scholars who tried to understand and describe the complex and rich history of this part of the world. However, it was the 19th-century Anglo-Russian competition, known as the "Great Game," and British and Russian advances into the Central Asian region that promoted scholarly studies of this land and its peoples in the West. During the 19th century a number of scholars, geographers, military cartographers, and simply adventurers traveled through the mysterious Kyrgyz land putting on the world's map the latest geographical details of one of the last "terra incognita" unexplored by Western scholars. Yet most of the works were devoted to the Central Asian region per se but very seldom specifically to the Kyrgyz land and Kyrgyz people.

Although a number of studies on Central Asian history, which included the history of the Kyrgyz people, appeared in the late 18th and early 19th centuries, probably the most comprehensive work on the Kyrgyz people was done by Russian monk and diplomat Nikita Bichurin (1777–1853) called *Sobraniye svedenii o narodakh, obitavshikh v Srednei Azii v drevniye vremena* [Collection of Resources about People, who Lived in Central Asia in Ancient Times] (1851). His works largely relied on thoroughly recorded Chinese sources and chronologies, which covered nearly two thousand years of the history of the nomadic regions northwest and west of the Chinese Empire. Another researcher, Arthur Conolly, who traveled through Central Asia in the early 19th century, published his book *Journey to the North of India, Overland from Russia, Persia and Afghanistan* (1838), which described customs and tradition of various people, including the Kyrgyzs.

In the middle of the 19th century the interest in the Kyrgyz region increased, as the Russians were advancing into this part of Central

Asia. During this time Chokan Valikhanov (1835–65), a Kazakh military officer in Russian service, completed several trips to northern Kyrgyzstan describing traditions, cultures, and political and economic development. His comprehensive written works, which include the article *Kirgizy* (Kyrgyzs) (1858), covered not only the contemporary situation in the area but also attempted to describe the history of the Kyrgyz people as it was kept in the people's memory. Several other expeditions to Central Asia were led by the naturalist Petr Semenov-Tianshanskii (1827–1914). The expeditions produced maps of the Tian-Shan and Pamir mountain ranges and collected materials about cultural and political developments in the region. He also was a key figure in planning and organizing the first Russian census in 1897, which covered the Kyrgyzs as well. Semenov produced interesting observations about the Kyrgyz land in his *Travels in the Tian'-Shan' 1856–1857.*

Meanwhile, in the second half of the 19th century the Russians sent several expeditions that had the specific purpose of studying Kyrgyz history and geography and collecting historical materials, including archeological artifacts, various documents, and narratives. The Russian scholars F. Poyarkov, H. Pantusov, and N. Veselovskii published numerous articles and reports on their findings. Among works published during this period was V. Nalivkin's *Kratkaya istoria Kokandskogo Khanstva* [The Concise History of the Kokand Khanate] (1885), which covered the political history of the Kyrgyz land in the 18th and 19th centuries. At the same time several books in English appeared in the West with not only narratives of travels, such as *Turkistan. Notes of a Journey in Russian Turkistan, Khokand, Bukhara and Kuldja* (1876) by E. Schuyler, but also with a detailed history of the region such as *The Heart of Asia. A History of Russian Turkestan and the Central Asian Khanates from Earliest Times* (1893) by F. Skrine and E. Ross.

In the late 19th and early 20th centuries the Russian school of oriental studies gathered momentum and produced much acclaimed and internationally recognized works on Central Asian history, including the history of the Kyrgyzs. The representatives of this school published very comprehensive historical research, which became classics of Russian orientalism. Among others, the famous Russian orientalist-turkologist Vasilii Radlow (1837–1918) published his *Narechiye dikokamennykh*

Kirgizov [The Dialect of the Wild-Stone Kyrgyzs] (1885) and some others. The Russian orientalist Vasilii Bartold (1869–1930) published his *Ocherk istorii Semirechya* [Essay on the History of Semirechie] (1898) and also *Kirgizy. Istoricheskii ocherk* [The Kyrgyz. A Historical Essay] (1927).

The Bolshevik revolution and especially the state delimitation in 1922–24 had a far-reaching impact on the study of the history of the Kyrgyz and the Kyrgyz land. Although initially historical studies absorbed the best traditions of the tsarist Imperial school of oriental studies, it became highly politicized and often heavily censored. It also had to justify and "scientifically" endorse the state delimitation in the region and creation of the Kirgiz Soviet Autonomous *Oblast* (Republic since 1926). Historical research on Kyrgyzstan often focus on the history of the Communist Party, civil war, and peasant movements and they often were a part of Soviet propaganda rather than scholarly studies.

Nevertheless, several scholars, especially from Leningrad (now Saint Petersburg) continued serious historical studies of the ancient and medieval past and culture, and conducted archeological excavations and ethnological studies. The Russian historian Aleksandr Bernsh'tam led several expeditions to Kyrgyzstan in the 1930s and 1940s and published a series of works based on the archeological findings. These included his books *Kultura drevnego Kirgizstana* [The Culture of the Ancient Kyrgyzstan] (1942) and *Architechturnye pamiatniki Kirgizii* [Architectural Monuments of Kyrgyzstan] (1950).

With the coming of the "iron curtain" in the 1930s, Western academia was severely limited in its access to historical data and archival documents in Kyrgyzstan. Yet several Western scholars continued their research on the history and culture of the Kyrgyz.

By the middle of the 20th century, however, a new native school of historians began to emerge. This development was particularly facilitated by the establishment of Kyrgyzstan's branch of the Academy of Science of the USSR in 1943. In 1956 a team of local scholars produced the first comprehensive work *Istoria Kirgizii* [The History of Kyrgyzstan], which covered the history of the Kyrgyz and Kyrgyz land from ancient times to the Soviet era. Yet highly politicized issues, such as the history of the Kyrgyz in the 18th and 19th centuries, the riot of 1916 in Turkistan, the Bolshevik revolution, the civil war, and collectivization, were covered very selectively or were hugely distorted. During this era a large number of books were published on the history of the Communist Party of Kyrgyzstan, most of them artificially constructed and heavily overloaded by Soviet propaganda.

Between 1967 and 1968 a team of Kyrgyzstan scholars produced *Istoria Kirgizskoi SSR* [The History of the Kyrgyz SSR], which presented a slightly different interpretation of Kyrgyz history. Again many topics, like history of the Russian advance into the Kyrgyz land, Stalin's purges, and many others, were covered selectively or not covered at all, although the work introduced some new archeological and archival findings and reinterpretation of certain events in the distant historical past.

Despite a definite stagnation of historical studies in Kyrgyzstan and in the Soviet Union in the 1970s, there were notable exceptions. In 1971 Semen Abramzon published his seminal *Kyrgyzy i ikh etnogeneticheskie i istoriko-kulturnye sviazi* [The Kyrgyzs and their Ethnological and Historical-Cultural Relations], which represented the best traditions of the Russian school of oriental studies. The book comprehensively assessed the historical and cultural development of the Kyrgyzs from ancient times to the modern era, but some ideas of the publication were considered at odd with the official Soviet interpretation of the history and too controversial. Therefore for almost a decade it remained outside of the mainstream of historical thought in Kyrgyzstan.

The Kyrgyz Academy of Science published three volumes of *Istoria Kirgizskoi SSR* [The History of the Kyrgyz SSR] between 1984 and 1986. However, the work prepared on the eve of Mikhail Gorbachev's *perestroika* was written in the old Soviet traditions and it avoided or simply ignored many issues in the history of the Kyrgyzs, especially in the 20th century. The publication was heavily inflated by numerous references to Soviet Marxist ideology and reinforced the official interpretation of the 19th- and 20th-century history of the Kyrgyzs and the Kyrgyz land. In the 1970s the "Kyrgyz Encyclopedia" publishing house produced six volumes of *Kyrgyz Soviet Encyclopediasy* [The Kyrgyz Soviet Encyclopedia] in Kyrgyz. In 1982 the encyclopedia *Kirgizskaia Sovetskaia Socialisticheskaia Respublika: Entsyklopedia* [The Kyrgyz Soviet Socialist Republic: Encyclopedia] was published in Kyrgyz and Russian. These two publications still remain among the most comprehensive reference works on Soviet Kyrgyzstan.

During the Gorbachev era and especially after Kyrgyzstan's independence there was a surge in research and publications on the history of the Kyrgyzs and Kyrgyz land. This time the Kyrgyz and foreign scholars have received wide access to the Kyrgyz national and party archives and they were able to discuss many issues that previously had not been discussed, including the tsarist policies in this part of the world in the late 19th and early 20th centuries, noncommunist political thought of the early 20th century, the history of the Basmachi movement, and the Stalin purges. Yet the monumental *Istoria Kyrgyzov i Kyrgyzstana* [The History of the Kyrgyzs and Kyrgyzstan] (2000) continued the established tradition in covering ancient and medieval history, though the history of the Soviet era was heavily rewritten and the Soviet phraseology was fully eliminated.

After independence Kyrgyz publishers began to publish a wide range of books, including encyclopedic series, specialized books on Kyrgyz culture, especially on the epic *Manas*, as well as numerous books on various historical topics. There were several scholarly publications, which are apart from the history books written for the general public. The Kyrgyz government sponsored the publication of the epic *Manas* both in Kyrgyz and English, and *Manas Entsyklopediasy* [Encyclopedia of *Manas*] in two volumes (1995). Between 1994 and 1996 the Kyrgyz Encyclopedia Publishing House also published a series of encyclopedias covering major Kyrgyzstan *oblasts: Talas Oblusu, Isyk Kol Oblusu, Chui Oblusu,* and so on in Kyrgyz, with some sections translated into Russian and English. In 2001 the Center for Kyrgyz Language and Encyclopedia published the first post-Soviet encyclopedia *Kyrgyzstan: Entsyklopedia* [Kyrgyzstan: Encyclopedia] in both Kyrgyz and Russian.

Since Kyrgyzstan's independence many new sources have become available to international scholars and a number of publications on Kyrgyz history appeared in the West in English. In 1993 the World Bank produced a comprehensive report on Kyrgyzstan's economy *Kyrgyzstan: The Transition to a Market Economy.* In 1999 John Anderson published his *Kyrgyzstan: Central Asia's Island of Democracy?* Collections of documents on Central Asia, which included a large section on Kyrgyzstan, were published by M.E. Sharpe in *The Soviet*

Multinational State: Readings and Documents in 1990 and *Russia and the Commonwealth of Independent States: Documents, Data, and Analysis* in 1996. In 2002 a comprehensive illustrated guidebook, *Kyrgyzstan*, was published by the Odyssey Publications.

There are several annual publications that cover the postindependence history of the republic. The most authoritative are the annual *Kyrgyzstan: Human Development Report* sponsored by the United Nations Development Program (UNDP), *The Kyrgyz Republic: Recent Economic Development* published by the International Monetary Fund (IMF) (semiannually, Washington, D.C.), *The Kyrgyz Statistical Annual Books* published in Kyrgyz, Russian, and frequently in English by the National Statistical Committee (quarterly, Bishkek), the *Kyrgyz Republic* published by the Economist Intelligence Unit (London), and *Kyrgyz Republic* published by Freedom House's project Nations in Transit (Washington, D.C.).

Major collections of historical documents on Kyrgyzstan may be found at the National Archive of the Kyrgyz Republic, the Central Archive of Political Documentation and other major archives. The most comprehensive and systematically organized collections of books, periodicals, and documents are to be found in the Central Library, in the library of the Academy of Science, and in the library of the Kyrgyz State National University. The National Statistical Committee has a substantial archive of the statistical materials. All collections are open to the public, although the authorities may impose some limitations on foreign users, especially on access to classified publications marked *"dlia sluzhebnogo polzovaniya"* [for restricted use only]. Several small but noteworthy collections can also be found overseas: at Indiana University, University of Washington, and the School of Oriental and African Studies Library in London.

For people who research the current history and political development of Kyrgyzstan, several media outlets have become available on the Internet, including all major magazines and newspapers in Russian, some major newspapers in Kyrgyz, and locally produced newspapers in English. For example, *The Times of Central Asia* (its predecessor was *The Central Asian Post*) is published in English and available both in a hard copy version and online. Major laws and legal documents have also become available on the Internet through numerous projects sponsored by the TACIS, Soros Foundation, USAID, and other sources.

CONTENTS

GENERAL

Websites

The major websites on Kyrgyzstan are:

Embassy of Kyrgyzstan to the U.S. and Canada	http://www.kyrgyzstan.org/
Gateway Kyrgyzstan	http://eng.gateway.kg/
Government of Kyrgyzstan	http://www.gov.kg/
International Crisis Group	http://www.crisisweb.org/
Kabar News Agency	http://www.kabar.kg
President of Kyrgyzstan	http://www.president.kg/
Parliament of Kyrgyzstan	http://www.kenesh.gov.kg/
Soros Foundation Kyrgyzstan	http://www.soros.kg/
The Times of Central Asia	http://www.times.kg
Vechernyi Bishkek (Daily newspaper in Russian)	http://vb.kyrnet.kg/
UNDP Kyrgyzstan	http://www.undp.kg
UN in Kyrgyzstan	http://www.un.org.kg

Annual Reports and Yearbooks

Kyrgyz Republic. Human Development Report. Bishkek: United Nations Development Program (annually from 1995 onward).

The Kyrgyz Republic. London: The Economist Intelligence Unit (quarterly from 1992 onward).

"The Kyrgyz Republic." *Freedom in the World: The Annual Survey of Political Rights and Civil Liberties.* Piscataway, N.J.: Transaction Publishers (annually from 1992 onward).

"The Kyrgyz Republic." In *Nations in Transit.* Washington, D.C.: Freedom House (annually).

The Kyrgyz Republic: Recent Economic Development. Washington, D.C.: International Monetary Fund, 1995; 1996; 1998; 1999; 2000.

"Kyrgyzstan." In *Europa World Yearbook.* London: Europa Publications (annually).

United Nations Development Program. *Human Development under Transition: Europe and CIS.* Bishkek: United Nations Development Program (semi-annually).

Bibliography

Allworth, Edward. *Soviet Asia Bibliographies: A Compilation of Social Science and Humanities Sources on the Iranian, Mongolian, and Turkic Nationalities, with an Essay on the Soviet-Asian Controversy.* New York: Praeger, 1975.

Astaf´eva, A. L. *Istoriia Kirgizii v zarubezhnoi pechati: Period s drevneishikh vremen do 1917 g.: bibliograficheskii ukazatel* [History of Kyrgyzstan in the Foreign Press: From the Ancient Times to 1917: Bibliographical Reference Book]. Frunze: [s.n.], 1985.

Beishekeev, Namasbek. *Kirgizskii iazyk: Bibliograficheskii ukazatel, 1960–1970 gg.* [The Kyrgyz Language: Bibliographical Reference Book: 1960–1970]. Frunze: Ilim, 1985.

Bregel, Yuri (ed.). *Bibliography of Islamic Central Asia.* Three volumes. Bloomington, Ind.: Research Institute for Inner Asian Studies, 1995.

Kyrgyz Respublikasynyn Basma Soz Zhylnaamasy [The Chronicles of the Kyrgyz Press]. (annual publication).

Ploskikh, V. M. et al. *Istochnikovedenie Kyrgyzstana: s drevnosti do XIX v* [Historical Sources on Kyrgyzstan: From Ancient Times to the 20th Century]. Bishkek: Ilim, 1996.

Ploskikh, V. M. et al. (ed.). *Trudy kirgizskikh istorikov, 1975–1980 gg.: Referativnyi sbornik* [Works of Kyrgyz Historians, 1975–1980]. Frunze: Ilim, 1985.

Tchoroev, Tyntchtykbek. "Historiography of post-Soviet Kyrgyzstan." *International Journal of Middle East Studies*, vol. 34, no. 2 (May 2002): 351–375.

Dictionaries

Abduldaev, E. et al. (ed.). *Kyrgyz tilinin frazeologiialyk sozdugu* [Kyrgyz Language Phrase Dictionary]. Frunze: Ilym, 1980.

Alieva, V. *Arkhitektura terminderinin oruscha-kyrgyzcha sozdugu, Russko-kirgizskii terminologicheskii slovar´ po arkhitekture* [Russian-Kyrgyz Dictionary of the Architectural Terms]. Frunze: Ilim, 1983.

Iudakhin, K. K. *Kirgizsko-russkii slovar (Kïrgïzcha-oruscha sözdük)* [Kyrgyz-Russian Dictionary]. Two volumes. Frunze: Glavnaia Redaktsiia Kirgizskoi Sovetskoi Entsiklopedii, 1985.

———. *Kirgizsko-russkii slovar (Kïrgïzcha-oruscha sözdük)* [Kyrgyz-Russian Dictionary]. Moscow: Sovetskaia Entsiklopediia, 1965.

Krippes, Karl A. *Kyrgyz: Kyrgyz-English/English-Kyrgyz Dictionary: Glossary of Terms.* New York: Hippocrene Books, 1998a.

———. *Kyrgyz-English Dictionary.* Kensington, Md.: Dunwoody Press, 1998b.

Musaeva, V. I., and E. K. Tashbaltaeva. *Kirgizsko-russkii i russko-kirgizskii slovar* [Kyrgyz-Russian and Russian-Kyrgyz Dictionary]. Bishkek: Raritet Info, 1999.

Oztopcu, Kurtulus. *Dictionary of Turkic Languages: English, Azerbaijani, Kazakh, Kyrgyz, Tatar, Turkish, Turkmen, Uighur, Uzbek.* London: Routledge, 1996.

Shambaev, Syrgabek and Dzholdosh Dzhusaev. *Kyrgyzcha-oruscha-anglische sozduk* [Kyrgyz-Russian-English Phrasebook]. Bishkek: Kyrgyzstan, 1994.

Shambaev, Syrgabek, Suiunbaeva Galia Dushombievna, and Zholdoshbekov Abdykerim. *Kyrgyzcha-oruscha-nemetsche sozduk* [Kyrgyz-Russian-German Phrase Book]. Frunze: Mektep, 1977.

Urstanbekov, B. U. and T. K. Choroyev. *Kyrgyz tarykhy: Kyskacha Entsyklopedialyk Sozduk.* [The Kyrgyz History: Concise Encyclopedic Dictionary]. Frunze: Kyrgyz Soviet Encyclopedianyn Bashky Redaktsiiasy, 1990.

Encyclopedias and Reference Books

Akiner, Shirin. *Islamic People of the Soviet Union.* London: Kegan Paul International, 1983.

Curtis, Glen (ed.). *Kazakhstan, Kyrgyzstan, Tajikistan, Turkmenistan, and Uzbekistan: Country Studies (Area Handbook Series).* Washington, D.C.: Federal Research Division, Library of Congress, 1997.

Encyclopedia of Nationalism: Leaders, Movements and Concepts. Vol. Two. San Francisco: Academic Press, 2001.

Isyk-Kol Oblusu: Entsyklopedia [Isyk-Kol *Oblast*: Encyclopedia]. Bishkek: Kyrgyz Entsyklopediasynyn Bashky Redakcyasy, 1995.

Kambaraly, Botoiarov, Raisa Momunbaeva, B. Ryspaev et al. *Pisateli Sovetskogo Kirgizstana: spravochnik* [Writers of Soviet Kyrgyzstan: Reference Book]. Frunze: Adabiiat, 1989.

Katz, Zev (ed.). *Handbook of Major Soviet Nationalities.* New York: Free Press, 1975.

Kirgizskaia Sovetskaia Socialisticheskaia Respublika: Entsyklopedia [Kyrgyz Soviet Socialist Republic: Encyclopedia]. Frunze: Kirgizskaya Entsiklopedia, 1982.

Kyrgyz Soviet Entsyclopediasy [Kyrgyz Soviet Encyclopedia]. Six vols. Frunze: Kyrgyz Soviet Encyclopedianyn Bashky Redaktsiiasy, 1976.

Kyrgyzstan: Entsyklopedia [Kyrgyzstan: Encyclopedia]. Bishkek: Kirgizskaya Entsiklopedia, 2001.

Manas Entsyklopediasy [Encyclopedia of Manas]. Two vols. Bishkek: Kyrgyz Entsyklopediasynyn Bashky Redakcyasy, 1995.

The Supplement to the Modern Encyclopedia of Russian, Soviet, and Eurasian History. Gulf Breeze, Fla.: Academic International Press, 1995–2003.

Readers and Collections of Documents

Akayev, A. *21 kylymda Kyrgyzstanda sotsialdyk cheirenu enekturuu modeli* [The Model of Social Development of Kyrgyzstan on the Eve of the 21st Century]. Bishkek: Uchkun, 1998a.

———. *Diplomacy of the Silk Road* (official document). Bishkek: Ministry of Foreign Affairs, 1998b.

Baktygulov, Dzh. S., et al. (ed.). *Sovetskii Kirgizstan v dokumentakh, 1917–1967* [Soviet Kyrgyzstan in Documents]. Frunze: Kyrgyzstan, 1983.

Brzezinski, Zbignev, and Paige Sullivan (eds.). *Russia and the Commonwealth of Independent States: Documents, Data and Analysis.* New York: M.E. Sharpe, 1996.

Hebert, Raymond J., and Nicholas Poppe. *Kirghiz Manual.* Bloomington: Indiana University Press, 1963.

Hu, Chen-hua, and Guy Imart. *A Kirghiz Reader.* Bloomington: Indiana University, Research Institute for Inner Asian Studies, 1989.

Kyrgyz Respublikasynyn Konstitutsiasy [The Constitution of the Kyrgyz Republic]. Bishkek: Uchkun, 1996.

Olcott, M., (ed.). *The Soviet Multinational State: Readings and Documents.* Armonk, N.Y.: M. E. Sharpe, 1990.

Paksoy, H. B., (ed.). *Central Asia Reader: The Rediscovery of History.* Armonk, N.Y.: M. E. Sharpe, 1994.

Ploskikh, V. M., et al. *Kyrgyzstan—Rossiia: istoriia vzaimootnoshenii (XVIII–XIX vv.): sbornik dokumentov i materialov* [Kyrgyzstan—Russia: History of the Interrelations (18th–20th centuries): Reader]. Bishkek: Ilim, 1998.

Russia and Eurasia Documents Annual 1995 (Formerly USSR Documents Annual). Volume 2 Central Eurasian States. Gulf Breeze, Fla.: Academic International Press, semiannual publication, from 1992 onward.

Statistics

Hunter, Brian (ed.). *The Statesman's Yearbook.* New York: St. Martin's Press (Annual publication).

International Monetary Fund. *Kyrgyz Republic: Recent Economic Trends (IMF Staff Country Report).* Washington, D.C.: International Monetary Fund, 1999.

Itogi Vsesouznoi perepisi naseleniya 1959 goda: Kirgizskaya ASSR [All-Union Census of 1926: Kyrgyz ASSR]. Vol. 8. Moscow, 1963.

Kratkii sbornik. Itogi vsesouznoi perepisi naselenia 1989 goda po Kirgizskoi SSR [Concise Collection of the Results of the 1989 Census in the Kyrgyz SSR]. Bishkek: Goskomstat, 1990.

Kyrgyzstan za 50 let Sovetskoi vlasti [Kyrgyzstan during the 50 Years of the Soviet Power]. Frunze, 1967.

Lawrence, R. R. *Russia and Eurasia Facts and Figures Annual.* Gulf Breeze, Fla.: Academic International Press (annually, from 1992 onward).

Mel'nik, O. P. (ed.). *Strany Tamozhennogo soiuza: Belarus', Kazakhstan,* Kyrgyzstan, *Rossiia i Tadzhikistan: Statisticheskii sbornik* [Countries of the Custom Union: Belarus, Kazakhstan, Kyrgyzstan, Russia, and Tajikistan: Statistical Compilation]. Moscow: Mezhgosudarstvennyi statisticheskii kom-t Sodruzhestva nezavisimykh gosudarstv, 2000.

Narodnoe Khoziaistvo SSSR [National Economy of the USSR]. Moscow: Finansy i Statistika (annually until 1991).

Sodruzhestvonezavisimykh gosudarstv: Statisticheskei ezhegodnik [The Commonwealth of Independent States: Statistical Yearbook]. Moscow: Statkomitet SNG (annually from 1992 onward).

State Committee on Statistics of the USSR. *Chislennost' naseleniya soyznykh respublik po gorodskim poseleniyam I raionam* [Size of the Population of the Union Republics by Urban and Settlements and Districts]. Moscow: Goskomstat, 1991.

———. *Demograficheskii ezhegodnik SSSR* [Demographic Yearbook of the USSR]. Moscow: Goskomstat (annually until 1991).

Vsesouznaya perepis naseleniya 1926 goda: Kirgizskaya ASSR [All-Union Census of 1926: Kyrgyz ASSR]. Vol. 8. Moscow, 1928.

Travel and Descriptions

Curzon, George. *The Pamirs and the Source of the Oxus.* London: Royal Geographic Society, 1896.

Danmore, the Earl. *The Pamirs. Being a Narrative of a Year's Expedition on Horseback and on Foot through Kashmir, Western Tibet, Chinese Tartary, and Russian Central Asia.* Two vols. London: John Murray, 1893.

Fleming, P. *News from Tartary.* London: 1903.

Gibb, H. A. R. *The Travel of Idn Battuta.* London: 1929.

Komroff, M. *Contemporaries of Marco Polo.* London: 1928.

Kyrgyzstan (Odyssey Illustrated Guides). New York: Odyssey Publications, 2002.

Latham, R. E. (transl.). *The Travels of Marco Polo.* London: 1958.

Parks, George B. (ed.). *The Book of Ser Marco Polo, the Venetian.* New York: Macmillan, 1927.

Rockhill, W. *The Journey of William Rubruck.* London: 1900.

Semenov, Petr Petrovich. *Travels in the Tian'-Shan' 1856 – 1857.* Ed. by Colin Thomas. Translated by Liudmila Gilmour, Colin Thomas, and Marcus Wheeler. 1998.

Valikhanov, Ch. *Sobranie Sochinenii* [Collection of the Work]. Two vols. Alma-Ata: Kazakhstan, 1985.

Zhumabaev, B. M. *Iuzhnyi Kyrgyzstan glazami rossiiskikh puteshestvennikov: vtoraia polovina XIX-nachalo XX vv* [History of Kyrgyzstan in the Eyes of the Russian Travelers: The Second Half of the 19th and Beginning of the 20th Centuries]. Bishkek: [s.n.], 1999.

CULTURE

General

Bernshtam, A. N. *Po sledam drevnikh kultur* [On the Footsteps of Ancient Cultures]. Moscow: 1954.

——. *Kultura drevnego Kirgizstana* [The Culture of Ancient Kyrgyzstan]. Moscow: 1942.

Daniiarov, S. S. *Stanovlenie kirgizskoi sovetskoi kul'tury, 1917–1924 gg* [Establishment of the Kyrgyz Soviet Culture, 1917–1924]. Frunze: Ilim, 1983.

——. *Kul'turnoe stroitel'stvo v Kirgizkoi SSR v gody dovoennykh piatiletok* [Cultural Building in Kyrgyz SSR during the Pre-War Years]. Frunze: Ilim, 1980.

Gross, Jo-Ann (ed.). *Muslims in Central Asia: Expression of Identity and Change.* Durham, N.C.: Duke University Press, 1992.

Knobloch, Edgar. *Beyond the Oxus. Archaeology, Art and Architecture of Central Asia.* London: Ernest, 1972.

Kulturnoye stroitelstvo v Kirgizii. Sbornik dokumentov i materialov [Cultural Building in Kyrgyzstan. Compilation of Documents and Materials]. Two vols. Frunze: 1957–1972.

Masson, V. M. *Osh i Fergana: arkheologiia, novoe vremia, kul'turogenez, etnogenez* [Osh and Ferghana: Archaeology, New Time, Culture and Ethnogenesis]. Bishkek: Muras, 2000.

Pechat Kirgizskoi SSR, 1926–1963 [Mass Media of the Kirgiz SSR, 1926–1963]. Frunze, 1964.

Urazgil´deev, R. G. *Bibisara Beishenalieva: vospominaniia sovremennikov* [Bibisara Beishenaliyeva: Memories]. Bishkek: Kyrgyzstan, 1996.

Architecture

Bernshtam, A. N. *Architechturnye pamiatniki* Kirgizii [Architectural Monuments of Kyrgyzstan]. Moscow: 1950.

Denike, B. P. *Arkhitekturnyi ornament Srednei Azii* [Architectural Ornament of Central Asia]. Moscow: 1939.

Goriacheva, V. D. *Pamiatniki istorii i kul´tury Talasskoi doliny* [Monuments of History and Culture in the Talas Valley]. Bishkek: Kyrgyzstan, 1995.

——. *Gorod zolotogo verbliuda: krasnorechenskoe gorodishche* [The City of the Gold Camel: Krasnorechenskoye Burial]. Frunze: Ilim, 1988.

——. *Srednevekovye gorodskie tsentry i arkhitekturnye ansambli Kirgizii: Burana, Uzgen, Safid-Bulan. Nauchno-populiarnyi ocherk* [Medieval City Centers and Architectural Ensembles of Kyrgyzstan: Burana, Uzgen, Safid-Bulan. Scholarly-and-Popular Review]. Frunze: Ilim, 1983.

Goriacheva, V. D., V. I. Deev, and S. Ia. Peregudova. *Pamiatniki istorii i kul´tury goroda Bishkeka. Pod redaktsiei S.S. Daniiarova* [Historical and Cultural Monuments of Bishkek City]. Edited by S. S. Daiarov]. Bishkek: Ilim, 1996.

Kurbatov, V. V,. *Arkhitektura sovetskoi Kirgizii* [The Architecture of the Soviet Kyrgyzstan]. Moscow: Stroiizdat, 1972.

Kurbatov, V. V. and Pisarskoi E.G. *Arkhitektura goroda Frunze* [The Architecture of Frunze City]. Frunze: Kyrgyzstan, 1978.

Nusov, V. E. *Sovremennaia arkhitektura Kirgizii* [Modern Architecture of Kyrgyzstan]. Frunze: Kyrgyzstan, 1982.

Zakharova, A. (Antonina). *Istoriko-arkhitekturnoe nasledie goroda Osh: Konets XIX-nachalo XX vv* [Historical and Architectural Heritage of Osh City: The End of the 19th and Beginning of the 20th Centuries]. Bishkek: Institut obshchestvennykh nauk, 1997.

Arts

Baltabaeva, T. M. *Kyrgyzdyn eldik kenchi = Narodnye sokrovishcha* Kirgizii [People's Treasures of Kyrgyzstan]. Frunze: Kyrgyzstan, 1974.

Fiel´strup, F. A. *Iz obriadovoi zhizni kirgizov nachala XX veka* [From the Traditional Life of the Kyrgyz of the Beginning of the 20th Century]. Moscow: Nauka, 2002.

Knobloch, Edgar. *Monuments of Central Asia: A Guide to the Archaeology, Art and Architecture of Turkestan*. London: I.B. Tauris, 2001.

Sadykov, T. S. et al. *Khudozhniki sovetskoi Kirgizii* [Painters of Soviet Kyrgyzstan]. Frunze: Kyrgyzstan, 1982.

Umotov, Zhumabai. *Kyial duinosundo. V mire ornamentov* [In the World of Ornaments]. Frunze: Kyrgyzstan, 1982. (In Kyrgyz, Russian, and English).

Usubaliev, K. N. et al. *Kyrgyz mamlekettik surot iskusstvo muzeii, Kirgizskii gosudarstvennyi muzei izobrazitel'nykh iskusstv* [The Kirghiz State Art Museum]. Frunze: Kyrgyzstan, 1985. (In Kyrgyz, Russian, and English).

Language and Script

Abduldaev, E. *Azyrky kyrgyz tili: fonetika, orfoepiia, grafika zhana orfografiia, leksikologiia zhana frazeologiia* [The Modern Kyrgyz Language: Phonetics, Orphoepia, Graphics and Orthography, Lexicology and Phraseology]. Bishkek: Kyrgyzstan, 1998.

Abduldaev, E., et al. (ed.). *Grammatika kirgizskogo literaturnogo iazyka* [The Grammar of the Literary Kyrgyz Language]. Frunze: Ilim, 1987.

Akhmatov, T. K., and S. Omuralieva. *Kyrgyz tili: fonetika, leksika* [The Kyrgyz Language: Phonetics and Lexicology]. Frunze: Mektep, 1990.

Allworth, Edward. *Central Asian Publishing and the Rise of Nationalism*. New York: New York Public Library, 1965.

Baskakov, N. A. *The Turkic Languages of Central Asia*. Translated by S. Worm. London: Central Asian Research Center, 1960.

Batmanov, I. A. *Sovremennyi kirgizskii iazyk* [The Modern Kyrgyz Language]. Frunze: Academy of Science, 1953.

Huskey, E. "The Politics of Language in Kyrgyzstan." *Nationalities Papers*, vol. 23, no. 3 (1995): 549–772.

Landau, Jacob M., and Barbara Kellner-Heinkele. *Politics of Language in the ex-Soviet Muslim States: Azerbaijan, Uzbekistan, Kazakhstan, Kyrgyzstan, Turkmenistan, Tajikistan*. London: Hurst, 2001.

Oruzbaeva, B. O. *Kyrgyzskii iazyk: kratkii grammaticheskii ocherk* [The Kyrgyz Language: A Concise Review of the Grammar]. Bishkek: Ilim, 1998.

——. *Kyrgyz terminologiiasy* [Kyrgyz Terminology]. Frunze: Mektep, 1983.

——. *Slovoobrazovanie v kirgizskom iazyke* [Word Creation in the Kyrgyz Language]. Frunze: Ilim, 1964.

Literature and Folklore

Akmataliev, A. (Amantur). *Kyrgyzdyn uz-ustalary: antologiia* [Kyrgyz Masters of Words: Anthology]. Bishkek: Kyrgyz entsyklopediiasynyn bashky redaktsiiasy, 1997.

Batmanov, I. A. *Talasskie pamiatniki drevneturskoi pis'mennosti* [The Talas Materials of Ancient Turkic Writing]. Frunze: Ilim, 1971.

Chadwick, Nora. K., and Victor Zhimunsky. *Oral Epic of Central Asia*. Cambridge: Cambridge University Press, 1969.

Kebekova, B. *"Kurmanbek" eposunun variantary* [The Variations of the "Kurmanbek" Epic]. Frunze: Ilim, 1961.

Kydyrbaeva, R. Z., K. Kyrbashev, and A. Zhainakova. *Varianty eposa "Manas," "Manas" eposunun varianttary* [The Variations of the Manas Epic]. Frunze: Ilim, 1988.

Malov, S. E. *Pamiatniki drevnetiurkskoi pis'mennosti Mongolii i Kirgizii* [The Monuments of Ancient Turkic Writing in Mongolia and Kyrgyzstan]. Moscow: Academy of Science, 1959.

Manas: kirgizskii epos. Velikii pokhod [Manas: Kyrgyz Epic. The Great Campaign]. Translated by Semena Lipkina, L´va Pen´kovskogo, and Marka Tarlovskogo. Moscow: Khudozhtvennaia literatura, 1946.

Mirza, Momun. "The World According to *Sovettyk Kyrgyzstan:* A Survey (January–November 1982)." *Central Asian Survey,* vol. 2, no. 4 (1983): 109–126.

Radlow, V. V. *Das Kudatku-Bilik des Yusuf Chass-Habshib aus Balasagun.* Vols. 1 and 2. Saint Petersburg, 1891–1900.

———. *Narechiye dikokamennykh Kirgizov* [The Dialect of the Wild-Stone Kyrgyzs]. Sant-Petersburg, 1885.

Music

Daniiarov, S. S. *Stanovlenie kirgizskoi sovetskoi kul´tury, 1917–1924 gg.* [Establishment of Kyrgyz Soviet Culture, 1917–1924]. Frunze: Ilim, 1983.

Diushaliev, K. *Pesennaia kul´tura kyrgyzskogo naroda: zhanrovo-istoricheskii aspect* [Song Culture of the Kyrgyz People: Historical Aspect]. Bishkek: Academy of Science, 1993.

———. *Kirgizskaia narodnaia pesnia: issledovanie* [Kyrgyz Folk Song: Research]. Moscow: Sovetskii kompozitor, 1982.

Iankovskii, V. (Vladimir). *Muzykal´naia kul´tura Sovetskoi Kirgizii, 1917–1967 gg.* [Music Culture of the Soviet Kyrgyzstan, 1917–1967]. Frunze: Ilim, 1982.

Skliutovskaia, T. M. *Kirgizskaia kamerno-instrumental´naia muzyka* [Kyrgyz Instrumental Music] Frunze: Adabiiat, 1989.

Slobin, Mark. *Kirgiz Instrumental Music.* New York: Society for Asian Music, 1969.

Subanaliev, Sagynaly. *Kirgizskie muzykal´nye instrumenty: idiofony, membranofony, aerofony* [Kyrgyz Musical Instruments]. Frunze: Kyrgyzstan, 1986.

ECONOMY

General

Abazov, R. "Policy of Economic Transition in Kyrgyzstan." *Central Asian Survey,* vol. 18, no. 2 (1999): 197–223.

Akayev, A. *Kyrgyzstan: An Economy in Transition*. Canberra: Australian National University, 2001.

——. *O strategii socialno-ekonomicheskogo razvitia Kyrgyzskoi Respubliki* [About the Strategy of Social-Economic Development of the Kyrgyz Republic]. Bishkek: Kyrgyzstan, 1993.

Anderson, Kathryn and Richard Pomfret. *Consequences of Creating a Market Economy: Evidence from Household Surveys in Central Asia*. Northhampton, Mass.: Edward Elgar, 2003.

The Comprehensive Development Framework of the Kyrgyz Republic to 2010. Bishkek, 2001.

Dabrowski, Marek, and Vladislav Jermakowicz. "Economic Reforms in Kyrgyzstan." *Communist Economics and Economic Transformation*, vol. 7, no. 3 (1995): 269–297.

Filatochev, Igor, and Roy Bradshaw. "The Soviet Hyperinflation: Its Origins and Impact throughout the Former Republics." *Soviet Studies*, vol. 44, no. 5 (1992): 739–759.

Henley, John S., and George B. Assaf. "Re-integrating the Central Asian Republics into the World Economy." *Intereconomics*, vol. 30, no. 5 (September/October 1995): 235–246.

International Monetary Fund. *Kyrgyz Republic. Recent Economic Development*. Washington, D.C.: International Monetary Fund, 1998.

——. *Kyrgyz Republic: IMF Economic Reviews*. Washington, D.C.: International Monetary Fund, 1993.

Kyrgyz Republic Foreign Investment Agency. *Kyrgyz Republic: Information for Prospective Investors*. Bishkek: Kyrgyz Republic Foreign Investment Agency, May 1998.

Nove, Alec, and J. A. Newth. *The Soviet Middle East: A Communist Model for Development*. New York: Allen and Unwin, 1967.

Pomfret, R. *The Economies of Central Asia*. Princeton, N.J.: Princeton University Press, 1995.

Rumer, Boris (ed.). *Central Asia in Transition: Dilemmas of Political and Economic Development*. Armonk, N.Y.: M.E. Sharpe, 1996.

Sherstobitov, V. P. *Lenin i krestianstvo Sovetskogo Vostoka* [Lenin and the Peasants of the Soviet Orient]. Frunze, 1969.

World Bank. *Kyrgyzstan: Agricultural Sector Review*. Washington, D.C.: World Bank, 1995a.

——. *Kyrgyzstan: Energy Sector Review*. Washington, D.C.: World Bank, 1995b.

——. *Kyrgyzstan: Social Protection in a Reforming Economy*. Washington, D.C.: World Bank, 1993a.

——. *Kyrgyzstan: The Transition to a Market Economy*. Washington, D.C.: World Bank, 1993b.

Yasuda, Osamu, and Yasutami Shimomura (eds.). *Economic Reform in Kazakhstan and Kyrgyzstan: Lessons from the East Asian Development Experience.* 2 vols. Tokyo: Sasakawa Peace Foundation, 1997.

HISTORY

General

Abramzon S. *Kyrgyzy i ikh etnogeneticheskie i istoriko-kulturnye sviazi* [The Kyrgyzs and Their Ethnological and Historical-Cultural Relations]. 2nd ed. Frunze: Kyrgyzstan, 1989.

Asankanov, A. A., and O. Dzh. Osmnov. *Istoriia Kyrgyzstana: S drevneishikh vremen do nashikh dnei* [History of Kyrgyzstan: From Ancient Times to Modern Days]. Bishkek: "Kyrgyzskii gos. pedagogicheskii universitet," 2002.

———. *Turkestan Down to the Mongol Invasion.* Translated by H. A. R. Gibb. London: Luzac, 1928.

Bartold, V. V. *Four Studies on the History of Central Asia.* Translated by V. and T. Minorsky. Leiden: E. J. Brill, 1956–1963.

Bernshtam, A. *Izbrannye trudy po arkheologii i istorii kyrgyzov i Kyrgyzstana* [Selected Works on Archaeology and the History of Kyrgyzs and Kyrgyzstan]. 2 vols. Bishkek: Aibek, 1997–1998.

Chotonov, U. (ed.). *Istoriia Kyrgyzstana—XX vek* [History of Kyrgyzstan—The 20th Century]. Bishkek: Kyrgyzstan, 1998.

Gibb, H. A. R. *Arab Conquest of Central Asia.* London: 1923.

Kwanten, Luc. *Imperial Nomads. A History of Central Asia, 500–1500.* Philadelphia: University of Pennsylvania Press, 1979.

Lunin, B. V. *Iz istorii russkogo vostokovedeniia i arkheologii v Turkestane; Turkestanskii kruzhok liubitelei arkheologii (1895–1917 gg.)* [From the History of Russian Oriental Studies and Archaeology in Turkistan; Turkistan Club of Enthusiasts of Archaeology (1895–1917)]. Tashkent: Akademiia nauk Uzbekskoi SSR, 1958.

Manz, Beatrice F. (ed.). *Central Asia in Historical Perspective.* Boulder, Colo.: Westview Press, 1993.

McGovern, W. M. *The Early History of Central Asia. A Study of the Scythians and the Huns and the Part They Played in World History.* Chapel Hill: University of North Carolina Press, 1939.

Ploskikh V. (ed.). *Khrestomatia po Istorii Kyrgyzstana* [The Reader of the History of Kyrgyzstan]. Bishkek: Ilim, 1997.

Saliev, A. A. (ed.). *Osh 3000.* Bishkek: Ilim, 2000.

Pre-Islamic Period

Adshead, S. *Central Asia in World History*. London: Macmillan, 1993.

Akmoldoeva, Sh. *Drevnekyrgyzskaia model mira: Na materialakh eposa Manas*. [Ancient Model of the World: On the Manas Epic Materials]. Bishkek: Ilim, 1996.

Alram, Michael, and Deborah E. Klimburg-Salter (ed.). *Coins, Art, and Chronology: Essays on Pre-Islamic History of the Indo-Iranian Borderlands*. Vienna: Österreichischen Akademie der Wissenschaften, 1999.

Aristov, N. A. *Usuni i kyrgyzy ili kara-kyrgyzy: Ocherki istorii i byta naseleniia zapadnogo Tian´-Shania i issledovaniia po ego istoricheskoi geografii* [Usuns and Kyrgyz or Kara-Kyrgyzs: Historical Reviews of the Everyday Life of the People in the West Tian-Shan and Research on Their Historical Geography]. Bishkek: Ilim, 2001.

Davidovich, E. A. (ed.). *Kirgiziia pri Karakhanidakh* [Kyrgyzstan under the Karakhanids]. Frunze: Ilim, 1983.

Harmatta, J. (ed.). *From Alexander the Great to Kül Tegin: Studies in Bactrian, Pahlavi, Sanskrit, Arabic, Aramaic, Armenian, Chinese, Türk, Greek, and Latin Sources for the History of pre-Islamic Central Asia*. Budapest: Akadémiai Kiadó, 1990.

Istoriya Kirgizskoi SSR [The History of the Kyrgyz SSR]. Vol. 1. Frunze: Nauka, 1984.

Litvinsky, B. A. *Zhan Guang-Da and Shabani Samghabadi. History of Civilizations of Central Asia*. Vol. 3. (Multiple History Series). Paris: UNESCO Publishing, 1996.

Masson, V. M. *Srednyaya Azia i drevnii vostok* [Central Asia and Ancient Orient]. Moscow: Nauka, 1964.

Musaev, K. *Istoriia Velikoi Kyrgyzskoi imperii* [History of the Great Kyrgyz Empire]. Bishkek: Kyrgyzstan-Ala-Too, 1999.

Roemer, Hans Robert (ed.). *Histoire des peuples turcs à l'epoque pre-islamique* [History of the Turkic Peoples in the Pre-Islamic Period]. Berlin: K. Schwarz in Kommission, 2000.

Islamic Period

Altmyshbaev, Asylbek Altmyshbaevich. *Ocherk istorii razvitiia obshchestvenno-politicheskoi i filosofskoi mysli v dorevoliutsionnoi Kirgizii* [Review of the Development of Public, Political and Philosophical Thought in Pre-revolutionary Kyrgyzstan]. Frunze: Ilim, 1985.

Bartold, V. V. *Cultural History of the Muslims*. Translated from the Russian by Shahid Suhrawardy. New Delhi: Mittal Publications, 1995.

Doronbekova, R., V. Mokrynin, and V. Ploskikh. *Kyrgyzdyn zhana Kyrgyzstandyn tarykhy: Sovettik doorgo cheiinki mezgil* [The Kyrgyz and Their History: The Pre-Soviet Era]. Bishkek: Ilim, 1993.

Esen uulu, Kylych. *Drevnekyrgyzskoe gosudarstvo Khagias: Kaganat Kyrgyz (840-nach. X v.)* [Ancient Kyrgyz State Khagias: Khaganate Kyrgyz (840 - X century)]. Bishkek: Renessans, 1994.

Galitskii, V. I., and V. Ploskikh. *Starinnyi Osh: ocherk istorii* [Ancient Osh: Historical Review]. Frunze: Ilim, 1987.

Haidar, Mirza Muhammad. *The Tarikh-i-Rashidi* [A History of the Moghuls of Central Asia]. An English version translated by E. Denison Ross. First published in 1895. Patna: Academica Asiatica, 1973 (reprint).

Il'iasov, S. I., et al. *Iz istorii dorevoliutsionnogo Kirgizstana* [From the History of Pre-revolutionary Kyrgyzstan]. Frunze: Ilim, 1985.

Ivanov, P. P. *Ocherki po istirii Srednei Azii (16 - seredina 19 vekov)* [Essays on the History of Central Asia (16th–19th centuries)]. Moscow: 1958.

Karaev, O. *Istoriia karakhanidskogo kaganata: X-nachalo XIII vv.* [History of the Karakhanid Khanate: 10th–beginning of 13th centuries]. Frunze: Ilim, 1983.

Khasanov, Anvarbek Khasanovich. *Narodnye dvizheniia v Kirgizii v period Kokandskogo khanstva* [Peoples Movement in Kyrgyzstan during the Kokand Khanate Era]. Moscow: Nauka, 1977.

Masson, V. M. *Izuchenie drevnego i srednevekovogo Kyrgyzstana* [Study of Ancient and Medieval Kyrgyzstan]. Bishkek: Muras, 1998.

Ploskikh, V. M. *Kirgizy i Kokandskoe khanstvo* [The Kyrgyz and the Kokand Khanate]. Frunze: Ilim, 1977.

Skrine, F. H., and E. Ross. *The Heart of Asia. A History of Russian Turkestan and the Central Asian Khanates from Earliest Times.* London: Methuen, 1893.

Russian and Soviet Period

Allworth, Edward (ed.). *Central Asia: 130 Years of Russian Dominance. A Historical Overview.* Durham, N.C.: Duke University Press, 1994.

——. (ed.). *Central Asia: A Century of Russian Rule.* New York: Columbia University Press, 1967.

Benningsen, Alexandre, and Chantal Lemercier-Quelquejay. *Islam in the Soviet Union.* New York: Praeger, 1967.

Clubb, O. E. *China and Russia: The "Great Game."* New York: Columbia University Press, 1971.

Curzon, George Nathaniel. *Russia in Central Asia in 1889 and the Anglo-Russian Question.* London: Cass, 1967.

Demko, George J. *The Russian Colonization of Kazakhstan, 1896–1916.* Bloomington: Indiana University Press, 1969.

Dzhamgerchinov, B. *Dobrovolnoe vhozhdenie kyrgyzskogo naroda v sostav Rossii* [Voluntary Accession of the Kyrgyzs to Russia]. 2nd ed. Frunze: Kyrgyzstan, 1963.

Istoriya Kirgizskoi SSR [The History of the Kyrgyz SSR]. Vol. 2. Frunze: Nauka, 1985a.

Istoriya Kirgizskoi SSR [The History of the Kyrgyz SSR]. Vol. 3. Frunze: Nauka, 1985b.

Karakeev K. K. (ed.). *Kirgiziia v trekh rossiiskikh revoliutsiiakh* [Kyrgyzstan in the Three Russian Revolutions]. Frunze: Ilim, 1987.

Kasymbekov, Tologon. *Syngan kylych: Tarykhyi roman* [Broken Sword: Historical Novel]. Frunze: Kyrgyzstan, 1979.

Kerimbaev, S. K. *Sovetskii Kirgizstan v Velikoi Otechestvennoi voine 1941–1945 gg* [Soviet Kyrgyzstan in the Great Patriotic War]. Frunze: Ilim, 1985.

Khalfin, N. A. *Russia's Policy in Central Asia, 1857–1868.* Condensed and translated by Hubert Evans. London: Central Asian Research Center, 1964.

Khelimskaia, Regina. *Taina Chon-Tasha* [The Secrets of the Chon Tash]. Bishkek: Ilim, 1994.

Mackenzie, David. *The Lion of Tashkent: The Career of General M. G. Cherniaev.* Athens: University of Georgia Press, 1974.

Meyer, Karl Ernest, and Shareen Blair Brysac. *Tournament of Shadows: The Great Game and the Race for Empire in Central Asia.* Washington, D.C.: Counterpoint, 1999.

Neilson, Keith. *Britain and the Last Tsar: British Policy and Russia, 1894–1917.* New York: Oxford University Press, 1995.

1916-zhylky Kyrgyzstandagy kcortcorculcush: dokkumenter zhana materialdar [The Revolt of 1916 in Kyrgyzstan: Documents and Materials]. Bishkek, Kyrgyzstan, 1996.

Pahlen, K. K. *Mission to Turkestan.* London: Oxford University Press, 1964.

Pierce, Richard. *Russian Central Asia, 1867–1917: A Study of Colonial Rule.* Berkeley: University of California Press, 1960.

Polykovskii, M. *Konets Madamin-beka: Zapiski o grazhdanskoi voine [The End of Madamin-Bek: Notes on the Civil War].* Tashkent: "Izd-vo lit-ry i iskusstva im. Gafura Guliama," 1984.

Rawlington, (Sir) Henry. *England and Russia in the East.* Reprint. New York, Praeger, 1970 (first published: London, 1875).

Rywkin, Michael. *Moscow's Muslim Challenge.* London: C. Hurst, 1982.

Zhantuarov, Sultan Baiturovich. *Grazhdanskaia voina v Kirgizii, 1918–1920 gg.* [The Civil War in Kyrgyzstan, 1918–1920]. Frunze: Izd-vo Akademii nauk Kirgizskoi SSR, 1963.

Zima, A. G. *Velikii Oktiabr´ v Kirgizii* [Great October in Kyrgyzstan]. Frunze: Ilim, 1987.

Post-Soviet Period

Bauer, Armin, and David Green. *Women and Gender Relations: The Kyrgyz Republic in Transition.* Manila: Asian Development Bank, 2000.

Dawisha, Karen, and Bruce Parrott. *Conflict, Cleavage, and Change in Central Asia and the Caucasus.* Cambridge: Cambridge University Press, 1997.

Gleason, Gr. *The Central Asian States: Discovering Independence.* Boulder, Colo.: Westview Press, 1997.

Haghayeghi, Mehrdad. *Islam and Politics in Central Asia.* New York: St. Martin's Press, 1995.

Hiro, Dilip. *Between Marx and Muhammad: The Changing Face of Central Asia.* London: HarperCollins, 1994.

Hyman, Anthony. *Political Change in Post-Soviet Central Asia.* London: Royal Institute of International Affairs, 1994.

Koichuyev, T. and A. Brudnyi. *Nezavisimyi Kyrgyzstan: Tretei put* [Independent Kyrgyzstan: The Third Way]. Bishkek: Ilim, 1993.

Kosmarskaia, N. P. and S. A. Panarin. *Etnosotsial'nye protsessy v Kyrgyzstane: Po materialam polevykh issledovanii 1992–1993 gg* [Ethnic and Social Processes in Kyrgyzstan: Results of the Field Studies in 1992–1993]. Moscow: RAN, 1994.

Razakov, Talant. *Osh koogalangy: KGBnyn maalymattary boiuncha* [The Osh Events According to the KGB Materials]. Bishkek: Renessans, 1993.

Sagdeev, Roald, and Susan Eisenhower (eds.). *Islam and Central Asia: An Enduring Legacy or an Evolving Threat?* Washington, D.C.: Center for Political and Strategic Studies, 2000.

Usubaliev, T. U. *Kak menia presledovali gorbachevtsy: moral'nyi i politicheskii terror* [How I Was Persecuted by Gorbachev's People: Moral and Political Terror]. Bishkek: Sham, 1997.

Vassiliev, A. (ed.). *Central Asia: Political and Economic Challenges in the Post-Soviet Era.* London: Saqi Books, 2001.

Vohra, N. N. (ed.). *Culture, Society, and Politics in Central Asia and India.* Delhi: Shipra Publications, 1999.

POLITICS

General

Akiner, Shirin. *Central Asia: Conflict or Stability and Development.* London: Minority Rights Group, 1997.

Anderson, John. *Kyrgyzstan, Central Asia's Island of Democracy?* Amsterdam: Harwood Academic Publishers, 1999.

Cummings, Sally N. (ed.). *Oil, Transition and Security in Central Asia.* New York: Routledge, 2003.

Hopkirk, Peter. *The Great Game: The Struggle for Empire in Central Asia.* New York: Kodansha International, 1992.

Huskey, Eugene. "The Rise of Contested Politics in Central Asia: Elections in Kyrgyzstan, 1989–1990." *Europe-Asia Studies,* vol. 47, no. 5 (1995): 813–834.

International Crisis Group. *Kyrgyzstan at Ten: Trouble in the "Island of Democracy." 28 August 2001.* Osh: International Crisis Group, 2002.

Koichuev, T. K., et al. *U istokov Kyrgyzskoi natsional'noi gosudarstvennosti* [At the Beginning of the Kyrgyz Nation State]. Bishkek: Ilim, 1996.

Luong, Pauline Jones. *Institutional Change and Political Continuity in Post-Soviet Central Asia: Power, Perceptions, and Pacts.* Cambridge: Cambridge University Press, 2002.

Mandelbaum, Michael (ed.). *Central Asia and The World: Kazakhstan, Kyrgyzstan, Tajikistan, Turkmenistan and Uzbekistan.* New York: Council on Foreign Relations Press, 1994.

Roy, Oliver. *The New Central Asia: The Creation of Nations.* New York: New York University Press, 2000.

Tismaneanu, Vladimir. *Political Culture and Civil Society in Russia and the New States of Eurasia.* Armonk, N.Y.: M.E. Sharpe, 1995.

United States Congress. Commission on Security and Cooperation in Europe. *Report on the Parliamentary Elections in Kyrgyzstan, February–March 2000.* A report prepared by the Staff of the Commission on Security and Cooperation in Europe. Washington, D.C.: Commission on Security and Cooperation in Europe, 2000.

——. *Report on the Parliamentary Election in Kyrgyzstan: February 5, 1995 Bishkek, Kyrgyzstan.* Prepared by the staff of the Commission on Security and Cooperation in Europe. Washington, D.C.: Commission on Security and Cooperation in Europe, 1995.

Zhenshchiny Kyrgyzstana posle Pekinskoi konferentsii 1995 goda: Analiz situatsii; kontseptsiia i strategiia deistvii do 2000 goda [Kyrghyzstan's Women after Beijing Conference 1995: Situation Analysis, Actions Conception and Strategy up to 2000]. Bishkek: Institut ravnykh prav i vozmozhnostei, 1998.

Political Parties and Organizations

Anarbekov, Abzhalbek. *Politicheskie partii v Kyrgyzstane: 1991–1999 gg.* [Political Parties in Kyrgyzstan: 1991–1999]. Bishkek: Tsentr Gusudarstvennogo Iazyka i Entsiklopedii, 1999.

Chinaliev, U. K. *Politicheskie partii Kyrgyzstana: monografiia* [Political Parties in Kyrgyzstan: Monograph]. Moscow: NIK, 1999.

Elebayeva, A. (ed.). *Grazhdanskiye Dvizhenia v Kyrgyzstane* [Civil Movements in Kyrgyzstan]. Bishkek: Institute of Ethnography, 1990.

Fukalov, A. I. (ed.). *Sbornik otchetov o deiatel'nosti Soveta Assamblei naroda Kyrgyzstana, natsional'no-kul'turnykh tsentrov i obshchestvennykh ob"edinenii, vkhodiashchikh v sostav Assamblei naroda Kyrgyzstana, 1996–2000 gg.* [Compilation of Reports on Activities of the Council of Assembly of People of Kyrgyzstan, National-Cultural Centers Public Organisations, Members of the Assembly of People of Kyrgyzstan]. Bishkek: Assambleia naroda Kyrgyzstana, 2000.

Ibragimov, T. R., and G. T. Iskakova. *Kyrgyzstandyn Sayasii Partiasalary* [Political Parties in Kyrgyzstan]. Bishkek: Razvtie Gumanitornogo Prostranstva, 2000.

International Crisis Group. *Kyrgyzstan's Political Crisis: An Exit Strategy. 20 August 2002.* Osh: International Crisis Group, 2002.

Ishiyama, John T., and Ryan Kennedy. "Superpresidentialism and Political Party Development in Russia, Ukraine, Armenia and Kyrgyzstan." *Europe-Asia Studies*, vol. 53, no. 8 (2001): 1177–1191.

"Kyrgyz Republic." In *Nations in Transit, 2003, Civil Society, Democracy and Markets in East Central Europe and the Newly Independent States.* Washington, D.C.: Freedom House, 2003.

"Kyrgyz Republic." In *Nations in Transit, 1999–2000, Civil Society, Democracy and Markets in East Central Europe and the Newly Independent States.* Washington, D.C.: Freedom House, 2001.

Nikishov, P. P. *Iz istorii krakha levykh eserov v Turkestane* [From the History of Collapse of the Left-*ESSERs* in Turkistan]. Frunze: Kyrgyzstan, 1965.

Ponomarev, Vitalii. *Samodeyatelnye obchestvennye organizatsii Kazakhstana i Kyrgyzstana, 1987–1991* [Independent Public Organizations of Kazakhstan and Kyrgyzstan, 1987–1991]. Moscow: 1991.

Ruffin, Holt M., and Daniel C. Waugh (ed.). *Civil Society in Central Asia.* Seattle: University of Washington Press, 1999.

Vybory v Zhogorku Kenesh Kyrgyzskoi Respubliki: Itogovyi otchet. 20 fevralia–12 marta 2000 [Elections to the Parliament of the Kyrgyz Republic: Final Report. 20th February–12th March 2000]. Bishkek: Za demokratiiu i grazhdanskoe obshchestvo, 2000.

Defense and Security

Allison, Roy, and Lena Jonson (eds.). *Central Asian Security: The New International Context.* Washington, D.C.: Brookings Institution Press, 2001.

Bertsch, Gary K. *Crossroads and Conflict: Security and Foreign Policy in the Caucasus and Central Asia.* New York: Routledge, 2000.

Clark, S. L. *Security in Russia and Central Asia: The New National Militaries and Emerging Defence Policies*. Boulder, Colo.: Westview Press, 1995.

De Cordier, Bruno. "The Economic Co-operation Organization: Toward a New Silk Road on the Ruins of the Cold War?" *Central Asian Survey*, vol. 15, no. 1 (1996): 47–58.

Fletcher, Joseph F., and Boris Sergeyev. "Islam and Intolerance in Central Asia: The Case of Kyrgyzstan." *Europe-Asia Studies*, 54 (March 2002).

International Crisis Group. *Central Asia: Border Disputes and Conflict Potential. 4 April 2002*. Osh: International Crisis Group, 2002a.

———. *Central Asia: Water and Conflict. 30 May 2002*. Osh: International Crisis Group, 2002b.

Legvold, Robert (ed.). *Thinking Strategically: The Major Powers, Kazakhstan, and the Central Asian Nexus*. Cambridge, Mass.: MIT Press, 2003.

Marcus, Ustina, and Daniel Nelson (eds.). *Eurasian and East Europe Security Yearbook*. Washington, D.C.: Brassey's, 2000.

Mekenkamp, Monique, Paul van Tongeren, and Hans van de Veen (ed.). *Searching for Peace in Central and South Asia: An Overview of Conflict Prevention and Peacebuilding Activities*. Boulder, Colo.: Lynne Rienner Publishers, 2002.

Menon, Rajan, Yuri E. Fedorov, and Ghia Nodia (eds.). *Russia, the Caucasus, and Central Asia: the 21st Century Security Environment*. Armonk, N.Y.: M.E. Sharpe, 1999.

Pirseyedi, Bobi. *The Small Arms Problem in Central Asia: Features and Implications*. Geneva: United Nations Institute for Disarmament Research, 2000.

Tabassum, Firdous. *Central Asia, Security, and Strategic Imperatives*. Delhi: Kalpaz Publications, 2002.

United States Senate. *Contributions of Central Asian Nations to the Campaign against Terrorism: Hearing before the Subcommittee on Central Asia and South Caucasus of the Committee on Foreign Relations*. United States Senate, 107th Cong., 1st sess., December 13, 2001. Washington, D.C.: U.S. Government Printing Office, 2002.

Winrow, Gareth M. "A Region at the Crossroads: Security Issues in Post-Soviet Central Asia." *Journal of South Asian and Middle Eastern Studies*, vol. 8, no. 1 (Fall 1994): 1–18.

Interethnic Relations

Abazov, Rafis. "Central Asia's Conflicting Legacy and Ethnic Policies: Revisiting a Crisis Zone of the Former USSR." *Nationalism and Ethnic Politics*, vol. 5, no. 2 (1999): 62–90.

Ahmar, Moonis. "Conflict Resolution and Confidence Building in Central Asia." *Strategic Studies*, vol. 16, no. 3 (Spring 1994): 58–96.

Elebayeva, A. *Razvitiye mezhnatsionalnykh otnoshenii v novykh nezavisimykh gosudarstvakh Tsentralnoi Azii* [The Development of Interethnic Relations in the Newly Independent States of Central Asia]. Bishkek: Ilim, 1995.

Elebayeva, A., and Nurbek Omuraliev. *Oshskii konflict: Sotciologicheski analiz* [The Osh Conflict: Sociological Analysis]. Bishkek: Ilim, 1991.

Khazanov, A. *After the USSR: Ethnicity, Nationalism, and Politics in the Commonwealth of Independent States*. Madison: University of Wisconsin Press, 1995.

Naumkin, Vitaly (ed.). *Central Asia and Transcaucasia: Ethnicity and Conflict*. Westport, Conn.: Greenwood Press, 1994.

Tishkov, V. *Ethnicity, Nationalism and Conflicts in and after the Soviet Union: The Mind Aflame*. London: Sage, 1997.

SCIENCE AND TECHNOLOGY

Education

Aitmambetov, Diuishe. *Dorevoliutsionnye shkoly v Kirgizii* [Schools in Pre-revolutionary Kyrgyzstan]. Frunze: Academy of Science, 1961.

Akaev, A. A. et al (eds.). *Akademicheskaia nauka Kirgizstana: Istoriia i problemy* [Academy of Science of Kyrgyzstan: History and Problems]. Frunze: Ilim, 1990.

Bauer, Armin, and Nina Bochman. *A Generation at Risk: Children in the Central Asian Republics of Kazakhstan and Kyrgyzstan*. Manila: Asian Development Bank, 1998.

Berryman, Sue E. *Hidden Challenges to Education Systems in Transition Economies*. Washington, D.C.: World Bank, 2000.

Demir, Cennet Engin, Ayse Balci, and Fusun Akkok. "The Role of Turkish Schools in the Educational System and Social Transformation of Central Asian Countries: The Case of Turkmenistan and Kyrgyzstan." *Central Asian Survey*, vol. 19, no. 1 (2000): 141–155.

Kudabaev, Z. I. et al. Obrazovanie v Kyrgyzskoi Respublike: Statisticheskii sbornik [Education in Kyrgyzstan: Statistical Collection]. Bishkek: Natsional´nyi statisticheskii komitet Kyrgyzskoi Respubliki, 2000.

Obrazovanie i nauka v meniaiushchemsia mire: Materialy Mezhdunarodnoi konferentsii, Kyrgyzstan, 22–27 sentiabria 1999 g. [Education and Science in a Changing World: Materials of the International Conference, 22–27 September, 1999]. Bishkek: Ilim, 2001.

Rysalieva, Symbat Dj., and Gulmira A. Ibraeva. *Educational Financing and Budgeting in Kyrgyzstan*. Paris: UNESCO/International Institute for Educational Planning, 1999.

Wile, James M. "A Literacy Lesson in Democracy Education." *The Social Studies*, vol. 91, no. 4 (July 2000): 170–178.

Geography

Academy of Science of the Kyrgyz SSR. *Atlas Kirgizskoi Sovetskoi Sotsialisticheskoi Respubliki* [Atlas of the Kyrgyz Soviet Socialist Republic]. Moscow: Glavnoe upravlenie geodezii i kartografii pri Sovete ministrov SSSR, 1987.

Aristov, N. A. *Usuni i kyrgyzy ili kara-kyrgyzy: ocherki istorii i byta naseleniia zapadnogo Tian´-Shania i issledovaniia po ego istoricheskoi geografii* [Usuns and Kyrgyzs or Kara-Kyrgyzs: Essays on the History and Everyday Life of the Population of Western Tian-Shan and Research on Its Historical Geography]. Bishkek: Ilim, 2001.

Dienes, Leslie. "Economic Geographic Relations in the Post-Soviet Republics." *Post-Soviet Geography*, 34 (October 1993): 497–529.

Economic and Social Commission for Asia and the Pacific. *Atlas of Mineral Resources of the ESCAP Region: Geology and Mineral Resources of Kyrgyzstan*. New York: United Nations Publications, 2000.

Kaiser, R. J. *The Geography of Nationalism in Russia and the USSR*. Princeton, N.J.: Princeton University Press, 1994.

Klerkx, J., and Beishen Imanackunov (eds.). *Lake Issyk-Kul: Its Natural Environment (NATO Science Series. 4, Earth and Environmental Sciences, V. 13)*. Dordrecht: Kluwer Academic Publishers, 2002.

Konkobaev, Kadyrali. *Toponimiia Iuzhnoi Kirgizii* [Topography of Southern Kyrgyzstan]. Frunze: Ilim, 1980.

Kyrgyzstan. Prepared by Geography Department, Lerner Publications. Minneapolis, Minn.: Lerner Publications, 1993.

Montgomerie, T. G. "On the Geographical Position of Yarkund, and Some Other Places in Central Asia." *Journal of the Royal Geographic Society*, no. 36 (1866): 157–172.

Pilkington, John. "Kyrgyzstan: A Tale of Two Journeys." *Geographical Magazine*, 65 (April 1993): 8–12.

Rayfield, Donald. *The Dream of Lhasa: The Life of Nikolay Przhevalsky (1839–88): Explorer of Central Asia*. London: Elek, 1976.

United Nations Economic Commission for Europe. *Environmental Performance Reviews: Kyrgyzstan*. New York: United Nations, 2000.

Wessels, C. *Early Jesuit Travelers in Central Asia, 1603–1721*. The Hague: M. Nijhoff, 1924.

SOCIETY

Anthropology and Ethnography

Abdyraimova, Roza. *Kyrgyzskaia etnopedagogika i vospitanie detei: Monografiia* [Kyrgyz Ethnic Pedagogy and Education of Children: Monograph]. Kiev: Izd-vo Dovira, 1997.

Asanaliev, K. (ed.). *Akyndar chygarmachylygynyn tarykhynyn ocherkteri* [History according to the National Bards]. Frunze: Ilim, 1988.

Attokurov, S. *Kyrgyz etnografiiasy: Okuu kuraly* [Kyrgyz Ethnography: Textbook]. Bishkek: Kyrgyz maml. ul. unstituti, 1997.

———. *Kyrgyz sanzhyrasy* [Genealogy of Kyrgyzs]. Bishkek: Kyrgyzstan, 1995.

Fierman, William (ed.). *Soviet Central Asia: The Failed Transformation.* Boulder, Colo.: Westview Press, 1991.

Horowitz, Michael M., and Forouz Jowkar. *Pastoral Women and Change in Africa, the Middle East, and Central Asia.* Binghamton, N.Y.: Institute for Development Anthropology, 1992.

Pestriakov, A. P. *Antropologiia naseleniia iugo-vostoka Srednei Azii* [Anthropology of the Population of South-East Central Asia]. Moscow: Staryi sad, 2000.

Poliakov, S. *Istoricheskaia etnografia Srednei Azii i Kazakhstana* [The Historical Ethnography of Central Asia and Kazakhstan]. Moscow: Moscow State University, 1980.

Seaman, Gary, and Jane S. Day (eds.). *Ancient Traditions: Shamanism in Central Asia and the Americas.* Niwot: University Press of Colorado, 1994.

Shakerim Kudaiberdy-uly. *Shazhere. Rodoslovnaia Turkov, Kazakhov, Kyrgyzov* [Genealogy. Origins of Turks, Kazakhs, Kyrgyzs]. Reprint. Alma-Ata: "Dastan," 1990 (First Publication: Orenburg, 1911).

Health

Becker, Charles M., Damira I. Bibosunova, Grace E. Holmes, and Margarita M. Ibragimova. "Maternal Care vs. Economic Wealth and the Health of Newborns: Bishkek, Kyrgyz Republic and Kansas City, USA. (Special Issue: The Demographic Crisis in the Former Soviet Union)." *World Development*, vol. 26, no. 11 (November 1998): 2057–2061.

Feshbach, Murray, and Alfred Friendly Jr. *Ecocide in the USSR: Health and Nature under Siege.* New York: Basic Books, 1992.

Howell, Jude. "Poverty, Children and Transition in Kyrgyzstan: Some Reflections from the Field." *Journal of International Affairs*, vol. 52, no.1 (Fall 1998): 131–136.

——. "Household Coping Strategies in Kyrgyzstan." *Development in Practice*, vol. 5, no. 4 (November 1995): 361–364.

"Kyrgyz Republic 1997: Results from the Demographic and Health Survey. (Statistical Data Included)." *Studies in Family Planning*, vol. 30, no. 4 (December 1999): 347–351.

Storey, J. Douglas, Alisher Ilkhamov, and Brit Saksvig. *Perceptions of Family Planning and Reproductive Health Issues: Focus Group Discussions in Kazakhstan, Turkmenistan, Kyrgyzstan, and Uzbekistan.* Baltimore, Md.: Johns Hopkins School of Public Health, Center for Communication Programs, 1997.

World Bank. *A Survey of Health Reform in Central Asia.* Washington, D.C.: World Bank, 1996.

Law

Anderson, John. "Creating a Framework for Civil Society in Kyrgyzstan." *Europe-Asia Studies*, vol. 52, no. 1 (January 2000): 77–93.

——. "Constitutional Development in Central Asia." *Central Asian Survey*, vol. 16, no. 3 (1997): 301–320.

Butler, W. E. *Encyclopedia of Soviet Law.* 2nd rev. ed. Dordrecht: Martinus Nijhoff, 1985.

Guttman, Cynthia. "Kyrgyzstan: Breaking Out of the Old Shell." *UNESCO Courier* (November 1999): 21–22.

Heinen, Joel T., Emil Shukurov, and Chinara Sadykova. "Legislative and Policy Initiatives in Biodiversity Conservation in Kyrgyzstan." *Post-Soviet Geography and Economics*, vol. 42, no. 7 (October–November 2001): 519–522.

Koenig, Matthias. "Social Conditions for the Implementation of Linguistic Human Rights through Multicultural Policies: The Case of the Kyrgyz Republic." *Current Issues in Language and Society*, vol. 6, no. 1 (1999): 57–84.

Kyrgyzstan Business Law Handbook. Bloomfield Hills, Mich.: International Business Publications, 2000.

Satybekov, S. S. *Grazhdanskoe sudoproizvodstvo Kirgizskoi SSR: Istoriko-pravovoe issledovanie* [Civil Court of the Kyrgyz SSR: Historical and Legal Research]. Frunze: Ilim, 1987.

Migration and Demographic Trends

Abazov, R. "Economic Migration in Post-Soviet Central Asia: The Case of Kyrgyzstan." *Post-Communist Economies*, vol. 11, no. 2 (June 1999): 237–252.

Altay, A. "Kirgiziya during the Great Purge." *Central Asian Review*, vol. 12, no. 2 (1964): 97–107.

372 • BIBLIOGRAPHY

Commander, S., and John McHale. "Unemployment and the Labour Market in Transition: A Review of Experience in East Europe and Russia." In Bartlomeij Kaminski, ed., *Economic Transition in Russia and the New States of Eurasia,* pp. 277–314. Armonk, N.Y.: M.E. Sharpe, 1994.

Devereux, John, and Bryan Roberts. "Direct Foreign Investment and Welfare in the Transitional Economies: The Case of Central Asia." *Journal of Comparative Economics,* vol. 24, no. 3 (1997): 297–312.

Garibaldi, P., and Zuzana Brixiova. *Labour Market and Unemployment Dynamics in Transitional Economies.* International Monetary Fund Working Paper. Washington, D.C.: International Monetary Fund, 1997.

Hisao, Komatsu, and Obiya Chika. *Migration in Central Asia: Its History and Current Problems.* Osaka: JCAS, 2000.

Krongardt, G. K. *Nemtsy v Kyrgyzstane: 1880–1990 gg.* [Germans in Kyrgyzstan: 1880–1990]. Bishkek: Ilim, 1997.

Lewis, Robert (ed.). *Geographic Perspective on Soviet Central Asia.* London: Routledge, 1992.

Russell, Sharon Stanton. *International Migration in North America, Europe, Central Asia, The Middle East and North Africa: Research and Research-Related Activities.* Geneva: United Nations, 1993.

Shlapentokh, Vladimir, Munir Sendich, and Emil Payin. *New Russian Diaspora: Russian Minorities in the Former Soviet Republics.* Armonk, N.Y.: M.E. Sharpe, 1994.

Religion

Abazov, Rafis, Vasilivetskii Aexei, and Vitalii Ponomarev. "Political Islam in Central Asia: Leaving the Scene or Gathering Momentum?" *International Journal of Central Asian Studies,* vol. 3 (1998): 120–148.

———. *Islam I politicheskaya borba v stranakh SNG. Spravochnik* [Islam and Political Struggle in the CIS Countries. Reference Book]. Moscow: Panorama, 1992.

Akbarzadeh, Shahram. "Islamic Clerical Establishment in Central Asia." *South Asia: Journal of South Asian Studies* (December 1997): 73–102.

Alisheva, Atyrkul. "Religioznaia situatsia v Kyrgyzstane" [Religious Situation in Kyrgyzstan]. *Tsentralnaia Azia I Kavkaz,* vol. 4, no. 5 (1999): 51–55.

Anderson, John. *Religion, State, and Politics in the Soviet Union and Successor States.* Cambridge: Cambridge University Press, 1994.

Benningsen, Alexandre. *Muslims of the Soviet Empire: A Guide.* London: Hurst, 1986.

———. *Mystics and Commissars: Sufism in the Soviet Union.* Berkeley: University of California Press, 1985.

Benningsen, Alexandre, and Marie Broxup. *The Islamic Threat to the Soviet State.* New York: St. Martin's Press, 1983.

Benningsen, Alexandre, and Wimbush S. Enders. *Muslim National Communism in the Soviet Union.* Chicago: University of Chicago Press, 1979.

Benningsen, Alexandre, and Chantal Lemercier-Quelquejay. *Islam in the Soviet Union.* London: Pall Mall Press, 1967.

Bourdeaux, Michael (ed.). *The Politics of Religion in Russia and the New States of Eurasia.* Armonk, N.Y.: M.E. Sharpe, 1995.

Carrere d'Encausse, Helene. *Islam and the Russian Empire: Reforms and Revolution in Central Asia.* Berkeley: University of California Press, 1988.

Fletcher, Joseph F., and Boris Sergeyev. "Islam and Intolerance in Central Asia: The Case of Kyrgyzstan." *Europe-Asia Studies,* vol. 54, no. 2 (March 2002): 251–276.

Haghayeghi, Mehrad. *Islam and Politics in Central Asia.* New York: St. Martin's Press, 1995.

Pryde, Ian. "Kyrgyzstan: Secularism vs. Islam." *World Today* 48 (November 1992): 208–211.

Rashid, Ahmed. *Jihad: The Rise of Militant Islam in Central Asia.* New Haven, Conn.: Yale University Press, 2002.

———. *The Resurgence of Central Asia, Islam or Nationalism?* London: Zed, 1994.

Ro'I, Yaacov (ed.). *Muslim Eurasia: Conflicting Legacies.* Portland, Ore.: Frank Cass, 1995.

Shukurov, Emil´, Amyrkul´ Alisheva, and Anara Tabyshalieva (eds.). *Renessans ili regress* [Renaissance or Regression?]. Bishkek: Tsentr issledovanii mira Kyrgyzstana, 1996.

Taheri, Amir. *Crescent in a Red Sky.* London: Hutchinson, 1989.

KYRGYZSTAN AND ITS NEIGHBORS

Foreign Relations

Abazov, Rafis. *The Formation of Post-Soviet International Politics in Kazakhstan, Kyrgyzstan and Uzbekistan.* The Donald W. Treagold Papers, No. 21. Seattle: University of Washington, Henry M. Jackson School, 1999.

Abdyraimova, R. A. *Printsipy demokratii i vneshnei politiki v konstitutsii Kyrgyzskoi Respubliki* [The Principles of Democracy and Foreign Policy in the Constitution of the Kyrgyz Republic]. Bishkek: 1999.

Anderson, John, *The International Politics of Central Asia.* Manchester: Manchester University Press, 1997.

Cholponkulova, A. O. *Konstitutsionnye osnovy vneshnepoliticheskoi deiatel'nosti Kyrgyzskoi Respubliki* [Constitutional Basis of the Foreign Policy Activities of the Kyrgyz Republic]. Bishkek: Biiktik, 2000.

Dawisha, A. I., and Karen Dawisha (eds.). *The Foreign Policy Interests of Russia and the New States of Eurasia.* Armonk, N.Y.: M.E. Sharpe, 1994.

Gillard, David. *The Struggle for Asia 1828–1914: A Study in British and Russian Imperialism.* London: Methuen, 1977.

Mesbahi, Mohiaddin. *Central Asia and the Caucasus after the Soviet Union: Domestic and International Dynamics.* Gainesville: University Press of Florida, 1994.

Olkott, M. *Central Asia's New States: Independence, Foreign Policy, and Regional Security.* Washington, D.C.: USIP, 1996.

Osmonov, O. Dzh. *Mezhdunarodnye sviazi Kyrgyzstana v sfere kul'tury* [International Relatins of Kyrgyzstan in the Cultural Area]. Bishkek: Kyrgyzskii s.-kh. institut imeni K.I. Skriabina, 1996.

United States Congress. House Committee on Foreign Affairs. Subcommittee on Europe and the Middle East. *United States Policy toward Central Asia: Hearing before the Subcommittee on Europe and the Middle East of the Committee on Foreign Affairs.* United States House of Representatives, 102nd Cong., 2nd sess. April 28, 1992. Washington, D.C.: U.S. Government Printing Office, 1992.

Afghanistan

Belokrenitsky, V. Ya. "Russia and Greater Central Asia." *Asian Survey*, vol. 34, no. 12 (December 1994): 1093–1108.

Gaulier, Simone, Robert Jera-Bezard, and Monique Maillard. *Buddhism in Afghanistan and Central Asia.* Leiden: Brill, 1978.

Lee, J. L. *The 'Ancient Supremacy': Bukhara, Afghanistan and the Battle of Balkh, 1731–1901.* Leiden: Brill, 1996.

Nyrop, R. F., and Donald M. Seekins (eds.). *Afghanistan: A Country Study.* Washington, D.C.: Federal Research Division, Library of Congress, 1986.

Rashid, Ahmed. "The New Struggle in Central Asia: A Primer for the Baffled." *World Policy Journal*, vol. 17, no. 4 (2000–2001): 33–45.

——. *Taliban: Militant Islam, Oil, and Fundamentalism in Central Asia.* New Haven, Conn.: Yale University Press, 2000.

Rezun, Miron. *Intrigue and War in Southwest Asia: The Struggle for Supremacy from Central Asia to Iraq.* New York: Praeger, 1992.

Rubin, Barnett. *The Fragmentation of Afghanistan: State Formation and Collapse in the International System.* New Haven, Conn.: Yale University Press, 1995.

Saikal, Amin, and William Maley (eds.). *The Soviet Withdrawal from Afghanistan.* Cambridge: Cambridge University Press, 1989.

Shahrani, Nazif. *The Kirgiz and Wakhi of Afghanistan: Adaptation to Closed Frontiers.* Seattle: University of Washington Press, 1979.

Weisbrode, Kenneth. *Central Eurasia: Prize or Quicksand? Contending Views of Instability in Karabakh, Ferghana and Afghanistan.* Adelphi Paper 338. Oxford: Oxford University Press, 2001.

China

Dorian, J. P., Wigdortz, and D. Gladney. "Central Asia and Xinjiang, China: Emerging Energy, Economic and Ethnic Relations." *Central Asian Survey,* vol. 16, no. 4 (December 1997): 461–486.

Craig Harris, Lillian. "Xinjiang, Central Asia and the Implications for China's Policy in the Islamic World." *China Quarterly,* no. 133 (March 1993): 111–129.

Ethnic Challenges Beyond Borders: Chinese and Russian Perspectives of the Central Asian Conundrum. New York: St. Martin's Press, 1998.

Forbes, Andrew D. W. *Warlords and Muslims in Chinese Central Asia: A Political History of Republican Sinkiang 1911–1949.* Cambridge: Cambridge University Press, 1985.

Fuller, Graham E. "The Emergence of Central Asia." *Foreign Policy,* no. 78 (Spring 1990): 49–67.

Gleason, Gregory. "Inter-State Cooperation in Central Asia from the CIS to the Shanghai Forum." *Europe-Asia Studies,* vol. 53, no. 7 (2001): 1077–1095.

Melet, Yasmin. "China's Political and Economic Relations with Kazakhstan and Kyrgyzstan." *Central Asian Survey,* vol. 17, no. 2 (1998): 229–252.

Kazakhstan, Tajikistan, and Uzbekistan

Allworth, Edward. *The Modern Uzbeks. From the Fourteenth Century to the Present.* Stanford, Calif.: Hoover Institution Press, 1990.

Bekmakhanova, N. E. *Mnogonatsional'noe naselenie Kazakhstana i Kirgizii v epokhu kapitalizma, 60-e gody XIX v.-1917 g.* [Multiethnic Population of Kazakhstan and Kyrgyzstan during the Era of Capitalism, the 60s of the 19th century to 1917]. Moscow: "Nauka," 1986.

Critchilow, James. *Nationalism in Uzbekistan: A Soviet Republic's Road to Sovereignty.* Boulder, Colo.: Westview Press, 1991.

Juska, Arunas. "Ethno-political Transformation in the States of the Former USSR." *Ethnic and Racial Studies,* vol. 22, no. 3 (May 1999): 524–530.

Karimov, Islam A. *Uzbekistan—svoi put' obnovleniya i progressa* [Uzbekistan—Its Own Road of Renovation and Progress]. Tashkent: Uzbekistan, 1992.

Lunin, B. V. (ed.). *Vzaimosviazi kirgizskogo naroda s narodami Rossii, Srednei Azii i Kazakhstana, konets XVIII–nachalo XIX vv.* [Relations between the Kyrgyzs and Peoples of Russia, Central Asia and Kazakhstan at the End of the 18th–Early 19th Centuries]. Frunze: Ilim, 1985.

Olcott, Martha B. *The Kazakhs.* 2nd ed. Stanford, Calif.: Hoover Institution Press, 1995.

Thomas, Paul. *The Central Asian States: Tajikistan, Uzbekistan, Kyrgyzstan, Turkmenistan.* London: Franklin Watts, 1992.

Russia/Soviet Union

Belokrenitsky, Vyacheslav Ya. "Central Asia in the New Eurasian Geopolitics: Implications for Pakistan and Russia." *Pakistan Horizon*, vol. 48, no. 3 (July 1995): 25–38.

Chufrin, Gennady (ed.). *Russia and Asia: The Emerging Security Agenda.* New York: Oxford University Press, 1999.

Dzhamgerchinov, B. D. *Prisoedinenie Kirgizii k Rossii* [Kyrgyzstan Merges with Russia]. Moscow: Izdatelstvo sotsial´no-ekonomicheskoi literatury, 1959.

Joshi, Nirmala. "Russia and Central Asia: The Strategic Dimension." *Strategic Analysis*, vol. 18, no. 9 (December 1995): 1273–1284.

Kubichek, Paul. "Regionalism, Nationalism and Realpolitik in Central Asia." *Europe-Asia Studies*, vol. 49, no. 4 (June 1997): 637–655.

Menon, R. "After Empire: Russia and the Southern 'Near Abroad.'" In Michael Mandelbaum, ed. *The New Russian Foreign Policy.* New York: Council on Foreign Relations, 1998.

Odom, William, and Robert Dujarric. *Commonwealth or Empire? Russia, Central Asia, and the Transcaucasus.* Indianapolis, Ind.: Hudson Institute, 1995.

Ploskikh, V. M. *Pervye kirgizsko-russkie posol´skie sviazi (1784–1827 gg.)* [Development of Kyrgyz—Russian Relations (1784–1827)]. Frunze, Ilim, 1970.

Snyder, Jed C. (ed.). *After Empire: The Emerging Geopolitics of Central Asia.* Washington, D.C.: National Defense University Press, 1995.

Starr, Frederick (ed.). *The Legacy of History in Russia and the New States of Eurasia.* Armonk, N.Y.: M.E. Sharpe, 1994.

Voropaeva, V. A., D. Dzhunushaliev, and V. Ploskikh. *Iz istorii kyrgyzsko-rossiiskikh otnoshenii (XVIII–XX vv.): kratkii kurs lektsii i metodicheskoe posobie* [From the History of Kyrgyz-Russian Relations (18th–20th centuries): Concise Course of Lectures and Textbook]. Bishkek: Ilim, 2001.

Zviagelskaia, Irina. *The Russian Policy Debate on Central Asia*. London: Royal Institute of International Affairs, 1995.

Middle East and South Asia

Ahmar, Moonis. "India and Its Role in the New Central Asia." *Pakistan Horizon*, vol. 45, no. 3 (July 1992): 57–70.

Aron, Leon. "The Soviet Union's Underbelly: Muslim Central Asia." *Global Affairs*, vol. 5, no. 4 (Special issue 1990): 31–62.

Banuazizi, Ali, and Myron Weiner (eds.). *The New Geopolitics of Central Asia and Its Borderlands*. Bloomington: Indiana University Press, 1994.

Belokrenitskii, V. Ia., and O. I. Zhigalina (eds.). *Islamskie strany i regiony: Istoriia i sovremennost': Tsentral'naia, Zapadnaia, Iuzhnaia Aziia, Severnaia Africa v XVII–XX vv.* [Islamic Countries and Regions: History and Present: Central, West and South Asia, North Africa in the 17th–20th centuries]. Moscow: Institut vostokovedeniia, 1994.

Dannreuther, Roland. *Creating New States in Central Asia: The Strategic Implications of the Collapse of Soviet Power in Central Asia*. Adelphi Papers 288. London: Brassey's, for the International Institute for Strategic Studies, 1994.

Ehteshami, Anoushiravan (ed.). *From the Gulf to Central Asia: Players in the New Great Game*. Exeter: University of Exeter Press, 1994.

Ferdinand, Peter (ed.). *The New Central Asia and Its Neighbours*. London: Pinter Publishers, 1994.

Karaev, O. (ed.). *Vostochnye avtory o kyrgyzakh* [Oriental Authors about Kyrgyzstan]. Bishkek: Kyrgyzstan, 1994.

——. (ed.). *Arabo-persidskie istochniki o tiurkskikh narodakh* [Arab and Persian Sources about Turkic People]. Frunze: Ilim, 1973.

Pasha, S. A. M. "Turkey and the Republics of Central Asia: Emerging Relations and Dilemmas." *International Studies*, vol. 34, no. 3 (July/September 1997): 343–357.

Peimani, Hooman. *Regional Security and the Future of Central Asia: The Competition of Iran, Turkey, and Russia* Westport, Conn.: Praeger, 1998.

Saray, Mehmet. *Kirgiz Türkleri tarihi* [History of the Kyrgyz Turks]. Istanbul: M. Saray, 1993.

Singh, Anita Inder. "India's Relations with Russia and Central Asia." *International Affairs* (Royal Institute of International Affairs (United Kingdom)), vol. 71, no. 1 (January 1995): 69–81.

Sowerwine, James. "Nation-Building in Central Asia: The Turkish Connection." *Journal of South Asian and Middle Eastern Studies*, vol. 18, no. 4 (1995): 25–38.

IX. SCHOLARLY JOURNALS

Central and Inner Asia Studies. New York City.
Central Asia and Caucasus. Lulea, Sweden. Bi-monthly.
Central Asia Monitor. Fair Haven, Vermont.
Central Asian Collection. Washington, D.C.
Central Asian Files. London.
Central Asian Survey. Abington, UK. Quarterly.
Central Asiatic Journal. Wiesbaden.
Contemporary Central Asia. New Delhi, India. Quarterly.
Eurasian Studies. Ankara, Turkey. Quarterly.
Evraziiskoiye Soobchestvo [Eurasian Community]. Almaty, Kazakhstan. Quarterly.
Himalayan and Central Asian Studies. New Delhi, India. Quarterly.
International Journal of Central Asian Studies. Seoul, South Korea.
Nationalities Papers. Abington, UK. Quarterly.
Perceptions. Ankara, Turkey. Bi-monthly.
Strategic Analysis. Ankara, Turkey. Monthly.
Vostok/Orient. Moscow, Russia.

LOCAL AND REGIONAL PERIODICAL PUBLICATIONS

English Language

Almaty Herald. Almaty, Kazakhstan. Weekly.
The Central Asian Post (1992–1996). Bishkek, Kyrgyzstan. Weekly.
Far Eastern Economic Review. Hong Kong. Weekly.
Russia and Moslem World. Moscow, Russia. Bi-monthly.
The Times of Central Asia. Bishkek, Kyrgyzstan. Weekly.

Kyrgyz Language

Aalam. Bishkek, Kyrgyzstan.
Ala-Too. Bishkek, Kyrgyzstan.
Agym. Bishkek, Kyrgyzstan.
Asaba. Bishkek, Kyrgyzstan (1990–2001).
Chui Bayany. Bishkek, Kyrgyzstan.
Erkin Too. Bishkek, Kyrgyzstan.
Kyrgyz Ordo. Bishkek, Kyrgyzstan.
Kyrgyz Ruhu. Bishkek, Kyrgyzstan.
Kutbilim. Bishkek, Kyrgyzstan.

Kyrgyz Tuusu. Bishkek, Kyrgyzstan.
Osh Zhanyragy. Osh, Kyrgyzstan.
Talas Turmushu. Talas, Kyrgyzstan.

Russian Language

AKI-Press. Bishkek, Kyrgyzstan.
Chuiskiye Izvestia. Bishkek, Kyrgyzstan.
Delo No. Bishkek, Kyrgyzstan.
Erkin Too. Bishkek, Kyrgyzstan.
Literaturnyi Kyrgyzstan. Bishkek, Kyrgyzstan.
Moia Stolitsa. Bishkek, Kyrgyzstan.
Res Publica. Bishkek, Kyrgyzstan.
Slovo Kyrgyzstana. Bishkek, Kyrgyzstan.
Vechernii Bishkek. Bishkek, Kyrgyzstan.
Vesti Issyk-Kulia. Karakol, Kyrgyzstan.

About the Author

Rafis Abazov is a visiting scholar at the Harriman Institute at Columbia University. He graduated from the Kyrgyz National University (1989) and earned his Ph.D. (*Kandidat Nauk*) in political science in Moscow, Russia (1994). He conducted survey studies on conflict resolution in the Ferghana valley for the Centre for Social Research of the Kyrgyz Academy of Science (1989–90). He also worked as a Central Asian regional analyst for Moscow-based news agencies and newspapers. He was awarded the NATO research fellowship for research on foreign policy formation in Central Asia, the Institute of Advanced Studies of the United Nations University research fellowship for his doctorate research on post-Soviet Central Asian development, and the British Academy visiting fellowship for research on Kyrgyzstan's economic transition. The areas of his research interests include economic development, public policy and governance, and conflict resolution in the former Soviet Union with focus on Central Asia. As an independent consultant he regularly contributes annual reports on the Kyrgyz Republic to the Freedom House's *Nations in Transit* and annual reports on Kazakhstan and Kyrgyzstan to the Transition On Line. He is a member of the editorial committee of the *Central Eurasian Studies Review* journal and *Journal of Central Asian Studies*.

Rafis Abazov has authored two books and a number of other publications in various Kazakhstani, Russian, and international academic journals. Most of his recent articles have been published in *Eurasian Studies, Central Asian Survey, International Journal of Central Asian Studies, Nationalities Papers, Post-Communist Economies,* and some others. He has also contributed articles to *Encyclopaedia of Modern Asia* (2002), *Encyclopaedia of Nationalism* (2001), *Encyclopaedia of National Economies* (2002), Supplement to the *Modern Encyclopaedia of Russian, Soviet, and Eurasian History,* and others.

CPSIA information can be obtained at www.ICGtesting.com
Printed in the USA
LVOW10*1755260615

444047LV00004B/8/P